ROBERTSON COUNTY TENNESSEE

Court Minutes

1796–1807

Carol Wells

HERITAGE BOOKS
2014

HERITAGE BOOKS

AN IMPRINT OF HERITAGE BOOKS, INC.

Books, CDs, and more—Worldwide

For our listing of thousands of titles see our website
at
www.HeritageBooks.com

Published 2014 by
HERITAGE BOOKS, INC.
Publishing Division
5810 Ruatan Street
Berwyn Heights, Md. 20740

International Standard Book Numbers
Paperbound: 978-1-55613-734-1
Clothbound: 978-0-7884-8408-7

TABLE OF CONTENTS

ABBREVIATIONS

acc^t	account
ack^d	acknowledged
ag^t	against
appt^d	appointed
br	branch
B/S	Bill of Sale
comm^{rs}	commissioners
cr	creek
def^t, df^t	defendant
Doll^s	Dollars
fk	fork
judg^t	judgement
N^o	North
P/A	Power of Attorney
pl^f, pl^{tf}	plaintiff
sec	security, securities
vs	versus

FOREWORD

The first Robertson County Court met in July 1796. Since
the first extant census is 1820, minutes--more than deeds or
wills--can reveal the names of persons in Robertson during
those exciting, tumultuous early years--the onrush of popu-
lation, some staying for a crop or two, some leaving sooner,
some becoming permanent residents. They served on juries,
opened roads, cared for aged, orphans, and indigent, were
licensed to keep ordinaries, build mills, or to serve in
some public capacity. They went to jail, they sued, and they
got into brawls. Some residents leave the records when in
1803 part of Robertson became part of a new county--Dickson.

This book was transcribed and abstracted from microfilm.
While original pages were not faded, and the handwriting was
competent, the spelling was often original. I visited
Robertson County to check the spelling of names. Although
names appear in this transcription as they looked to me on
the microfilm, in cases of illegibility, I used the more
correct spelling. Some letters look alike in handwriting:
L and S often cannot be distinguished, t & l, e & i, u & n,
r & s, and other letters can be hard to determine. Please
use imagination in seeking ancestors in the index, and then
check with the original volume. Are Stak and Stark the same
name; Show and Shore? Samuel, Lamuel and Lemuel? To add a
sense of age, many words are retained in their old spelling.

Repeated phrases are omitted. Jurors are "good and lawfull
men...elected and sworn the truth to speak." Deeds were
"proven in open Court by the oath of..." and then "ordered
to be registered." Wills are "the Last Will & Testament of."
Please check the entire page when the index gives a page
number. Once in Court, other business was often transacted.
There is often more than one item for a name on a page.

First Court in Robertson

By an Act of General Assembly in April, Tennessee County was laid off into Two Counties, Robertson & Montgomery. William Fort, Chas Miles, Wm Miles, Benjamin Menees, Isaac Philips, Bazel Boren, Martin Duncan, Jno Philips, Hugh Henry, Zebulon Hobart, James Crabtree were appointed Justices of the Peace to hold Courts of Pleas & Quarter Sessions in Robertson. At Jacob McCarty's house the following took the oaths appointed by law for qualification of Justices: Wm Fort, Isaac Philips, Wm Miles, Benjamin Menees, Bazel Boren, Martin Duncan, John Philips, Zebulon Hobart and James Crabtree

Court elected Thomas Johnson clerk; Bond Two thousand Dollars; security Jacob McCarty, Bazel Boren & Melcher Oyler
Court elected Hugh Henry sheriff; Bond Two Thousand Dollars with John Donelson & William Duncan securities
Elected Isaac Brown coroner, Bond one Thousand Dollars, with Stephen Boren and Daniel McKindley securities

p.2 The Court appointed William Fort Esquire their chairman

Bill/Sale William Fort to James Dean ack^d in open Court
Deed James Smithers to Edward Cheatham proven by Hugh Lewis
Power/Attorney James and Isabella Duncan to Melcher Oyler proven by Martin Duncan
Deed Jacob McCarty to Daniel Hogan ack^d
Deed Thomas Kilgore to Wm Crabtree proven by James Crabtree
Deed Joseph Barns to Jonathan Dardin proven by Isaac Brown
Deed Jacob Penington to John Donelson proven by John Couts & Hugh Henry
Deed Thomas Kilgore to John Carter proven by Zebulon Hobert
Deed Charles Wheaton to Francis Boren proven by Thos Johnson
Deed Jesse Cain to Robert Lancaster proven by Thomas Johnson
Deed John Boren to Anderson Cheatham ack^d
Court Adjourns untill tomorrow Morning 9 OClock

Tuesday Morning July 19th 1796
Present the Worshipfull Bazel Boren, James Crabtree, William Miles & Martin Duncan, Esquires

Deed John Boren to Bazel Boren proven by Isaac Brown
Deed John McCoy Alston to Jesse Williams proven by Isaac Brown
Deed John McCoy Alston to Jesse Williams proven by Isaac Brown
Deed John McCoy Alston to Jesse Williams proven by Isaac Brown

1

Deed William Hinds to Jacob McCarty proven by James Herod

Tavern Licence granted to Isaac Brown, bond 330 Dollars, Anderson Cheatham & Stephen Boren securities

Ordered one acre condemned for the use of Maj^r Charles Miles mill to include his mill where it at present stands

Tavern Rates till Next Court, half pint Whiskey 16 2/3 Cts, half pint Brandy 21 Cents, half pint rum or Wine 25 Cents, Breakfast or supper 25 Cents, Dinner 33 1/3 Cents

John Philips Esquire appointed Ranger for the County

p.4   Court message to Montgomery County concerning Legality of Montgomery Collecting the County Tax within the Bounds of Robertson. Wish Montgomery Collector to stop collecting Tax and to refund what he has Collected.
Wm Miles Esqr to carry foregoing message & superintend business with Montgomery Court. Thomas Johnson Clk, Wm Fort C C

Bazel Boren Esq elected Register, bond Two Thousand Dollars, Isaac Brown & Stephen Boren securities
Stephen Boren apptd Constable; bond 250 Dollars, Isaac Brown & Willis Hicks securities
Isaac Menees appointed Constable; bond 250 Dollars, Josiah Fort & Jacob McCarty securities
Josiah Fort app^{td} Trustee for County, Bond Two Thousand Dollars, Isaac Menees & Jacob McCarty securities
Daniel McKindley app^{td} Constable, bond 250 Dollars, Benjamin McIntosh & Richd Martin securities
William Brown appointed Constable, bond 250 Dollars, Benjamin McIntosh & Cornelius Dabney securities
p.5   John Mercer app^{td} Constable, bond 250 Dollars, Zebulon Hobert & Josiah Fort securities
Deed Benjamin Harden to Willis Hicks proven by Wm Fort
Anderson Cheatham, Isaac Brown, Henry Johnson, David Ronsavall, Anthony Sharp and George Martin apptd Jurors to attend next Superior Court
Thomas Johnson clerk gives Bond 2 thousand Dollars, Anderson Cheatham & Daniel Holeman securities
Order Scire fa issue agt Nancy Lemar to bring to next Court her daughter Milley Loggans
Court Adjourns untill Court in Course, to Meet at Benjamin McIntosh's house. Wm Fort, Benjamin Menees, James Crabtree, Bazel Boren, John Philips, Martin Duncan, Wm Miles

p.6 Octr 17th 1796. Court met at house of Benjamin McIntosh.
Present Ja^s Crabtree, Bazel Boren, Wm Fort, Zebulon Hobart,
Martin Duncan, Isaac Philips, and John Philips, Esquires

Jurors   Jonathan Price, Jesse Martin, Joseph Carmack, Moses
Boren, John Crain, Philip Parchment, Nimrod McIntosh, Thomas
Yates, John Couts, Archer Cheatham Jr, John Johnson, William
Byrd, James Stark, William Duncan, John Husk, Joseph Payne,
Robert Lancaster, Walter Stark, Francis Boren, James Yates,
John Powers, Wm Briscoe, Charles McIntosh and Isaac Flannery

Sworn as Grand Jurors   Jonathan Price foreman, Jesse Martin,
Joseph Carmack, Moses Boren, John Crain, Philip Parchment,
Nimrod McIntosh, Thos Yeats, John Couts, Archer Cheatham Jr,
John Johnson, Wm Byrd, James Stark, Wm Duncan, John Husk

Depositions of George Walker & William Murray of Fayette Co,
Kentucky, to be taken for purpose of recording deed in this
County Joseph Brock to Thos Hopkins

Bazel Boren register bond to his Excellency John Sevier 500
Dollars for collecting & paying Taxes during his continuance
in office, Martin Duncan & Charles McIntosh his securities

Samuel Donelson Esqr appointed County Solicitor
Deed Andrew Miller to John Irwin proven by Thos Johnson

p.7   Ordered a road laid off from Wills fork of Sharps Road
to the ford of the fur fork of River where the Old Kentucky
Road crosses same. Appointed to mark sd Road James Crabtree
Sen, Wm Byrd, Joseph Crabtree, Wm Wills, Wm Gilbert, William
Harrington, Daniel Holeman Senr, Wm Crabtree and James Yates
or any five of them. William Byrd to oversee afsd Road, and
hands to work thereon are all in bounds of the company commanded by Capt Abraham Young, Wills & Havards excepted

Deed Robert Prince sheriff to Saml McMurry ackd
Deed Robert Prince sheriff to George Wills ackd
Deed Wm Betts to Thomas Ross Senr proven by James McDonald
Deed Robert Hays to Thomas Johnson proven by Martin Duncan
Deed Robert Lancaster to Thomas Johnson ackd
Deed Thomas Johnson to Wm Binson ackd
Deed Isaac Miller to John McIntosh ackd
Deed Thos Johnson to Charles McIntosh ackd
Bill/Sale Jesse Cain to Robert Lancaster proven by Thomas
Johnson
Deed Charles Wheaton to John Duncan proven by Thomas Johnson
Deed Elijah Hamilton to George A Sugg ackd
Deed Ezekiel Cloyd to Thomas Strain proven by James Crabtree

p.8   B/S John Doss to Anthony Sharp proven by Nicholas Hull
Deed Robert Nelson to Benjamin Wood proven by Hugh King
Deed Ralph Fleming & George Scott to Jesse Martin proven by
Robert Ewing
Deed Ralph Fleming & George Scott to Archibald Mahan proven
by Robert Ewing
Deed Philip Trammel to Joseph Payne proven by James Wheeler
Deed John Nichols to George Briscoe proven by Thomas Johnson
B/S William Rasco to Archibald Mahan proven by James
Norfleet
Deed George Briscoe to Thomas McIntosh ackd
Deed Philip Trammel to James Wheeler proven by Joseph Payne
Court Adjourns untill tomorrow Morning Nine OClock

Tuesday Morning October the 18th 1796. House of Benjamin Mc-
Intosh. Present the Worshipfull Wm Fort, Benjn Menees, James
Crabtree, Bazel Boren, Esquires

Deed Daniel McIver to Sampson Matthews ackd
James Crabtree Jr appointed Constable, bond 250 Dollars, Wm
Haggard and David Havard his securities; took oaths

p.9 John Sutton vs Thomas Woodard. Appeal. Summons: Debt under 20 Dollars, Martin Duncan JP; executed by Stephen Boren,
returned to John Philips, who gave Judgement favour of pltf
for 10½ Dollars and costs. James Doherty atty; Pltf by Seth
Lewis attorney. Jury Robert Lancaster, Joseph Payne, Isaac
Flannery, John Powers, Walter Stark, Francis Boren, Charles
McIntosh, James Yates, Wm Briscoe, Thomas McIntosh, Benjamin
Shaw & John Duncan who find for plaintiff his damage 4 Dollars fifty cents & Costs of suit

p.10   State vs James Stuart. Assault & Battery. James Stuart
on 25 Sepr at the Race paths in the Barrens in Open company
committed assault & battery on Isaac Brown. Samuel Donelson,
solicitor; true bill, Jonathan Price. James Stuart submits
to Mercy of the Court; fined two Dollars and costs.

Hugh Henry sheriff protests against the Gaol of Robertson C°
on acc^{t} of its being Insufficient
Joseph Barns apptd constable, bond 250 Dollars, Wm Rasco and
Archer Cheatham Jr his securities; took the oaths

p.11 John Crane vs Edward Cheatham. Certiorari. Petition of
Edwd Cheatham sheweth that March 24 1795 he agreed with John
Crane to raise a crop on his land, Crane to furnish tools,
horses, & board. When crop completed, petitioner to receive
one third thereof. Crane was to help but this was not in the
Articles; Crane now charges him 6 Dollars 94 cents & Costs 1

Dollar 30 Cents before Benjamin Menees J P. Petition asks a
Writ to certify the cause to this Court.
p.12 Edward Cheatham before Martin Duncan J P 2 Sepr 1796.
October Session, Pl^{tf} by James Doherty. Def^{dt} by Seth Lewis
his att^y. Jury Robt Lancaster, Joseph Payne, Isaac Flannery,
John Powers, Walter Stark, Francis Boren, Chas McIntosh, W^m
Briscoe, Thos McIntosh, Benjn Shaw, John Duncan find for De-
fendant. Def^t to recover Ag^t plt^f his Costs expended
Court Adjourns untill Tomorrow Morning 10 OClock

Wednesday Morning October the 19th 1796
Present Bazel Boren [page torn] John Philips

p.13 James Mason vs Daniel Menees. Case. Pl^{tf} dismisses suit

Summons to Nancy Lemarr to shew cause why her daughter Milly
Loggins, not receiving proper care, should not be taken from
her. Thos Johnson, clerk. Returned by Sheriff indorsed Not
found. Hugh Henry Shff

Ordered Stephen Boren & Daniel McKindley constables allowed
Two Dollars each for their attendance on Court
William Clarke app^{td} overseer of road from Sulpher fork [un-
readable because of patched page] to Davidson County line a-
bove Zach Betts, hands of Capt Duncans Company south side of
Sulpher fork from below John Donelsons down to include the
inhabitants of War trace Creek

William McAdoe app^{td} overseer of Road from Sulpher fork near
Meeting House to the Logan County line & hands to work under
him are all in Capt Duncans Company in Red River settlement
[torn] lower side of Beaver Dam Creek on North side Sulpher
[torn] bounds of sd Company as low as Nimrod McIntosh

p.14 Daniel McKindley apptd overseer of road from John Donelsons to Karrs Creek, all Hands from Warr trace Creek settlement (them not included) on the South side of the Sulpher
fork crossing sd Creek & including Settlement on other side
as far as opposite the mouth of Karrs Creek thence to mouth
of sd Creek and up same to Davidson County line

Ordinary Licence granted to Benjamin McIntosh; bond 100 Dollars, Daniel McKindley & Charles McIntosh securities

Tavern Rates: half pint Whiskey 12½Cents, half pint Brandy
25 Cents, half pint Rum 25 Cents, Dinner 25 Cents, Breakfast
or Supper 16 2/3 Cents, Lodging per night 8 Cents, Corn or
Oats 4 Cents per quart
Court Adjourns untill Court in Course to Meet at House of

Benjamin McIntosh. John Philips, James Crabtree, Bazel Boren

p.15 Monday January 16th 1797 at house of Benjamin McIntosh.
Present   Wm Fort, Wm Miles, Benjamin Menees, Isaac Philips

Mark Noble excused for Nonattendance as a Jurror last Term

Letters/Administration granted to Ann Hart and Noah Sugg on
estate of Joseph Hart decd; bond 5 thousand Dollars, James
Norfleet and Isaac Dortch securities

John Kilgore excused from serving as Jurror this Term

Grand Jurors Daniel Holeman foreman, Jno Duncan, Wm Baldwin,
Archibald Mahan, Ephraim Pratt, John Coughran, Samuel Sugg,
Thos Sellars, Lewis Barker, William Haggard, Caleb Winters,
Wm McAdoe, Abram Tippy, Thos Woodard, Alexr Cromwell

Ordinary Licence granted to Moses Winters; bond with William
Brown & Nath' Dickison securities

Letters/Admn granted to William Harrington on estate of William Stair decd; bond 5 Thousand Dollars, Abraham Young and
Thomas Havard securities

Danl Holeman Jr excused for Nonattendance last Term as Juror

Deed Stephen Boren to Isaac Brown ackd
Deed Bazel Boren to Stephen Boren ackd
Deed Stephen Boren to Isaac Brown ackd
Deed John Couts to James Appleton ackd

p.16 Timothy Demumbro vs Moses Larisy. At Oct'' Term 1796 pl'
by Seth Lewis his att'', Def' by James Doherty, cause continued. Def' Confesses Judgement 25 Dollars & assumes cost

Bond Joseph Hath[?Hash] to Henry Johnson Sen'' proven by Tho⁰
Johnson
Deed Wm Cage shff to Jonathan Latimer proven by Seth Lewis

Order John Crain, Caleb Winters, Isaac Menees, Joseph Barns,
Jonathan Dardin, Matthew Johnston, Moses Winters, Benjn Min-
ces, Wm Brown Sr, Wm Fort, Hugh Lewis, Archer Cheatham Junr,
Archer Cheatham, Ephraim Pratt, David Hamilton & Elijah Hamilton lay off a Road from Browns fork of Karrs Creek to the

road leading from Winters to John Donelsons about half mile
above sd Winters, to Browns ford on Red River, thence to the
Kentucky Line, crosses Elk fork at mouth of Hoopers Hollow,
Jurors above to alter the publick Road by Winters plantation
as much as they think fit doing Justice to sd Winters farm &
also to Publick Road, above order granted October Term 1796
on which Jury return Nothing Done for want of the Sheriff

Power/Attorney John Carter to Thomas Kilgore proven by John
Kilgore
Deed Thos Johnson to Thomas Woodard ackd
Deed Archibald Mahan to Henry Gardner proven by John Gardner
p.17 B/S Joseph Tribble Still to Mary Warner proven by Mary
Hardin
Deed Richd Martin to Jacob McCarty ackd
Deed Richd Harman to Isaac Dortch proven by James Norfleet
[Norfloch?]
Deed Joseph and Sarah Barns to Miles Kerby proven by Archer
Cheatham Jr
Deed Hugh Henry to George Pool ackd
Deed Jacob McCarty to Richd Martin ackd
Deed John Carter to William Crabtree ackd by Thomas Kilgore
atty in fact for John Carter
Deed John Philips to Elias Fort ackd
Deed Nicholas Conrod to George Sadler proven by Wm Miles

Ann Hart and Noah Sugg delivered Inventory of part of estate
of Joseph Hart deceased

Ordered following Magistrates take Lists in Respective Mili-
tia Companies hereafter Named, of Taxable poles & property,
William Miles for Capt Lockarts Company, Wm Fort for his own
Company, John Philips for Captain Coughrans Company, Bazel
Boren for Captain Duncans Company, James Crabtree for Capt
Youngs Company

James Appleton records his mark and brand. Marks and brands
also recorded by Geo Gordin, Samuel McMurry, Jno Couts, Hugh
Henry, John Philips, Amos Rounsavall

p.18 Elihu Howard vs John Neal & Abraham Dean. Benjamin Shaw
security for sd Deans appearance delivered him
Court Adjourns untill Tomorrow Morning Ten OClock

Tuesday 17th of January 1797
Present Wm Miles, Martin Duncan, John Philips, Esquires

Order Deposition of Philip Trammel of Logan County, Kentucky
be taken to prove an Article of Agreement between Wm Stair &

Jethro Sumner

Archer Cheatham Junr appointed Constable, bound 620 Dollars,
William Rasco & Miles Kerby securities
Abraham Young excused for Nonattendance at last Term
Deed Richard Dodge to Bazel Boren ackd
Deed Bazel Boren to Aaron Perry ackd

Order Road laid off from house of Benj McIntosh to Montgom-
ery County line where Road strikes same from Davis ferry on
Cumberland River; & following to mark same, James Norfleet,
Arch Mahan, Jesse Martin, Isaac Titsworth, Wm Rasco, Archer
Cheatham, David Patterson or any five of them

Deed John Young to James Haynes ackd
Deed David Hughs to James Hayns proven by John Young
Deed Robert Hays to Joseph Hart proven by Thos Johnson
Deed Robert Hays to Joseph Hart proven by Thomas Johnson
Deed Isaac Brown to John Porter ackd
Deed Morgan Brian to Bazel Boren proven by Melcher Oyler
Deed Joseph Brock to Thomas Hopkins proven by Geo Walker of
Kentucky whose Depositon was taken for that purpose

p.19 State vs Isaac Brown. A/B. At Race paths in the Barrens
in Open Company Isaac Brown committed assault & Battery upon
James Stuart. James & Isaac did then & there in publick Company strip themselves & did fight. Samuel Donelson, solicitor; True Bill Jonathan Price foreman. Brown pleaded Guilty.
Jury John Hutchison, Wm Duncan, Richd Dodge, Abraham Young,
John Grimes, Benjn Shaw, Melcher Oyler, Wm Wills, David Hamilton, Thomas Strain, William Spiller, and Andrew Irwin, who
find Defendant Guilty and fine him Six Cents.

Deed Isaac Brown to John Porter ackd

Bond, Wm Renfro to James Renfro. At Court held for Franklin
County 7 March 1796 within Bond was proven by two witnesses
thereto subscribed. Signed James Callaway, to which County
Seal is affixed, and presiding Justice Peter Saunders certifying James Callaway to be Clerk of sd Court

William Fort records his mark and brand
Thomas Woodard obtains an order for a Mill on his own Land
near where he lives

p.20 State vs William Brown. October Term 1796, Jurors present William Brown, Constable, 5 September 1796, for going
contrary to Law in administering his office. Samuel Donelson
solicitor; endorsed True Bill Jonathan Price, foreman. Brown
by James Doherty his attorney; Bill was Quashed

Jurors next Court   Joseph Hamilton, Ja^s Lockart, Elias Fort
J^r, Wm Deloach, Jesse Martin, Elias Fort (Millers Cr), James
Elliott, James Walker, Mark Noble, Wm Grimes, Wm Matthews,
Chas Kilgore, Johnson Kilgore, Barton Coats, Wm Coats, Ge^o
Hobert, Jiner Lacy, Jno Price, Jonathan Price, William Lusk,
David Henry, Arther Pitt, James Cannon, Henry Johnson, John
McIntosh J^r, Bazel McIntosh, Thomas McIntosh & John Matthews
Court Adjourns untill tomorrow Morning 10 OClock

Wednesday Morning January 18th 1797
Present John Philips, Isaac Philips, Bazel Boren, Esquires

Deed Thomas Johnson to John White ackd
Deed Thomas Johnson to Nimrod McIntosh ackd
Deed George Wills to Saml McMurry ackd by Hugh Henry his at-
torney in fact
Deed John McCoy Alston to Jesse Williams proven by Charles
Crouch
Isaac Philips records his stock mark
William Boren records his stock mark

p.21   Nathaniel Dickeson vs Joseph Barns. Debt. Plaintiff
dismissed the Suit at his own costs

Nathl Dickeson vs Joseph Barns. Attachment. Pltf appeared,
also wife of the Defendant.   Parties ordered suit dismissed
as they had compromised

State vs John Vaughn. Poligamy. Presentment- John has been
twice married & doth at this time live in Adultery with Isabella Duncan which is 18th of October 1796, Samuel Donelson,
Solicitor, indorsed & true Bill, Jonathan Price foreman, on
which capias issued at Jany Term 1797, the sheriff returned
Not found, left the state, signed Hugh Henry shff

Isaac Titsworth excused for his nonattendance last term as a
Juror on the oath Hugh Henry
Daniel McKindley records his stock mark

Tavern Rates allowed: half pint whiskey 16 2/3 cents, half
pint Brandy, Rum or Wine 25 cents. Dinner 33 1/3 cents, supper or Breakfast 25 cents, Lodging per night 8 Cents. Corn
or oats per Quart 4 Cents

Court Adjourns untill Court in Course   to Meet at the House
of Benjamin McIntosh. Bazel Boren, Isaac Philips, John Philips, Martin Duncan

p.22 Robertson County. Monday, April 17th 1797, at home of
Benjamin McIntosh. Present Worshipfull William Miles, John
Philips, Bazel Boren, James Crabtree

Grand jurors Henry Johnson foreman, John Price, Wm Deloach,
John Matthews, Sampson Matthews, Wm Matthews, John McIntosh
Junr, Elias Fort, William Lusk, Barton Coats, James Lockart,
James Walker, Johnson Kilgore, Jesse Martin

State vs George Havard, Henry Havard, Anderson Cheatham, Edward Cheatham and Isaac Brown. Assault & Battery. Defdts did
with force of arms unlawfully & riotously assemble together
16 January 1797 and in publick company did strip themselves
& fight & then Henry and George Havard did commit an assault
on Anderson Cheatham and Anderson then did beat, wound & ill
treat & that Anderson Cheatham Edward Cheatham & Isaac Brown
assaulted George Havard and did beat wound & ill treat contrary to the peace & dignity of our state. Samuel Donelson
solicitor. True Bill Daniel Holeman foreman. The Court fine
Geo Havard six cents, Henry Havard six cents, Anderson Cheatham six cents & Isaac Brown one cent

p.23 John Caffery vs George Havard. Covenant. At Jany Term,
Pltf by Seth Lewis his atty. Defdt failing to appear, Judgment by Default entered agt him at April term 1797.   Defdt
confesses Judgment 42 Dollars 25 Cents & Costs

Samuel Mason excused for nonattendance as a juror last Term
Deed Jonathan Price to Thomas Stark ackd
Deed James Taylor to Isaac Dortch proven by James Norfleet
Deed James McElyea to William Crockett ackd
B/S William Reasons to James Elliott Jr ackd
B/S Benjn Kovel to Matthew Williams proven by Elias Fort
Deed Hugh Henry to George Pool ackd
Court Adjourns untill tomorrow Morning 9 OClock

Tuesday Morning April 18th 1797
William Fort Esqr returns Lists of Taxable property for his
Company. William Miles Esqr for Captain James Lockarts Com-
pany. James Crabtree Esqr for Capt Abraham Youngs Company

Robert Searcy Esqr produced a licence to practice Law as an
attorney in this State

Article/Agreement between Jethro Sumner and Wm Stair; Philip
Trammel was called on to prove sd Articles; being blind his
handwriting was proven by oath of James Crabtree Esqr. Said
Trammel on oath was examined & related substance of Article

p.24 Jonathan Price vs Samuel Crocket. Covenant. October Term 1796 pl^t^f by Seth Lewis & James Doherty Esq^rs^, Def^t^ by Bennet Searcy Esqr. Cause continued to April 1797 Term. Jury Thomas Woodard, Jacob McCarty, Benjamin Shaw, Josiah Ramsey, Nimrod McIntosh, James Karr, Joseph Carmack, Isaac Dorris, George Briscoe, Arther Pitt, David Henry, Thomas McIntosh, who find in favor of Pl^t^f, assess his Damages to 234 Dollars and his Costs. Def^t^ prayed and obtained appeal to Superior Court of Mero Dis^t^; bond 500 Dollars, John Crocket, security

James Crabtree Esq paid 3 Dollars fine he has Collected

C^t^ unanimously elected David Henry coroner, Bond 1 thousand Dollars, James Norfleet & Henry Johnson securities; too oath

Jonathan Price agt Saml Crocket. Benj Nail a witness proved 4 days attendance. Thomas Stark 4 days, Jane Norris 3 days, John Tucker 4 days. Richard Martin 4 days. Martin Duncan 4 days. Wm Kar 1 day. Daniel McKindley 4 days

p.25 Andrew Snody vs Abram Hardin. Case. Oct 1796 Term, pl^t^f by Seth Lewis, Def^t^ by James Doherty. Cont. Jury James Norfleet, Abraham Dean, Jn° Hutchison, Wm Havard, Thomas Mills, James Mason, Wm Rasco, Samuel Crocket, Benjamin Nail, George Havard, Elijah Lancaster & David Havard, who find for pl^t^f, assess his damage to 29 Dollars 36 Cents, also Costs of Suit

County Tax laid as High as the Law will Admit
Orphan Patrick Murphey bound to William Crocket until he arrives to age twenty one years
Henry Johnson Jr records his stock mark
Deed Demsy Coffield & Grisham Coffield to Elias Fort proven by Giles Kelley
Wm Harrington adm^r^ on estate of William Stair dec^d^ returned on oath an Inventory of s^d^ Stairs Estate
Deed Demsey Coffield and Polly Coffield to David Patterson proven by Elias Fort
Deed John Nichols to Joseph Castleberry ack^d^
Deed Andrew Irwin to Jn° Hutchison proven by Samuel Donelson

p.26 Article/Agreement between Wm Stair & Jethro Sumner assigns to Charles Harrington, the assignemnt of which by Sumner to Harrington is proven by Abraham Dean

Order road from Moses Winters to Clarksville turned to cross Millers Cr 150 yards above the old ford, intersect old road oppisit Wm Rascoes House; Wm Miles, Ja^s^ Norfleet, Arch^d^ Mahan, Jesse Martin, Wm Rascoe, Holland Dardin lay off same

Deed John Nichols to Richard Miles & William Miles, minors,

sons of Charles Miles ack^d
Deed William Duncan to Wm Johnson proven by Thos Johnson
Deed Samuel Hollis to Elisha Bellemey proven by Isham A
Parker
Deed Daniel Young to John Crocket proven by Samuel Crocket
Court Adjourns untill tomorrow Morning 9 OClock

Wednesday Morning April 19th 1797   Present
John Philips, James Crabtree, Bazel Boren & Martin Duncan

Deed George Briscoe to John Cheatham proven by Wm Briscoe
Wm Brown Junr proves two days attendance as a witness behalf
of State against Cheatham, Havards & Brown
Bazel Boren Esq returns Lists of Taxable property in Captain
Duncans Company

Order Noah Sugg & Ann Hart admrs Estate of Joseph Hart decd
deliver to Sheriff perishable property of sd estate they see
cause to have sold, which Sh^{ff} shall sell agreeable to Law

p.27 James Karr vs Cornelius Dabney. Detinue. Jany Term 1797
Pltf by Bennett Searcy, Deft by Seth Lewis; cont. Jury John
Sayrs, Anderson Cheatham, Wm Farmer, Abraham Dean, Jonathan
Price, Arther Pitts, Willis Hicks, James Norfleet, David
Henry, David Rounsavall, Thomas McIntosh, Nathan Perry, who
find for pl^{tf}, assess damages 38 Dollars, also costs of suit

Orphan Peggy Murphey bound to Jane Crocket untill age eight-
een years
Moses Winters security for Griffith Dickison, Certiorari by
sd Dickison against John Cheatham
Pr/Atty Margaret Karr, William Karr, Henry Johnson, Willis
Hix, William Briscoe, Margaret Karr J^r, Agness Karr, Robert
Karr & John Karr to James Karr ack^d by parties in open Court

William Brown Jr at his own request dismist from serving any
longer as Constable
Bill/Sale Joseph T Still to James Karr proven by Mary Hardin

David Henry records his stock mark
Benjn McIntosh records his stock mark
Benjn Menees records his stock mark

p.28 Matthew Sellars vs Executors of Jesse Reed dec^d. Eject-
ment. Jany Session, pl^{tf} by Ja^s Doherty Es^q, def^t by Bennett
Searcy. Notice served on Tenant in possession, Ezekiel Clam-
pet. Pl^{tf} declares John Din complains of Richd Fin who with
force of arms entered the messuage of 640 acres that Matthew
Sellars on 27 October 1795 demised to John Din for a Term of

ten years not yet expired, lying on North waters of Cumberland River below fork of Nelsons Creek [details omitted] and
ejected him from his farm to his great damage on 28th day of
October 1795 with force & arms
p.29 against the peace & dignity of the State whereby John
Din saith that he is injured to the Value of 50 Dollars, and
therefore he brings his suit. James Doherty atto
    To Ezekiel Clampet informing him to appear first day
next County Court at house of Benjamin McIntosh by some atto
Richd Finn. 22 Decr 1796
    April 1797 comes pltf by atto as also Extra of Jesse
Reed by Bennett Searcy. Say they are not guilty of Trespass.
Jury Jno Sayres, Anderson Cheatham, Wm Farmer, Abraham Dean,
Jonathan Price, Arther Pitt, Willis Hix, James Norfleet, David Henry, David Rounsavall, Thos McIntosh, Nathan Perry who
find Defts not Guilty as charged in Declaration of Ejectment
by reason of pltfs having no Entry; it is considered of by
the Court that the Defts keep possession

Ordered that Cornelius Dabney, John Cheatham, Thomas Christmas, William Armstrong Senr, Josiah Fort & Josiah Ramsey attend next Superior Court as Jurors

Samuel Crocket appointed Overseer of Road from Brown fork to
Sulpher fork; all hands on No side sd fork in 5 miles of sd
road work on the same

Jonathan Darden appointed Overseer of Road from Sulpher fork
to Browns ford on Red River; hands within 5 miles of sd Road
No side Sulpher fork work on same

Samuel Sugg apptd Overseer from Browns ford on Red River to
Kentucky State Line; all hands within 5 miles of sd Road on
No side of Red River work on same

p.30 Deed Samuel Allen, atty/fact for Wm Allen, to Stephen
Boren proven by Thomas Johnson
John Philips Esqr allowed 19 days from present to return to
Clerk the List of Taxable property for the company for which
he was appointed
Archer Cheatham records his stock mark

Order Bazel Boren, Thomas Johnson, John Philips, Martin Duncan, William Duncan & William Haggard lay off Road from John
Donelsons to Bledsoes Lick as far as the County Line

Court Adjourns until Court in Course to meet at the House of
Benjamin McIntosh.   Wm Fort, John Philips, Benjamin Mences,
Martin Duncan

April Term 1797. David Stephenson vs William McKee. Case.
Isham A Parker for pl^{tf}, defendant in proper person. Plaintiff ordered suit dismised at his own costs

July Term 1797
Jesse Williams vs Thomas Christmas. Case. Pl^{tf}'s attorney in
fact John Cheatham in proper person ordered suit dismised, &
assumed the costs

p.31 Monday July 17th 1797
Present Benjn Menees, John Philips, Martin Duncan, Esquires

Jurors George Briscoe, John Johnson, John Pike, John Hutchi-
son, Thomas Hutchison, Sampson Matthews, William Matthews,
Thos Smith carpenter, Adam Clap, Wm Hust, Wm Wills, Thomas
Strain, Samuel Crocket, William Fleuellen, Benjn Wood, Caleb
Winters, Grisham Coffield, Isaac Titsworth, Archibald Mahan,
Miles Kerby, William Deloach, Samuel Sugg, Azariah Dunn, Jno
Coughran, Thomas Little, Richard Martin, John Couts, Nathan
Perry, Chas Wheaton, Francis Boren

Grand Jurors   Miles Kerby foreman, Francis Boren, Thomas
Little, Archibald Mahan, Benjn Wood, Jno Couts, Thos Strain,
Adam Clap, John Hutchison, John Coughran, Sampson Matthews,
Nathan Perry, Isaac Titsworth, Wm Fleuellen, Caleb Winters

Saml Hollis records his stock mark
Wm Crunk excused for nonattendance as juror at Jany Term
Thomas Molloy called out for nonattendance to give Testamony
in suit Ge^o A Sugg ag^t Elijah Hamilton fined Ni Si
Robert Hamilton Esqr produced licence to practice law as an
attorney in this State & was Admited according
Francis Hall Esq produced licence to practice law as an att^y
in this State & was admited accordingly
Charles Smith released from paying tax for 320 acres lying
in Montgomery County altho given in
Martin Duncan Esqr released from paying tax for his land ly-
ing in Montgomery County notwithstanding given in here
John Hutchison records stock mark and brand
Deed James Haynes to James Ewing ackd

Deed Wm Brown heir of James Brown decd to Elisabeth Airs &
Patrick Martin heir of Joseph Martin deceased proven by Asa
Woodworth
Deed John Hutchison to James Sawyers ackd
Deed Jonathan Lattemer to Joseph Lattimer proven by Griswell

Lattimer
B/S John Bridges to Jesse Williams proven by John Williams
B/S Thos Sellars to Philip Parchment proven by Benjn Menees
B/S Wm Crichloe to Jesse Williams proven by John Williams

Sheriff returned into Court the amount of sales of estate of
Joseph Hart deceased

p.32 Power/Attorney William Flinn to Capt James Maxwell ack^d
Court Adjourns untill tomorrow Morning 9 OClock

Tuesday July 18th 1797
Present Benjn Menees, Zebulon B Hobart, Isaac Philips Esq^{rs}

John Tucker security for Asa Woodworths appearance at Court
delivers up s^d Woodworth

Martin Grider gives bond 50 dollars for guardianship of minors Sampson Conrod & Peggy Conrod, Benjn Menees and Charles
Miles his security; previous to which the minors afsd chose
sd Grider for their Guardian

John Tygard agt Philip Shackler on attachment, continued for
nine months
Samuel Donelson Esqr resigns his appointment of County Solicitor & Court appoints Isham A Parker

Thomas Johnson vs William Hinds. Case. April Term 1797 Pl^{tf}
by Bennet Searcy, Def^t failing to appear, judg^t by default
entered ag^t him, cause continued untill July Term. Came pl^{tf}
by att^y, def^t still fails to attend; Jury Grisham Coffield,
Thos Smith, William Deloach, Richd Martin, Charles Wheaton,
Wm Hust, George Briscoe, William Wills, Jno Johnson, Azariah
Dunn, William Matthews who find for pl^{tf} damages 37 Dollars
12 2/3 cents, also costs of suit

Benjamin Nail vs Aseph Woodard being the Return Term of the
writ, the Plaintiff comes & dismisses suit as his own costs

p.33 Jno Cheatham vs Griffith Dickeson. Certiorari. Petition
of Griffith Dickeson sheweth in 1794 he assigned a note/hand
to John Cheatham on Richard Pearl for one cow & calf and ten
gallons Whiskey for which petitioner received half the value
of sd Note, he taking note at risque that if he recovered he
should have it, if not he should not call on your petitioner
for any part thereof; petitioner not being scholar knew not
the manner assignment was made, knows Pearl was in the country long after note was due, and that Cheatham never brought
suit to recover from Pearl, that he rec^d three Dollars from

Pearl for which he gave a credit on sd note But now Cheatham
hath sued a Warrant agt petitioner, & hath judgement against
petitioner for 11 Dollars 66 cents and one Dollar & 25 cents
costs of suit for same before Wm Fort Esqr, and is about to
cause execution to be levied on petitioners property. Begs
Writ of Certiorari to certify cause to Court.
    Certification by Griffith Dickison before John
Philips, J P, 24 February 1797
p.34 Writs issued agreeable to prayer of petitioner. John
Philips J P
    Pl^{tf} appeared by Seth Lewis, def^t by James Doherty.
Moses Winters def^t's security, proceedings continued to July
Term. Parties by attorneys. Jury Thomas Hutchison, Grisham
Coffield, Thomas Smith, Wm Deloach, Richard Martin, Charles
Wheaton, Wm Hust, Ge° Briscoe, Wm Wills, John Johnson, Azar-
iah Dunn, Wm Matthews who say upon oath that the issue is in
favour of def^t; Def^t to recover ag^t pl^{tf} his costs Expended

Philip Alston S^r allowed Fifteen Dollars for the County Seal
furnished this County
Wm Brown Sr proves two days attendance as a witness in suit
Jno Cheatham vs Dickison
John Kitts proves five days attendance as a witness in suit
Jno Cheatham agt Griffith Dickison

Deed Elijah Robertson to John Caffery proven by Seth Lewis
Deed Hugh McMillion to Jacob McCarty proven by Hugh Lewis
Deed William Harrington to Thomas Harrington ackd
P/A Barnabas King to John Ewing ackd in open Court
P/A Geo Wills to Hugh Henry proven by John Donelson

Will of Matthew Williams dec^d proven by Saml Sugg. Sugg Fort
& Wm Deloach, executors, took oath, delivered into Court an
inventory of estate of Matthew Williams decd

Deed John Tucker to Saml Tucker ackd
Deed Thomas Johnson to Matthew Johnson ackd
P/A Moses Larisy to David Burney ackd
Ann Hart delivered into Court a supplementary inventory of
estate of Joseph Hart decd
Deed William Cage shff to Jonathan Lattimer proven by Seth
Lewis

p.35 Tatum & Wiggin vs Isaac Handley. Return, executed July
11th 1797 and escaped same day. Acceptions were taken at return for want of Security being taken by Sheriff; Sh^{ff} noti-
fyed of such exceptions; on motion by Sheriffs counsel, Sh^{ff}
was released from standing Special Bail in said Cause

B/S Thomas Johnson to Matthew Johnson ackd

OCTOBER 1797

Court Adjourned untill tomorrow Morning 10 OClock

Wednesday Morning July 19th 1797
Present Wm Fort, Bazel Boren, William Miles, Martin Duncan

Charles McIntosh registers his stock mark
Isaac Dorris registers his stock mark
Order Wm Miles, Bazel Boren, David Henry to attend as Judges
to superintend ensuing Election for governor & assembly
B/S Danl Lyons to Benjn McIntosh proven by Lucy Murphy

Order John Tucker to oversee the Road from Karr Creek to Jno
Donelsons in place of Danl McKindley with same hands
Clerk and Sheriff allowed 25 Dollars each for exoficio services for past year
Hugh Henry Shff gives Bond 5 thousand Dollars for collection
and accounting of Publick & County Tax for 1797, Bazel Boren
and Stephen Boren his securitys

Clerk to make out Certificate of land reported by Sheriff to
bring about sale of said land

Jurors to next Court John Donelson, Cornelius Dabney, Robert
Lancaster, Thomas Woodard, Eli Jones, Melcher Oyler, William
Spiller, John Tucker, Jas Delany, Benjn McIntosh, James Con-
yers, Josiah Ramsey, Wm Johnson, David Hamilton, Wm Duncan,
Wm Coates, Wm Crabtree, Joseph Crabtree, Michael Gilbert,
Andw Irwin, John Payton, Chas Colgin, Jno Robins, Wm Tucker,
Edmond Turpin, James Haynes, John Crane, John Tolley, Robert
Black, Elijah Hamilton.

Court Adjourns until Court in Course to Meet at the House of
Benjn McIntosh.   Wm Fort, Bazel Boren, Wm Miles

The suit by Judicial attachment James Haynes agt Nehemiah
Motia was dismised, the Defendant assuming costs

p.36 Monday October 16th 1797
Present Bazel Boren, Benjamin Menees, Martin Duncan, Esqrs

Jurors John Donelson, Cornelius Dabney, Robt Lancaster, Thos
Woodard, Eli Jones, Melcher Oyler, Wm Spiller, John Tucker,
James Delany, Benjn McIntosh, James Conyers, Josiah Ramsey,
Wm Johnson, David Hamilton, Wm Duncan, Wm Coates, Wm Crab-
tree, Joseph Crabtree, Michael Gilbert, Andrew Irwin, John
Payton, Chas Colgin, John Robins, Wm Tucker, Edmond Turpin,

17

James Haynes, John Crane, John Tolley, Robert Black, Elijah
Hamilton

Grand Jurors sworn   Wm Johnson foreman, Joseph Crabtree, Wm
Spiller, John Robins, Andw Irwin, Robert Black, Wm Crabtree,
John Tucker, Josiah Ramsey, Wm Tucker, James Haynes, Charles
Colgin, Elijah Hamilton

Isaac Menees Constable sworn to attend the Grand Jury

Jonathan Dardin appointed admr of estate of Ann Darden
Deed William Johnson to William Sale was ackd in open Court
Deed James McElyea to David Spencer proven by Peter Spencer
Deed William Johnson to Sampson Trammel ackd
Deed Henry Johnson to William Coates ackd
Deed William Dobbins to Andrew Mitchel proven by Edward Gwin
Deed James Henderson to William Saunders ackd
Deed James McElyea to Matthew Day proven by David Spencer

Deed Philip Philips and Michael Campbell executor   by Bennet
Searcy their attorney in fact   to James Henderson   proven by
Isaac McNutt a subscribing witness thereto

Deed Jonathan Price to Martin Duncan ackd
Deed James Henderson to William Perry ackd
Deed James Byrn to Robt Lauter[Sauter?] proven by Jno Rhodes

p.37 George A Sugg vs Elijah Hamilton. Covenant. Jany Session 1797 Plaintiff by James Doherty his attorney, Defendant
by Bennet Searcy his attorney, cause continued. Jury Sampson
Matthews, John Johnson, Nimrod McIntosh, William Duncan, Jno
Crane, Edmond Turpin, William Haggard, Thos Woodard, Michael
Gilbert, Melcher Oyler, Eli Jones, Robert Lancaster who find
in favour of plaintiff, assess his damage by Defendants Nonperformance of Covenant to 169 Dollars 60 cents; also costs
of Suit in that behalf expended
Deft prayed new trial, motion over Ruled; Deft prayed appeal
to Superior Court for Mero District; gave David Hamilton and
Joseph Hamilton his Securities

B/S Margaret McElhainy to Charles McIntosh proven by Thomas
Johnson
B/S William Russel to Anthony Sharp proven by John Neill
Deed Caleb Doug to Daniel Choen proven by Benjn Choen
Cornelius Dabney excused from serving as juror this Term

p.38 State vs William Wills & Richd Matthews. Assault & Battery. Defts submit to Court; fined fifty cents each
Court Adjourns untill tomorrow Morning Ten OClock

Tuesday October the 17th 1797   Present
Bazel Boren, John Philips, Isaac Philips, Zebulon B Hobert

Thomas Talbot vs Isaac Brown. Debt. July Term 1797 pl^{tf} by
Isham A Parker his att^y, Def^t failing to attend, judgment by
Default. At October 1797 Session pl^{tf} by att^y, James Doherty
for Defendant. Jury Thomas Woodard, Michael Gilbert, Melcher
Oyler, Eli Jones, Robert Lancaster, Wm Duncan, John Crane,
Edmon Turpin, David Hamilton, Elijah Lancaster, Richard Mar-
tin, James Karr who find for Pl^{tf}, assess his Damage 31 Dol-
lars 19 Cents; also costs of suit in that behalf expended

p.39 Michael Gleaves vs Grisham Coffield. Case. July 1797
pl^{tf} by Isham A Parker, Def^t by Seth Lewis. Continued to Oc^t
Term. Jury Thos Woodard, Michael Gilbert, Melcher Oyler, Eli
Jones, Robert Lancaster, Wm Duncan, Jno Crane, Edmon Turpin,
David Hamilton, Elijah Lancaster, Richard Martin, James Karr
who find for plaintiff damage 23 Dollars; also costs of suit

John Tucker vs John Sayre. Debt. July 1797, pl^{tf} by Samuel
Donelson, Def^t by Isaac McNutt and James Doherty. Oc^t Term
1797 Def^t in proper person confessed judgment for 42 Dollars
& costs of suit; Stayed by pl^{tf} for 2 months

p.40 Wm Haggard vs Daniel Lyons. Attachment. July 1797 pl^{tf}
by Seth Lewis. Def^t failing to attend, judgement by default
ag^t him, Sheriff having previously levied the attachment on
a stud horse the property of def^t, after which proceedings
continued untill October Term. Jury Thomas Woodard, Michael
Gilbert, Melcher Oyler, Eli Jones, Robert Lancaster, William
Duncan, Jno Crane, Edmon Turpin, David Hamilton, Elijah Lancaster, Richard Martin, James Karr who find pl^{tf} damages 205
Dollars; also costs of suit

p.41 Tatum & Wiggin vs Isaac Standley. Case. July Term 1797
Sh^{ff} returned Writ executed, escaped same day, at which Term
Pl^{tf} by Isaac McNutt his att^y entered exception for the want
of Bail, after which proceedings continued untill Octr Term
1797. Jury John Hutchison, Henry Hires, Benjamin Chapman,
Jno Couts, Wm Williams, David Havard, David Hamilton, Nathan
Clark, Wm Clark, Isaac Dorris, Thos Yates, Benjn Porter, who
find for plaintiff damages 37 Dollars 27 cents; also costs

Deed Martin Duncan to Thomas Johnson ackd
Deed Robert Lancaster to Thomas Johnson ackd
Deed William Johnson to Joel Vaughn ackd
Deed William Hood to John Chislom ackd
Deed Joseph Barns to Kerby Vick proven by Archer Cheatham
Deed Robert Nelson to Benjamin Menees Senr proven by Martin

19

Duncan

Mary Johnson admx estate of Matthew Johnson decd bound one
thousand Dollars, Benjn Menees and William Flinn securities

Josiah Fort Esqr apptd County Trustee, bond 2 thousand Dollars, Anderson Cheatham & Isaac Henry his securities

p.42 Deed James Wheeler to Zachariah Oneal proven by William
Harrington
Court Adjourns untill tomorrow Morning 10 OClock

Wednesday Morning October 18th 1797   Present
John Philips, Bazel Boren, Benjamin Menees, Martin Duncan

Deed Jesse Williams to George Briscoe for 110 acres ackd
Deed Jesse Williams to George Briscoe for 365 acres ackd

Shadrick Nye & Cº vs Cornelius Dabney. Debt. Plᵗᶠ by Seth
Lewis; Defᵗ in proper person confessed Judgement 29 Dollars
35 Cents & Costs of suit; stay of Execution untill next Term

Joseph Boren Senr released from paying Pole Tax present year

Jurors to next Superior Court   Benjamin Menees, Wᵐ Haggard,
Samuel Crocket, John Crocket, Jonathan Price & Martin Duncan

Henry Gardner apptd overseer Road from Brush Creek to Calebs
Creek, all hands convenient work on sd road
James Long apptd overseer from Calebs Creek to Karrs Creek,
overseer to nominate hands convenient to sd road
Charles Wheaton appointed overseer of road from Sulpher to
Kentucky State Line
Joseph Wray apptd Deputy Sheriff, takes oaths & qualifies
Zebulon B Hobert records his stock mark
Wm Johnson records his stock mark
Thomas Johnson records his stock mark

p.43 Andrew Snody vs Philip Parchment & John McCarty. Si fa.
Andrew Snoddy obtained judgement agᵗ Abraham Hardin at April
Term for 29 Dollars 36 Cents and 7 Dollars 3 ½ cents costs;
John McCarty & Philip Parchment special bail for appearance
of Abraham Hardin, bond 24 Septʳ 1796 notified to appear at
October 1797 County Court to shew cause why Judgement should
not be entered agᵗ them for debt & costs afˢᵈ. Plᵗᶠ appeared
by Seth Lewis, Defᵗˢ failing to appear, judgement by Default

John Sayre vs Benjamin McIntosh. Case. Plᵗᶠ came in proper
person & dismissed suit at his own costs

Benjamin McIntosh vs John Sayre. Case. Pl^{tf} came in proper person and dismissed suit at his own costs

George Hacker vs Joseph Crabtree. Saml L Crawford plaintiffs attorney dismissed suit and assumed the Costs
Court Adjourned untill Court in Course to meet at the House of B McIntosh. Benjn Menees, Z B Hobert, Martin Duncan, John Philips

p.44 Monday January the 15th 1798 at House of Benjamin McIntosh. Present Bazel Boren, James Crabtree, Martin Duncan

James Norfleet took oath & qualified as Justice of the Peace

Jurors Jacob McCarty, Caleb Winters, John Dorris (Baptist), George Briscoe, James Stark, Walter Stark, James Conyers, John Donelson, John Tolley, Charles McIntosh, William Karr, Jn° Barr, Jn° Tucker, Francis Conner, Jn° Price, Lewis Barker, Wm Benson, Wm Flinn, Amos Rounsavall, Ezekiel Clampet, Patrick Martin, Benjn Nail, Philip Parchment, Wm Fleuellen, Richd Matthews J^r (Blackhead), John Parchment, Peter Spencer

Grand Jurors George Briscoe foreman, Walter Stark, Wm Karr, Benjn Nail, Jacob McCarty, Wm Benson, John Parchment, Chas McIntosh, Caleb Winters, James Stark, Jno Barr, John Tolley, John Dorris

April 1797 Peggy Murphey and Patrick Murphey orphans of Patk Murphey decd bound to Wm & Jane Crocket; these children were brought from Montgomery County where their property was inventoryed; order Orphans delivered to their Mother, and they and Crockets Released from their obligations

Charles Wheaton records his stock mark
Deed Philip Parchment to Margaret Guffey proven by William Fleuellen
Deed John Wilson to Archer Cheatham Jr & Miles Kerby proven by John Kilts
Deed Hugh Henry Sheriff to John Simmons ackd
Deed Philip Parchment to Margaret Guffey proven by William Fleuellen
Deed Sampson Trammel to Eli Jones ackd

p.45 Tavern licence granted to Benjamin McIntosh, bond 200 Dollars, Bazel Boren and James Norfleet his securities
Tavern licence granted to Moses Winters, bond 200 Dollars,

21

Joseph Carmack and Miles Kerby his securities
Wm Flinn excused from serving present Term as a juror
B/S Philip Parchment to Margaret Guffey proven by William
Fleuellen

Order Jn° Crane, Ezekiel Clampet, Archer Cheatham Sʳ, Samuel
Crocket, Jacob McCarty, Moses Winters Sʳ, Benjn Menees, Jaˢ
Long to alter road from Springfield to Clarksville at ford
of Hoods Br, crossing sd branch as near Old Road as ground
admits for a waggon road, falling into road from Brown fork
to Red River about half a mile from where it falls into Old
County Road, thence to Moses Winters.

Deed Thomas Winningham to Thos Yates proven by Thos Kilgore
Deed Thomas Hamilton to Jno Dobins proven by Alexander McKee
Deed William Coates to Eli Jones ackd
Deed John Caffery to Arthur Pitt proven by Thomas Johnson
Deed Thomas Johnson to Richard Nuckolls ackd
Deed John Duncan to William Edwards ackd
Deed Daniel McKindley to Meredith Walton proven by Francis
Conner
Court Adjourns untill tomorrow Morning 9 OClock

Tuesday Morning January 16ᵗʰ 1798
Present Wᵐ Miles, James Norfleet, Martin Duncan, Bazel Boren

p.46 James Dromgoole & Abram Hardin released from penalty of
a forfeited Recognizance they gave for appearance of Henry
Havard, crime of Adultery, Securities pay costs on Suit

Thomas Stuart & William P Anderson produced licences to
practice law as attorneys, took oaths and qualified

John Murry bound in sum 500 Dollars, Chaˢ McIntosh and Benjⁿ
McIntosh his securities, his appearance at next county Court

Mary Johnson admˣ estate of Matthew Johnson decᵈ delivered
inventory of estate of decd
Mary Johnson appᵗᵈ Guardian to orphans James Johnson & Betsey Johnson, children of Matthew Johnson decᵈ; bond 1 thousand Dollars, John Parchment & Benjamin Nail securities

Deed John Williamson to Ezekiel Cloyd proven by John Young
Deed John Young to Abraham Young ackd
Deed Thomas Smith to Jacob Warren proven by John Young
Deed Ephraim Pratt to Benjamin Menees proven by David Enoch
Deed Robert McConnel to William Macbean proven by Bennet
Searcy
Deed Grisham Coffield to Archibald Mahan ackd

Deed Elisha Bellamy to Charles Parker proven by Allen Parker
Deed Samuel McMurry to David Huddleston ackd
Power/Atty George Flinn to James Yates ackd
P/A James Renfro to James Norfleet proven by George Neville
B/S Arthur Pitt to Samuel McMurry ackd

p.47 John Den on Demise of John Moore vs Ricd Fen alias Jno
Hutchison & Others. July 1797 pltf by Isham A Parker; defts
by James Doherty & Samuel Donelson, plead Not Guilty; a copy
of each Entry to be brought from Entry Book; continued. John
Den complains of Richd Fen in custody of Sheriff; John Moore
10 May 1797 let to John Den 428 acres in Robertson Co (former Tennessee Co) on Sulpher fork of Red River two mile above
Jacob Penningtons...on Montflorences line...from 10 May 1797
to end of five years. On 10 June 1797 Richd Fen with force &
arms entered and withholds possession thereof to the damage
of sd John Den 500 Dollars.
p.48 William Hutchison, John Hutchison and John Kelly notified by Richd Fenn of his ejection. Jno Hutchison and others
by James Doherty & Saml Donelson their attornies standing on
merits of title, in no wise guilty of trespass. Jury John
Price, Patk Martin, Richd Matthews, Amos Rounsavall, Francis
Conner, Wm Fleuellen, John Roberts, Saml Sugg, Saml McMurry,
Wm Haggard, Nathan Clark, Wm Crocket, find Defts not Guilty
as set forth in plaintiffs Declaration; Defendants continue
in possession
Court Adjourns untill Tomorrow Morning 10 OClock

Wednesday Morning January the 17th 1798   Present
Zebulon B Hobert, Bazel Boren, James Crabtree, Martin Duncan

Sheriff to sell personal estate of Matthew Johnson decd

Jacob McCarty apptd overseer of road from ford of Sychamore
at Rileys Old Place to Junction of sd road with Betts Road;
persons on Sychamore and all within two miles of sd road at
the lower ford work on same, including Hollis

Deed George Gordon to James & David Jones proven by James
Appleton
Deed Thomas Hutchins to Nathan Clark proven by Wm Haggard
Deed Wm Baldwin to James Cambell proven by Elijah Flannery

p.49 William Haggard vs John Sayre. Case. July 1797 pltf by
Seth Lewis; deft by Isaac McNut; cause continued until Octr
Term when jury Jno Hutchison, Henry Airs, Benjn Chapman, Jno
Couts, Wm Williams, David Havard, Wm McAdoe, Nathan Clark,
Wm Clark, Isaac Dorris, Thomas Yates, Benjn Porter found for
Defendant, Plaintiffs attorney moved for New Trial; ordered;

23

continued; January 1798 plaintiff in proper person dismissed
suit and assumed costs

W^m McKee vs Jonathan Stephenson. To Sheriff Montgomery County: Feb 1797 Jonathan Stephenson entered in Bond as security
sum 200 Dollars, condition that David Stephenson would prosecute a suit by him commenced against W^m McKee. David Stephenson hath failed to prosecute or to pay . You are commanded
to cause Jonathan Stephenson to appear before our Court held
at house of Benjn McIntosh 3rd Monday January to show cause
why execution should not issue ag^t his goods chattels lands
for amount of s^d Costs. Jonathan Stephenson comes into Ct in
proper person & confessed judgment according to scire facias

p.50 Elener Logue vs Michael Purtle. Detinue. Octr 1797 pl^tf
by Seth Lewis; def^t by James Doherty; continued to Jany 1798
Session; plaintiffs att^y dismissed suit at plaintiffs costs

John Den on Demise of James Karr vs Richard Fin alias Cornelius Dabney. Ejectment. October 1797 pl^tf by Bennet Searcy;
def^t by Seth Lewis pleads Common Rule, not Guilty; continued
till January Session. Pl^tf declares that Richard with force
entered into 270 acres on Sulpher fork of Red River about 2
miles below War trace Creek...where J Karr now lives...James
Karr one of heirs of Robert Karr dec^d demised to Jno Den for
a term not yet expired; Fin ejected Den to his great damage,
James Karr 15 Feb 1796 had demised to John Den from 15 Feb^y
1796 to term of seven years. Afterwards on 10 November 1796
Richd Fen entered in manner af^sd .
p.51 Notice by Richd Fen to Cornelius Dabney July 18 1797.
January Term 1798 comes pl^tf by att^y af^sd and Cornelius Dabney by Seth Lewis as defendant in the cause. Def^t in proper
person confesses judgment for one penny and costs; plaintiff
to Recover of def^t one penny & costs of suit expended

Federick Stump vs James Dromgoole. Debt. Jany Term 1798, Return of Writ, pl^tf by Seth Lewis, def^t by Ja^s Doherty. Pl^tf
dismissed suit at Def^t's cost; def^t, present, gave consent

Andrew Snoddy vs Jesse Cain. Attachment. Jany 1798 Sheriff
levied on 3 cows & 2 calves. Pl^tf by Saml Donelson. Def^t by
James Doherty. Robert Lancaster entered interpleader, claims
the property attached. Plaintiffs attorney dismissed suit

Mason & Smith vs Cornelius Dabney. Jany 1798 return of Writ
indorsed "Not found." Pl^tf dismissed suit & assumed costs

Andrew Snoddy vs Thomas Havard. Plaintiff by Saml Donelson.
Plaintiff in proper person dismissed suit at his own cost

Nancy Hart vs James King. Attachment. Writ Executed. Josiah Ramsey garnishee. Joseph Wray D S. Pl[tf] dismissed suit and assumed costs

William Bray vs David Havard. Attachment. Pl[tf] by Sam[l] Donelson, def[t] by Ja[s] Doherty. Pl[tf] dismissed suit at own costs

Wm Byrd to oversee Road called Gaspers River Road from where it leaves the Kentucky Road below Wills to Harrington Creek; James Wheeler to oversee from Harringtons Creek to Kentucky line, overseers to divide the hands

Jonathan Darden adm[r] estate of Ann Darden dec[d] delivered to Court an Inventory of the estate of the s[d] dec[d]

Justices of the Peace to take Lists of Taxable property in Districts assigned for present year

Captain Messers Company	William Fort, Esquire
Captain Pattersons	William Miles Esqr
Capt Coughrans	Benjamin Menees Esqr
Capt Johnsons	Martin Duncan Esqr
Capt Hutchisons	Bazel Boren Esqr
Capt Youngs	Zebulon B Hobert Esqr

Court Adjourns untill Court in Course to Meet at the House of Benjamin McIntosh. Bazel Boren, James Crabtree, Martin Duncan

p.53 April Term 1798   Monday, 16th of April 1798
Present Benjn Menees, John Philips, Martin Duncan

John Alston vs David Havard. Covenant. January 1797 pl[tf] by James Doherty; deft by Seth Lewis. Continued term to term to April 1798. Jury Wm Edward, Thos Barker, Anderson Cheatham, Joseph Hamilton, Jno Dorris, Daniel Lerew, James Menees, Jno Parchment, John Robins, Thos Woodard, John Young, Adam Clap, who find for Deft. Plaintiff prayed & obtained an appeal to Superior Court, Robert Lancaster and Moses Larisy securities

Grand Jurors Saml Crocket foreman, John Crocket, John Crane, Nicholas Conrod, Mark Noble, Wm Lusk, Abraham Tippy, Joseph Carmack, John Tucker, Jno Hudson, Moses Larisy, Thomas Simpson, Wm Wills

Alexr McIntosh records his stock mark

James Yates and Wm Byrd delivered up Joseph Philips for whom they were security for his appearance in suit Thomas Hickman agt Saml Philips. Jos Philips gives John Robins & Wm Tucker as his securities in suit Thos Hickman agt Philips
John C Hamilton produced Licence to practice law; took oaths by Law Required
Deed James Lockart to John Gardner and Elias Laurence proven by Richd Whitehead
Deed Hardy Murfre to Wm Glover was proven by John Gardner
Deed William Prince to Wm Connel was proven by Giles Connel
Deed Thomas Perry to James Shannon was ackd
Deed Isaac Philips to Matthew McClain was ackd
Deed William Duncan to Wm Johnson proven by Thomas Johnson
Deed Stephen Boren to Charles Colgin ackd
p.54 Thomas Henry excused from serving as juror this Term
Deed Aaron Perry to Saml Tucker proven by John Robins
Deed Aaron Perry to John Robins proven by Thos Johnson

Bond Christian Crops to Saml Hendley; assignment of sd Bond to Adam Hampton proven by James Fort
Court Adjourns untill Tomorrow Morning 9 OClock

Court Met in Springfield on Tuesday 17th of April 1798
Present   John Philips, Benjn Menees & Isaac Philips Esquires

Thomas McIntosh records his stock mark

State vs Jesse Hill. Assault & Battery. Defendant submitted, Court fine him six Cents

Frederick Stump vs William Henry. Debt. January 1798 pltf by Seth Lewis; Defdt by Samuel Donelson. Cont. Jury Wm Edward, Anderson Cheatham, Thomas Woodard, Adam Clap, James Sawyers, William Haggard, William Hust[Hirst?], Benjn Chapman, Isaac Weakley, Wm Briscoe, Wm Crocket, Jacob Pickrell who find for pltf, assess his damage 53 Dollars 36 Cents; costs of suit

p.55   Federick Stump vs William Henry. Covenant. Jany 1798, pltf by Seth Lewis, Deft by Saml Donelson. Cont. Jury Wm Edwards, Anderson Cheatham, Thos Woodard, Adam Clap, Jas Sawyers, Wm Haggard, Wm Hust, Benjn Chapman, Isaac Weakley, Wm Briscoe, Wm Crocket, Jacob Pickrell, who find for plaintiff, assess his damages 29 Dollars 32 Cents; also costs of suit

John Hughs vs John Stuart. Orig¹ Attachment. Jany 1798 Shff returned "Levied on Corn & Other Articles. H Henry" Jesse Martin, garnishee, states he is indebted to Stuart 15 Shillings to be paid in Linnen and that John Tolley has a Jacket patren;   Stuart failing to appear, Judgt by Default was en-

tered agt him; cont. Shff reports message from B Boren, John
Philips, Martin Duncan 17 feby 1798 authorizing him to sell
corn levied upon. Sale brought 36 Dollars 25 cents.
p.56 Jury Jno Hutchison, Jno Price, Archabal Mahan, Francis
Boren, Elijah Lancaster, Benjamin Nail, William Matthews, Wm
Johnson, Benjamin Porter, Isaac Dorris, Jesse Martin, James
Jones, who find for Pltf, assess his damage to 75 Dollars 40
cents; pltf to recover, & also costs of suit

Wm Lusk records his stock mark
Wm Fort Esq returned into Court the List of Taxable property
in Capt Messers District
Wm Miles...in Capt Lockarts District
Zebulon B Hobert...in Capt Youngs District

Grisham Coffield vs Samuel Crocket. Appeal. Summons 26 Aug
1797 to Samuel Crocket signed by John Philips J P, executed
by Daniel McKindley. Philips gave Judgment in favour of pltf
for eleven Dollars & Costs of Suit from which pltf obtained
appeal. Deft by James Doherty, pltf by Seth Lewis. Jury William Edwards, Anderson Cheatham, Adam Clap, Jas Sawyers, Wm
Haggard, Wm Hust, Benjn Chapman, Isaac Weakly, Wm Briscoe,
Robert Lancaster, Arthur Pitt, Wm Farmer, who find for pltf
damage eleven Dollars; also costs.

Benjn Nail apptd overseer of road Browns fork to Sulpher Crk
in place of Saml Crocket.
In suit Grisham Coffield agt Saml Crocket, David Fort proves
two days attendance & 60 miles traveling. Benjamin Coffield
proves 2 days, (blot) Tucker 5 days, Daniel McKindly 7 days

p.57 John Tucker, security for Wm Farmer & Benjamin McIntosh
in two suits George Bell agt sd McIntosh & Farmer, delivered
them up in exhonoration of himself

B/S Joseph Hart to Stephen Boren proven by Thomas Johnson

John Siglar appointed Constable; bond 625 Dollars, Jnº Young
and Zebulon B Hobert securities; took required oaths
B/S Wm Clark to Stephen Boren proven by Thomas Johnson
Daniel Holman excused from serving present Term as a Juror
Deed John Hogan to John Johnson ackd
Deed John Porter to Benjamin Porter ackd
Deed John Porter to Benjamin Porter ackd
Deed Melcher Oyler to Wm Johnson proven by Wm Spiller
Deed John Hogan to Saml McMurry ackd
Deed Abraham Young to Thomas Smith proven by Josiah Smith
Deed Moses Larisy to Nathaniel Rogers ackd
Sheriff delivered into Court the amount of the sale of per-
sonal Estate of Matthew Johnson decᵈ

Benjamin Menees Esq[r] returned list of Taxable property in Captain Coughrans District.
Likewise, Bazel Boren...Capt Hutchisons District
Martin Duncan...Captain Johnsons District

Deposition of Dennis Dendry to be taken to prove bond given by William Stuart to Thomas Jemeson

Deed Benjamin Loyd to Matthew Brooks Junr proven by Matthew Brooks
Deed Elisabeth Airs Patrick Martin & George Martin to Samuel Crocket proven by oath of Isaac Robertson

p.58 William Brown Senr vs John Knight on Certiorari. July 1797 pltf appeared, deft by Seth Lewis; refered to arbatrament; award of William Fort & Stephen Boren to be Judgement of Court; proceeding continued; award: in consequence of Jno Knight bringing an Ox which he has in possession of sd Brown we find Brown to be in debt to Knight eleven shillings nine pence, but if the Ox is not brought, we find the sum of nine shillings three pence in favour of Brown. Knight came into Court and delivered up the Ox; Clerk takes possession of Ox for sd Brown & the suit is in favour of sd Knight.
Court Adjourns Untill Tomorrow Morning 10 OClock

Wednesday Morning April 18th 1798
Present Isaac Philips, John Philips, Wm Fort, Martin Duncan, Bazel Boren

Charles Hutton agt Samuel Crocket, John Buckhannon proves three days attendance and 52 miles riding
John Chislom released from paying tax for 1797 for 640 acres Hood preemption, reason Jas Long paid for sd Land

Samuel Crocket ackd himself satisfyed for a Note given by Archer Cheatham Senr to Joseph Price which Crocket has Lost or mislaid

p.59 Eneas McCalister vs Jonathan Price. Jan[y] 1798 pl[tf] by Thomas Stuart; def[t] by James Doherty; cont. Jury Wm Edwards, Anderson Cheatham, Cha[s] Kilgore, Wm Farmer, Wm Dorris, Amos Rounsavall, Asa Woodworth, John Huddleson, David Rounsavall, Benj[n] Porter, Benj[n] McIntosh, David Havard find pl[tf] damages 34 Dollars 61 1/3 cents; & costs. Wm Briscoe proves 3 days attendance as witness; John Philips Esq[r] proves 3 days

Ordered County Tax for present Year be 12½ cents on each 100 acres, 12½ cents each white pole, 25 cents each black pole

for purpose of defraying County Contingencies
Ordered a Tax for present year laid for purpose of defraying
expences of the Publick Building in Springfield as follows,
100 acres 5½ cents, white pole 5½ cents, black pole 11 cents

James Long to oversee Road from Karrs Creek as lately marked
to Moses Winters, all hands each side within 4 miles work on
same

Order Joseph Dorris, Thomas Johnson, John Hutchison, Richard
Matthews, Sampson Matthews, Wm Wills, James Appleton, George
Briscoe and Wm Johnson to lay off a Road from John Donelsons
to Bledsoes Lick as far as the County line; they to nominate
the overseer; all convenient hands to work on same

p.60 Beverley A Allen vs James Bulgin & Isaac Herberts. Sh^ff
Hugh Henry notified by Thomas Johnson returns "Not found,"
January 1797. Order to Sheriff: Beverley A Allen commences
action of Trespass, Damage 30000 Dollars ag^t James Bulgin &
Isaac Herbert, they not being inhabitants of this government
order Judicial attachment be issued. April 1797. July Term
1797 issued; returned October 1797. Continued to Jany Term
1798, Judg^t by Default, attached property to be sold.
p.61 Order by Thos Johnson to Sheriff to sell attached property of James Bulgin & Isaac Herbert; levied on books. April
7th 1798 two books sold, one by Alex^r Pope for 50 Cents, a
spelling dictionary for 25 cents. Hugh Henry sh^ff. Jury W^m
Edwards, Anderson Cheatham, Chas Kilgore, Wm Farmer, Wm Dorris, Amos Rounsavall, Asa Woodworth, John Huddleston, David
Rounsavall, Benjamin Porter, Benjamin McIntosh, David Havard
who find for pl^tf damages 14 083 Dollars 55 cents; plaintiff
to recover; also costs

D/Gift Beverly Allen to Ann Coke Allen, Jn° Hays Allen, Mary
Allen, Beverley Allen J^r, Sarah Allen ackd

Wm Rasere[Rasin?] app^td overseer from Brush Creek to Calebs
Creek on the Clarksville Road, and all hands work on s^d Road
the south side of the Sulpher fork between s^d Road and Creek

p.62 Wm Armstrong Senr app^td overseer of the Kentucky Road
from Harrington fork of Red River to the Kentucky State Line
& Ja^s Crabtree Esqr divide the hands between s^d overseer and
Wm Byrd & Ja^s Wheeler former overseers

William Fleuellen app^td overseer of Road from Millers Creek
to Browns fork on road called Betts Road

Deed Isaac Titsworth to John Fort proven by Elias Fort

Benjamin McIntosh and William Farmer give Joseph Dorris, Jn° Dorris and Robert Lancaster as their securities in two suits brought ag' them by George Bell, returned to present Term

Hugh Henry gave Bond 5000 Dollars, Bazel Boren, George Briscoe and Benjamin McIntosh his securities for faithfull Collection of County & State Tax for 1798 in Robertson Co

Thomas Talbot vs Cornelius Dabney & Stephen Boren. S f. 17 March 1797 Isaac Brown entered Bond with Cornelius Dabney & Stephen Boren securities, sum 60 Dollars, Bond to be void on condition Isaac Brown appeared before County Court at Benjn McIntosh house July 1797 to answer Thomas Talbot in plea of Debt which Brown detains; he hath failed to appear and debt costs & charges hath failed to pay. Cornelius Dabney & Stephen Boren to appear in April next to show cause why Execution should not issue against their goods chattels lands and Tenements for the amount of the debt & costs. Thos Johnson. Came to hand Feby 5th 1798. Feby 6th made known to Stephen Boren in presence of Ge° Prince & Wm Montgomery. Feby 15th 1798 made known to Corn^s Dabney in presence of M Duncan & J Barr. At April Term 1798 pl^{tf} appeared by Isham A Parker and Judgement entered ag' def^{dts}
Court Adjourns untill Court in Course.   Z B Hobert, John
                                   Philips, Isaac Philips

State vs Thomas McIntosh. Presentment. Def^{dt} submits and is fined 6 cents

p.63 Monday July the 16th 1798   Present
William Fort, Benjamin Menees, Martin Duncan, & Ja^s Crabtree

Grand Jurors James Appleton foreman, David Jones, James Elliott, John Carr, Holland Dardin, John Robins, Nathan Clark, James Jones, Elijah Hamilton, Isaac Dorris, Johnson Kilgore, John Couts, Wm Gilbert, Alexander Cromwell, Elijah Lancaster

John Tygard vs Philip Shackler. Attachment. July 1797 Sh^{ff} returned on s^d attachment Levied on 274 acres; pl^{tf} by James Doherty; proceedings cont^d to April 1798. Judg^t by Default ag' Def'; cause cont^d to July 1798. Jury John Krisel, Wm Deloach, Isaac Dortch, John Dorris, Caleb Winters, Elias Fort Jr, Benjamin Wood, Jonathan Dardin, George Sprouse, Richard Matthews, William Johnson, Aaron Angling who find for pl^{tf} & assess his damage to 9 Dollars 47 cents. Ordered so much of Property attached be sold as will pay debt & Costs of suit

Edward Cheatham on application is allowed to build a mill on
Spring Creek of Sulpher fork on his own Land

Thomas Christmas records his stock mark

Miles Kerby app^td Constable, gives Bond 625 Dollars, Archer
Cheatham Senr & Edward Cheatham his securities; took oaths

p.64   Deed Isaac Miller to Abraham Tippey proven by William
Duncan
Deed Edward Saunders to Volentine Choate ackd
Deed Edward Saunders to Thomas Bounds ackd
Deed George Saddler to Matthew Luter ackd
Deed James Norfleet to Laurence Karr ackd
Deed Elisha Billing to Allen Parker proven by Saml Hollis
Deed Thomas Smith to Willis Whilford & Thos Whilford ackd
B/S Lewis Pipkin to Wm Johnson proven by Thos Johnson

Ordered Clerk receive lists of Taxable property
Court Adjourns untill Tomorrow Morning 9 OClock

Tuesday morning July the 17th 1798.   Present
Wm Fort, William Miles, Z B Hobert, John Philips, Esquires

James Maclin, summoned as witness in suit W^m B Powel against
Daniel Lyons, George Havard and Benjamin McIntosh, failed to
attend; Order that he forfeit unless at first Court he shows
sufficient cause to the Contrary

Josiah Fort Esqr appt^d County Trustee; bond 10 000 Dollars,
Wm Deloach, Elias Fort J^r and Anderson Cheatham his security

Election for Sheriff. Present Wm Fort, William Miles, James
Norfleet, John Philips, Isaac Philips, Bazel Boren, Martin
Duncan Esq^rs when James Menees J^r was elected

Joseph Herndon Esqr, licenced to practice Law, admitted

Joseph Dorris & John Dorris delivered Benjamin McIntosh & W^m
Farmer for whom they were securities in suit George Bell ag^t
McIntosh & Farmer

p.65 William Baxter Powel vs Danl Lyons, Ge^o Havard & Benjn
McIntosh. Debt. Oct Term 1797 Sheriff returned execution on
George Havard & Benjamin McIntosh; pl^tf by Samuel Donelson;
def^ts by James Doherty. Cont. Death of George Havard; Scire
facias issued ag^t rep^s of Ge^o Havard, return July 1798
"Made known to Mary Havard, wife of Ge^o Dec^d, in presence of

Stephen Boren & Meredith Walton. J Wray, D.S." Jury John
Krisel, Wm Deloach, John Dorris, Caleb Winters, Elias Fort
Jr, Benjn Wood, Jonathan Dardin, Jacob McCarty, Benjn Coats,
George Campbell, John Johnson, John Huddleston, who find for
Plaintiff Damage 58 Dollars 30 cents; Def^{ts} obtained appeal
to Superior C^t, David Havard and Cornelius Dabney securities

Charles Hutton vs Samuel Crocket. Case. January 1798 pl^{tf} by
Thos Stuart; def^t by James Doherty. Cont^d to July. Jury John
Krisel, Wm Deloach, John Dorris, Caleb Winters, Elias Fort
Jr, Benjn Wood, Jonathan Dardin, Jacob McCarty, Benjn Coats,
George Campbell, John Johnson, John Huddleston who find for
pl^{tf} Damages 69 Dollars; also costs of suit. John McGaugh
proved two days attendance as a witness & sixty miles travel
Wm McGaugh two days attendance & sixty miles travel

p.66 Elener Logue J^r by Next friend Elener Logue vs Michael
Purtle. Case. April 1798 pl^{tf} by Seth Lewis; def^t by James
Doherty. Cont^d to July. Jury Charles Wheaton, Abraham Tippy,
Peter Lerew, Jno Briscoe, Wm Briscoe, Wm Matthews, Volentine
Choate, James Sawyers, John Parchment, Samuel Todd, Patrick
Martin, Richard Matthews, who find for pl^{tf}, assess her dam-
age to 125 Dollars; def^t obtained appeal to Superior Court,
James Ford & George Purtle his securities
David Young wit one days attendance & sixty miles traveling
Samuel Crocket   "   30   "
Adam Young   "   30   "
Robert Barnet   "   24   "
Zachariah Betts   "   24   "
John Byrn   "   30   "
John Boren   3   30   "
Sarah Boren   3   30   "

Samuel Sugg apptd Constable to attend next Court
Deed William Johnson to Lewis Pipkin proven by Thos Johnson

P/A Margeret Karr widow, William Karr, Henry & Mary Johnson,
Welles and Elender Hicks, William and Sarah Briscoe to James
Karr ackd

B/S Henry Gardner to Isaac Flannery proven by James Norfleet
Court Adjourns untill Tomorrow Morning 9 OClock

Wednesday July 18th 1798   Present William
Fort, John Philips, James Norfleet, and Bazel Boren Esquires

p.67 George Bell vs Joseph Hamilton & David Hamilton. Debt.
Jan 1798 pl^{tf} by Joseph Herndon; def^t by Thos Stuart. Cont^d.
Jury Isaac Dortch, William Deloach, Elias Fort J^r, Jonathan

Dardin, Benjn Wood, John Krisel, John Dorris, Abraham Tippy,
Nicholas Conrod, Chas Miles, John Hutchison, Patrick Martin,
who find for pl^{tf} his debt 79 Dollars, assess his damages 7
Dollars 61 cents & 6^d costs

Ltrs/Admn granted to Robert Barnet on estate of Ann Kanedy
decd; bond with David Henry and Isaac Henry his securities.
Ordered sale of personal estate of Ann Kenedy

Elener Logue Jr by her Next friend vs Michael Purtle. Order
name of Robert Barnett as security for pl^{tf} be struck out &
Jas McDaniel & John Dorris be inserted, being by their consent freely given in April court previous to the Trial

Robert Barnet delivered Inventory estate of Ann Kenedy dec^d
Deed Isaac Miller to Nathan Clark proven by Elijah Lancaster
Order adm^{rs} of the estate of Ann Dardin dec^d expose to sale
agreeable to law the Estate of the Dec^d
Order Thomas Johnson Clerk of Court be allowed for his exof-
ficio services 26 Dollars for services to present Term
Order Sheriff receive same pay as Clerk above mentioned

Joseph Barns vs Benjamin Nail. Case. April 1798 Pl^{tf} by Seth
Lewis; def^t by Jas Doherty. July jury Samuel Crocket, Thomas
Conner, Jno Huddleston, Henry Johnson, Joseph Hamilton, Nim-
rod McIntosh, William Karr, Edward Cheatham, Nicholas Couts,
Jno Smeathers, George Briscoe, Wm Farmer who find for pl^{tf},
damage 119 Dollars 66 2/3 cents; def^t obtains appeal to Su-
perior Court, Patrick Martin his security
Archer Cheatham witness proves three days attendance
Anderson Cheatham   "
Thomas Cheatham   "
Peter Cheatham   "
Patrick Martin   two
Nimrod McIntosh   one
John Crane   "
David Henry   three
Abraham Tippy   "

Matthew McCance vs James Menees J^r. Case. April 1798 pl^{tf} by
Bennet Searcy; def^t by James Doherty. July Term jury Isaac
Dortch, Wm Deloach, Elias Fort J^r, Jonathan Dardin, Benjamin
Wood, John Krisel, John Dorris, Abraham Tippy, Nicholas Con-
rod, Charles Miles, John Hutchison, Patrick Martin, who find
for pl^{tf}, damage 115 Dollars 83 cents & costs
John Mcfarlin witness proves 3 days attendance & 40 miles

Lands of John G Blount, reported for not being given in as
Taxable for 1797, released as same not in this County

p.69 Daniel Burford agent for Henry Lester vs Cornelius Dabney. Debt. April 1798 pl't by John C Hamilton; def' by Seth Lewis. July jury Isaac Dortch, Wᵐ Deloach, Elias Fort Junʳ, Jonathan Dardin, Benjᵘ Wood, John Krisel, John Dorris, Abraham Tippy, Nicholas Conrod, Charles Miles, John Hutchison, Patrick Martin, who find for pl'ᶠ, assess damage to 46 Dollars 83 cents, also costs of suit
Robert Tait witness proved two days attendance & sixty miles

James Karr vs Cornelius Dabney. Covenant. April 1798 pl'ᶠ by Samˡ Donelson; def' failing to appear, Judgement by default against him, cause cont'ᵈ. July jury Samuel Crocket, Francis Conner, John Huddleston, Joseph Hamilton, Nimrod McIntosh, Edward Cheatham, Nicholas Couts, John Crane, George Briscoe, John White, John Wilson, Ezekiel Clampet, who find for pl'ᶠ & assess his damage to 95 Dollars 21 cents, & costs of suit
Henry Johnson witness proved two days attendance
William Karr   "
James Robertson   one

Wᵐ Fort Esqr added to the number of arbitrators appointed to decide a suit between Nicholas Conrod extr for J Conrod decᵈ ag' Martin Grider and John Alston; make return to next Court

p.70   Martin Duncan vs Andrew Irwin. Covenant. April Term 1798 pl'ᶠ by Thoˢ Stuart; def' by Samˡ Donelson. Cont. July Jury Isaac Dortch, Wᵐ Deloach, Elias Fort Jʳ, Jonathan Dardin, Jnᵒ Krisel, John Dorris, Charles Miles, John Hutchison, Patrick Martin, Jacob McCarty, Jaˢ Karr, Jacob Pickrell, who find for pl'ᶠ, assess damage 51 Dollars 75 cents; also costs

George Briscoe vs Hugh Dobins. Attachment. Apˡ 1798 Sheriff levied on Negro Boy; pl'ᶠ by Samuel Donelson, Js Herndon & I McNutt Esqˢ; deft by S Lewis; cont'ᵈ. July jury Isaac Dortch, Wᵐ Deloach, Elias Fort Jʳ, Jonathan Dardin, John Krisel, Jnᵒ Dorris, Abraham Tippy, John Hutchison, Patrick Martin, Jacob McCarty, Jaˢ Karr, Jacob Pickrell, who find for pl'ᶠ 92 Dollars debt and 2 Dollars 37 cents damages; also costs of suit

William B Powell vs Danl Lyons, Geo Havard & Benjn McIntosh. Joseph Herndon, witness, proves 3 days attendance & 60 miles

George Bell vs Joseph and David Hamilton. Cornelius Dabney, witness, proves 3 days attendance

James Norfleet Esqʳ apptd to take enumeration of inhabitants in Cap' Pattersons District in stead of Wᵐ Miles Esqʳ who is about to Remove

p.71 Order John Brooks oversee Road from Karrs Creek to John

34

Donelsons in place of John Tucker, & that he strike West end
of Main Street & clear out sd street in town of Springfield

Order that Saml Crocket, John Wilson, Patrick Martin, Henry
Aires, Wm Conyers, Grisham Coffield, Ja^s Elliott Senr, James
Walker, James Elliott J^r, Isaac Moore, Benjn Wood, & Philip
Parchment are hands assigned to Wm Fleuellen to work on Road
of which he is overseer & all within their bounds
Court Adjourns untill Tomorrow Morning 6 OClock

Thursday Morning, July the 19th 1798. Present Wm Fort, John
Philips, Isaac Philips, James Norfleet, Martin Duncan Esq^{rs}
Court Adjourns for half an hour. Court Met according to Ad-
journment, Present the same as above

Richard Matthews app^{id} overseer of Road from John Donelsons
plantation to Sumner County line leading to Bledsoes Lick as
lately marked, hands formerly assigned work on same

Ordered County Trustee advance loan to James Norfleet & John
Young, Springfield commissioners, 100 Dollars Publick money

Sheriff presented list of Insolvents from whom he cannot
collect 1797 Tax

George Bell vs Wm Farmer & Benjamin McIntosh. Debt 183 Dollars 71 Cents. Def^{ts} in hands of Sheriff; pl^{if} called & not
praying them to satisfy said judgement, order def^{ts} released

George Bell vs Benjamin McIntosh & Wm Farmer. Debt 172 Dollars 72 Cents. Def^{ts} in hands of Sheriff; pl^{if} not praying
that they remain in custody to satisfy s^d judgment; released

Hugh Henry Sh^{ff} took Oath for Collection of Tax present year

p.72 Ordered Clerk forthwith transmit a Return of lands not
given in, or tax paid for, for year 1797 Agreeably to Sheriffs Report to the Knoxville Gazette to be published

Whereas William Dennis agent for Eli West returned 500 acres
for 1797 & Hugh Henry Shff made Report that Taxes due thereon not paid & that there is no personal goods of Eli West on
which he can distress it is ordered that Clerk cause copy of
this order to be published in Knoxville Gazette three times
together with Taxes due on sd lands & costs

Edward Douglass & Co vs Joseph Dorris. Case. July 1798 pl^f
by Saml Donelson, def^t in proper person confessed Judgement
31 Dollars 87 cents & costs

Jacob Harrow vs William Williams. Covenant. July 1798 Plaintiff dismised Suit and Def[t] assumed costs

William Montgomery vs William Dorris. Case. July 1798 pl[f] by
Sam[l] Donelson also in proper person dismised Suit, and Def[dt]
in proper person assumed all costs

Mich[l] Campbell & And[w] Hinds Ext[rs] of Philip Philips Dec[d] vs
Joseph Dorris Def[t]. Case. July 1798 pl[tf] by Bennet Searcy &
in proper person confessed judgement for 11 pounds 13 shillings nine pence Virginia Money equal to 39 Dollars & 26 cts
and costs

p.73 William Taitt vs William Miles. Debt. July 1798 pl[f] by
Bennet Searcy; def[t] by Seth Lewis came in proper person and
confessed Judgement 73 Dollars 4 cents being Debt & Interest
on the Bond filed; & Costs

William Taitt vs William Rascoe. Case. July 1798 plf by Bennet Searcy; deft in proper person came & Confessed Judgement
10 pounds 5 shillings Virginia Money, equal to 34 Dollars 20
cents, & costs

Thomas Hickman vs Joseph Philips. Case. July 1798 plf by S
Lewis; deft in proper person Confessed Judgement, £15.17/77p
Equal to fifty two Dollars & ninety three 3/4 cents, & costs

George Bell vs W[m] Farmer and Benj[n] McIntosh. Debt. July 1798
pl[f] by W[m] P Anderson & Joseph Herndon; Def[dts] in proper person confessed Judgement 183 Dollars 71 cents and costs

George Bell vs Benj[n] McIntosh and W[m] Farmer. Debt. July 1798
pl[f] by W[m] P Anderson & Joseph Herndon Esq[rs]; Def[ts] in proper
persons Confessed Judgment 172 Dollars 72 Cents & Costs

Court Adjourned untill Court in Course to Meet in the Town
of Springfield. Signed Wm Fort, John Philips, Martin Duncan, Isaac Philips, James Norfleet

p.74 Robertson County. Monday October 15th 1798. Springfield
Present John Philips, Martin Duncan, Benjn Menees, Esquires.
Court Adjourns half Hour to Meet at Store House of Geo Bell.
Court Met According to Adjournment at George Bells House in
Springfield. Present John Philips, Martin Duncan, Benjamin
Menees, Esqrs

James Menees Esqr produced Commission from Governor to serve as Sheriff; gave bond 12500 Dollars, Nathan Arnet, William Fleuellen, Isaac Menees, Laurence Carr & John Karr his securities, took Oaths required for qualification of Sheriff

Grand Jurors Anderson Cheatham foreman, Elijah Flannery, Wm Spiller, Thomas Simpson, Edward Cheatham, Laurence Carr, Wm Elliott, Jno Crane, Jno Parchment, Saml McMurry, Chas Colgan [Colyar?], William Coates, William Fleuellen, Josiah Ramsey

Elisabeth Locust who has been in Slavery and supposed she is free, produced Ann Barker to prove her freedom; agreeable to her Testamony, Court are of Opinion she is Free, & Liberates her as such

Will of Moses Winters decd proven by Wm Fleuellen; Elisabeth Winters extx took oath; Letters Testamentary to issue

Resignation of Isham A Parker as County Solicitor; Joseph Herndon is appointed; took the Oath by law required

p.75   Will of George Wills decd proven by Robert Johnston; William Wills and Robert Wilson extrs took oath; Letters Testamentary to issue

John Gardner excused from serving as Juror at present Term

Benjamin Menees delivered enumeration of free Taxable inhabitants within his District

Taxable property of James Shannon by mistake twice given in; sd Shannon released from one of the charges

Deed Mark Noble to Ezekiel Smith ackd
Deed James Henderson to Nicholas Choate ackd
Deed Hugh Lewis to Joseph Washington proven by Miles Kirby
Deed John Boren to Charles McIntosh proven by Thos Johnson
Deed Margaret Mcfarlin extx of Jas Mcfarlin decd to John Crane proven by Miles Kirby
Deed Robert Weakley to Luke Rawls proven by Jacob Lewis
Deed Robert Weakly to Isaac Saunders proven by Jacob Lewis
Deed Edward Harris to John Powers proven by Wm McAdoe
Deed Robt Weakley to Jacob Moake proven by Jacob Lewis
Deed Robert Weakley to Jacob Lewis proven by Luke Rawls

Azariah Dunn excused from serving as Juror at present Term
p.76 Court Adjourns untill tomorrow Morning 10 OClock

Tuesday Morning October 16th 1798

Present Wm Fort, Benjamin Menees, Martin Duncan, Esquires

Nicholas Conrod vs Philip Conrod. Detinue. April 1798 pl^{tf} by Samuel Donelson and Seth Lewis; defend^t by James Doherty. Cont^d. Octr Jury Philip Parchment, William Conyers, Nimrod McIntosh, David Havard, Caleb Winters, William Crocket, John Hutchison, Benjn Nail, John Barr, Walter Stark, Patrick Martin, Matthew Day who find for Def^t. Pl^{tf} prayed and obtained appeal to Superior C^t, George Bell & John Jones securities

Samuel Crocket vs Nicholas Conrod. Case. April 1798 pl^f by Ja^s Doherty; def^t by Seth Lewis & Jo^s Herndon. Cont^d. Octr Jury Philip Parchment, Wm Conyers, Nimrod McIntosh, David Havard, Caleb Winters, John Hutchison, Benjn Nail, Jno Barr, Walter Stark, Patrick Martin, Matthew Day, Elijah Lancaster

p.77 Andrew Snoddy vs Jesse Cain. Attachment. April 1798 Sheriff H Henry levied on 41 acres where Elisabeth Cain now resides. Pl^{tf} by Saml Donelson. Court ordered Judicial attachment issue. J Wray Sh^{ff} levied on 2 feather beds, 1 pot, 2 pewter dishes & 6 small pewter plates. Pl^{tf} by att^y; def^t failing to appear, Judgement by Default; cause cont^d. Octr Jury Philip Parchment, Wm Conyers, Nimrod McIntosh, David Havard, Caleb Winters, Jno Hutchison, Benjn Nail, John Barr, Walter Stark, Patrick Martin, Matthew Day, Elijah Lancaster who find for pl^{tf} and assess damage to 30 Dollars 46 cents; also costs of suit

Saml Crocket vs Nicholas Conrod. James Adams witness proves 4 days attendance, 120 miles riding. David Tully wit proves 2 days, 60 miles. John Willson witness proves 3 days

Nicholas Conrod vs Philip Conrod. John Jones witness proves 3 days attendance & 80 miles riding

Deposition of Peter Lerew to be taken in suit Jacob McCarty agt Mary Warner as an interpleader in suit Jacob McCarty agt Joseph T Still on an attachment before Isaac Philips, Esqr

Deed James McElyea to Henry Jones proven by David Spence

p.78 Jesse Carter vs Cornelius Dabney. Debt. July 1798 pl^{tf} by George Smith, def^t by James Doherty. Cont^d. October Jury Philip Parchment, William Conyers, Nimrod McIntosh, David Havard, Caleb Winters, Jno Hutchison, Benjn Nail, John Barr, Walter Stark, Patrick Martin, Matthew Day, Elijah Lancaster, who find for plaintiff 48 Dollars 40 cents; also costs

Sheriff of Robertson County protests agt Gaol of sd county James Norfleet Delivered Enumeration of Taxable Inhabitants

in Bounds of Capt⁰ Pattersons Company
Deed Eli Jones to Meredith Walton ackd

Bond Christian Crips to Samuel Hendley proven by Danl Hogan;
also the assignment on s^d Bond made by Adam Hampton to David
Shelby proven by William Taitt

Deed John Payton to Joseph Dickson proven by Henry Wigle
James Stark to oversee Road from Sulpher fork on Logan Road
to Kentucky state line
William Johnston, Red River, records his stock mark

p.79   Nicholas Conrod Ext^r of Joseph Conrod dec^d vs Martin
Greider. Debt. October 1797 Pl^f by Seth Lewis; def^t by James
Doherty, Cont^d to Jany 1798, to Ap^l 1798 at which Term cause
refered to Arbratrament & award of James Norfleet & Benjamin
Menees. July 1798 Wm Fort app^{ld} to act with those before ap-
p^{ld}. Oct 1798 arbitrators award: Martin Greider allowed 160
Dollars as a sett upon Note of Hand given by s^d Greider
& Jn° Alston for 237 Dollars 42 Cents. Signed Oct 13th 1798.
Wm Fort, Ja^s Norfleet, Benjn Menees. Considered by Court the
Pl^l f to recover 85 Dollars 12 cents; also his Costs of suit

Court Adjourns untill tomorrow Morning 10 OClock

Wednesday Morning October 1798
Present Wm Fort, Benjn Menees, John Philips, Martin Duncan

p.80 Anderson Cheatham brought 4 Dollars 45 cents, the sum
due Hannah Porter on Judgement obtained by sd Porter agt sd
Cheatham before Wm Fort Esqr; appeal to this Court

Ordered one acre condemned for purpose of building a fulling
mill on the branch below Charles Miles's mill for the use of
Charles Miles

Lemuel Sugg gave Bond 620 Dollars, William Fleuellen & Alexander Cromwell his securities for his duty as Constable

Sugg Fort, Miles Kirby & Charles Wheaton apptd Commissioners
to settle with County Trustee, give bond & security next Ct

Thomas Johnson made oath he lost one Certificate for service
of Benjn Hardin on Road Guard which is now payable in County
Tax, that after credits were deducted there was a balance of
£7 unpaid; ordered that s^d Johnson be intitled to afsd £7

Martin Duncan delivered Enumeration of Taxable Inhabitants
in Captn Wm Johnsons District

Bazel Boren Delivered Enumeration of Taxable Inhabitants in Capt^u Hutchisons Company
Zebulon B Hobert Delivered into Court Enumeration of Taxable Inhabitants in Captn Youngs District

George Briscoe allowed tavern licence in Robertson County at his own house, Saml Donelson & Anderson Cheatham, securities

Jurors to Superior Court: Archer Cheatham Senr, James Crabtree Senr, John Hutchison, Isaac Philips, Samuel Crocket, David Hamilton

p.81   Nicholas Conrod vs Jonathan Price. Appeal. Jany 1798 pl^tf by S Lewis & Joseph Herndon; def^t by Ja^s Doherty. Cause cont^d each Term to Octr 1798; suit dismissed at pl^tfs costs

Vachel Lovelass vs Thomas Christmas. Debt. July Term 1798. Pl^tf by Ja^s Doherty; def^t by Seth Lewis; cont^d. October Term Def^t by att^y and in proper person confesses Judgement for 31 Dollars 25 cents with interest on the Note to this Day, and Costs. The Interest is 87 cents

William Clement & Co vs Lamuel Sugg. Debt. Pl^tf by S Lewis; def^t by Ja^s Doherty, Bennet Searcy & Isaac McNutt. Pl^tfs attorney dismissed suit & assumed all costs

Vachel Lovelass vs Thomas Christmas. Augustine Cook, witness, proved 3 days attendance

p.82   George Briscoe vs James Ford & James Taylor. Si fa. Writ to Sheriff Montgomery County relating that 3 March 1798 Hugh Dobins entered, James Ford and James Taylor securities, sum 184 Dollars, void on his appearance at next Robertson C^t at Benj^u McIntosh's house to prosecute his action ag^t George Briscoe for taking his Negro Boy; Dobins hath failed to appear and Debt & Costs hath failed to pay to s^d Briscoe. Sh^ff is told to have two good men of his county make known to Ja^s Ford & James Taylor personally to be before Robertson Court in Springfield on third Monday October to shew cause why Execution should not issue against their goods & chattels for amount of s^d debt & costs. Sh^ff returns "Made known to James Ford & James Taylor in presence of Ge^o Bell & Wm Montgomery. G. Neville Sh^ff."
October Term 1798 pl^tf by Samuel Donelson, J Herndon & Isaac McNutt; def^t failing to appear Judgement was entered against them according Scire facias, & it is considered by the Court that the pl^tf recover ag^t def^t 94 Dollars 37 cents being the amount of Debt due from Dobbins to pl^tf also costs of suit

Ordered that Briton Bryan, Joseph Hamilton, Wm Johnson (Red

River), Lam¹ Sugg, Joseph Wimberley, Wᵐ Byrd, Elias Fort Jʳ,
Epaps Lawson, Isaac Dortch, Archᵈ Mahan, Azariah Dunn, John
Gardner, Elias Laurence, Holland Dardin, Jonathan Dardin,
Alexander Cromwell, Jesse Martin, Walter Stark, John Duncan,
Jonathan Price, Thomas Woodard, Richard Nuckolls, Wᵐ Benson,
Wᵐ Johnson, Sampson Trammel, John Price, Samuel Crocket, Abᵐ
Tippy, David Cane, Arther Pitt, John Young, Abram Young at-
tend our next Court as Jurors.
Court Adjourns untill Court in Course   Isaac Philips, Benjⁿ
                          Menees, Martin Duncan, John Philips

p.83   Robertson County. Monday January 21sᵗ 1799   At the
House of George Bell, Springfield. Present Benjamin Menees,
John Philips, Martin Duncan, Esquires

Commission from his Execllency John Sevier presented commis-
sioning John Hutchison, George Bell and Hardy Bryan Justices
of the Peace for this County. Hutchison and Bell took oaths

Grand Jurors Wm Johnson (Red River) foreman, Wm Byrd, Elias
Fort Junr, Sampson Trammel, Arthur Pitt, John Gardner, Abraham Tippy, Jesse Martin, Epephroditus Lawson, Archibald Mahan, Walter Stark, Azeriah Dunn, Wm Benson, Abraham Young,
Jonathan Price

Thos Smith brought Thos Yates who deposeth that Silas Smith,
son of afsd Thomas, has part of an ear bit off; he was present when it happened and knows it was done in the fights

Benjamin Sewel produced licence to practice law; admitted

Will of Joseph Carmack decd proven by Abraham Tippy. Mary
Carmack & Thomas Johnson extx & extr of will of Joseph Carmack decd took the oath of executor

Nathan Arnet, who was security for appearance of Samuel Musgrove in suit Mary Crolly agt Musgrove, delivered Musgrove

Nimrod McIntosh, who was security for the appearance of John
White in suit Joseph Motheral agt Benjn McIntosh & Jno White
delivered up sd White

Ordered Executors of Joseph Carmack decd are at Liberty to
sell as much of Estate of Decd as they see cause, giving 12
days notice of sale and 12 months credit

p.84 Benjamin Porter apptd overseer/Road in place of William Crunk

George Campbell apptd Constable, gave Joseph Dorris and John Dorris as his Securities and took Oaths by Law required

Jonathan Dardin excused from serving as a Juror this Term

B/S William Melone to Nicholas Conrod proven by Zebulon B Hobert

Deed James Menees Shff to Jane Asbell ackd

Deed James Menees Shff to Jane Asbell, lot in Springfield, acknowledged

D/G William Armstrong to Jane, Sally, and Nancy Armstrong, proven by Richard Clark

Deed Edward Harris to George Henley proven by Wm McAdoe

Deed George Walker to John Patterson proven by Jas Hewit

Deed Isaac Flannery to William Spiller proven by Bazel Boren

Isaac Weakley excused from serving as a Juror this Term

William B Powel licenced to keep a Tavern, bond 200 Dollars with Jacob Young and Francis Byrd his securities

Court Adjourned untill tomorrow Morning 10 OClock

Tuesday Morning, January 22nd 1799   Present John Philips, Z B Hobert, John Hutchison, Benjn Menees, Martin Duncan, Esqrs

p.85 William Campbell vs Philip Parchment. Case. July 1798 Plⁱᶠ by Joseph Herndon; Defⁱ by James Dorris. Dispute over ownership of 3 Negroes at house of Robert Scott in Bladen Co North Carolina named York, Peter & Ceazer

p.86 S Lewis for Defᵈᵗ, J Herndon for plⁱᶠ. Contᵈ. January jury John Price, Richard Nuckolls, Alexander Cromwell, John Duncan, Isaac Dortch, Wᵐ Johnson, Holland Dardin, Jonathan Dardin, Samuel Crocket, Thoˢ Yates, Matthew Day, Wᵐ Elliott who find for plⁱᶠ, assess damage 200 Dollars. Defⁱ obtained appeal to Superior Cᵗ, Martin and William Elliott securities

Asa Woodworth proves 2 days attendance as a witness

Wᵐ McAdoe, who has in possession a Negro Elisabeth or Betsey Locust, ackd her a Free person, prays same be Recorded. Ordered Hannah Locust, James Locust, Austin Locust, and Moses Locust children of above Elisabeth or Betsey Locust continue in possession of Wᵐ McAdoe untill they arrive at age 21 provided he continue to live within Jurisdiction of this Court during that period

Archer Cheatham Junr resigned being Constable

p.87 John Philips Esqʳ security for appearance of Jaˢ Adams in suit Geᵒ Briscoe agⁱ sᵈ Adams delivered him up. Wᵐ Boren ack^d himself security for James Adams in above suit

Charles Wheaton, Miles Kerby and Sugg Fort, Commissioners to
settle with Collectors of County Tax, gave Bond 100 Dollars
with David Smith security

Deed Daniel Welburn to David Smith proven by Briton Bryant
Deed John Young and James Norfleet, Commissioners of Spring-
field, to Richard Matthews Senr ackd
Deed Philip Trammel to John Young proven by Abraham Young
Deed Henry Johnson Sh^ff to Thomas Johnson ackd
Deed Thomas Smith to John Young proven by Abraham Young
Deed Christopher Taylor adm^r of Wm Renfro decd to Wm Connel
proven by James Norfleet
Deed James Norfleet & Jno Young Commissioners of Springfield
to Wm Luck J^r ackd
Deed Hugh Henry Sh^ff to John Young ackd
Deed Jno Young & Ja^s Norfleet Com^rs for Springfield to Rich^d
Matthews Junr ackd
Miles Kerby returns List of Taxable property for 1798: 499
acres, one white pole, one black pole
Inventory, estate of Moses Winters dec^d delivered by extx
Inventory, estate of Joseph Carmack dec^d delivered by extrs

p.88 Deed Christopher Taylor Adm^r of William Renfro dec^d to
Robert Black proven by Ja^s Norfleet
Deed George Briscoe to Wm Briscoe proven by Thomas [blank]
Deed Zebulon B Hobert [to] John Hudson ack^d
Deed Christopher Taylor Adm^r Wm Renfro dec^d to Isaac Dortch
proven by James Norfleet
Deed Elias Fort to Obedience Smith proven by Sugg Fort
Deed Elias Fort to Esther Jackson proven by Sugg Fort
Deed Elias Fort to Elisabeth Lawson proven by Sugg Fort
Deed Elias Fort to Catherine Williams proven by Sugg Fort
Deed John Young and James Norfleet Comm^rs for Springfield to
George Bell ackd
P/A Edward Harris to Thomas Johnson proven by Willie Blount

George Briscoe was constitutionally elected Coroner; bond
1000 Dollars, Hugh Henry & James Menees Jr, securities
Court Adjourns untill Tomorrow Morning 10 OClock

Wednesday Morning January 23rd 1799   Present
John Philips, Martin Duncan, James Norfleet, Esquires

John White gave Bond to Sh^ff in place of Nimrod McIntosh who
this Term delivered up s^d White in the Suit Joseph Motheral
ag^t Benjamin McIntosh & John White, Securities are Ja^s Adams
& Moses Boren as p^r Bond filed

John Young registered his stock mark and brand

p.89 State vs George Briscoe. Def^{dt} ack^d bound 200 Dollars, attendance at this Court from day to day during this Term to answer such things as may be alledged against him in behalf of the State

Wm Montgomery vs Wm Miles. Case. Octr 1798 pl^{tf} by Saml Donelson & Isaac McNutt; def^d by Ja^s Doherty. Cont^d. Jany jury Thos Hutchison, Thos Christmas, Jacob R Pickrel, John Parchment, John Brooks, James Henderson, John Briscoe, Patrick Martin, Thos Simpson, William Boren, Moses Boren, Thos Yates who find for Defendant

The Sheriff entered protest against Jaol of Robertson county

James Adams & Moses Boren delivered John White for whom they were security in suit Joseph Motheral ag^t Benjn McIntosh and John White

Ordered a Road laid off from Springfield to Maj David Smiths mill on Elk fork of Red River as far as Kentucky State Line; following to mark same Charles McIntosh, Lamuel Sugg, David Hamilton, John Philips, Alexander Cromwell, Joseph Hamilton, Isaac Philips, Wm Fort, Sugg Fort, James Norfleet, any five

Deed John Young and James Norfleet Comm^{rs} for Springfield to Archer Cheatham J^r ack^d

p.90 Benjn Hicks vs Thos Christmas. July 1793 pl^{tf} by George Smith; def^t by James Doherty. Cont^d to Jany 1799. Arbratrament of Francis Hall & William Miles; award Def^t pay pl^{t}f 40 Dollars, each pays own costs of suit. Francis Hall, Wm Miles

Deed John Young and James Norfleet Comm^{rs} for Springfield to Archer Cheatham J^r ack^d
Deed Kirby Vick to Noel Vick proven by John Cheatham
Deed John Young and James Norfleet Comm^{rs} for Springfield to Thos Johnson ackd
Deed John Young and James Norfleet Comm^{rs} &c to Thos Johnson ackd
Deed James Henderson to Archibald Huddleston ackd
Deed John Young and James Norfleet Comm^{rs} &c to John Philips ackd
Ordered that Thos Johnson County Clerk be allowed 15 Dollars for three bound books purchased by him for use of County

p.91 Joseph Motheral vs Benjn McIntosh & John White. Debt. Octr 1798 pl^{tf} by Bennet Searcy; def^t by James Doherty, Jos-

eph Herndon & Thos Stuart, pleads payment. Cont^d. Jany jury
Thos Hutchison, Jacob Pickrel, John Parchment, John Briscoe,
Patrick Martin, Thos Simpson, Wm Boren, Moses Boren, Matthew
Day, Asaph Parker, Peter Spence, Jeffery Lively who find for
pltf his debt 161 Dollars 55 cents, Damage 6 Dollars 46 cts;
also costs of suit
Court Adjourns untill tomorrow Morning 10 OClock

Thursday Morning January 24th 1799   Present John Philips,
Zebulon B Hobert, John Hutchison, James Norfleet, Esquires

State vs George Briscoe. Def^t ack^d bound 100 Dollars for his
attendance at next Court to answer charge of State agt him

John White who was Delivered to Sheriff in Suit Joseph Motheral ag^t Benjn McIntosh & John White, released from custody
because pl^{tf} did not pray him in custody to satisfy the debt

p.92 William Mackey vs Kissey Evans. Octr 1798 pl^{tf} by Seth
Lewis; def^t by James Doherty her attorney. Cont^d to January;
cause dismissed at pl^{tfs} Costs. Wit^s proved attendance: Thos
Yates 4 Days, Patience Lively 4 Days, Thomas Simpson 4 days

George Frazer vs Nathan Smith. Octr 1798 pl^{tf} by Ja^s Doherty
& cause cont^d. Jan^y, def^t in own person; jury Ja^s Henderson,
Peter Spencer, Asaph Parker, Jeffery Lively, James Herod, W^m
Boren, Anderson Cheatham, Jno Parchment, Thomas McIntosh, W^m
Farmer, David Young, Philip Parchment, who find for pl^{tf} his
Damage 25 Dollars; also costs

The Following Justices to take Lists of Taxable property
John Hutchison for Captn Hutchisons Company
James Crabtree for Captn Abraham Youngs Company
John Philips for Captn Wm Johnsons Company
George Bell for Captn Edward Cheathams Company
Isaac Philips for Captn Isaac Philips Company
James Norfleet for Captn Pattersons Company and to include
the Inhabitants of Sychamore formerly within s^d Company
p.93 Court Adjourns Unitll tomorrow Morning 10 OClock

Friday Morning January 25th 1799
Present John Philips, Martin Duncan, George Bell, Esquires

Anderson & John Cheatham being bound for their appearance to
this Court & in the mean time to keep the peace, at Instance
of George Briscoe, who not appearing to pray Continuance of
same. it is Ordered by Court they be Released

45

Order the property of estate of Jesse Cain be sold to satisfy the Judgement of Andrew Snoddy

Tavern Rates: half pint spiritous Liquor 12½ cents; Dinner 25 cents; Breakfast/Supper 16 2/3 cents; 12½ pr gallon for Corn; Stabling horse 12 hrs with plenty of fodder or Hay 12½ cents; Lodging pr night in a bed 6¼ cents

An Instrument of Writing Benjamin McIntosh to John White was ack^d & ordered to be Registered, dated 16th July 1798

Deed Benjamin McIntosh to John White for 70 acres Joining Springfield was ackd

Hardy Bryant took oath of a Justice of the Peace

Order a Road laid off out of the Logan Road running through Springfield Direct to Nashville as far as Sychamore, Davidson County Line, any five of following to mark same: Nathan Smith, Lovick Ventress, Henry Johnson, James H Bryant, John Tucker, Patrick Martin, Thomas Norris, Isaac Weakley, Nimrod McIntosh

Persons who have neglected to Return Lists of Taxable property for 1798 and make return to Clerk & pay Taxes on or before first of Next Court shall be Exhonarated from fine and double Tax as inflicted by Law

p.94 Order Lands reported by Hugh Henry Shff for Nonpayment of 1797 Taxes which have been published in Knoxville Gazette be sold, or so much thereof as shall be sufficient to satisfy Tax & Costs due on each tract, as follows John Herritage 640 acres, Wm Smith 640, Henry Martin 640, Thomas Amis 6140, David Ivy 274, Wm Farrow 228, Francis Wilks 228, David Jones 1096, Joshua Cheason 274, Fred^k Desorn 274, James Evans 228, Wm Fryer 228, Miles McShehees Heirs 2410 ac, Jn° Bowers 228, Martin Striker 228, Dugal McCays Heirs 640, Richd Douge 640, David Edwards 640, Col° Andrew Hampton 640, John Faith 640, Nehemiah Peay 640, Wm Jackson 274, John Sugg 274, Isaac Hudson 357, Wm Whitehead 274, Anthony Black 640, Abraham Colrean 640, Jn° Poe 640, Wm Jinkins 274, Abraham Fulkison 640, Andrew Armstrong 640, Daniel Turners Heirs 6140, William Alford 640, Benjn Sheppard 274, Thomas Ross 640, Adam Fleeners Heirs 320, Daniel Mcfatter 640, Col° Jno Armstrong 228, William Campbell 640, John Hall 2560, John Eastin & Wm Tyrell 274, Eli West 500, And that Clerk issue execution for Tax & Costs due on each Tract, and Sheriff proceed to sell

As Printer hath made Mistake in Publishing Lands in the Gazette, Order Clerk Transmit to Printer the following Tracts:

John and James Bonner 274 acres, David Davis 640 acres, together with Tax & Costs due thereon

Court Adjourns untill Court in Course to meet in the Town of Springfield. John Philips, Martin Duncan, Hardy S Bryan

p.95 Robertson County, Monday April the 15th 1799, at the House of George Bell Esqr in Springfield. Present Benjamin Menees, James Crabtree, John Hutchison, Esquires

Elected as Grand Jurors Bazel Boren foreman, James Sawyers, David Jones, William Deloach, Francis Boren, Thomas McIntosh, Archer Cheatham Junr, Spen Coffield, Nimrod McIntosh, Caleb Winters, Joseph Washington, Johnson Kilgore, Charles Kilgore

James Dromgoole delivered Wm Henry in discharge of himself as bail for sd Henry in suits Federick Stump agt Wm Henry

Land of Philemon Thomas given in to pay 1798 Tax by George Neville is reduced to 340 acres, that is the whole amount of his land & by mistake was given in for 640 acres

Archer Cheatham Junr licenced to keep an Ordinary in this County gave Bond 500 Dollars, Miles Kerby his security

Will of Alexr McIntosh decd proven by Bazel Boren; no Extr apptd, Elizabeth McIntosh is granted Ltrs/Admn will annexed; gave bond with John McIntosh her Security & took oath

Deed Robert Weakley to Henry Tarr proven by Wm P Anderson
Deed Samuel Allen to Charles Simmons ackd
Deed Elias Fort Senr to Milbery Deloach proven by Sugg Fort
Deed Jonah Smith to William Everett proven by William Brown

James Menees Sheriff gave Bond 6000 Dollars for Collection State & County Tax, Samuel Donelson & Miles Kerby securities

p.96 Elisabeth McIntosh admx estate of Alexr McIntosh decd delivered an Inventory of the Estate

Jno Hardin Jr apptd Overseer of Road in room of Wm Armstrong

Isaac Dorris app'd Constable gave Bond 620 Dollars, George Briscoe & Abram Tippy his securities

James Crabtree Esq[r] delivered a list of Taxable property in Capt[n] Abraham Youngs Company

Wm Grimes excused from serving as a juror this Term Court Adjourns untill tomorrow Morning 9 OClock

Tuesday Morning April 16th 1799   Present James Crabtree, William Fort, Martin Duncan, Benjamin Menees, Esquires

William Bray vs David Havard. Case. April 1798 pl[tf] by Sam[l] Donelson; def[t] by James Doherty. Cont[d]. April 1799 jury John Price, Elijah Lancaster, Abraham Tippy, Thomas Hutchison, Francis Byrd, W[m] Wills, William Matthews, Sam[l] McMurry, John Crane, David Henry, Edward Cheatham, Lawrence Carr.   After argument thereon Court orders pl[tf] be NonSuited. Samuel Mc-Murry a witness proves 4 days attendance

W[m] Crunk who was bail for John Crunk came into Court and de-livered s[d] John, suit W[m] Tucker ag[t] s[d] Crunk

John Siglar resigned being Constable

p.97 State vs George Briscoe. Pettit Larceny.   January 1799 Grand jury presents George Briscoe late of s[d] County, Tavern keeper, on first December 1798, a Hog called a Barrow colour white & ear marked of a person to the Jurors afs[d] unknown of value Nine Cents, being found & did feloniously steal to the great Injury of the person unknown, to evil Example of all others in like case offending contrary to statute & against the dignity of our State. Herndon C[ty] att[o]. Signed William Johnston foreman. Def[t] pleads Not Guilty. Continued.   April 1799 Def[t] by Seth Lewis, Sam[l] Donelson & Isaac McNutt. Jury Thomas Woodard, Thomas Yates, Thomas Christmas, Matthew Day, James Elliott Jun[r], Ja[s] Walker, Thomas Henry, Sam[l] Crocket, Volentine Choate, W[m] Crunk, Jesse Martin, W[m] Fleuellen find defendant Not Guilty.   Charles Colgan witness proves 4 days; David Howser 4 days; Philip Parchment 4 days, Cha[s] McIntosh 2 days. Robert Adams summoned as witness in behalf the State failing to attend forfeits; si fa issues.

p.98 State vs Henry Airs. Assault/Battery. July 1798. Grand jury presents Henry Airs planter on 1st June at Patrick Mar-tins on Benjamin Nail with force & arms assaulted & beat to his great Damage, an Evil example and ag[t] peace. J A Parker True Bill, James Appleton, foreman. Def[t] pleads Not Guilty. Contd. April 1799 def[t] by Seth Lewis. Jury Jn[o] Price, Elijah Lancaster, Abraham Tippy, Thomas Hutchison, Francis Byrd, W[m] Wills, W[m] Matthews, Samuel McMurry, John Crane, David Henry, Edward Cheatham, Lawrence Carr, find def[t] Guilty. Court fine defendant Three Dollars and Costs. Jinsey Hicks a witness proves 3 days attendance

Deed Isaac Miller to Joseph Carmack proven by Isaac Dorris
Deed William Johnson to Richard Hart proven by Thos Johnson

James Bryan app^{td} Overseer of Road from Sychamore leading to Clarksville as far as fork of the road leading to Mr Betts, the inhabitants of Sychamore below the road as far as Spring Creek & inhabitants of Spring Creek settlement work on same

p.99 William Tucker vs John Crunk. July 1798 pl^{tf} by Thomas Stuart, def^t by Saml Donelson, pleads Not Guilty. Continued. April 1799 Jury Abraham Tippy, Samuel Crocket, Thomas Hutchison, Jno Crane, Francis Byrd, Thos Henry, Thos Yates, Jesse Martin, David Henry, Volentine Choate, John Dorris, Mark Noble who find for pl^{tf}, assess damage fifteen Dollars; also costs. Thos Christmas witness proves six days attendance; Wm Haggard 6 days, David Cain 2 days, Elijah Lancaster 7 days

Jno Pankey licenced to keep an Ordinary in this County, bond 620 Dollars, John Dorris & Elijah Lancaster his Securities

B/S Martin Greider to William Dickson proven by Wm Given

County Tax for 1799: 6¼ cents each hundred acres and same on each white Pole, 12½ cents each Black pole, 25 cents each Town Lot, 6 Dollars 25 Cents each Billard Table, 25 cents each stud Horse kept for the covering of Mares

John Hutchison Esqr delivered list of Taxable property for 1799 in Captn Hutchisons Company
p.100 Isaac Philips Esqr [as above] Captn Philips Company
John Philips Esqr...Captn Johnsons Company
Ja^s Norfleet Esqr for Captn Pattersons Company
George Bell Esqr for Captn Cheathams Company
James Crabtree Esqr for Captn Youngs Company

Robert Barnet adm^r of the estate Ann Kenedy dec^d delivered the amount of the sales of s^d Estate

Ordered Road laid off from Springfield to Ma^j Smiths mill on Elk fork of Red River to State Line, crossing Red R at mouth of Isaac Philips Esqr Spring branch, any 5 of following mark same, Samuel Sugg, Josiah Sugg, Britain Bryant, Josiah Fort, William Johnston (R.R.), Jacob Philips, Charles McIntosh and John Philips

Deed John Young and James Norfleet Comm^{rs} for Springfield to George Bell ackd

Deed John Young and James Norfleet Comm^{rs} for Springfield to John Hutchison ackd
Deed Rhody Richards to James Coghlin proven by Thomas Farmer
Court Adjourns untill tomorrow Morning 9 OClock

Wednesday Morning   April 17th 1799   Present
John Philips, Benjamin Menees, and James Crabtree Esquires

William Lowry licenced to keep an Ordinary in this County
gave Bond 620 Dollars, Henry Airs & Asa Woodworth securities

p.101 Jacob McCarty vs Mary Warner Interpleader of the property of Joseph T Still. In suit Jacob McCarty ag^t Joseph T Still sheriff Levied on one Bay Mare, one Bay Horse, one cow & Calf, one two year old; one waggon & harness, two beds and furniture, one trunk, pewter, pots, a womans saddle together with all household and kitchen furniture belonging the house of Elisabeth Still & one shovel plough. July Term 1798 Mary Warner appeared by William P Anderson Esqr; on motion is allowed to interplead and try the right of attached property, which she claims as her own property. Jacob McCarty likewise appeared by Thomas Stuart & Isaac McNutt Esq^{rs}. Cont^d. April 1799 Jury John Crain, David Henry, Edward Cheatham, Lawrence Carr, Mark Noble, Wm Boren, Robt Head, Francis Byrd, Anderson Cheatham, John Cheatham, Volentine Choate & David Rousavall, who say the property belongs to Joseph T Still, except one Chest and one side saddle. Interpleader obtained appeal to Superior Court, Bond 200 Dollars, Wm P Anderson and Seth Lewis her securities.   At July Session 1799 Def^{dt} came into Court & dismised her appeal. Ordered that Vandiones expones issue to sheriff to sell property af^{sd} to satisfy the Judgement of McCarty ag^t Joseph T Still
p.102   Philip Parchment witness in above suit proves 7 days attendance; Thos Herod 5 days, Caleb Winters 6 days, Daniel Lerew 4 days, James Herod 7 days, Jesse Martin 6 days

Jacob McCarty vs Joseph T Still. Attachment. July Term 1798 pl^{tf} by Isaac McNutt & Thomas Stuart; def^t by W^m P Anderson. Cause cont^d. April 1799 Judg^{mt} by Default. Jury John Brooks, John Briscoe, Asa Woodworth, Matthew Day, Wm Elliott, John Parchment, Samuel Gallaway, Isaac Moore, Dempsey Coffield, Thos Byrd Junr, Moses Larisy, John Dorris who find for pl^{tf} damage three Hundred seventy three Dollars; & costs of suit. Property not attached by Mary Warner ordered to be sold, and applyed to payment of Judgement

Benjamin McIntosh security for James Adams in suit George Briscoe ag^t s^d Adams

Deed John Young and James Norfleet to Jacob Young   proven by
Bazel Boren
Deed John Young & James Norfleet to James McGill ackd
p.103 Deed John Young and James Norfleet Comm^rs Springfield
to John Cheatham ackd
Deed John Young & James Norfleet to Joseph Pankey   proven by
Thos Johnson
Deed John Young and James Norfleet to Joseph Wray   proven by
Thos Johnson
Court Adjourned untill tomorrow Morning 9 OClock

Thursday Morning   April 18^{ih} 1799   Present
Benjamin Menees, John Philips, George Bell, James Norfleet

Mary Harrow vs Thomas Byrd. Slander. Octr 1798 pl^{tf} by James
Doherty; def^t by Jno C Hamilton pleads Not Guilty & Justifi-
cation. Cont^d. April 1799 Jury Lawrence Carr, David Henry,
John Price, Asa Woodworth, John Parchment, Samuel Gallaway,
Edwd Cheatham, John Cheatham, John Briscoe, George Campbell,
Amos Cohean & William Lowry who made mistrial. By consent of
Parties, refered to arbratrament; award of Benjn Sewel, Hugh
Stephenson, John Young, Thos Harrison & William Stephenson
to become Judgement of Court. They awarded that Mary Harrow
dismiss her suit; def^{dt} pay all costs.   Hugh Henry witness
proves 5 days attendance; Joseph Dorris 9 Days, Thos Hutchi-
son 9 days

p.104 Francis Byrd who was Security for Thos Byrd's appearance in suit Mary Harrow ag^t s^d Byrd surrendered s^d Thos

Deed John Young & James Norfleet Comm^rs to Robert Curry ackd
Deed John Young & James Norfleet Comm^rs to Charles Simmons
proven by Thos Johnson

William Lowry vs James McGill. On 26th March 1799 Wm Lowry
obtained Judgement against Ja^s McGill for Three Dollars Debt
& fifty Cents Costs before George Bell Esqr; 18th April 1799
John Philips Esqr issued Execution, Isaac Dorris, Constable
levied Lot #7 in Springfield. Ordered that sheriff sell said
Lot to discharge Plaintiffs Judgement & costs

Deed Thomas Johnson to John Young and James Norfleet Commissioners for Springfield ackd

A Bond given by John Stuart 2nd Feby 1785 to Thomas Jamison
was proven by Dennis Condry before Andrew Evins Esq Justice/
Peace for Grainger County by Virtue of Commission from this
Court; order Bond be recorded

Order Archer Cheatham Junr, Jonathan Dardin, Archer Cheatham Senr, Thomas Johnson, George Briscoe and Archibald Mahan attend next Superior Court as Jurors

p.105 Henry Airs vs Benjamin Nail. Slander. Octr Term 1798 pl^{tf} by Seth Lewis; def^t by James Doherty pleads Not Guilty. Contd. April 1799 Jury Thomas Hutchison, Francis Byrd, Allen Parker, Jacob Young, William Dorris, Volentine Choate, David Young, Ge^o Chapman, Wm Karr, William Boren, Jacob Pickrell, George Martin find for pl^{tf}, assess Damage to One Hundred Dollars. Def^t obtained an appeal to Superior Court; bond 500 Dollars, Allen Parker & William Karr securities. John Wilson witness proves 6 days attendance, 30 miles riding, 2 ferriages; Asa Woodworth proves 8 days; Samuel Crocket proves 10 days, John Parchment proves 8 days

Henry Airs vs Benjamin Nail. Assault & Battery. October 1798 pl^{tf} by Seth Lewis, def^t by James Doherty pleads Not Guilty. Contd. April 1799 jury Lawrence Carr, David Henry, Thomas Cheatham, Asa Woodworth (p.106) Jno Parchment, Saml Gallaway, Edwd Cheatham, John Cheatham, John Briscoe, Ge^o Campbell, Amos Cohea and Samuel Crocket who find for Plaintiff & assess damage to Six Cents & Costs
Court Adjourns untill tomorrow Morning 9 OClock

Friday Morning April 19th 1799.   Present
John Philips, James Norfleet, Ge^o Bell, John Hutchison Esq^{rs}

George Briscoe vs John Cheatham. Assault & Battery. At Jany Session 1799 pl^{tf} by Seth Lewis & Isaac McNutt; def^t by Ja^s Doherty & John C Hamilton pleads Not Guilty. Cont^d. Ap^l 1799 Jury Lawrence Carr, Jacob Pickrell, James Powel, W^m B Powel, Ge^o Chapman, Joseph Philips, Lawrence Howse, Benjn McIntosh, Jacob Young, Charles McIntosh, Henry Airs, Wm Lowry who find for Defendant. Pl^{tf} obtained appeal to Superior Court, bond 500 Dollars, Hugh Henry & David Hooser security. Robert Head witness proves 5 days attendance; Martha Head 5 days; Nimrod McIntosh 5 days; Stephen Boren 5 days.

George Brisco presented to Court a Commission from the Governor for office of Coroner; took required oaths

p.107 Isaac Dorris to oversee the new Road from Karrs Creek through Springfield to Logan County Road as marked by Jury of View; all hands within One Mile and half work on same in clearing it out

Samuel Crocket to oversee Road from Karrs Creek to Sychamore (lately marked from Springfield to Nashville) all Hands liv-

ing on Browns creek & those living on Sychamore waters above
the road leading from Nashville to Clarksville work on same

Ordered Jurors who served County of Tennessee who at Time of
Service lived within present bounds of Robertson County, on
those Certificates being produced, Also Guard Certificates
granted by Auditors of Tennessee County to persons who lived
at Time of Services in present bounds of Robertson County Be
Discharged by Collector or Trustee as far as Funds for that
purpose will extend

Jesse Carter vs Thomas Christmas. Si fa. To Sh^{ff} Octr 1798
Jesse Carter obtained Judg^t ag^t Cornelius Dabney for 48 Dollars 40 cts & Costs of suit 7 Dollars 3½ cts, but Execution
remains to be made. Thomas Christmas became Dabneys bail in
manner according to intent of an Act of Assembly, These are
to Command you that by two good & lawfull men of your County
you cause to be made known to Thomas Christmas personally to
appear before our County Court (p.108) third Monday April
to shew cause why Execution should not issue ag^t his goods &
chattels lands & tenements for amount of Judgement and costs

Joseph Crabtree vs John Price. To Sheriff. On 16 Jany 1798
George Hacker entered Bond, John Price security, condition
George Hacker would prosecute a suit he commenced ag^t Joseph
Crabtree. Ge^o Hacker hath failed to prosecute. You are commanded that by two good lawfull men of your County you cause
to be made known to John Price personally to appear before
our County Court to be held third Monday April next, to shew
cause why Execution should not issue ag^t his goods, chattels
lands & tenements for amount of s^d costs. To which at April
Term 1799 Def^t failing to appear Judg^t was entered ag^t Def^{dt}
for amount of costs & charges in s^d suit expended

Court Adjourned untill Court in Course.
John Philips, George Bell, James Norfleet, John Hutchison

p.109 Robertson County. Monday Morning July the 15th 1799
Court met at the House of George Bell Esqr. Present Martin
Duncan, John Philips, James Norfleet, Esquires
Court adjourned one quarter of an Hour to meet in the Court
House. Court met in the Court House in Springfield. Present
William Fort, Jno Philips, Zebulon B Hobert, John Hutchison,
Benjn Menees, Esquires

Grand Jurors Wm Given[Gwin?] foreman, Zachariah Oneal, Danl

Holman, Charles Wheaton, William Elliott, David Huddleston, John Carr, Charles Bradon, Andrew Irwin, Thomas Christmas, Thomas Little, Dempsey Coffield, Samuel Miles, William Perry

Ordered Clerk receive Lists of Taxable property for 1799
Deed Robert Weakly to Jacob Hunter proven by Wm Fort
James Sawyers appointed overseer of Road in room of Richard Matthews J^r

Philip Parchment to oversee Road in room of Samuel Crocket; all hands on Sychamore above Hollis's mill creek, and Calebs and Karrs Creek, above the Road leading from Springfield to Clarksville work on same

Mary Harrow vs Thomas Byrd. John Briscoe, witness, proves 11 days attendance & 60 miles traveling

p.110 Spur Coffield who was Security for appearance of David Patterson in suit James Menees agt s^d Patterson delivered up s^d Patterson in exhoneration of himself

On petition of Elisha Chick, ordered one acre Condemned for purpose of building a water grist mill across North fork Red River at or near where Chicks lower line crosses the river, Sheriff to summons John Young, Wm Armstrong, Bartimas Pack, Ja^s Haynes, Abraham Young, Jacob Warren, Joseph Payne or any four to value s^d land & make report next Court

Deed John Duncan to son Martin Duncan proven by John Price
Shaderick Rawls excused for nonattendance as Juror last Term

Deed James Norfleet to Andrew Washington ackd
Deed Ezekiel Smith to Noel Watkins proven by Henry Hyde
Deed Nehemiah Wroten to Henry Wroten proven by Nehemiah Wroten
Deed Robert Ewing to Henry Wroten proven by Nehemiah Wroten
Deed John Young & James Norfleet Commrs to Lucy Parker ackd

Elisha Chick licensed to keep an Ordinary at his house, bond with John Young his security

James Yates excused for nonattendance as a juror last Term [same wording]: James Haynes, Thomas Bounds, James Ewing
Thomas Kilgore excused from serving as Juror at present Term

p.111 Clerk & Sheriff allowed 35 Dollars each for Exoficio Services for the past year
Court Adjourns untill tomorrow Morning 9 OClock

Tuesday Morning July the 16th 1799. Present William Fort, James Norfleet, Benjamin Menees, Zebulon B Hobert, Esquires

William Stephenson vs Samuel Gallaway. Case. Oct[r] 1798 pl[tf] by Samuel Donelson; def[t] by James Doherty pleads Not Guilty. Cont[d]. July 1799 Jury Abraham Tippy, Richard Matthews J[r], William Wills, William Matthews, John Tucker, Thomas Strain, Nimrod McIntosh, David Hamilton, Rich[d] Nuckells, Josiah Ramsey, James Bell, Patrick Martin who find for def[t]; plaintiff obtained an appeal to Superior Court; bond 500 Dollars, Hugh Stephenson & John Stephenson his securities. John Briscoe a witness proves 10 days attendance, 60 miles travel; George Campbell proves 10 days, Amos Cohea proves 6 days

Deed William Rascoe to John Carr proven by Lawrence Carr

p.112 Chrisley Connelly vs Lewellen Phips. Debt. April 1799 pl[tf] by Seth Lewis; def[t] by Joseph Herndon pleads payment & set off; cont[d]. July 1799 Jury Matthew Day, Benjamin Coates, Rob[t] Black J[r], Josiah Sugg, William Coates, Obediah Bounds, Samuel Henry, Ja[s] Yates, William B Powel, John Young, Elijah Lancaster, David Hamilton who find for plaintiff his debt 30 Dollars & damage one Dollar 57½ cents also his costs of Suit

John Hutchison Esq[r] and George Campbell, securities for the appearance of Samuel Gallaway in suit William Stephenson agt sd Gallaway delivered him in exhoneration of themselves

Sheriff protests against Jaol of Robertson County

George Campbell & John Dorris ack[d] themselves Samuel Gallaways security in suit William Stephenson ag[t] s[d] Gallaway

Deed George M Deaderick to Mary Searcy wife of Bennet Searcy was proven by Samuel Donelson; also consent of Bennet Searcy to his wife's receiving s[d] deed ack[d] in Open Court

Robert Black Sen[r] excused for nonattendance as juror at last Term. Robert Black J[r] excused for not serving as a juror at this present Term

p.113 Ordered that Holland Dardin, John Gardner, James Gardner, & Elias Lawrence be Patrolers, and that Jonathan Dardin be considered as Captain thereof

Ordered that Josiah Sugg, William Deloach & Micajah Fort be Patrolers and that Lamuel Sugg be considered Captain thereof

Charles McIntosh to oversee Road in place of Isaac Dorris
John Gardner to oversee Road in place of Jonathan Dardin

Court Adjourned untill tomorrow Morning Nine OClock

Wednesday Morning July 17th 1799
Present William Fort, John Philips and Isaac Philips, Esq^{rs}

Charles Miles took oaths as a Justice of the Peace

Ordered that Joseph Herndon be admitted to transact business
of the Clerk Thomas Johnson for this Day, and that his Acts
shall be considered valid in this Court

Grand Jury made Report and were Discharged

Thos Johnson apptd Commissioner for Robertson County to settle & liquidate claims of Daniel Roan, with persons apptd by
Davidson & Montgomery counties according to Act of Assembly

p.114 W Jno Den on Demise of Wm Covey & wife Jane vs Richard
Fen alias William B Powel & Ja^s Powel. Ejectment. April 1799
plt^{f}s by Saml Donelson & John C Hamilton; def^{dt} by James Doherty & Benjamin Seawell pleads Not Guilty. July jury Jacob
Pickrel, Josiah Ramsey, Jesse Jones, John Duncan, Aaron Anglin, James Bell, John Cheatham, Abraham Tippy, Bazel Boren,
Robt Head, Richd Matthews, Josiah Fort, who find Def^t guilty
of the Trespass & Ejectment as stated in Declaration, assess
Plt^f damage one cent & costs. De^{ft} obtained appeal to Superior C^t, bond 500 Doll^s, David Spence & Henry Airs securities

Jurors apptd to attend next Term David Hamilton, John John-
son, Britain Bryan, Epaphroditus Lawson, Elias Fort Jr, Da-
vid Cain, Robt Lancaster, Josiah Sugg, Walter Stark, Thomas
Woodard, Wm Wills, John Couts, Obediah Bounds, Wm Gilbert,
Adam Clap, James Yates, John Gardner, Lawrence Carr, Caleb
Winters, Philip Parchment, Edward Cheatham, Samuel Musgrove,
Jas Dromgoole, Alexr Cromwell, Moses Larisy, Isaac Weakley,
John Crocket, William McAdoe, John Powers, Bazel Boren, John
Bryant, Thomas McIntosh, John Johnston
Court Adjourned untill Tomorrow Morning 9 OClock

p.115 Thursday Morning July the 18th 1799
Present William Fort, Charles Miles, Isaac Philips, Esquires

Ge^o Bell vs John White. Attachment. Levied by Constable by
virtue of Judgement before a Justice/Peace on title of John
White to 70 acres joining Springfield; so much as may satisfy debt & costs to be sold by Sheriff

George Bell vs William Lowry. Execution levied by Constable by virtue of two Judgements before Justice/Peace on title of William Lowry to 70 acres joining Springfield; s^d land or so so much as may satisfy debt and costs to be sold by Sheriff

William Lowry who had bound John Pankey to the peace before a single Justice came in proper person and released s^d Panky

James Menees, Sheriff, took the Oath required for Collection of State & County Tax for 1799

p.116 William Lowry licenced to keep an Ordinary & he & his securities exhonerated by consent of Court from any breach of his Ordinary Licence bond which might hereafter accrue

Hugh Henry Esqr Collector of the State & County Tax for 1797 reports that at sale of lands for Taxes for sd Year it fell short of raising the monies due to the Treasurer 4 Dollars & 78 cents. Order Treasurer of Mero District credit Collector for afsd sum; same sum to have a credit for County trustee

Ordered that Charles Miles, James Crabtree, & Thomas Johnson Esqrs be inspectors of our ensuing Election

Court Adjourns untill Court in Course.
Benjamin Menees, Isaac Philips, Hardy S Bryan, Martin Duncan

p.117 Robertson County, Monday October the 25th 1799
Present Isaac Philips, Martin Duncan, John Hutchison, Esq^rs

Grand Jurors James Dromgoole foreman, William Gilbert, John Couts, John Johnson, Obediah Bounds, Thomas Woodard, David Hamilton, Elias Fort J^r, Thomas McIntosh, Isaac Weakley, Jno Crocket, James Yates, Edward Cheatham

Deed George Allen to William Allen proven by Samuel Allen
Deed William Allen to Jesse Jones ackd
Deed Anthony Crutcher to Charles Nabb proven by Henry Small

Will of Richard Matthews decd proven by James Sawyers & William Renick. Sampson Matthews and William Matthews extrs of will of Richard Matthews decd received Letters Testamentary

Deed Anthony Sharp to Elisha Chick proven by Reubin Searcy & Richard Clark
Deed Anthony Crutcher atty for William Crutcher to George Ury proven by Robert Heaton

Deed Noah Woodard to Thomas George proven by Thomas Woodard
Deed Thomas Kilgore to Charles Kilgore proven by Thos Strain
Deed/Gift Jane Asbell to her children ackd

p.118 Benjamin Nail vs Henry Airs. Assault & Battery. Octr
1798: pltf by James Doherty; deft by Seth Lewis pleads Not
Guilty. October Term 1799, Jury Walter Stark, John Gardner,
Philip Parchment, Caleb Winters, Moses Larisy, Robert Lancaster, Samuel Musgrove, Josiah Ramsey, John Cheatham, Abraham Young, John Dobins, John Hardin who find for the Pltf, &
assess damage to 12½ cents & costs of suit. Patrick Martin,
witness, proves 2 days attendance; David Ramsey 8 days
Court Adjourns untill tomorrow Morning 9 OClock

Tuesday Morning October 22nd 1799   Present Charles Miles,
Isaac Philips, George Bell, John Hutchison, John Philips

Benjamin Chapman who was security for James Powel in Suit W^m
Lowry ag^t s^d Powel delivered s^d Powel

Jurors to next Superior Court Isaac Philips, Charles Miles,
Lamuel Sugg, James Crabtree Sr, Thos Johnson, John Hutchison

p.119 State vs James Powel. Assault & Battery. Def^t submits,
fined Two Dollars

Deed Zebulon B Hobert to Thos Yates proven by Isaac Johnson
Deed John Cheatham to W^m P Anderson ackd
Deed Moses Larisy to Emanuel Skinner ackd
William Crabtree to Elias Fort proven by Wm Fort
Deed Bazel Boren to Isaac Dorris proven by W^m B Powel
Deed James Henderson to Isaac Moore ackd
Bryant Oneal is released from paying Tax for 228 acres with
which he is charged through mistake
Court Adjourns untill Tomorrow Morning 9 OClock

Wednesday Morning October the 23rd 1799
Present Wm Fort, John Hutchison, Isaac Philips, Esq^{r}s

John Tucker for refusing to obey order of Sheriff as a guard
is fined one Dollar which he paid into the office

Elisabeth White (minor) bound to Charles McIntosh untill she
arrives to age eighteen years
Deed Alex^r Allen to William Allen proven by Saml Allen

p.120   James Head vs Anderson Cheatham. Assault & Battery.
April 1799 pl^{ff} by Saml Donelson; def^t by James Doherty &

John C Hamilton pleads Not Guilty. Cont^d. October 1799 Jury
Walter Stark, Philip Parchment, Caleb Winters, Moses Larisy,
Robert Lancaster, Saml Musgrove, Lewellen Phips, Wm Farmer,
James Powel, Abraham Tippy, David Jones, Wm Boren, who find
for the Defendant

Robert Wilson who was security for John Dobins in suit Ed^{wd}
James ag^t s^d Dobins caused Dobins to be Delivered to Court.
John Hardin & Saml Allen s^d Dobins security in af^{s}d suit

Joseph Dorris security for Wm Lowry & his wife Jane in suit
Danl Burford ag^t s^d Lowry delivered them into Court

Ordered Abraham Tippy exhonerated from payment of County and
State Tax on a town lot in Fayetteville, out of this County

In Suit Wm Lowry & wife Jane ag^t W^m B Powel & Ja^s Powel in
Ejectment which was determined at last Term, Ja^s Menees wit-
ness proved 3 days attendance.
Court Adjourned untill Court in Course.
                    Wm Fort, George Bell, Isaac Philips

p.121   Robertson County. Monday Morning January 20th 1800
Present Benjamin Menees, Isaac Philips, James Crabtree, John
Philips, James Norfleet

Grand Jurors Wm Johnson (RR) foreman, Anderson Cheatham, Ja^s
Elliott, Jo^s Payne, Wm Lusk, Thos Hutchison, Jno Tucker, Geo
Sprouse, William Fort Jn^r, Elias Lawrence, Arch^d Mahan, John
Brooks, Alexander Cromwell, Richard Matthews, Adam Clap

David Patterson vs Wm Miles and George Saddler. Attachment.
Matthew Lester summoned as garnishee is indebted to William
Miles sixty some odd Dollars

Lawrence Carr fined five Dollars for absenting himself from
Jury after being sworn, without consent of Court, which ab-
sence was previous to decision of case Hannah Porter ag^t Anderson Cheatham on appeal

Lucy Parker licenced to keep an Ordinary in Springfield for
one year, gave bond with Daniel Young her security

Deed Lovick Ventress to James H Bryan, 2717 acres, ackd
p.122   Will of John Patterson proven by Anthony Sharp
Deed James Henderson to Warren Sams for 120 acres proven by

JANUARY 1800

John Wade
Deed Joseph Hamilton to Alexander Johnston for 87 acres
proven by Wm Johnston
B/S James H Bryan to Lovick Ventress ackd

John Dorris son of Joseph app^td Constable; bond 250 Dollars
with Joseph Dorris & Wm Dorris securities

Will of Noah Sugg proven by George Sugg Allen. Aquilla Sugg,
executor, took oath and received Letters Testamentary
Court Adjourns untill tomorrow Morning 10 OClock

Tuesday Morning January 21st 1800   Present William Connel,
John Stuart, George Bell, Martin Duncan, James Norfleet

John Stump vs Wm Harper. Attachment. Benjn Menees Esqr summoned as Garnishee owes Harper nothing, and has none of his
property, knows no person that has
Shaderick Rawls same as above

James Menees witness in suit Wm Lowry & wife Jane ag^t Benjn
McIntosh proved eleven days attendance

p.123 Ordered William Fort, James Norfleet and Isaac Dortch
Esqrs to settle with County Trustee and make Report

Ordered that William Matthews be overseer of Road from John
Donelsons to Bounds Spring branch
Ordered that Charles Bradon be overseer of Road to Bledsoes
Lick from Bounds Spring branch to County Line; Wm Wills and
Isaac Dorris to divide the hands between Matthews and Bradon

Daniel Burford vs Wm Lowry & Jane his wife. Case. July 1799
pl^tf by Seth Lewis & Thomas Stuart; def^ts by Samuel Donelson
plead Non Asst. Cont^d. Jany 1800 Jury Peter Spence, George
Pool, Elijah Lancaster, Matthew Day, Barton Coates, John
Chewning, Titus Benton, Wm Edwards, Chas Wheaton, Andrew Irwin, John Bryan, Robert Black, who find for Pl^tf, and assess
damage to 25 Dollars & Costs

Order County Trustee pay Josiah Fort 32 Dollars 49 Cents 8
mills for balance of Certificates overpaid in settlement for
the year 1797

Isaac Menees, witness in suit State ag^t Jane Lowry, proves 3
days attendance

Ordered that Wm Williams, Thos Henry, Ja^s Jones J^r, Anthony
Jones, Titus Benton, & John Appleton be Patrolers, & that W^m

66

Williams be their Captn, to act within the bounds of Captn
Bounds Company

p.124 Ordered that Lewis Pipkin, Augustine Cook, Elijah Lancaster, Robt Lancaster, Nathan Clark & John Bryan be patrolers in Captn Johnsons Comp^y, Lewis Pipkin Captn of the party

Bond Joseph Carmack to Martin Duncan for 6½ acres proven by
John Duncan
John Bryan app^{td} Constable, Bond 620 Dollars, Thomas Yates &
Abraham Tippy his securities
Ordered a Road laid off from James ferry on Cumberland River
to intersect a Road ordered laid off by Court of Montgomery
from Richard Miles old place to James ferry. Road is to meet
at County line. Aaron Choate, Joseph Choate, Thomas Weakley,
John Jennings, Isaac Weakley, Andrew Stuart, Wm Long, Nelson
McDowal, Benjn Weakley, David McGraw, Thos Hill & Washington
Ryburn mark same and make return to our next Court

Deed Jeremiah Lofton to Levi Moore for 274 acres proven by
Thos Yates
Hardy S Bryan admitted to keep an Ordinary; gave bond, Danl
Young his security
Samuel Grayson app^{td} Constable; bond 640 Dollars, Danl Young
his security
Ordered following Justices/Peace take Lists of Taxable prop-
erty in this County for the present year:
        Hardy S Bryan for New Company South of Cumberland R
        Isaac Dortch   his own Company
        Benjn Menees   Captn Cheathams Company
        Isaac Philips   his own Company
        Wm Johnson   his own Company
        Thos Strain   Captn Youngs Company
        Joseph Dorris   Captn Bounds Company
        John Stuart   Sychamore Company lately laid off

Deed Andrew Bowman to John E Long for 640 acres proven by
Peter Binkley

p.125 Isaac Dortch, James Norfleet & Wm Fort Esqrs apptd to
settle with County Trustee, reported a final settlement for
year 1797 as per Account Lodged in the office
Court Adjourned untill tomorrow Morning 10 OClock

Wednesday Morning January 22nd 1800
Present William Fort, Isaac Philips, Martin Duncan, Esquires

James Elder & Co vs Lewellen Phips. Debt. Octr 1799 pl^{tf} by
Bennet Searcy; def^t by Joseph Herndon pleads payment. Cont^d.

January Term 1800 Jury Lawrence Carr, Jn° Pike, Arthur Pitt, Elias Fort (MC), Eppa Lawson, Thomas Smith, Joseph Hamilton, Benjamin Porter, Joseph Wimberley, Wᵐ B Powel, John Chowning, Henry Lawson, who find for plᵗᶠ 59 Dollars 4 cents, also his Costs of Suit

Archer Cheatham to oversee Road from Karrs Cr to John Donelsons in place of Jn° Brooks; Thomas Johnson & George Bell to divide Hands between sᵈ Cheatham & Charles McIntosh

John Hardin who was summoned to give Testamony in behalf the State against William Bond, failing to attend was called out agreeable to Law, order Scire facias issue

p.126   John McPherson vs William Bond. A/B. Octʳ Term 1799 plᵗᶠ by J C Hamilton & James Doherty; defᵗ by Wᵐ P Anderson pleads Not Guilty. Contᵈ. Janʸ Term 1800 Jury Lawrence Carr, John Pike, Arthur Pitt, Elias Fort (MC), Eppa Lawson, Thomas Smith, Joseph Hamilton, Samˡ Crocket, Benjamin Porter, Wᵐ B Powel, John Chowning, Matthew Day, who find for plᵗᶠ, assess Damage to 12½ cents, also costs

William Lowry vs James Powel. A/B. October 1799 pltf by J C Hamilton; deft by Jas Doherty pleads Not Guilty. Continued. Jany Term 1800 Jury John Bryant, Aaron Anglin, Wm Briscoe, Amos Cohea, Thos Yates, Robert Curry, Nimrod McIntosh, Nathl Rogers, Saml Gallaway, Jacob Pickrell, John Dorris, Wm Karr, who find for plaintiff; assess damage to 37 Dollars 50 cts; also his costs. Thomas Hamilton, witness, proved 5 days attendance and 56 miles traveling

p.127   Robert Stothart & Co vs Lewellen Phips. Case. Octʳ Term 1799 plᵗᶠ by Bennet Searcy; defᵗ by Joˢ Herndon pleads Non Assumpset, Set off. Contᵈ. Janʸ Term 1800 Jury Lawrence Carr, John Pike, Arthur Pitt, Elias Fort MC, Eppa Lawson, Thoˢ Smith, Joseph Hamilton, Samˡ Crocket, Benjⁿ Porter, Jn° Chowning, Matthew Day, Joseph Wimberley, who find for plᵗᶠ, assess damage to 31 Dollars 75 cents; also his costs of Suit

Anderson Cheatham and Edward Cheatham admʳˢ estate of Archer Cheatham decᵈ delivered an Inventory of estate of the decᵈ. Order admʳˢ sell perishable property of estate

Deed James Menees Sheriff to George Bell 70 acres ackd
Deed James Menees Sheriff to George Bell 70 acres ackd
Deed James Menees Sheriff to Thomas Johnson 41 acres ackd
Deed Robert Lancaster to James Cain, Jesse Cain Jr, and John Cain for 41 acres proven by Thoˢ Johnson
Deed Thomas Johnson to James Cain, Jesse Cain Jr, & Jn° Cain for 41 acres ackd

p.128 Samuel Wilson vs Joseph Prior. Covenant. Octr 1799
plts by Saml Donelson; def^t failing to attend, judgement by
default. January 1800 Jury Lawrence Carr, John Pike, Arthur
Pitt, Elias Fort MC, Eppa Lawson, Thos Smith, Joseph Hamilton, Saml Crocket, Benjn Porter, John Chowning, Matthew Day,
John Parchment who find for pl^{tf}, assess damage 200 Dollars;
also costs of suit in that behalf expended

Order Abraham Tippy Overseer of Road from Sulpher fork leading to Betts's in room of Benjn Porter

Ltrs/Admn granted Anderson Cheatham & Edward Cheatham on the
estate of Archer Cheatham decd; bond 4000 Dollars with Elias
Lawrence & Joseph Wimberley their securities; took oath

Bill/Sale Robert Lancaster to Elisabeth Cain proven by Thos
Johnson
B/S Thomas Johnson to Peggy Cain, Nancy Cain, and Rebeckah
Cain ackd
Court Adjourns untill tomorrow Morning Ten OClock

Thursday Morning January 23rd 1800
Present Martin Duncan, James Crabtree, Joseph Dorris, Esq^{rs}

p.129 Thomas Johnson vs John Burgess. Attachment. Pl^{tf} having filed Declaration, def^t being solemnly called to put in
special Bail and replevy property returned by Sh^{ff} as having
been attached in hands of Jno Pankey, summoned as garnishee,
who declareth he oweth s^d John Burgess 44 Dollars 10½ cents,
failing to appear, therefore it is considered by Court that
pl^{tf} recover of John Burgess 60 Dollars as in Declaration, &
Costs of suit

Thos Johnson vs John Pankey. Garnishee of John Burgess. John
Pankey being sworn as garnishee of John Burgess declared he
owed John Burgess 44 Dollars 10½ cents; considered by Court
that execution issue accordingly to satisfy part of Debt recovered by Thomas Johnson agt John Burgess

Archibald Mahan to oversee Road from Brush Cr to Calebs Cr

Matthew Luter to oversee Road, from Wm Givings on Nashville
Road, passing by his House to Sychamore at Danl Youngs & the
hands living on Spring Creek of Sychamore & up Sychamore to
the road; all hands between that Road & the Springfield Road
as far as Winters Creek, work on the same

Moses Hardin, Jn° Hurt, Robert Wilson, Wᵐ Findley, Volentine Choate, Sampson Matthews, Wᵐ Huddleston, Titus Benton, James Jones, Jonathan Price, Vachel Lovelass, George Henley, Lewis Pipkin, Thomas Woodard, Levi Moore, Wᵐ Briscoe, John Powers, Dann Lynn, Wᵐ McAdoe, Wᵐ Sale, Moses Larisy, Joseph Miller, Nathˡ Rogers, Wᵐ Gwin, Wᵐ Conyers, Walter Stark, John Crane, Jesse Martin, John Carr, Jn° Chowning, Holland Dardin, Jonathan Dardin, Caleb Winters attend next Court as jurors.

Court Adjourns untill Court in Course
                    John Philips, Joseph Dorris, Martin Duncan

p.130   Robertson County.   Monday Morning April 25ᵗʰ 1800
Present Benjamin Menees, John Philips, Martin Duncan, Esqʳˢ

Grand Jurors Levi Moore foreman, James Jones, Walter Stark, Vachel Lovelass, Robᵗ Wilson, Thomas Woodard, Joseph Miller, George Hendley, Titus Benton, Jesse Martin, William McAdoe, Wᵐ Conyers, Jonathan Price

Mary Patterson & George Patterson extˣ & extʳ of the will of John Patterson decᵈ took oath required for executors

John Hutchison Esquire and Richard Matthews security for the appearance of Joseph Philips in the suit William T Lewis agᵗ sᵈ Philips surrendered him in exoneration of themselves. Sᵈ Philips brought into Court George Briscoe who acknowledged himself sᵈ Philips bail

Ordered that Dedimus Potestation issue to State of Virginia, Southampton County, to take Depositions of James Edwards and James Griswill or any one of them to prove the will of Zorabable Stark Decᵈ

Thomas Johnson appᵗᵈ guardian to Henry Hart orphan of Joseph Hart, bond 2 Thousand Dollars with Martin Duncan and William Johnson his securities

James Norfleet, John Baker & Hugh Henry to divide Negroes of the Estate of Joseph Hart decᵈ and allot to widow and orphan each their part

Ordered that Francis Graham be at Liberty to build a mill on his own land on Brush Creek
Ordered that Polly Brickey be allowed Twenty Dollars for her support to be collected in County Tax to be laid this Term

p.131 Henry Johnson and Abraham Tippy securities for appearance of Sam¹ Grayson in suit John Barr agᵗ him delivered him
& George Bell & Dempsey Coffield ackᵈ selves Graysons security in sᵈ suit

Order James Crabtree Esqr and Abraham Young divide hands between John Hardin overseer of one road and James Wheeler of
the other

Securities of Josiah Hendley in suits Black & Williams · and
James Maxwell ag¹ sᵈ Hendley which are Washington Ryburn and
Benjamin Weakley delivered Hendley. Josiah Hendley brought
into Court Isaac Weakley & Sam¹ Henry who ackᵈ themselves sᵈ
Hendleys security in both the afˢᵈ suits

Deed William Betts to Martin Duncan town lot in Fayetteville
proven by George Briscoe
Deed John Duncan to Isaac Weakley for a lot in Fayetteville
ackd
Deed Andrew Washington to Archer Cheatham for 100 acres was
proven by Jaˢ Menees
Deed William Coates to John Baker for 320 acres proven by
Bazel Boren
Deed/Gift Josiah Hundley to Nancy Ryburn was proven by John
Stuart
Deed Thomas Johnson to Archer Cheatham for 129 acres ackd

Thoˢ Strain Esqr delivered the list of Taxable property for
Captain Youngs Company

Richard Cook petitions that persons may meet on a tract belonging to Cook on Brush Creek, and examine sᵈ survey in order to perpetuate Testimony. Order John Baker, Henry Gardner
& Josiah Fort meet and act agreeable to petition

p.132 Aquilla Sugg executor of estate of Noah Sugg decd delivered inventory of the estate & amount of sales

B/S John Couts to Thomas Woodard proven by Thomas Johnson
Deed Thos Molloy to Aquilla Sugg extr of Noah Sugg decd 640
acres proven by Bennet Searcy
Deed Richard Hart to John Tenison for 200 acres proven by Wm
Sale
Deed James Menees shff to John Childress 640 acres ackd
Deed James Menees shff to John Childress 640 acres ackd
Deed Daniel James to Robert Weakley for lot in Fayetteville
proven by Benjⁿ Weakley

Isaac Weakley apptd overseer of Road from James's ferry to

Clarksville as far as county line with hands: Andrew Stuart, Jas Farmer, James Jennings, Cornelius McGraw, Uriah McGraw, Paul McGraw, David McGraw's hands, Jesse Sibley, Tendale Whitworth, William Ryburn's hands, Matthew Ryburn, Samuel Handley, Jordan Handley, John Kimbrel, Wm Long

John Chewning excused from serving as juror the present Term Court Adjourns untill tomorrow Morning 9 OClock

Tuesday Morning April 22nd 1800   Present Benjn Mences, Martin Duncan, John Philips, Wm Johnson, & John Stuart Esqrs

Samuel Crocket who purchased at Sheriff Sale part of tract belonging to Benjamin Koen whereon he now lives for nonpayment of 1797 Taxes came into Court & ackd himself satisfyed by sd Koen for the part he had purchased & Relinquishes his Right to any part by Virtue of purchase afsd

Edmond Turpin exhonarated from paying State & County Tax for his Negro Matt which is so afflicted he is rendered useless, this Order continues during his inability

p.133 Hannah Porter vs Anderson Cheatham. Appeal. Octr 1798 defl pd into Office 4 Dollars 50 Cts agreeable to Judgement of Wm Fort, Esqr, before whom it was tried on a Warrant, To which at Jany Term 1799 pltf by Thos Stuart; Defl by S Lewis Contd. Jany 1800 Jury found for pltf 6 Dollars 74 cents from which Verdict defdt obtained a new trial. Cause contd until April 1800, Jury John Carr, Jno Hust, Caleb Winters, William Sale, Dann Lynn, Wm Findley, Jno Powers, Moses Larisy, Sampson Matthews, Wm Huddleston, Volentine Choate, Moses Hardin who find for pltf and assess Damage to 7 Dollars & Costs. David Hamilton witness proves seven days attendance James Butler witness in behalf defl failing to attend agreeable to summons it is ordered he forfeit

Hardy J Bryan Esqr to oversee Road to Clarksville from ford of Sychamore to fork of road below Ramseys Old place & that Lovick Ventress, James H Bryan, Edmond Hatch, Ezekiel Smith, Henry Hyde, John Hyde, Isaac Robert & Wm Farmer

Deed Lucy Parker to James Doherty for 2 lots in Springfield ackd by Saml Grayson her attorney in fact
Deed Josiah Ramsey to Jacob Pinkley for 100 acres ackd

p.134 Archer Cheatham admitted to keep an Ordinary for one year; bond 500 Dollars, Wm Fleuellen his security

George Chapman, reputed father of Polly Pankey's child, gave

Bond 500 Dollars, Wm Dorris & Jno Crunk securities. S^d Chapman fined 3 Doll^s 12½ c^{ts}; execution stayed till next Court

Benjn Menees Esqr delivered the List of Taxable property in Captain Cheatham's Company

John Pankey admited to keep Ordinary in Springfield for year bond 500 Dollars, Volentine Choate & W^m B Powel securities

Deed John Young & James Norfleet to John J Dorris for Lot in Springfield ackd
Deed John Young & Ja^s Norfleet to Thos Stuart lot in Springfield ackd
Deed John Young and Ja^s Norfleet to heirs of Joseph Carmack for lot in Springfield was ackd
Deed William Lurey to George Bell 399 acres proven by Archer Cheatham
Deed Benjamin Wood to Henry Airs 180 acres proven by Caleb Winters
Deed William Everet to Hugh Brown 228 acres proven by William Brown
Deed John Dobins to John Syreker 200 acres proven by John James
Deed James Menees Sheriff to Richard Matthews Senr 652 acres 115 poles ackd
Deed James Menees Sh^{ff} to Wm Dorris, son of Isaac, for 198 acres 148 poles ackd
Deed Thos Woodard to John Couts for 100 acres proven in open Court by Thos Johnson
Deed Ja^s Menees Sh^{ff} to David Young 39 acres 36 poles ackd
Deed Benjn Nail to Isham Rogers 125 acres ackd
Deed Wm Betts to Ge^o Bell lot in Fayetteville proven by Saml Donelson

p.135 Hardy S Bryan Esqr returned List of Taxable property for New Company South of Cumberland River
Isaac Dortch Esqr returned List of Taxable property for Capt Dortch's Company
Isaac Philips Esqr delivered List of Taxable property for his own company
Joseph Dorris Esqr delivered List of Taxable property for Capt Thos Bounds Company
Anderson Cheatham and Edward Cheatham adm^{rs} of the estate of Archer Cheatham decd delivered inventory

Titus Benton, Anthony Jones, John Waters, Richd Jones, James Jones & Hugh Henry to be patrolers, Titus Benton the captain

Order County Tax for 1800: 12½ cents on each hundred acres; 6¼ cts each white pole, 12½ cts each black pole, 25 cts each stud horse kept for covering mares, 12½ cents each town lot; 5 Dollars each Billard Table

Deed John Young & James Norfleet to Thomas Stuart for Lot in Springfield ackd
P/A Henry Shore Senr to Geo Briscoe proven by Jacob Shore
William Johnson Esqr delivered List of Taxable property in his own Company
John Stuart Esqr delivered List of Taxable property for Capt Benjn Weakleys Company
Court Adjourned untill tomorrow Morning 8 OClock

Wednesday morning April 23rd 1800   Present Benjn Mences, John Stuart, Isaac Philips, & John Hutchison Esqrs

Deed Josiah Ramsey to Elijah Carny for 100 acres was ackd
Deed Richard Cook atty/fact for Robt Burton & Josiah Watson to John Hinds for 300 acres proven by Moses Hardin
Deed Richard Hart to John Vaughn 100 acres proven by Thomas Johnson
Deed Thos McIntosh to Jesse Williams for 100 acres proven by Thomas Johnson
Deed Jesse Williams to George Briscoe for 100 acres proven by Thos Johnson

William Lowry vs Wm B Powel. Case. July 1799 pltf by Samuel Donelson; deft by Jas Doherty. Octr 1799 Jury find for pltf 29 Dolls 2 cts; deft obtained New Trial. Cause contd. April 1800 Jury John Carr, John Hust, Caleb Winters, Dann Lynn, Wm Findley, Jno Powers, Moses Larisy, Sampson Matthews, Wm Huddleston, Volentine Choate, William Sale, Moses Hardin who find for defdt

Daniel McKenly apptd Constable gave bond 640 Dollars, Volentine Choate & Moses Larisy his securities; took Oath

p.137 George Bell vs James Doherty. Attachment. On 2 attachments which Sheriff levied on 2 lots & house in Springfield. Ordered lots & house sold to satisfy 2 judgements & costs

Thomas Tabot vs James Doherty. Attachment. Sheriff levied on house & lot in Springfield. Ordered house & lot sold to satisfy judgement & costs

Thomas Jones vs Anderson Cheatham & Edwd Cheatham Admrs. Appeal. Pltf by Thos Stuart; deft by Jno C Hamilton. Jury John Crane, Nathl Rogers, Jonathan Dardin, Holland Dardin, Barton Coates, John Baker, Peter Spence, Moses Boren, Matthew Day, John Tucker, Marmaduke Mason, John Dorris who find for pltf

damage 6 Dollars 50 cents & costs.
Henry Fleuellen a witness proves two days attendance

p.138 Matthew Sellars vs William Tyrrell. Attachment. July
1799 Sheriff levied 66½ acres near Mr Winters property of Wm
Tyrrell. Pltf by Samuel Donelson & Bennet Searcy; six-month
stay. Jany 1800 Judgi by default agt deft. Contd. April Jury
John Carr, John Hust[Hirst?], Caleb Winters, Wm Sale, Dann
Lynn, Jno Powers, Moses Larisy, Sampson Matthews, Wm Huddleston, Moses Hardin, Lewis Pipkin, Volentine Choate, who assess pltf damage to 960 Dollars; also costs of suit. Order
attached property sold

John Dorris vs Jonathan Price. Appeal. Pltf by Thos Stuart;
deft by Isaac McNutt. Jury John Carr, John Hirst[Hust?],
Caleb Winters, Wm Sale, Wm Findley, Sampson Matthews, Volentine Choate, Edward King, John Crane, Nathl Rogers, Wm Tucker, William Huddleston, who find for pltf damage 6 Dollars &
costs. John Hutchison witness proves 3 days attendance. Joseph Dorris Junr proves 3 days attendance

Edward Cheatham security for Robert Warren in suit Thos Talbot agt sd Warren delivered sd Warren

p.139 Joseph Dorris vs Cornelius Dabney. Case. Jany 1800
pltf by Saml Donelson; deft by John C Hamilton. Contd. April
1800 Jury John Carr, John Hust, Caleb Winters, Wm Sale, Wm
Findley, Sampson Matthews, Volentine Choate, Edward King,
Nathl Rogers, John Tucker, Wm Huddleston, Dann Lynn who find
for pltf damage 40 Dollars & costs

Order Writ/Certiorari issue to bring up proceedings of suit
tryed before single Justice, John Pankey agt Shaderick Rawls

James Menees Sheriff appid to Collect State & County Tax for
1800; bond 5000 Dollars with John C Hamilton & George Bell
securities & took oath by law required
Court Adjourns untill Court in Course
    Isaac Philips, Benjn Menees, John Philips, John Hutchison

p.140 Robertson County. Monday Morning July 21st 1800
Present Benjamin Menees, James Norfleet, William Connel, and
John Philips, Esquires

Grand Jurors Samuel Crocket foreman, Ezekiel Smith, John
Chewning, Samuel McMurry, Edward Cheatham, Thomas George,

Josiah Hundley, Joseph Choate, Samuel Musgrove, Lamuel Sugg, John Hyde, Joseph Payne, William Wills

Deed John Blackwell to William Graham 150 acres proven by Nathan Arnet
Deed William Johnson to William Edwards 146 146/160 acres ackd
Deed William Johnson to James Mark 236 acres ackd
Deed Thomas Palmer to John Simmons 182 3/4 acres proven by Charles Simmons
Deed Luke Rawls Junr to Luke Rawls Senr 85 acres proven by Saml Miles
Deed Ann Hart surviving adm^x to Joseph Hart dec^d to Henry Johnson Senr 90 acres proven by Thos Johnson
Deed John Young & James Norfleet to Zerobable Stark for town lot ackd by James Norfleet
Deed Robert Black Senr to Martha Stark 50 acres proven by Henry Gardner
Deed Jonathan Magness to William Byrd 213 1/3 acres proven by William Findley

John McElhainy records his stock mark
Nicholas Perkins Esqr produced licence to practice as an attorney; qualifyed agreeable to Law & was admitted
John Dickison Esqr produced licence; admitted as above

p.141 Eli Jones and James Vaughn, security for Sampson Trammel in suit Wm Johnson vs s^d Trammel delivered Trammel; Thos Yates, Elijah Lancaster, Daniel McKindley, & Meredith Walton ack^d themselves Sampson Trammels Security in above suit

Giles Connel appointed Constable, gave bond with Wm Connell and Isaac Dortch his securities, and took necessary oaths

Thomas Bell app^{td} guardian to Sarah Robey, orphan; bond one Thousand Dollars, Stephen Boren and Abraham Tippy securities

Inventory, estate of John Patterson dec^d returned by ex^{tr}

Will of Luke Rawls proven by Samuel Miles; Elizabeth Rawls, one of the executors, qualified

William Findley app^{td} Constable; bond with Thomas Strain and George Patterson, securities, in Six Hundred Twenty Dollars

Philip Russel app^{td} Constable; bond, with Benjamin Weakley & Isaac Weakley securities, Six Hundred Twenty Dollars

Commissioners app^{td} to divide Negroes of Joseph Hart decd made their return

John Johnson excused from further attendance as a juror this
Term

Edward Cheatham app^{td} Overseer of Road in place of Ja^s Long;
all hands within Two Miles of the road work thereon

Lewis Pipkin app^{td} Guardian to his own Children; bond Two
Thousand Dollars with Hugh Henry & Wm Johnson his securities

Isaac Dorris appointed Constable; bond Six Hundred Twenty
Dollars with John Hutchison Security

Scire facias to issue ag^t Jacob Lewis, Abraham Young, Elias
Lawrence, Ja^s Walker, and Elijah Hamilton, delinquent Jurors

p.142 Court Adjourns until Tomorrow Morning 9 Oclock

Tuesday Morning July 22nd 1800
Present William Fort, John Hutchison, Benjamin Menees, Esqrs

Lamuel Henry produced Licence to practice as an attorney and
was admitted

Josiah Ramsey vs Wm Fleuellen. Saml Crocket a witness proved
seven Days attendance

Jacob McCarty vs Samuel Todd. Attachment. July 1799 pl^{tf} by
Thomas Stuart & Isaac McNutt; proceedings stayed six months;
April Session 1800 Judg^t by Default; July jury John Hardin,
William Crunk, David Young, Robt Black Jr^r, Moses Boren, John
Price, David Rounsevall, Bazel Boren, Barton Coates, Britain
Bryan, John Robins, Wm Sale who assess pl^{ffs} damage to Eigh-
teen Dollars and twenty five Cents; also Costs

Article of Agreement after nature of Indenture made between
William Crocket and Jane Crocket of one part and John Wilson
of the other, proven by Saml Crocket

Charles Miles & Wm Connel ack^d themselves Ja^s Dohertys Security in suit John Barr ag^t s^d Doherty in place of Wm Johnson
& John Bryan who surrendered s^d Doherty

p.143 John Burgess vs John Pankey. Debt. Octr 1799 pl^{tf} by
Samuel Donelson; def^t by Thomas Stuart. January 1800 Def^t as
garnishee in case Johnson ag^t Burgess, swore he owed 44 Dol-
lars 10½ cents. July 1800 jury John Hardin, Francis Boren,
Jo^s Hamilton, Barton Coates, Jno Barr, Jonathan Dardin, Saml
Henry, Dann Lynn, John Dorris, Nathan Clark, Joel Vaughn,

Elijah Lancaster, who find for the defendant

James Jones, John Krisel, & Silas Tucker as witnesses prove
that the left ear of s^d Jones was bit off in a fight; Depon-
ants say on 24th May 1800 s^d James Jones & Richard Crunk had
a fight at house of Nathan Clark at which time the ear of s^d
Jones was bit off by s^d Crunk

Sugg Fort, Charles Wheaton, and Miles Kirby allowed Fifteen
Dollars each for services as commissioners for settling with
the County Trustees & Collectors

John Crunk who was security for George Chapman in suit State
ag^t s^d Chapman delivered s^d Chapman

Clerk & Sheriff allowed Twenty five Dollars each for Exoficio services for the past year

B/S for a Negro: James Menees, sheriff, to Beverley A Allen
ack^d; also assignment from Allen to David McGraw ack^d

p.144 Lovick Ventress vs Daniel Young. Ejectment. Pl^tf by
Thomas Stuart; def^t by Bennet Searcy. Jury John Couts, John
Price, Henry Airs, Abel Williams, Ezekiel Mace, William Wil-
son, Jacob Pickrel, John Flynn, Jesse Joiner, Anthony Jones,
Robert Currey, Wm Simpson, who find Deft guilty of Trespass;
assess damage to 6 1/4 cents

Deed William Grimes to Saml McMurry for 100 acres ack^d
Deed William McAdoe to Dann Lynn for 74 acres proven by
Joshua Rice
Deed Robert Hays to William Johnson for 477 acres 67 poles
was proven by William Sale
Deed Simon Totevine to Thomas Hanks for 100 acres proven by
John Hanks
Deed Simon Totevine to John Hanks for 200 acres proven by
Thomas Hanks
Deed Edmond Turpin to William Reed 100 acres ackd

Miles Kerby app^td Constable; bond 620 Dollars, Ja^s Norfleet
& Edward Cheatham securities
B/S Wm Fort to Nancy Hart and Henry Hart for Negroes ackd

Isaac Sanders to Oversee Road marked from head of Sugar fork
of Spring Creek to meet a road from Robertson Court house to
Weakley ferry, to begin at Widow Rawls sugar camp, thence to
Turnbulls Stamp where roads intersect; hands to work thereon
William Perry, Luke Rawls, Samuel Miles, Jacob Moake, Thomas
Hunter[?], Jacob Binkley, Fred^k Binkley, Jno Shanon, Gabriel
Sanders, William Sanders, Jacob Lewis [illeg], James Lewis,

Wm Hunt, Arch^d Huddleston, Jesse Simmons, [name illegible]

p.145   Order a road laid off from Springfield to near Turn-
bulls Horse Stamp from the iron works on Bartons Creek; fol-
lowing to view & mark same Patrick Martin, Ja^s H Bryan, John
Tucker, Samuel Binkley, Thomas[faded], Thos Norris, Wm Karr,
Lovick Ventress, Henry Airs, [name faded], Saml Crocket, and
Benjamin Koan

James Menees reelected Sheriff;   bond 12500 Dollars,   Edward
Cheatham, Jo^s Payne, Saml Donelson, Ge^o Briscoe, securities

Order a road laid off from Robert Weakleys ferry to the Cum-
berland furnace on Bartons Creek;   to view & mark same   Maj^r
George Ross,   Robt Weakley, Geo Ross Jr, Stephen Ward, Moses
Furgeson, Jno Burgan, Isaiah Hamilton, Thos Hamilton, Nathan
Johnson, John Johnson, Ja^s Ross & [faded] Matthews

Josiah Fort Esqr   was duly elected County Trustee;   bond two
thousand Dollars, Hugh Henry & Britain Bryant his securities

Petition of Jno Russel McShehee praying Court to order Clerk
to certify to secretary of North Carolina in issuing a grant
upon military warrant #1087,   favour Miles McShehee for 2560
acres in Robertson, having been read & proof to support same
having been heard which appears satisfactory,   Ordered Clerk
Certify facts in sd petition to Secretary of North Carolina.
Court Adjourns untill tomorrow Morning 9 OClock

Wednesday Morning July 23rd 1800   Present Benjn Menees,
Charles Miles, James Norfleet, Martin Duncan, John Hutchison

p.146 Wm T Lewis vs Joseph Philips. Covenant. Jany 1800 pl^tf
by Joseph Herndon; def^t by Isaac McNutt pleads Covenant performed. July 1800 Term Jury Jno Dorris, Jesse Jones, Ezekiel
Mace, Melcher Oyler, John Hardin, John Price, Thomas Little,
John Flynn, Charles Colgin, Edward King, John Wilson, Abraham Tippy who find for pltf, assess damage to 100 Dollars 30
cents; also his costs

Nimrod McIntosh to oversee road in place of Charles McIntosh

Deed Thomas Christmas to William Christmas,   70 acres proven
by Thomas Johnson
Deed Thomas Hampton to James Crabtree 320 acres proven by Wm
Harrington

Joseph Robertson who was security for Samuel Grayson & John
Grayson delivered them in exhonaration of himself & Geo Bell

in two suits John Barr ag[t] s[d] Graysons, also exonaration of William Karr

John J Dorris and Shederick Rawls ack[d] themselves George Chapmans security in place of John Crunk and William Dorris

George Bell vs Shederick Rawls. Judg[t] before single justice for 41 Dollars 90 c[ts] & 50 c[ts] costs levied by John J Dorris constable on 603 acres on Buzzard Creek; order land sold

William Crunk fined one Dollars for a Breach of the peace in fighting with Jacob Riggs

p.147   John Barr vs James Doherty & Other Def[ts]. Assault & Battery. April 1800 pl[tf] by Seth Lewis dismisses suit only as ag[t] James Dromgoole, Bazel Boren, J & Thomas McIntosh J[r]; Def[t]s James Doherty, Samuel Grayson, Jn[o] Grayson, Daniel Mc-Kindley appeared by Thomas Stuart, pleads Not Guilty. Judgement by Default entered ag[t] Stephen Boren. July 1800 Isaac McNutt for Stephen Boren moved that Judgement by Default be set aside. Default set aside on his paying costs heretofore accruing except service of Writ on persons named & their appearance bonds. Jury Jesse Jones, Melcher Oyler, Jn[o] Hardin, Thomas Little, John Flynn, Charles Colgin, Edward King, John Wilson, Abraham Tippy, W[m] Briscoe, Rob[t] Simpson, Benj[n] Weakley who find Defts Not Guilty. John Pankey witness proves 3 days attendance.   Nancy Pankey 3 days, Ezekiel Mace 3 days, John Price 3 days, Solomon Wilson 3 days, John Couts 3 days

Jacob Riggs fined 2 Dollars for a Breach of the Peace for fighting with William Crunk J[r]

p.148 John Pankey vs Shaderick Rawls. July 1800 pl[tf] by Tho[s] Stuart; def[t] by John C Hamilton. Jury Jesse Jones, John Dorris, Ezekiel Mace, Melcher Oyler, Cha[s] Colgin, John Wilson, W[m] Crunk Jr, Joel Harvey, Thomas McIntosh, Tho[s] Dorris, John Couts, Nimrod McIntosh, who find for pl[tf] & assess damage to Ten Dollars 66 2/3 cents; also his costs. Isaac Dorris witness proves 3 days attendance. Thomas Settle 3 days.   Archer Cheatham 3 days, proves the succeeding Court.

State vs John Tenneson. Adultry. April 1800 Grand Jury found bill ag[t] def[t]. July 1800 def[t] pleads Not Guilty. Jo[s] Herndon for State; Thomas Stuart for def[t]. Jury W[m] Grimes, Britain Bryan, Rob[t] Simpson, Sam[l] Henry, Henry Airs, Henry Johnson, Matthew Day, David Spence, John Tucker, Nath[l] Hardin, Jacob Pickrel, Shaderick Rawls, find def[t] Not Guilty
Court Adjourned untill Tomorrow Morning 9 OClock

Thursday Morning July 24th 1800
Present John Philips, Joseph Dorris, Charles Miles, Esqrs

Archer Cheatham app^{td} Joaler; bond one thousand Dollars,
Isaac Dorris his security

p.149 Ordered the prison bounds in Springfield be: the whole
East end of Town including that part of Black Branch within
the publick Land, and as far West in Town as Second Cross St
West of main North & South Street

Joseph Dorris Esqr app^{td} to build a stray Pen on the publick
Square in Springfield, following dimensions, posts well sunk
in ground, forty feet square with five posts of a side, good
gate, 4 rails to each pannel, mortised into posts at proper
distances; John Philips, Charles Miles, and Wm Johnson Esq^{rs}
inspect work when compleated, on or before first day of next
County Court; sd Dorris to receive Ten Dollars

Ordered Clerk transmit to printer of Knoxville Gazette the
lands reported by Hugh Henry Esqr Collector for nonpayment
of Taxes for year 1798, to be published agreeable to Law

Court Adjourns untill Court in Course.
John Philips, Joseph Doris, William Johnson

p.150   Robertson County.   Monday Morning October 20th 1800
Present   Benjamin Menees, William Johnson, Isaac Dortch

Grand Jurors Henry Gardner foreman, Arthur Pitt, Nathan
Clark, Wm Benson, Jno Siglar, James Elliott, Jas Stark, John
Appleton, John Hudson, Ephraim Rees, Elias Fort Jr, Joseph
Washington, John Baker. John Bryant Cnstable sworn to attend
the Grand Jury

Matthew Luter vs Robert Black J^r. Appeal. July 1800 pltf by
Thomas Stuart, def^t by Bennet Searcy. Cont^d. Octr 1800 Jury
Andrew Irwin, Azariah Dunn, Elias Lawrence, Robert Guttery,
Chas Bradon, Jonathan Stephenson, George Pool, Joseph Payne,
Ja^s H Bryan, Jno McIntosh, Nimrod McIntosh, William Briscoe,
who find for pl^{tf} damage one Dollar 25 cents; also his costs
of suit. Giles Connel witness proves 3 days, Isaac Dortch 3
days, Wm Connel 3 days

Luke Rawls Junr sworn as executor to will of Luke Rawls Senr

Isaac Flannery vs Edward Harris. Jn° Powers garnishee swears he is indebted on his Bond given to Edward Harris sum of Two Hundred Dollars

p.151 William Johnson ag^t Sampson Trammel. Daniel McKinley & Meredith Walton, Trammel's securities, delivered Trammel

Deed Simon Totevine to Richard Hanks for 100 acres proven by Edward Gatlin
Deed Wm Prince to Ephraim Reese 60 or 70 acres proven by Wm Connel
Deed Thomas Bounds to Obediah Bounds for 223 acres proven by Joseph Bounds
Deed John Hutchison to Wm Hutchison 50 acres proven by Thos Hutchison
Deed John Hutchison to Wm Wilson for 50 acres proven by Thos Hutchison
Deed Jacob Moake to Thomas Hunter 34½ acres proven by Samuel Miles
Bond Joseph Carmack to Jesse Carmack for 225 acres assigned by Jesse Carmack to John Carmack and by John Carmack to John Fleanor J^r, which Bond & assignments were ack^d in Open Court by the executors of s^d Joseph Carmack

Barton Coats, Jn° McMillion, Bartimeas Pack, Francis Boren & Richd Nuckles excused from serving as jurors at present term

Court Adjourned untill tomorrow Morning 9 OClock

Tuesday Morning October the 25th 1800   Present
Benjamin Menees, Martin Duncan, Wm Connel & Wm Johnson Esq^{rs}

James Simpson to oversee road from Weakleys ferry to Iron works; the whole of Captn Hamiltons Company to work on same

Deed Philip Parchment to David Shelby 320 acres proven by Saml Donelson

p.152 William Farmer vs Jesse Moore. Attachment. Octr Term 1799 Sheriff "levied on an old screw augur in hands of Benjn Chapman." Pl^{tf} by Thomas Stuart. Jany 1800 Judgement by default. Octr 1800 Jury And^w Irwin, Azariah Dunn, Elias Lawrence, Jonathan Stephenson, Sampson Matthews, Wm Edwards, Wm Crunk, Wm Karr, David Spence, Wm Matthews, Joel Vaughn, Eppa Lawson who assess damage to 42 Dollars 24 cents; also costs

John Jones Esqr commissioned by governor as a Justice/Peace took the Oaths by Law required

Edwd Ja^s vs Jn° Dobins. Ja^s Guttery, witness, proves 2 days attendance, 30 miles travel. Bostick Martin 2 days, 30 miles

Deed Henry Gardner to Lawrence Carr for 50 acres ackd
Deed Thomas Hardwick to Noah Sugg 60 acres proven by Samuel Donelson
Deed Daniel Burford to Henry Lawson 640 acres proven by Luke Dillard
Deed Henry Lawson to Joseph Wimberley 640 acres proven by Luke Dillard
Deed John Hudson to John Beason 100 acres ackd
Deed Francis Holmes to John James 157½ acres proven by Charles Simmons

p.153 Josiah Payne vs Wm Crunk & Martin Duncan. Debt. Jany 1800 pl^if by Saml Donelson; def^t by John C Hamilton. Cont^d. Octr Term 1800 Jury Charles Bradon, Richard Matthews, Lawrence Carr, Matthew Day, William Sale, William Spiller, Wm Grimes, Aaron Laws, Elijah Lancaster, Augustus Cook, David Henry, George Pool who find for def^ts. Margaret Keneday witness proves 5 days and 90 miles traveling

Thomas Woodard app^id Constable; bond with And^w Irwin & Danl Holland securities; took Oaths required by Law

B/S William Fort to Frederick Fort proven by James Menees

Nathan Arnet one of Executors of will of Luke Rawls dec^d delivered an Inventory of the Estate

James Robertson, John Bosley & R C Napier granted liberty to Erect a grist mill on Bartons Meat Camp Creek at place known by the name of Family Forge agreeable to their Petition

p.154 John Barr vs Saml Grayson. Ap^l 1800 pl^f by Seth Lewis; def^t by Thos Stuart pleads Not Guilty. July 1800 Jury Britain Bryan, Moses Larisy, Nathl Harbert, Matthew Day, Moses Boren, David Spence, David Ramsey, Wm Simpson, John Crunk, Jn° Young, Henry Airs, Jn° Duncan find for pl^tf, assess damage to 120 Dollars and Costs. Def^t granted New trial; cause cont^d. Octr 1800 Jury Andrew Irwin, Azariah Dunn, Elias Lawrence, Robert Guttery, Chas Bradon, Jonathan Stephenson, Ge° Pool, Sampson Matthews, Wm Edwards, William Crunk, Wm Karr & Wm Matthews who find for pl^tf, assess damage to 100 Dollars; also costs. John Pankey, witness, proves 3 days attendance, Ezekiel Mace 1 day
Barr vs Grayson. Patrick Lyons who was summoned as a witness failed to appear; he is to be subject to penalty of Law
Court Adjourned untill tomorrow Morning 9 O Clock

Wednesday Morning October 22nd 1800.
Benjn Menees, Martin Duncan, Wm Johnson, Esquires

p.155   David Patterson vs Wm Miles & Ge^o Sadler. Attachment.
Jany 1800 pl^f by Bennet Searcy. Sh^{ff} levied in hands of Mat-
thew Luke & him summoned as Garnishee who came into Court &
Swore he owed Def^t Wm Miles 60 odd Dollars. Cause cont^d.
July 1800 Judg^t by Default ag^i Def^{ds}. Octr 1800 Jury Elias
Lawrence, Andrew Irwin, Jonathan Stephenson, Jno Price, Mat-
thew Luter J^r, John Tennison, Bazil Boren, Lewellen Phips,
John Crunk, Ja^s McDaniel, And^w Job, Edward Cheatham who find
for plaintiff and assess his damage to one cent; also costs

Jonathan Stephenson admitted to keep an Ordinary in this
county for one Year; Bond 500 Dollars, Josiah Fort, Ephraim
Reese & Elias Fort J^r his security

Deed William Spiller to Vachel Lovelass for 30 acres proven
by John Bryant
James Elliott Jr to oversee road in place of Wm Fleuellen

Bazel Boren and Thomas Yates security for Philip Shackler in
suit John Young against sd Shackler

Jurors to Superior Court Thomas Johnson, Jonathan Dardin, W^m
Connel, Robert B Currey & Anderson Cheatham

p.156 Wm Johnson vs Sampson Trammel. Trespass. July 1800 pl^f
by Thomas Stuart; def^t by J C Hamilton & Ja^s Doherty pleads
Not Guilty. Octr Jury And^w Irwin, Azariah Dunn, Elias Law-
rence, Jonathan Stephenson, Charles Bradon, William Coates,
Lewellen Phips, James McDaniel, Matthew Day, Thomas Yates,
Nathaniel Hardin, Bazel Boren, who find for defendant. John
Baker, witness, proves 2 days attendance. Wm Sale, 3 days;
And^w Job, 3; John Tennison, 3; Mary Vaughn, 3; Mary Vaughn
Junr, 3; Mary Grimes, 3; John Bryant, 3; Elizabeth Bryan, 3;
Mary Harris, 3; Mrs Spiller, 2; Jeremah Harris 3, John T
Harris, 3

Johnson vs Trammel, pl^{tf} to pay only two of def^{t}s witnesses,
& def^{dt} Trammel pay rest. Johnson vs Trammel, John Grimes,
summoned as a witness for Johnson, failed to attend; order
he be subject to penalty of the Law

Martin Duncan exhonarated from payment of State & County Tax
for 1800 on 213 acres, said Land being given in by Melcher
Oyler

p.157 Isham Rogers to Oversee road from Karrs Creek to Turnbulls Stamp as lately marked; hands which work on Nashville Road to Sychamore to work in clearing out same

William Karr to receive from the Collector or County Trustee the amount allowed him by the Commissioners for Building the Jaol in Springfield

Orders for Stray Pen cont^d, to be compleated by next Term

Jurors to next Term Ja^s Blackwell, Mark Noble, Jesse Martin, Caleb Winters, John Crane, William Crocket, Matthew Day, Jacob Warren, George Patterson, James Atkins, William Grimes, Wm Elliott, Samuel Crocket, James Long, Patrick Martin, John Beason, Anderson Cheatham, Benjn Porter, Moses Hardin, John James, Jonathan Price, Elijah Lancaster, Chas McIntosh, John Duncan, John Powers, William Spiller, Jonathan Oyler, Wm Deloach, John Carr, Thos Hutchison

Court Adjourned untill Court in Course
            Benjamin Menees, Joseph Doris, John Philips

p.158   Robertson county. Monday Morning January 19th 1801. Town of Springfield.   Present the Worshipfull John Stuart, James Norfleet, William Johnson and John Hutchison, Esquires

Grand Jurors John James foreman, Anderson Cheatham, William Grimes, Patrick Martin, Jonathan Price, Jacob Warren, John Beason, Jonathan Oyler, Charles McIntosh, James Long, Benjn Porter, James Blackwell, William Miller, George Patterson

John Barr agt Samuel Grayson (determined last Court)   Archer Cheatham proves five days attendance as a witness

Wm Smith produced Licence to practice as an attorney in this State and is admitted accordingly.   Likewise, Jesse Wharton

State vs Robert Lancaster. Assault & Battery. Defendant in proper person submitted to Court, fined One Dollar and Costs

Property of John Pinkley decd be sold agreeable to Law

Peter Pinkley app'd Adm^r to estate of Jno Pinkley dec^d; bond 1200 Dollars with Anderson Cheatham & Matthew Day securities

Isham Rogers admitted to keep an Ordinary in this County at his own House for one year; bond 500 Dollars, John Tucker &

79

Matthew Day his securities

p.159 Edward James vs John Dobins. Covenant. Octr 1799 plt^f
by Jn° C Hamilton; def^t by Thos Stuart. Jany 1801 jury John
Carr, John Powers, John Duncan, William Edwards, Mark Noble,
Elijah Lancaster, Saml Crocket, Jo^s Washington, Jesse Martin, Meredith Walton, Abraham Tippy, William Crocket who find
for pl^{tf}, assess damage to 350 Dollars & costs of suit. Def^t
obtained an appeal to Superior Court; bond 700 Dollars, John
James and John Beason his securities. Bostick Martin, a witness, proves 8 days attendance & 150 miles, James Guttery 7
days, 120 miles, and John Shannon 4 days, 60 miles

Deed William Johnson to Alexander McNeely 127 acres ackd
Deed Aquilla Sugg to Thomas Hill 228 acres proven by Paul
McGraw
Deed Charles Parker to Willliam Huse 98 acres ackd
Deed John McCoy Alston to Hannah Porter 87 acres proven by
Joseph Brown

Thos Little apptd overseer of Road from Karrs Creek to Donelsons Old place in room of Archer Cheatham

p.160 Relinquishment of property signed by Legatees of Rich^d
Matthews dec^d, proven by James Sawyers

Will of Daniel Koen proven by Benjamin Koen

Lamuel Sugg app^{td} Surveyor of Road leading from Weakley ferry to Robertson Court House as far as Widow Rawls Sugar Camp
on Sugar fork of Spring Creek (where Isaac Sanders begins to
work on his part of s^d Road) and following Hands work under
him, to open the part not yet opened, & then keep s^d Road in
repair according to Law: Captn Benjn Weakley, David Weakley,
William Weakley, Jn° Weakley, Philip Russel, Wilson McDowel,
David Beasly, William Lewis, Jn° Hill, Benjamin Owens, Isaac
Matthews

John Tucker admitted to keep an ordinary in Springfield one
year, bond 500 Doll^s with Saml Crocket & Abraham Tippy, sec

B/S Martin Greider to Peggy Conrod proven by Sampson Conrod

Nathan Clark apptd Overseer of Road from Sulpher fork to
Bells in place of Abraham Tippy
Court Adjourns untill tomorrow Morning 9 OClock

Tuesday Morning January 20th 1801
Worshipfull James Norfleet, John Stuart & John Jones Esq^{rs}

Deed Thos Parker to Thos Jemison 320 acres ackd
Deed Thomas Jemison to Archibald Mahon 320 acres ackd

Bazel Boren & Thomas Yates, securities for the appearance of
Philip Shackler, delivered him in discharge of themselves

p.161 Andrew Bowman vs John Ed Long. Attachment. April 1800
Sheriff "Levied on 640 acres on Cooks Branch of Red River."
Pl'f by Joseph Herndon. Proceedings stayed until Octr 1800;
Judgement by default ag' def'. Jany 1801 jury John Powers,
John Duncan, Henry Airs, Richard Nuckles, John Carr, Archi-
bald Mahon, Elijah Lancaster, William Crocket, James Atkins,
Joel Harvey, Joseph Johnson, James Bell who find for plf and
assess damage to 726 Dollars 66 2/3 cents & Costs. Order to
sell the property attached.

John Young & James Norfleet, Commissioners, vs John Pankey.
Certiorari. January 1800 pl'fs by Thos Stuart; def^t by Isaac
McNutt. January 1801 Jury John Duncan, Mark Noble, Elijah
Lancaster, William Crocket, James Atkins, John Hardin, James
Bell, Thos Yates; previous to their Verdict, the Plaintiffs
suffered a Non Suit

p.162 Jn° Young vs Philip Shackles. Covenant. Octr 1800 pl'f
by Samuel Donelson; def^t by John C Hamilton. Jany 1801 Jury
Nathaniel Rogers, David Hamilton, James Stark, Arthur Pitt,
Francis Boren, Thos McIntosh, Jo^s Castleberry, David Spence,
Stephen Boren, John Appleton, Ezekiel Mace, Sam' Crocket who
find for def'. Pl'f obtained appeal to Superior Court; bond
200 Dollars, George Briscoe, sec. Hezekiah Robertson a witness proves 2 days attendance, John J Dorris the same

Josiah Fort, County Trustee, allowed one Dollar 37½ Cents, a
sum overpaid of County Tax for 1797

At an Election for Coroner, George Briscoe was elected; bond
1000 Dollars, John Hardin and John Hutchison his securities

Overseer of Road from Logan to Nashville through Springfield
to open sd road from Sulpher f^k nearest way, passing through
Springfield with the main North & South Street

Deed John Young & James Norfleet Comm^rs to Richd Nuckles for
Town Lot proven by T Johnson
Deed ditto
Deed Wm Duncan to Benjn McNow 213 acres proven by Jn° Bryant
Deed Hugh Henry Shff to Wm Fort 320 acres ackd
Deed Martin Duncan to Wm Duncan 213 acres ackd

p.163   Following persons to take Lists of Taxable property
for the present year:

John Jones Esqr Captn Hamiltons Company
James Crabtree Esqr Captn Youngs Company
William Connel Esqr Captn Blackwells Company
Hardy S Bryan Esqr Captn Weakleys Company
John Hutchison Esqr Captn Bounds Company
Martin Duncan Esqr Captn Johnsons Company
Charles Miles Esqr Captn Dardins Company
John Philips Esqr Captn Cheathams Company

Adam Sheppard & Co allowed to erect a mill dam on Iron fork
of Bartons Creek, at same place or fork of creek where Adam
Shepherd & Co have built Iron works & mill on their own land

Release 108 acres John Robins to Bazel Boren proven
Deed William Betts to David McGraw, Town Lot in Fayetteville
proven by John Stuart
Court Adjourns untill tomorrow Morning 9 OClock

Wednesday Morning January 21st 1801
Present   John Stuart, John Hutchison, Isaac Dortch, Esquires

B/S Howel Dupree to Samuel Sugg proven by Isaac Philips
B/S John Young to John Simmons proven by Thos Strain. Previ-
ous to registration, Jno Simmons orders this B/S given up to
Young, that he has rec^d full satisfaction as p^r order filed

Deed John Young to Saml Crocket 105 acres ackd
Deed Philip Shackler to John Young 274 acres proven by Jacob
Young

p.164 Thos McIntosh by next friend John McIntosh vs Anderson
Cheatham. Assault & Battery. Octr 1800 pl^{tf} by Thos Stuart;
def^t by John C Hamilton. January 1801 Jury Matthew Day, Thos
Hutchison, Mark Noble, Elijah Lancaster, Wm Crocket, James
Atkins, Arch^d Mahon, George Briscoe, Thos Christmas, Rich^d
Martin, William Edwards, John Hardin who find pl^{tfs} damage
Ten Dollars; also costs. Danl McKinley witness proves 3 days
attendance, Jacob Young, 3 days, Bazel Boren 2 days

George Gordon vs John Ellis. Attachment. Octr 1800 pltf by
John C Hamilton; judg^t by default ag^t Def^t. Sheriff "Levied
on 640 acres Buzzard Creek." Jany 1801 Jury Jacob Pickrel,
James Bell, Wm Briscoe, Wm Coates, Abel Williams, Asa Park-
er, Jacob Pinkley, Saml Gallaway, Wm Simpson, Peter Pinkley,
Joel Harvey, Jno McElhainey find for pl^t 640 Dollars & costs

p.165 Wm Johnson vs John Grimes. Scire facias ag^t def^t as a

delinquent witness in suit Wm Johnson ag^t Sampson Trammel.
Pl^{tf} to recover ag^t def^t 50 pounds equal to 125 Dollars and
Costs. Jemimah Harrison a witness proves 3 days attendance

Order Thomas Johnson as Surveyor attend on all Lands of John
Pinkley dec^d and lay them off, each Heir his part agreeably
to Law, and that Henry Johnson Junr, John Philips, & Anderson Cheatham attend on the premises as Jurors

Order a road laid off from Springfield to Richard Cavets on
Red River, passing John Couts mill on Beaver Dam creek. Wal-
ter Stark, Wm Grimes, Johnson Kilgore, Abraham Young, Thomas
Strain, John Young, James Yates, Jonathan Price Senr, James
Wheeler, or any five to mark same. Make immediate return to
Clerk who is to issue orders to William Grimes & Daniel Hol-
iman as Overseers to open same. All hands on North side of
Sulpher fork above the mouth of Beaver Dam Creek within two
miles of said Road work on the same in clearing it out

Order road laid off from Kentucky line near Harris's mill to
Weakleys ferry on Cumberland river, and if it should be any-
thing near the nearest way, to go by or near Joseph Choates.
Jesse Martin, Caleb Winters, Moses Winters, Moses Larisy,
Nathl Rogers, Joseph Miller, Aaron Choate, Nicholas Choate,
George Evans, John Sharod, Francis Grayham, Mark Noble, & W^m
Noble or any of them mark same & make return

p.166 Jurors to next County Court George Pool, David Jones,
David Huddleston Senr, Richd Matthews, Jno Somorville, Moses
Beason, Webster Gilbert, Zachariah Tucker, Henry Johnson,
Nimrod McIntosh, William Karr, Jas McKinley, Abraham Tippy,
Joseph Robertson, Thos McIntosh, Caleb Winters, Benjn Wood,
Jacob Young, Robt Simpson, Saml Musgrove, Elias Fort- Brush
Cr, Elias Fort Jr, Eppa Lawson, Jno Siglar, Levi Moore, Wal-
ter Stark, Bazel Boren, Wm Benson, Arthur Pitt, William Lusk
Court Adjourns untill tomorrow Morning 9 oClock

Thursday Morning January 22nd 1801
Present John Philips, Martin Duncan, Wm Johnson, Esquires

Levin & Cuthberth Powell did not give in their List of Taxable property for 1800, Order Clerk insert amount of taxable
property on Collectors List with what is due thereon so same
may be paid, and that forfeiture incured thereby be remited

Deed William Johnson to Thos Berry 640 acres ackd
Personal estate of Archer Cheatham dec^d to be sold by adm^{rs}

Suit Thos McIntosh by next friend John McIntosh agt Anderson

Cheatham, Beverley A Allen summoned as witness for McIntosh failed to appear; Scire facias to issue

John Young ag^t P Shackler. Bazel Boren, Anderson Cheatham, Wm Fleuellen, John Brooks, & Jonathan Oyler ack^d themselves s^d Shacklers security

p.167 Following tracts reported to Collector for 1798 for Nonpayment of Taxes, have been advertised agreeable to Law; Judgment is entered against s^d Lands: Miles McShehees heirs 1057 ac 45/160; Anders Armstrong 294 ac 60/160; Benjn Sheppard 75 ac 12/160; Wm Campbell 463 ac; Frederick Deseard 95 ac; Jno Sugg 235 ac 99/160; Frederick Hargett & Carney 2153½ acres; David Jones 712 ac 39/160; Wm Jinkins 157 ac 30/160; And^w Hampton 615 ac 130/160; Wm Jackson 221 ac 47/160, Isaac Hudson 255 ac 55/160; John Herritage 522 ac 153/160; Anthony Black 600 ac 124/160; Francis Wilks 196 ac 131/160; Nehemiah Pevy 536 ac 53/160; John Bowers 124 ac 73/160; Danl Mcfatter 537 ac 127/160; Abraham Fulkison 213 ac 19/160; Dugal McCays Heirs 431 ac 106/160; William Alford 458 ac 92/160; Abraham Colrean 582 ac 65/160; Jno Poe 584 ac 97/160; John Taitt 544 ac 23/160; Wm Farrow 191 43/160 ac; John Easten & Wm Tyrrell 233 ac; David Ivy 253 93/160 ac; David Davis 640 ac; Ja^s Lee 274; Lt James Moore 2560 ac; John Bosley 640 ac; John Pirky [blot]; John Bowman 640 ac; John Porterfield 640 ac; Benjn McCullock 640 ac; Benjamin McCullock 640 ac; Benjn McCullock 6140 ac; Benjn McCullock 640; Benjn McCullock 640 ac; Benjn McCullock 274 ac; Jno Clendennons heirs 428 ac; Stokely Donelson & Wm Tyrrell 2560 ac; Gubbins 640 ac; Daniel Wilburn 1000 ac; John Love [11 tracts 640 acres each]
Order Clerk issue execution for each tract for tax & costs; sheriff to sell agreeable to Law

p.168 Following Tracts ordered sold for nonpayment of Taxes for 1797: John and James Bonner 274 ac; David Davis 640 ac; & Clerk to issue execution for each Tract for Tax and costs; Sheriff to proceed to sell agreeable to Law

Tracts which heretofore had part sold for Taxes, part now to be sold for above Judgemts shall be laid off in a square to join side or end of the part heretofore sold; tracts which are to be sold of which never was any part sold before shall the part now sold by Virtue of above Judgements be laid off square, to begin at the beginning of the original surveys

Order Martin Duncan Esqr added to those heretofore apptd to receive the stray pen
Jacob Young produced acct for one Dollar for working on Jaol which was allowed
Archer Cheatham allowed Two Dollars 50 cents for Jaol fees

APRIL 1801

Commissioners apptd to receive the Stray Pen order Clerk to
issue a certificate to Joseph Dorris for amount allowed him

Court Adjourns untill Court in Course
                John Philips, Martin Duncan, Wm Johnson

p.169 Robertson County. Monday Morning April 20th 1801
Present the Worshipfull John Stewart, William Johnson,
Thomas Strain, Esquires

Grand Jurors elected: David Huddleston foreman, Nimrod McIn-
tosh, Abraham Tippy, Webster Gilbert, Elias Fort Jr, Walter
Stark, Arthur Pitt, Caleb Winters, Wm Benson, Elias Fort,
Moses Beason, John Siglar, Richard Matthews, Jacob Young

Joseph Choate, Security for Ambrose Hutchison in suit Adam
Shepherd & Cᵒ agᵗ sd Hutchison, surrendered him into Court

Benjn Nail on Judgement by Default in suit John Hays agᵗ sᵈ
Nail, being set aside, gives Matthew Day and David Spence as
special bail, who acknowledge themselves bound as such

Redmond D Barry Esqʳ produced his Licence to practice as an
attorney; took oaths and is admitted

Isham Rogers allowed to pay Collector the State & County tax
on 125 acres on Brown fork of Karrs Creek
Court Adjourns for One Hour. Court met accᵈᵍ to adjournment

A Shepherd & Co vs Ambrose Hutchison. Henry D Downs, Samuel
Crocket & Wm Connel ackd selves sd Hutchisons Security

Deed Jesse Jones to Augustine Cook 100 acres ackd

p.170 John Carr vs Samˡ Glover admʳ of William Glover decᵈ.
Attachment. 23 April 1800 John Carr obtained attachment agᵗ
Samˡ Glover admʳ of Wᵐ Glover for 25 Dollars 37½ cents on a
note of hand besides Interest.on sᵈ Note accruing. At July
1800 Sheriff "Levied May 30 on 640 acres on Sychamore near
Hollis's Mill." J Menees Shᶠᶠ, plᵗᶠ by Seth Lewis. Continued
9 months. Apˡ 1801 plᵗᶠ by Joˢ Herndon. Jury Wᵐ Lusk, Zachʰ
Tucker, Eppa Lawson, Henry Johnson, David Jones, Levi Moore,
John Somerville, Samuel Musgrove, John Crocket, Henry Airs,
John Chewning, Wᵐ Crocket who find for plᵗᶠ; also his costs

John W Crunk vs Volentine Choate. Wᵐ Wills, defᵗs security,

delivered s^d Choate. Joseph Payne, John Hutchison ack^d themselves s^d Choates security

Elisabeth Chambers bound as apprentice to Thomas Norris Senr
until she arrives to age eighteen years
Joseph Robertson excused from serving as juror present Term

Deed David Quick & William Quick to George Donnel 640 acres
proven by Joseph Gamble
Deed Wm Crutcher to Ge^o Ury 50 acres proven by Russel Gower

p.171 P/A John R McShehee to Thomas Britain proven by Isaac
Walton
Deed Benjn & Elisha Owens to Isham Matthews 100 acres proven
by Benjn Weakley
Deed Elizabeth Rawls to Wm Miles 30 acres proven by Henry
Johnson
Deed Jonathan Price Junr to Arthur Pitt 11 acres proven by
Thomas Johnson

Jonathan Downey app^{td} Constable; bond 640 Dollars, Henry D
Downs his security; took the necessary Oaths
Ltrs/Admn granted Jonathan Downey on estate of Benjn Rogers
decd; bond 200 Dollars, John Jones security
Court Adjourned untill untill Tomorning 9 OClock(sic)

Tuesday Morning April 25th 1801
Present Benjn Menees, Isaac Dortch, Isaac Philips, Wm Connel

John Philips Esqr delivered List of Taxable property for the
year 1801 in Captn Cheathams Company
Order Tavern keepers entitled to receive 25 Cents for Brake-
fast or supper
Deed Hugh Henry Sheriff to Josiah Fort 320 acres ackd
Deed John Young & James Norfleet Comm^{rs} for Springfield to
John C Hamilton one Town Lot ackd

Thos Smith bound to give testimony in behalf State agt Ezekiel Mace failed to appear, and David Henry his security was
called on Recognizance & forfeited

p.172 Aquilla Randal vs William Lusk. Covenant. January 1801
pl^{tf} by Bennet Searcy; def^t by Jno C Hamilton & Ja^s Doherty.
April 1801 Jury Zachariah Tucker, Appa Lawson, David Jones,
Levi Moore, John Somerville, Saml Musgrove, Wm Karr, David
Henry, Elijah Lancaster, Wm Grimes, Wm Wills, Wm Coates, who
find for Def^{dt}. Motion for new trial overruled. John Crocket
witness proves 2 days attendance; William Lusk 2 days & 180
miles travel, Edward Gatlin 2 days, 60 miles travel

Order Estate of Joseph Hart dec^d to pay estate of Noah Sugg
dec^d 20 Dollars for services of Noah Sugg as adm^r to estate
of s^d Hart

John Carr to oversee Road in room of Archibald Mahon; following hands to work under him: Isaac Dortch, Jonathan Stephenson, Robert Black, James Stewarts hands, Lawrence Carrs
hands, Mrs Ann Gardners hands, Jesse Martin

Deed Moses Laurisy to John Williams 195 acres proven by Dud-
ley Williams
Deed Wm Boren by Bazel Boren his att^o in fact to James Karr
100 acres ackd
Deed John Mann to Aquilla Sugg 228 acres proven by Thomas
Johnson
Deed Robert Nelson to Martin Duncan 113 acres proven by Danl
McKinley

p.173 Jesse Jones vs Bazel Boren Jr. Assault & Battery. Jan^y
1801 Pl^{tf} by John C Hamilton; def^t by Thomas Stewart. Cont^d
each Term untill July 1801. Jury Wm Perry, Benjamin Chapman,
James McDonald, Joseph Castleberry, Eli Jones, Samuel Miles,
John Sherod, John Carr, Wm Armstrong, Nicholas Conrod, David
Spence, Sampson Matthews who find for pl^{tf}, assess damage to
15 Dollars & costs. Benjamin Fort witness 4 days attendance

Jurors to Superior Court David Weakley, Thomas Strain, Isaac
Philips, Charles Miles, Wm Connel

James McDonald to oversee road from top of Ridge near Betts
to Browns fork. Hands to work under him: Henry Wigle, John
Keneday, Joshua Phips, James Shannon, all hands on waters of
Karrs down to where road crosses from Springfield to Nashville & hands above s^d road on Sychamore

Surveyor & Jurors app^{id} to divide lands of John Pinkley dec^d
between Legatees made report to Court

Wm Connel Esqr delivered list of Taxable property for Captn
Blackwells Company. John Hutchison for Captn Bounds Company.
Thos Strain for Captn Youngs Company

p.174 Archer Cheatham to keep an Ordinary in Springfield
for a year, bond 500 Dollars, James Menees security
John Pankey to keep an Ordinary in county for one year gave
bond 500 Dollars, Samuel Musgrove his security
Deed Thomas Molloy to James Robertson Adam Sheppard and John
Jones for 6 acres proven by Joseph Herndon
Deed George Briscoe to John Robins 365 acres proven by Thos

Johnson
Deed Henry Pinkley to Jacob Pinkley 50 3/4 acres proven by
Tho⁸ Johnson

Order Giles Connel to oversee Road from ford of Brush Creek
near Jonathan Stephensons to Clarksville as far as the line
of Montgomery County; Henry Gardner, Ephraim Reese, Thos Edwards, Thos Traviss & sd Giles Connel to make any amendments
as they may think proper so as not to injure any person
Court Adjourns untill tomorrow Morning 9 OClock

Wednesday Morning April 22nd 1801   Present the Worshipfull
Benjamin Menees, John Hutchison, Wᵐ Johnson, Isaac Philips

John Stewart delivered tax list for Captⁿ Weakleys Company

Wm Sale registered his stock mark

Peter Pinkley admr estate of estate of John Pinkley decd de-
livered supplementary inventory
Deed Josiah Ramsey to Marvel Loes(Low?) 200 acres proven by
Jonathan Ramsey
p.175 Charles Miles Esqʳ delivered tax list of Captⁿ Dardens
Company
Ordered that the Overseers of road from Springfield to Richᵈ
Cavets have all hands to work in clearing out said road that
reside within 2½ miles of same
George Clark oversees Kentucky Road in room of Wm Armstrong

John Jones Esqʳ delivered tax list of Captⁿ Hamiltons Compʸ

Ordered that each person who kills a wolf in this county
after this Day shall receive from County Trustee one Dollar
for each Wolf so killed
Order hands formerly ordered to view road from Springfield
to Port Royal to mark same

State vs John Tucker. Presentment quashed. Joel Harvey witness behalf State proves 3 days attendance, 20 miles travel

State vs Mark Noble. John James witness for State proves 4
days attendance; Same in State agt James Walker.

Order Wm Karr, Henry Johnson, Wm Coates, Jesse Williams, Edward King and Shaderick Rawls to view & mark a road Springfield to state line near Majr Smith on Elk fork, to near the
Spring Creek cabbin where Perdue lately lived, from thence
to Isaac Philips Spring branch to cross Red River

Jurors to next Court: Benjamin Owens, Joseph Choate, Squire Choate, Amos Cohea, Benjamin Chapman, James Sawyers, Samuel Miles, Wm Perry, Nicholas Conrod, John Sherod, Azariah Dunn, Wm Stark, Alexr Cromwell, Elijah Hamilton, Jno Crane, George Murphey, Wm Sale, Jno Price, George Hendley, Benjamin McNew, Bazel Boren, Lewis Barker, Jos Castleberry, Wm Haggard, Wm Armstrong Senr, William Armstrong Junr, George Clark, James Ewing, Elisha Chick, John Carr

p.176 Order County Tax for present year: 12½ cents on each hundred acres; 6¼ on each white pole; 12½ each black pole, 25 cents each stud horse kept for covering mares; 12½ cents each Town Lot; 5 Dollars each Billard Table

Deed Isaac Dorris to Amos Cohea seven acres proven by John Hutchison
Matthew Day to oversee road in room of Philip Parchment
Court Adjourns untill tomorrow Morning 9 OClock

Thursday Morning April 23rd 1801
Present Benjn Menees, Isaac Philips, Martin Duncan

Deed James Menees Shff to Jacob Johnson 50 acres ackd
Deed James Menees Shff to Wm Duncan 640 acres ackd
Deed James Menees Shff to Wm Duncan 640 acres ackd
Martin Duncan delivered tax list for Captn Bryants Company

William Coates overseer of the new road (from Weakleys ferry to Kentucky line) from Sulpher fork to sd line, all hands on North side Sulpher fork within 3 miles of the road and all Benjn Menees hands work on the same

Francis Graham to oversee from Sulpher fork to opposite the Man(Marr?) lick, same priviledge of hands above mentioned as to distance from the road. Thomas Choate to be overseer from opposite Man(Mare?) lick to its Junction with the road from Springfield to Weakleys ferry and hands to work the distance from the road as above mentioned

p.177 Deed Bazel Boren to Thos Christmas 60 acres proven by Joseph Robertson
Deed Thomas Christmas to Joseph Robertson 60 acres proven by John Young

State vs Daniel McKinly. Henry Johnson, a witness, proves 2 days; Isaac Dorris 2 days; Benjamin Porter 4 days; Anderson Cheatham 4 days

John Pankey vs John Tucker. Detinue. Jany 1801 plf by Thomas

Stuart & James Doherty; def^t by John C Hamilton. April Jury Benjn Porter, Zachariah Tucker, Wm Karr, James Atkins, Robt Lancaster, John James, Nathaniel Hardin, Ja^s Walker, William Briscoe, Moses Hardin, Levi Moore, Augustine Cook, who find for pl^{tf} and value waggon 40 Dollars which may be discharged by delivery of waggon to pl^{tf} and 8 Dollars for detainer. A Motion for New tryal overuled. Stephen Boren, witness, four days; Danl McKinley 4 days; Henry Johnson 4; Isaac Dorris 4; Perry Cohea 4; Samuel Wilson 4; Jacob Pickren 4; John Duncan 4; John J Dorris 4

p.178 Order lands reported for Nonpayment of 1799 taxes, Clk forthwith to transmit to printer of Knoxville Gazette a copy thereof with Tax & double tax & costs to be published

James Menees Sheriff app^{td} Collector of State & County Tax; bond 5000 Dollars, with John James, Joseph Robertson, Anderson Cheatham his securities; took oaths by law required

George Bell vs Ja^s Doherty. Judgement on two attachments, on Motion to reverse Judg^{ts}, Court takes advesari to next Court

State vs Ja^s Walker. Augustine Cook witness behalf the state proves 3 days attendance

Joseph Robertson app^{td} a Commissioner in room of Sugg Fort, removed, for purpose of Settling with the Collectors, gave bond 100 Dollars with Benjn Porter & Isaac Dorris securities

Whereas three scire facias has issued against Joel Hundley to bring orphan children into Court, That they may be dealt with as Law directs, Order Sheriff take said Orphan children (named in Grand Jury presentment) into his possession, and cause them to be brought to this Court

Robt B Currey vs James McCaleb & Samuel Grayson. Attachment. Ordered proceedings stayed six months
Court Adjourns untill Court in Course
                    Benjamin Menees, Isaac Philips, Martin Duncan

p.179   Robertson County.   Monday Morning   July 20th 1801 Springfield. Present the Worshipfull Benjamin Menees, Isaac Dortch, John Hutchison, Esquires

Grand Jurors   James Sawyers foreman, Elijah Hamilton, Elexr Cromwell, James Ewing, Benjamin Owens, Joseph Choate, George

Murphey, Wm Stark, Wm Haggard, Squire Choate, Amos Cohea, Wm Armstrong Senr, John Crane

Deed James Robertson to Thomas Hamilton 100 acres proven by Stephen Ward
Deed James Robertson to Hance Hamilton 150 acres proven by Stephen Ward
Deed John McShehee by Tho[s] Britton his att[y] in fact to And[w] Irwin 250 acres proven by David Huddleston
Deed John Young & Ja[s] Norfleet to Henry Pirkey for 1 lot in Springfield ackd
Deed Lewis Pipkin to Jonathan Oyler 218 acres proven by Wm Johnson

Order Hugh Brown to oversee Road in room of Francis Graham, having same priviledge of hands as Graham

Order Thomas Johnson apptd Surveyor; Benjamin Weakley, James Norfleet, David McGraw, Gabriel Allen, and Andrew Caldwell appointed Jurors to go on 2 tracts of 640 acres each claimed by Roger B Sappington & Harriett S Rice, and divide the same according to each of their claims

p.180 Jesse Martin garnishee in suit John Burris agt William Martin maketh oath that he is not indebted to Wm Martin nor was at time of serving the attachment; he is agent for sd Wm & has a pair of mill stones lying at Clarksville & 3 pair of mill stones lying at Nashville upper ferry & following notes & accounts: an acc[t] for 29 Doll[s] on Rob[t] Boyd dated 1799 who lives in Kentucky; on Tho[s] Harrison 24 Doll[s] dated July 15th 1799 living in Davidson; a note under seal on Jehu Harrison for 18 Doll[s] dated Dec[r] 13th 1799; acc[t] agt John Cennedy for money lent 10 Jan[y] 1800 for 8 Doll[s], believes Cennedy lives in Davidson; proven account on Jehu Davy of Davidson for 15 Doll[s] dated Nov[r] 13th 1799, a proven account agt Peter Johnson living in Davidson for 25 Doll[s] 87½ cents. Garnishee has heard s[d] Wm Martin say Mrs Randol living in Davidson was indebted to him a considerable am[t]; garnishee has no property other than af[sd] in his hands nor had at the time of levying attachment nor since of s[d] Wm nor does he know of any debts due to Wm or property of s[d] Wm in hands of any person than as af[sd]. S[d] garnishee now deposits notes and accounts in the Clerks office of this County

Deed Joel Vaughn to James Vaughn 51 acres 16 poles ackd
Court Adjourns untill tomorrow Morning 9 OClock

Tuesday Morning July 25th 1801
Present Benj[n] Menees, John Stewart, Martin Duncan

Order Isaac Dortch & Isaac Philips to settle with executors of Matthew Williams Dec^d; report this day delivered

p.181 John Hays vs Benjn Nail. Case. Octr 1800 pl^{tf} by Thos Stuart; Def^t failing to attend Judgement by default entered; April 1801; def^t by J C Hamilton; Default set aside on Def^t giving Special Bail. July 1801 Jury Bazel Boren, Wm Perry, Benjn Chapman, James McDonald, Jo^s Castleberry, John Sherod, John Carr, Nicholas Conrod, Elijah Lancaster, Jacob Pinkley, Abraham Tippy, Isaac Robertson. Pl^{tf} suffered himself to be Non Suited. Asa Parker a witness proves 5 days attendance; Thomas Jones 3 days, Joseph Jones 2 days, Ann Spence 3 days, Thomas Norris 2 days

Receipts Saml Henry, John Henry, James Henry, and Thos Henry to Hugh Henry proven by Isaac Henry and ordered Registered

Wm Findley resigned acting as a Constable
Grand Jury discharged

Ordered John Appleton to oversee road from John Donelsons to Bounds Branch; Ja^s Sawyers, David Huddleston & Thomas Bounds to divide the hands between s^d Appleton & Chas Bradon

p.182 Benjamin Stansberry vs Elisha Chick. Case. Jany 1801 pl^{tf} by J Herndon; def^t by J C Hamilton. April 1801 Jury for pl^{tf}, damages 175 Doll^s 50 cents. Def^t obtained a new tryal. July 1801 Jury Anthony Jones, Shaderick Rawls, Henry Gardner, Holland Dardin, Jacob Fry, John Appleton, Jesse Jones, Arthur Pitt, Isaph Parker, Isham Rogers, Benjamin Nail, Thos Yates find for pl^{tf}, assess damage 175 Doll^s 50 c^{ts}; & costs of suit. Philip Johnson witness proves 5 days attendance; Robert Johnson 2 days & 38 miles traveling; Wm Chick 2 days, 38 miles traveling

Deed Squire Choate to Thomas Choate 111 acres proven by John Stewart
Deed Archibald Mahon to Azariah Dunn 100 acres proven by Henry W Lawson
Deed Philip Parchment to Jacob Fry 105 acres proven by Jacob Pinkley
Deed John Jinnings to Allen Hunter 300 acres proven by John Stewart

p.183 Sheriff reported a tract of 640 acres on Bartons Creek in name of Moses Hobert; he can find no goods or chattels on which he can distress for State & County Tax for 1801. Order Clerk transmit to Knoxville Gazette the account of land, tax & costs to be published

William Perry excused from serving longer as juror this Term

Appoint Findal Whitworth overseer of road from Kentucky line to Weakley ferry on Cumberland R; begin at Nicholas Choates on Raccoon Creek and work to Capt[n] Benj[n] Weakleys; following hands: W[m] Ryburns hands, Matthew Ryburn, Isaac Weakley, And[w] Stewart, W[m] Hundley, Washington Ryburn, David McGraws hands, Paul McGraw, Henry Raglin, Lankston Hundley, Jesse Sibley, Samuel Hundley, Jurden Hundley, William Long, James Stewart, and with same he keep the road in repair

Hands to work under Thos Choate, overseer from Double licks to Stewart Road: Nich[l] Choate, Green B Choate, Dempsey Hunter, Allen Hunter, Aaron Choate, Thomas Choate Jun[r], David Choate, Jo[s] Choate, Squire Choate, Jn[o] Choate, Ge[o] Evans and John Wade

Elisha Chick excused from serving this Term as a Juror
Benj[n] McNew D[o]

Inventory of estate of Benj[n] Rogers dec[d] delivered by adm[r]

Deed Philip Parchment to Jacob Pinkley 215 acres proven by Jacob Fry
Deed Joseph Pinkly to Jacob Fry 50 3/4 acres proven by Jacob Pinkley
Deed William Betts to Benj[n] Porter Town Lot proven by George Briscoe
Deed William Betts to Benj[n] Porter Town Lot proven by George Briscoe

p.184 Jonathan Oyler app[td] Constable; bond 620 Dollars, Abraham Tippy and John Duncan securities; took oath

Deed James Menees Sh[ff] to Sampson Matthews 1057 acres and 45 poles ackd
Court Adjourns untill tomorrow Morning 9 OClock

Wednesday Morning July 22nd 1801
Present Benj[n] Menees, Isaac Philips, John Stewart, Esquires

W[m] Ryburn allowed to build a mill on Half Pone Creek on his own land

Tho[s] Britton agent for John R McShehee allowed to pay tax on 140 acres, the quantity of McShehees land remaining in his right, not yet sold for taxes; paying double tax

Order James Sawyers, Wm Hill, & Martin Duncan be inspectors for ensuing Election; Thos Johnson & Henry D Downs to act as Clerks

P/A Goodloe Warren & John Warren to James Stewart proven by Lem^l Henry

Jacob Pinkley S^r to oversee road in room of Edward Cheatham

Deed Josiah Ramsey to Jonathan Ramsey 640 acres; Ditto for 213 acres, Ditto for 200 acres, all proven by Thomas Johnson

Deed James McCaleb & wife Lucy McCaleb to Archer Cheatham 2 Lots in Springfield proven by Thos Johnson

p.185 Edward Cheatham vs Saml Crocket. Appeal. Pl^tf by Thos Stuart & Ja^s Doherty; def^t by J C Hamilton. Jury Saml Mills, Ja^s McDonald, Joseph Castleberry, John Carr, John Sherod, Wm Crunk J^r, Wm Armstrong J^r, Jacob Pinkley, David Spence, Joel Vaughn, John Simmons, Nicholas Conrod who find for def^t. New trial granted; also Def^dt to pay all Costs to the overruling of plea & abatement at October Term 1801. Pl^tf dismissed the suit. Isham Rogers a witness proves 5 days attendance; William Wilson 3 days

Order James Crabtree, John James, James Ewing, Johnson Kilgore, & Thomas Bounds to lay off a road from the ridge above David Stewarts to intersect with old Kentucky Road between Simmons Branch & Lucas's; report to next Court

Fees for ferry keepers on Cumberland River: each man & horse 6¼ cents, each waggon 1 Dollar, single horse, head of horned cattle 3 1/8 cents

p.186 Jurors to next County Court Richard Napier Senr, Thos Kilgore Jr, Jno Bush, Volentine Vanhooser, Wm Wills, Richard Matthews, Andrew Irwin, Obediah Bounds, Jonathan Price, John Price, Wm Lusk, John Krisel, Lovick Ventress, James H Bryan, Jas McKrow, George Ross S^r, Washington Ryburn, Richd Napier J^r, Nelson McDowel, Thomas Hunter, Jacob Moake, Nimrod McIntosh, Francis Boren, John Couts, James Walker, James Karr, Melcher Oyler, William Benson, John Bryan, Sampson Mathews

Wm Karr to oversee new road from Springfield to Smiths Mill, from town as far as Menees road near the head of Buzzard C^r; all hands within two miles of road clear out road

Jury app^td last Court to view road from Springfield to Port Royal make return to next Court
Deed Wm Betts to Abraham Tippy, 1 Lot in Fayetteville proven

by George Briscoe
Clerk and Sheriff allowed 25 Dollars each for Exoficio services for past year
David Henry to oversee road in place of Wm Grimes; to have a
reasonable number of hands to work on same

Order Daniel McKinley, John Tucker and Patrick Martin divide
hands to work on roads under the following overseers: Isham
Rogers, Jas McDaniel and Matthew Day

Hardy S Bryan admitted to keep an ordinary for 1 year; gave
bond with Isham Rogers & Matthew Day his securities

p.187 John Burris vs Wᵐ Martin. Attachment. Plᵗᶠ by Thomas
Stuart; Defᵗ failing to appear, Judgement by Default according to specialty filed with Interest, money reduced to money
of the United States. Jury George Browning, Ezekiel Robertson, Abraham Tippy, Levi Moore, Charles Colgin, Wᵐ Briscoe,
Sampson Matthews, Arthur Pitt, Jonathan Oyler, Vachel Lovelass, Elijah Lancaster, Samuel Miles, who find value of one
Hundred Pounds Pennsylvania Money in United States or State
of Tennessee Currency equals 266 dollars 66 2/3 cents. Clerk
calculated interest to 46 Dollars 62 cents on above sum. Order property attached be condemned; issue fi fa to Davidson
County
Court adjourns untill Court in Course
                    Benjⁿ Menees, Isaac Philips, John Philips

p.188 Robertson County. Monday Morning October 19ᵗʰ 1801
Present William Fort, Benjamin Menees, Wᵐ Johnson, Esquires

Grand Jurors Lovick Ventress foreman, Nimrod McIntosh, Fran-
cis Boren, Richard Matthews, Jonathan Price, Melcher Oyler,
John Couts, Sampson Matthews, Thomas Hunter, Thomas Kilgore,
John Busch, Jacob Moake, Nelson McDowel.

Mary Henry records her stock mark
Isaac Henry records his stock mark

Deed Thoˢ Molloy to Henry D Downs 114 acres proven by Daniel
Ross
Deed Thomas Molloy to Danˡ Ross 520 acres proven by William
Smith
Deed George Briscoe to Joseph Childress 64 acres 126 poles
proven by Thoˢ Johnson

Order revived; surveyor & jurors apptd last Court to divide lands between Roger Sappington & Harriett S Rice to make return to next Court

Ltrs/Admn granted Elisabeth Holland on estate of Daniel Holland decd; bond 2000 Dollars; Wm Stark & John Powers securities. Adm^x delivered inventory of estate; sale order issued

George Ross Senr & Washington Ryburn excused for nonattendance this Term as Jurors on deposition of Henry D Downs

Deed James Menees Sh^{ff} to Matthew Maning 228 acres ackd
John Strain to oversee road in room of Danl Holiman
James Crow minor bound by indenture to James Hunt untill he arrive to age 21 years
Rich^d C Napier excused from serving as juror this Term
Deed David Spence to Nathl Harbin 75 acres ackd

p.189 Peter Pinkley adm^r of John Pinkley dec^d vs Ge° Briscoe. Covenant. Ap^l 1801 pl^{tf} by J Doherty; def^t by Saml Henry. July 1801 Jury Ja^s McDonald, Jo^s Castleberry, John Carr, John Sherod, Wm Crunk, Jn° James, David Spence, Joel Vaughn, Amos Cohea, Nicholas Conrod, James Jones who found for pl^{tf} 164 Dollars & costs. New tryal granted. Octr 1801 Jury Obediah Bounds, James Walker, James Karr, David Henry, Barton Coates, Thos George, Wm Sale, Joseph Payne, Johnson Kilgore, Ambrose Hutchison, Saml Crocket, John Hinds, find for pl^{tf}, assess damage to 164 Doll^s & costs. Deft obtained appeal to Superior Court; bond 300 Dollars, Wm Briscoe his security
Court Adjourns until Tomorning 9 OClock

Tuesday Morning October 20th 1801
Present William Fort, Benjⁿ Menees, Hardy S Bryan, Esquires

Wm Smith elected County Solicitor for this County

p.190 Samuel Hammond vs Lemuel Sugg. Debt. Jany 1801 pl^{tf} by Thos Stuart; def^t by John C Hamilton. July Jury Bazel Boren, Wm Armstrong Jr, Wm Perry, Benjⁿ Chapman, Ja^s McDonald, Joseph Castleberry, Saml Miles, Jn° Sherod, John Carr, Nicholas Conrod, Jacob Pinkley, David Spence find for pl^f his debt 57 Dollars 5 7/9 cents & damage 5 Doll^s 22 cents. Def^t obtained new trial. Cause cont^d to Octr 1801 Jury Obed^h Bounds, Isham Rogers, Ja^s Karr, James Walker, John Robins, Joseph Washington, Wm Benson, Wm Coates, Edward Cheatham, John Brooks, Wm Milsap & Saml Crocket who find for pltf; assess damage to 60 Dollars 29 cents; also costs of suit

Robert Galespie bound 200 Doll^s for his appearance from Term to Term as prosecution until a suit is determined the State agt W^m B Vinson for assault & battery

Deed James Menees Sh^{ff} to Joseph Washington, And^w Washington & Martin Grider for 1876 acres ackd

p.191 Bond Wm Ross & Jane Buxton to Lovick Ventress proven by Hardy S Bryan

Order of last Term for laying off road from ridge above David Stuarts to intersect old Kentucky between Summers Branch and Lucas is now null & void
Court Adjourns untill tomorrow Morning 9 OClock

Wednesday Morning October 21st 1801
Present Wm Fort, John Philips, Isaac Philips, Benjn Menees

John Philips Esqr exhonarated from 2 Dollar tax for present year, being wrongfully charged with a stud
Volentine Vanhusir excused for his Non attendance as a Juror this Term
Isham Rogers bound 200 Doll^s to attend from Term to Term to prosecute James McDonald on Bill of Indictment

State vs Robt Galespie. Def^t bound 200 Dollars, Isham Rogers & Nathl Hardin his securities, that he will attend this Term from day to day to answer Bill of Indictment against him

Saml Crocket vs Edward Cheatham. Isham Rogers witness proves 2 days attendance; Wm Wilson 2 days

Order taxable property of Noel Walkers which is 93 acres be rec^d by Collector for years 1799, 1800 & 1801

Jacob Pickren app^{td} Constable; bond 620 Dollars, Abram Tippy & Nimrod McIntosh, securities

p.192 John Barr vs Patrick Lyons & Thos McIntosh. assault & Battery. July 1801 pl^f by Jno C Hamilton; def^{ts} by Thos Stuart & James Doherty. Octr jury Obediah Bounds, Abram Tippy, Jacob Pinkley, Jacob Pickrel, Silas Tucker, Robert Galespie, Jno Duncan, Wm Benson, Wm Wilson, Nathl Harbin, Peter Spence & John Chewning who find for def^t. John Pankey witness 1 day attendance, Danl McKinley 5 days attendance

Jurors to Superior Court Thomas Johnson, Elijah Lancaster, Josiah Fort, George Clark & Wm Hutchison
Peter Spence allowed credit for tax on 100 acres charged by

mistake
Daniel McDaniel allowed 25 Dollars per year for his support,
to be paid out of monies collected for that purpose

Instrument Joseph Childress to Jacob Pinkley conveying all
his real and personal estate to s^d Pinkley proven by oath of
Thos Johnson

Order Thos Strain, Jn° Hutchison & Benjn Menees Esq^{rs} be inspectors of ensuing Election for representative to Congress

George Briscoe, Coroner, rec^d si fa ag^t Sh^{ff}, failed to return same at time required, called; still failed to appear;
order Judgment by Default entered ag^t Coroner George Briscoe

Wm Grimes to oversee road in room of David Henry
Court Adjourns untill Tomorrow Morning 10 OClock

p.193 Thursday Morning October 22nd 1801
Present Benjn Menees, John Philips, and Martin Duncan, Esq^{rs}

Jurors to Next Court Thomas Yates, James Yates, John Beason,
Patrick Patterson, Zachariah Oneal, John Kilgore, Wm Wills,
John Simmons, Charles Wheaton, Solomon Squire, Wm Johnson,
Volentine Choate, David Huddleston, Wm Lusk, Levi Moore, Ep-
pa Lawson, Henry Gardner, Jonathan Stephenson, Maj^r Jn° Bak-
er, James Stark, William Spiller, Benjamin Spiller, Wm Sale,
John Bryan, John Baker, Caleb Winters, Elias Lawrence, James
Stewart, Philip Parchment, Augustine Cook

Deed James Menees Sh^{ff} to Joseph Johnson 640 acres ackd
Deed James Menees Sh^{ff} to Thomas Johnson 640 acres ackd

Lands published in Knoxville Gazette for nonpayment of Taxes
for 1799, Sheriff to sell agreeable to Law: John Bowman 190
ac, Ab^m Colrean 22 ac, Andrew Hampton 516 ac, Wm Gubbins 620
ac, Daniel Mcfatter 337 ac, Lieu^t James Moore 60 acres, John
Porterfield 590 ac, Jn° Sugg 197 ac, Fred^k Ward 340 ac, Danl
Wilburn 105 ac, Ja^s Montgomery 160 ac, Joseph Erwin 228 ac,
Robert Lasiter 320 ac, John Clendennons heirs 428 ac, Conrod
Strader[Shader?] 108 ac, Richard Fenner 3977 ac, Sarah Rich-
ardson 400 ac, Chas Robertson 640 ac, Abesha Thomas 640 ac,
Daniel Taylor 100 ac. The following for year 1800: Richard
Fenner 3977 ac, John Ellis 640 ac, Kirby Vick 100 ac.   The
following for year 1801 Moses Robert 640 acres

William B Vinson & Joseph Robertson bound 200 Doll^s, condition Vinson attend our next County Court to answer charge of
State against him for assault & Battery; also to prosecute a

suit State against Robert Galespie, assault

Court Adjourns untill Court in Course
Benjamin Menees, Martin Duncan, John Philips

p.195 Robertson County. Monday Morning, January 18th 1802
Town of Springfield. Present Benjamin Menees, John Philips,
and Joseph Dorris, Esquires

Grand Jurors Maj^r John Baker foreman, William Lusk, Henry
Gardner, Levi Moore, John Bryan, Wm Sale, Jonathan Stephen-
son, Caleb Winters, Pat^k Patterson, Volentine Choate, Thos
Yates, Charles Wheaton, James Stark

Peter Richardson Booker Esqr produced Licence as attorney, &
is admitted, having been previously sworn in Sumner County

Matthew Lodge Esqr produced licence as an attorney, took the
oaths necessary for qualification

Ninian Edwards is admitted to practice as an attorney having
also produced his Licence to the Court

Epphaphodetus Benton records stock mark
Miles Kirby resigned being Constable

John Crane vs Martin Grieder. Judgement before a Justice of
Peace for $15 & costs. Yet due on the Judgement $4.78.1 and
costs. Levied on 113 acres whereon Mr Pool now lives on Millers Creek; ordered sd land sold to satisfy sd Judgement and
costs

Deed James Menees Sh^{ff} to Roger B Sappington Two 640 acre
tracts proven in open Court

Will of John Kitts proven by Nicholas Conrod
p.196 Will of Wm Fort proven by David Smith. Josiah Fort &
Elias Fort Junr ex^{trs} took required oath
B/S Josiah Skinner to Danl Holland ackd
Ltrs/Admn granted Ann Cromwell and Dorsey Cromwell on estate
of Alexr Cromwell decd; bond; took oath; delivered inventory

P/A Melcher Oyler to Thomas Roberts proven by Augustine Cook

Ltrs/Admn granted Benjn Koen on estate of Abraham Koen decd;
bond 2 thousand Dollars; took oath

Miles Kerby produced Commission as Entry Taker for Robertson County; gave Bond; took required oaths

Samuel W Musgrove vs Martin Greider. Judgement before a Justice/Peace for 13 Dollars & $1.31 costs. Levied on 112 acres whereon Mr Pool now lives on Millers Creek; Ordered sd land be sold to satisfy afsd judgement

Deed Wm Christmas att° for Robt Fenner to Isaac Dortch proven by Bennet Searcy
Deed Saml Kendly to Josiah Ramsey 100 acres proven by Bazel Boren
Deed Nehemiah Wroten to Joshua Warren proven by Jacob Warren

Deed Josiah Ramsey to Silas Crane for 100 acres proven by Jonathan Ramsey
p.197 Deed Ezekiel Smith to George Murphey proven by George Murphey Junr
Deed Ephraim Reese to Noah Woodard proven by Henry Gardner
Deed Ephraim Reese to Noah Woodard proven by Daniel Woodard
Deed Robt Black S^r to Henry Gardner 110 acres proven by John Baker
Deed George Ury to Wm Dorris 50 acres proven by Bazel Boren
Deed John Baker to Thomas Traviss 100 acres proven by Jonathan Stephenson
Deed Wm Betts to John Duncan one Lot in Fayetteville proven by Ge° Briscoe

Adm^x of Danl Holland dec^d delivered supplementary return of estate
B/S Joseph Wimberley to Josiah Fort proven by Eppa Lawson
P/A John Walker to Thos Little ackd
Amount of sale estate of Danl Holland dec^d delivered by adm^x

Will of John Tucker proven by Peter Spence
William Edwards to John Duncan a Certificate proven by Thomas Johnson
B/S Elisabeth Rogers to Isham Rogers ackd
Court Adjourns untill tomorrow Morning 10 OClock

Tuesday Morning January 19th 1802   Present Benjn Menees, James Crabtree, Jno Hutchison, Isaac Philips, Thomas Strain, Charles Miles, Esqrs

p.198 Richard Cross exhonarated from payment of 1800 tax on 1800 acres, the land lies in Montgomery County; tax paid in Montgomery proven by a receipt

James Norfleet ex^{tr} Will of John Kitts took oath; delivered an inventory of the estate

James Doherty vs Joseph Robertson. Ass^t & Battery & faulse imprisonment. April 1801 pl^{ff} appeared; def^t by T Stuart, W Smith & Jo^s Herndon. Cont^d to Octr 1801. Jany 1801 pl^{tf} by N Edwards; def^t pleads Not Guilty & Justification. Jury James Yates, Wm Spiller, Benj^u Spiller, Augustine Cook, David Huddleston, Philip Parchment, Eppa Lawson, Wm Wills, John Simmons, Jesse Jones, Jonathan Vancleave and Elias Lawrence who find for pl^{tf} & assess damage to 150 Dollars. Def^t appealed to Superior Court; bond 300 Dollars, Josiah Fort & Wm Flewellen securities

Benjn Weakley surveyor to divide two 640-acre tracts between Roger B Sappington & Harriett S Rice, proves attendance as a surveyor five days & 2 chain carriers 3 days. Andw Caldwell a juror for purpose of dividing above land proves 5 days

p.199 William B Vinson vs Robert Galespie. Case. Octr 1801 pl^f by Lem^l Henry; def^t by Thos Stewart. Jan 1802 Jury Zachariah Oneal, Perry Cohea, David Henry, Benjamin Coates, John Krisel, Nicholas Young, Meredith Walton, Wm Edwards, Matthew Day, John Couts, Isham Rogers, Jo^s Payne find for def^t. New tryal granted. Def^t in proper person confesses judgm^t for 28 Doll^s 25 c^{ts}. Ex^{ctn} stayed 80 days; pl^f assumes costs. John Pankey wit^{ss} proves 2 days attendance; Stephen Boren 2 days

Benjn Koen at liberty to sell property of Abraham Koen dec^d agreeable to Law
Ex^{trs} of Wm Fort dec^d at liberty to sell perishable property and hire Negroes of estate as they think proper

Deed Edward Harris by Thomas Johnson his atty in fact to Eli Jones 200 acres ackd
Deed James Menees Sh^{ff} to Wm Edwards 640 acres ackd
Deed Vachel Lovelace to Eli Jones 30 acres proven by Geo Lovelace
Deed John Mann to Cornelius McGraw 213 acres proven by Easter Allen
p.200 B/S Noah Sugg to John Simmons proven by Thos Johnson
B/S David McGraw to Cornelius McGraw proven by Uriah McGraw
Benjn Koen admr estate Abraham Koen decd delivered inventory

Benjn Weakley & And^w Caldwell, surveyor & Juror app^{ld} to divide land of Roger B Sappington & Harriet S Rice, delivered plat & certificate of their proceeding

John Robins to oversee road in room of Nathan Clark, his road extends to fork of road from Springfield to Logan

Deed Josiah Ramsey to Marvel Law 200 acres   proven by Jonathan Ramsey

Deed John Vaughn to John Tennison 100 acres   proven by James Vaughn

Deed Charles Kilgore to Matthew Maning three acres proven by Zachariah Tucker

Edmond Haggard and John Haggard bound apprentices to Jesse Jones to learn the House Carpenter trade untill they arive to the age of Twenty one years

John Rogers bound apprentice to Isham Rogers to learn Trade of a Hatter untill he arrives to the age of Twenty one years

Court Adjourns untill tomorrow Morning 9 OClock

Wednesday Morning January 20th 1802   Present John Philips, Benjamin Menees, Isaac Philips, John Hutchison

Jacob Young, possessor of a cotton press, gave bond, Joseph Robertson & Abraham Tippy his securities; took oath

p.201 John Fort vs James Menees. Appeal. Pltf by Ninian Edwards; deft by Thos Stuart, J C Hamilton & J Doherty. Jury Wm Wills, John Simmons, Jas Yates, Wm Spiller, David Huddleston, Nimrod McIntosh, Augustine Cook, Benjn Spiller, Matthew Day, James Appleton, Wm Grimes, Jno Brooks who find for pltf, assess damage to fifty cents & costs. Asa Woodworth a witness proves two days attendance; Nathaniel Harbin 2 days

John and Edward Cheatham, possessors of a cotton press, gave bond, Jonathan Stephenson their security; took oath. Also Jonathan Stephenson, above, gave bond with John Cheatham his security & took the oath by law required

Anderson Cheatham to oversee road in room of Nimrod McIntosh

Deed Wm Dennis to Jonathan Price 45 acres proven by James Price

Jurors to next Court Bartimias Pack, Daniel Holeman, Robert Wilson, Jno Young, Moses Hardin, John Crocket, Wm Crunk, Nathan Clark, John Couts, Bazel Boren Senr, Wm McAdoe, Peter Pinkley, Nicholas Young, Geo Browning, John Crane, Asa Woodworth, Edward Cheatham, Andrew Cheatham, Isham Rogers, Archd Mahon, George Murphey Junr, Joseph Washington, Wm Karr, Lawrence Carr, James Gambril, Abraham Moore, Wm Benson, Willis Skinner, Anthony Jones

p.202 Hugh & Ralston vs George Briner. Attachment. Ap^l 1801 Sh^{ff} levied on 640 acres on Karrs Creek. Pl^{tf} by Lem^l Henry & Thos Stuart. Stayed 9 months. Jany 1802 Def^t failed to appear; pl^{tf} recovers 174 pounds 3 shillings 3 pence half penny Kentucky money with interest thereon at 6 percent per annum from first August 1798 until 7 Feby 1801 (date of original attachment), together with one penny s^d money. Court not knowing what that sum is in Dollars & Cents, a Jury summoned William Wills, John Simmons, James Yates, Wm Spiller, David Huddleston, Nimrod McIntosh, Augustine Cook, Matthew Day, Wm Grimes, John Brooks, Matthew Lodge, William B Vinson who say above Kentucky money is worth 666 Dollars 41½ cents. Pl^{tf} to recover s^d sum & costs. Attached property to be sold

Deed Robt Galispie to George Galispie 50 acres ackd John J Dorris app^{td} constable; gave bond 625 Dollars, Benjn Menees & John Brooks securities; took oath
p.203 Court Adjourns untill Tomorrow Morning 9 OClock

Thursday Morning January 21st 1802
Present John Philips, Benjn Menees, Isaac Philips, Esquires

State vs W^m B Vinson. Trespass Assault & Battery. State by Wm Smith, County Solicitor; def^t by att^y pleads Not Guilty. Jury Wm Spiller, Benjn Spiller, Augustine Cook, David Huddleston, Wm Wills, John Simmons, Zac^h Oneal, Stephen Boren, Asa Parker, Wm Crunk, David Spence, John Chewning find def^t Guilty as charged. Fined one Dollar & Costs. Tenor Danily a witness proves seven days attendance, Rachel Walker 7 days, Jacob Pickren 6 days

Former Order for roads from Springfield to Port Royal & from Springfield to Major Smiths mill as far as the Kentucky Line revived. Josiah Fort oversees from Red R to Kentucky Line, hands to work under him are s^d Forts hands & Wm Forts hands. Lem^l Sugg to oversee road from Red River to head of Buzzard Creek to Menees Road, with hands Mortons, Wm Philips, James Johnson, Josiah Skinner, Willie Skinner, Harrell, two Crumwells, Jesse Lawrence; same jury as formerly to view road to Port Royal

Joseph Wimberley to oversee from Browns ford to the Kentucky Line in room of Lem^l Sugg; Wimberleys & Johnstons hands work on sd road

James Williams app^{td} Constable gave bond 640 Dollars, Samuel Tucker & John Pankey his securities; took oaths

p.204 State vs Robert Galispie. Trespass assault. State by

Wm Smith, County Solicitor; def^t by att^y pleads Not Guilty.
Jury Wm Spiller, Benjn Spiller, Augustine Cook, Jno Simmons,
Wm Wills, David Huddleston, Zach^b Oneal, Stephen Boren, Asa
Parker, Wm Crunk, David Spence, John Chewning find the def^t
Guilty as charged; fined one Dollar & Costs

Deed William Christmas to Joseph Robertson 60 acres, being a
relinquishment of mortgage which Thomas Christmas gave to W^m
Christmas for s^d Land, proven by Thomas Johnson

Tract of 640 acres belonging to Nathl Perry granted to Bail-
ey Sutton exhonarated from double tax
Archer Cheatham Esqr Justice/peace, took required oaths
Joseph Choate exhonarated from payment of one Dollar Tax
charged on a stud
Court Adjourns untill tomorrow Morning 9 OClock

Friday Morning January 22nd 1802   Present the Worshipfull
Benjn Menees, Isaac Philips, Martin Duncan, Archer Cheatham,
Wm Johnson, Esquires

Wm B Vinson at liberty to pay Tax on 640 acres on Sulpher
fork for 1801

p.205 Order the Following Justices to receive lists of Taxable property for the present year

James Norfleet	Captn J Dardins Company
Wm Connel	Captn Blackwells
Archer Cheatham	Captn Jones
William Johnson	Captn Bryans
Hardy S Bryan	Captn Weakleys C^o --all of s^d

Company which shall be in this County after the line is run

Joseph Dorris	Captn Bounds Company
James Crabtree	Captn Youngs
Martin Duncan	Captn Isaiah Hamiltons,--all

that part of sd Company which shall remain in Robertson after the county line is run

County Trustee to pay Anderson Cheatham 54 Dollars 40 cents
3 mills, being balance due Cheatham for building Court House
in Springfield

Order James Wheeler & Adam Clap be patrolers in Captn Youngs
Company

Order John Williams oversee road from Weakleys ferry to Harris's mill, from State line to head of Buzzard Creek. Hands
on Spring Creek & Buzzard work on same. Joseph Washington to
oversee s^d road from Buzzard to Sulpher fork. Hands on Benjn

Menees Esqr plantation, Shad^k Rawls, Matt[?] Matthews, Asa
Parker, s^d Washington, And^w Washington, & the Fykes work on
same. Henry Airs given Sulpher fork to oppesite Man Lick,
hands of Moses and Aaron Winters, 2 Blankstones, Barny Bone,
Silas Crane, Whitmill Harrington, Wm Milsaps, & all hands on
Brush Creek convenient to s^d road

p.206 John Pankey vs John Tucker. Jacob Pickren, a witness,
proves 8 days attendance
Deed William Haggard to Robert Galespie 50 acres proven by
Thomas Johnson
Lemuel Sugg app^{td} Constable, bond 620 Dollars, Josiah Fort &
Wm Flewellen his securities; took oaths
Daniel McKinley app^{td} Coroner pro tem untill next Term; bond
with Isham Rogers & Wm Crunk securities

James Menees Collector State & County Tax for 1799 reported
land not given in for tax, & no personal property within the
county whereon Collector can distress. Clerk to cause a copy
of this order to be published together with Tax due & costs.
Wm Cox 228; Elijah Robertsons heirs 1920 acres; Jesse Nelson
640; Jesse Nelson 640; Noah Parr 640; Wm Nelson 640; Daniel
Sellars heirs 640; Joseph Cosway 640, Wm Bowman 640; Hum-
phrey Hogans heirs 640; Jno Harris 100; Joseph Barns 100; W^m
Glovers heirs 640; Edmond Jinnings 124; David Rounsavall as-
see Humphrey Hogan 100; John Boyd 43 acres
And the following Tracts for 1800: Jesse Nelson 640; D^o 640;
Noah Parr 640; Wm Nelson 640; Danl Sellars heirs 640; Joseph
Cosway 640; Richd Vaughns heirs 640; Wm Bowman 640; Humphrey
Hogans heirs 640; Danl Wilburn 95 acres; Andrew Hampton 476;
John Clendennon's heirs 389; Sarah Richardson 320; Charles
Robertson 610; Frederick Ward 240; Joseph Ennever 138; James
Moon 256; Wm Gubbins 533; Robert Lasiter 240; Ja^s Montgomery
71; John Porterfield 395; John Childress 1920; John Sugg 97;
Danl Mcfatter 308; Ja^s G Bickhouse 357; Ditto 1920; D^o 2232;
William Beck 510; Ge^o Bradly 3340; Rafford Crumpler 850; Ja^s
Glassgow 1000; Edward Givens 640; Ditto 400; D^o 640; D^o 220;
James Turner 3840; Hugh Williamson 4840 acres
p.207 Joseph Dickson 640 ac; Thomas Person 3840 ac; Benjamin
Bailey 3840; John Hardin 640; John Easten 640; Samuel Marsam
640; Lancelet Johnson 640; James Cummins 640; -- Kerby 640;
Benjⁿ Coffield 1746; Edmond Jinnings 124; James Harris heirs
100; Joseph Barns 100 acres; Wm Glovers heirs 640; John Boyd
43; Wm Cox 228; John Childress 1920; Lancelet Johnson 640;
David Rounsavall ass^{ee} Humphrey Hogan 100 ac; Stephen Hopkin
140; Saml Thompson 500. [Following names are lined through:
John Hanks 200; Thos Hanks 100; Richd Hanks 100; John Cryer
150; John Gordon 640; Wm Hogan 471; John Love 7040; Isaac
Moore 100; Matt^w McClain 150; Isaac Roberts 640; Henry Shore
640; Saml Cummins 914; John Fowler 640

The following Tracts for 1801: Jesse Nelson 640; Ditto 640; Wm Nelson 640; Daniel Sellars heirs 640; Joseph Cosway 640; Noah Parr 640; Richd Vaughns heirs 640; Wm Bowman 640; Humphrey Hogan's heirs 640; Daniel Wilburn 95; John Clendennons heirs 389; Sarah Richardson 320; Chas Robertson 610; Frederick Ward 240; Joseph Ennever 138 acres; James Moore 2560; Wm Gubbins 533; Robt Lasiter 240; John Sugg 97; Daniel Mcfatter 308; Joseph Barns 100; Wm Glovers heirs 640; Danl Hogan 100; John Boyd 43; F Harget & Carney 2560; James G Beckhoose 357; D^o 1920; D^o 2232; William Beck 510; Ge^o Bradley 3340; Raffred Crumpler 850; James Glasgow 1000; Edward Givings 640; D^o 640; D^o 400; D^o 220; James Turner 3840; Hugh Williamson 4840; Joseph Dickson 640; Thos Person 3840; Benjamin Bailey 3840; John Hardin 640; Jno Eastin 640; Wm Crafford 640; Saml Marsam 640; James Cummins 640; -- Kirby 640; Benjn Coffield 1746; Edmond Jinnings 124; James Harris's heirs 100; Wm Cox 228; John Childress 1920; George W Darnald 1500; David Rounsavall assee Humphrey Hogan 100 ac; Jacob McCarty 113; Saml Thompson 500 [lined through: Wm Caswell 538 acres].

p.208 Unpaid Taxes for 1800; the owners have no goods within County on which Collector can Distress: Martin Armstrong 960 acres; Jno Hanks 200; Thos Hanks 100; Richard Hanks 100; Philip Alston 590; John Cryor 150; Malaciah Fikes 240; John Fikes 200; Jno Gordon 640; William Hogan 471; Jno Love 7040; Isaac Moore 100; Matthew McClain 150; Benjn McCulloch 3474; Allen Walker 1000 acs; Isaac Roberts 640; Henry Shore[Show?] 640; Saml Cummins 914; John Fowler 640
For 1801: William Caswell 548 acres; Malakiah Fikes 240; Joseph Green 640; Andrew Hampton 640; Ja^s Montgomery 160; John Porterfield 640; Isaac Renfro 640; John Fikes 200; Wm Blackfan 640; Wm Hughs 98; John Haynes 320; George Hook 320; Thos Hogg 640; Anthony Jones 100; Alex^r Parish 200; Ezekiel Smith 100, Alex^r Walker 1000; Abraham Fulkison 640; William Herring 1000; John Hutchins 624; Samuel May 640; John Cox 640; John Fowler 640; Wm Jackson 274; John Gordon 640; Wm Hogan 471; Matt^w McClain 150; James McCowns heirs 400; Eli West 500; Anthony Gains 100; Eanis Ward 274.

Court Adjourns untill Court in Course
John Philips, Archer Cheatham, Isaac Philips
William Johnson, Martin Duncan

p.209 Robertson County, Monday Morning April 19th 1802
Present the worshipfull John Philips, Benjamin Menees,
Charles Miles, Wm Johnson, Esquires

Grand Jurors Archibald Mahon foreman, Nathan Clark, Wm
Benson, John Crocket, Abraham Moore, William Karr, George
Murphey, Lawrence Carr, Daniel Pinkley, John Couts, Edward
Cheatham, Anderson Cheatham, John Crane

B A Allen ag^t George Evans. Green Choate, Evans's appearance
bail delivered him. Def^t brought into Court Philip Parchment
& Isaac Robertson, who ack^d themselves his securities

John Barr vs George Briscoe. Jury Isham Rogers, Ge^o Brown-
ing, Asa Woodard, Peter Pinkley, Danl Holman, Anthony Jones,
Robert Wilson, Wm Crunk, Robert Galispie, Wm Dickison, Isaac
Robertson, James Stark say they find for Pl^{tf} agreeable to
Scire facias; Def^t prayed and obtained a new trial

Sheriff to summon a Jury of Freeholders to enquire into the
Lunicy of Jane Tucker, a supposed Lunitick; return their Inquisition on Oath signed with each of their proper Names

Wm Connell Esqr delivered List of Taxable property of Captn
Blackwells Company
Power/Atty John Dunn & Margaret Dunn to Ja^s Karr ackd
p.210 Benjn Koen adm^r Abraham Koen dec^d delivered amount of
sale of s^d Estate
Thos Johnson has Liberty to enter & pay Tax in name of John
Colman for years 1800 & 1801
Deed Jacob Pinkley to Peter Fry 50 3/4 acres ackd
Deed John Colman to Thomas Williams 640 acres proven by Bush
Rowland
Deed Noel Watkins to Isaac Robertson 92 acres proven by
Henry Hyde
Deed Isaac Weakley to Jonathan Oyler 300 acres proven by W^m
Johnson
Deed John Hardin Senr to John Hardin J^r and Moses Hardin 640
acres proven by Wm Armstrong
Deed Richard Cook to John Baker 500 acres proven by Jonathan
Stephenson
Richard Cook to Isaac Dortch & Wm Connell relinquishment to
claim of Land proven by Thomas Edwards
Jonathan Stephenson admited to keep an Ordinary 1 year, bond
500 Dollars, Wm Atkins & John Yoes securities
B/S James Henderson to Jane Henderson ackd
John Yoes app^{ld} Constable, bond 620 Dolls, Wm Atkins & Jona-
than Stephenson securities
David Spence to oversee road in room of Matthew Day, hands
as assigned to Day

Ltrs/Admn granted to Samuel Tucker on estate of John Tucker
decd; bond 10 thousand Dollars with And^w Irwin, John Robins,
Silas Tucker & Enoch Tucker securities

p.211 James Crabtree Esqr delivered List of Taxable property of Captⁿ Youngs Company. Archer Cheatham...Captⁿ Jesse Jones Company
Court Adjourns untill tomorrow Morning 9 OClock

Tuesday Morning April 20th 1802
Present John Philips, Benjⁿ Minees, William Johnson, Esqrs

William Flewellen vs Isaac Philips. Appeal. Jany 1802 pl^f by Ja^s Doherty; Def^t by Thos Stuart. Jury William Spiller, Benjamin Spiller, Augustine Cook, David Huddleston, Wm Wills, John Simmons, Zachariah Oneal, Stephen Boren, Asa Parker, Wm Crunk, David Spence, John Chewning who made Mistryal; cause continued. April 1802 pl^{tf} by J C Hamilton; def^t by Peter R Booker. Jury Danl Holman, Ge^o Browning, Isham Rogers, Benjⁿ Coates, Jno Alley, Anthony Jones, Nathl Harbin, Robt Wilson, Peter Pinkley, Jesse Williams, Nicholas Conrod, Asa Woodard, who find for Pl^{tf}, assess Damages to one Dollar; also costs

p.212 William Armstrong Junr vs Abraham Young Junr. Trespass January 1802 Pl^{tf} by Jno C Hamilton; Def^t by Peter R Booker. Cont^d. Ap^l 1802 Jury Nathl Dickison, Robert Galespie, James Stark, William Lusk, Jno Siglar, Azariah Dunn, Dann Lynn, Wm Dickison, Robert Lancaster, Nimrod McIntosh, James England, Abraham Dean who find for Pl^{tf}, assess damage to 12 Dollars; also costs of suit. James Wheeler, a witness, proves 2 days attendance; George Clark 1 day; Adam Clap 1 day

Hardy S Bryan Esqr delivered Tax List for Captⁿ Weakleys C^o
Executors of Wm Fort dec^d delivered Inventory of estate
Deed Thos Byrd Senr to Thos Byrd J^r ackd
Deed James Ewing to William Haynes 316 acres proven by Benjⁿ Johnson
Deed James Menees Sh^{ff} to And^w Jackson 640 acres ackd
Deed James Menees Sh^{ff} to Thos Hutchins 640 acres ackd
Deed John Nelson to Robert Nelson 640 acres proven by James Menees

p.213 Benjⁿ Menees J^r who had purchased at last sale of reported Lands part of 320 acres in name of Robt Lasiter, now acknowledges full satisfaction and relinquishes his claim to John Gardner, heir of s^d Lasiter

Samuel Tucker, adm^r estate of Jno Tucker dec^d, at Liberty to sell Perishable property of estate, also may Hire Negroes of estate untill next Christmas

Jurors summoned to enquire into Lunicy of Jane Tucker: Miles
Kirby, John Cheatham, Nicholas Conrod, Nathan Arnet, Samuel
Hollis, James Sawyers, John Brooks, Joseph Castleberry, William Flewellen, Hugh Henry, Jacob Pinkley, Bazel Boren, being sworn, say they believe Jane Tucker to be a Lunitick

Enoch Tucker app^{td} guardian for Jane Tucker a Lunitick, gave
Bond with Nathan Arnet security

Deed Thos Yates to Wm Ragsdale 100 acres ackd

Saml Tucker, Jno Robins, Charles Simmons, Enoch Tucker, Thos
Norris & Silas Tucker gave Bond 1000 Dollars for safekeeping
& well providing for children of John Tucker dec^d for 6 mos

James Norfleet Esqr delivered Tax List for Captn Dardins C^o

Order Clerk to enter 274 acres on 1801 Tax list belonging to
Joseph Washington

Deed James Haynes to Ezekiel Norman 274 acres proven by Thos
Byrd
Deed Isaac Johnson to Thomas Johnson & Benjn Porter 90 acres
proven by Wm Johnson
p.214   Deed Henry Johnson to Isaac Johnson 90 acres proven
by Thos Johnson
Henry W Lawson to Jane Keykendall and John Mitchel, a relinquishment to Land proven by Ja^s Norfleet
Deed Benjamin McNew to James Holland 147 acres proven by
Dann Lynn
Deed William Dorris to Christian Rominier 90 acres proven by
Bazel Boren
Deed William Dorris to James Holland 124 acres proven by
Bazel Boren
Deed/Gift William Fort to daughter Sarah Fort a Negro proven
by Josiah Fort
Deed Moses Winters to Joseph Washington 204 acres proven by
Miles Kirby
Deed John Young and James Norfleet, Commissioners, to John
Cheatham, Lot in Springfield, ackd
Deed James Minees Shff to Archer Cheatham 640 acres ackd
Deed Stephen Hopton to Absolam Hooper 140 acres proven by
David Robertson

Archer Cheatham Esqr admited to keep an Ordinary one year;
bond 500 Dollars, Joseph Robertson & Miles Kirby securities

William Johnson Esqr delivered List of Taxable property in
Captn John Bryants Company

Daniel Holman Esqr elected Coroner for two years; bond one thousand Dollars, John Crocket his security
Court Adjourns untill tomorrow Morning 9 OClock

p.215   Wednesday Morning April 25th 1802   Present John Philips, Benjn Menees, James Crabtree, Wm Johnson, Esquires

Ordered that Hannah Locust, James, Austin, & Moses Locust be released from William McAdoe, and all other persons claiming under him by Virtue of Order of this Court heretofore, Court being satisfyd from Testimony that McAdoe treated them in an improper and unjustafiable manner, and it being Necessary to the purpose of Justice consistant with Law that they should be discharged

Henry Airs gives up his Order for overseer of Road by Reason of Old Age; Court appoints James Stuart in his place

Samuel Crocket vs Thos Norris Senr. Danl McKinley a witness proves one Day attendance; Asa Barker 3 days; Ja^s Norris 2 days; Thos Norris Jr 2 days; Wm Wilson 3 days; Hannah Norris 2 days; Sally Isaacs one day.

State vs Philip Parchment. Ordered by Court that prosecutor pay all Costs. George Briscoe witness proves 2 days attendance; Asa Woodworth 2 days; Matthew Day 3 days; Henson Day 3 days; Benjn Nail 3 days, 25 miles traveling; Nicholas Boise 3 days, 48 miles traveling

John Powers, Peter Cartwright & Edmond Wilcox against whom a Bill/Indictment found, gave Bond 10 thousand Dollars for appearance at next Superior Court; Jacob Cook, William Grimes and Benjn Coates their securities

Deed Philip Parchment to Asa Woodworth 113 acres ackd

p.216 Benjn Coates vs John McMillon. Appeal. Pl^t by J C Hamilton; Def^t by Peter R Booker; Jury Wm Crunk, Danl McKinley, Abraham Tippy, Isham Rogers, George Briscoe, Asa Woodworth, Saml Crocket, Saml Henry, Anth^y Jones, Robert Wilson, Peter Pinkley, John Johnson who find for pl^{tf}, assess damage to 8 Dollars 25 cents; also his costs of suit

Hannah Locust, James, Austin, and Moses Locust, children of Elisabeth Locust, bound to Ninian Edwards untill they arrive to age 21, s^d Edwards & Jno Philips Esqr both signed the Indentures, s^d Edwards being resident of Kentucky State, gives John Powers security for faithfull performance of Indenture

James Stuart to oversee road in room of Henry Airs, hands W^m
Milsaps hands, Moses & Aaron Winters, Silas Bankstone, Silas
Crane, Francis Graham, Wm Atkins, John Yoes, Elisha Pilant,
Mark Noble, Stuarts own hands & Garner[Gaines?]

Joseph Dorris Esqr delivered Tax List for Captn Bounds Co

County Tax for this year: 12½ cents each hundred acres; 6¼
cents each white pole; 12½ cents each black pole; 25 cents
each stud horse for covering mares; 12½ cents each town lot,
5 Dollars each Billard Table
p.217   Court Adjourns untill tomorrow Morning 9 OClock

Thursday Morning April 22nd 1802
Present John Philips, Benjn Menees, Archer Cheatham, Esq^{rs}

Following Land was last Court Ordered published in Tennessee
Gazette; sd land has been published. Judgment entered agt sd
lands for Tax & Costs   [List being same as appeared in last
Court, pp 105 & 106 of this book, is here omitted]
p.218 [List continues]
p.219 [List continues]

On Oath of Enoch Tucker & Nathan Arnet respecting situation
of Jane Tucker, there is Danger of her doing herself Damage
or some Individual; therefore order she be imprisoned, that
the Jaoler safely keep, bailable on Security given

Wm McAdoe Burrel Pitts, Wm Hicks, witnesses behalf State agt
John Powers, Peter Cartwright & Edmond Wilcox gave Bond 2000
Dollars for appearance at Next Superior Court

Order Lands reported for Non payment of Taxes before next
Court, Clerk to send to Printer of Tennessee Gazette

Jurors app^{td} to view a road Springfield to Port Royal report
business compleated. Eppa Lawson to oversee above road from
Port Royal to Skiners Road, being road leading from Harrison
mill to the Iron work. Shaderick Rawls to oversee road from
Menees Road to Springfield; hands under each overseer: all
in 3 miles of s^d road on each side in clearing it out, Benj^u
Mencees Esqr hands to work on the upper part of s^d road

p.220 Jurors to next Superior Court Benjamin Menees, George
Murphey J^r, Benjamin Menees Junr, George Briscoe, Wm Johnson

Jurors to next County Court Henry Hyde, John Hyde, Thomas
Hunter, Joseph Choate, Samuel Miles, Wm Perry R R, Matthew
Lester J^r, Azariah Dunn, Wm Deloach, Nathan Wilkison, Rich^d

Matthews, George Sprowse, Adam Clap, Bryant Oneal, William Haynes, John Sigler, John Bryan, Eli Jones, Meredith Walton, Benj[n] Porter, John Robins, Jacob Pinkley, Peter Fry, David Spence, John Brooks, James Elliott, Abraham Tippy, Willis Skinner, Josiah Skinner

Martin Duncan Esq[r] allowed untill next Court to return list of Taxable property for 1802 in Capt[n] Isaiah Hamiltons C[o]
Court Adjourns untill Court in Course
John Philips, Benjamin Menees, Martin Duncan

p.221 Robertson County. Monday Morning, July 19th 1802.
Present the Worshipfull Benjamin Menees, Isaac Dortch, James Norfleet, John Hutchison, and William Johnson, Esquires

Grand Jurors John Siglar foreman, Nathan Wilkeson, Bryan O-neal, William Perry, Henry Hyde, Samuel Miles, David Spence, Richard Matthews, Abraham Tippy, Benjamin Porter, Thos Hunter, John Hyde, Meredith Walton

Isaac Robertson ass[ee] Cha[s] Quary vs Nicholas Conrod. Debt. Jan[y] 1802 pl[tf] by Matt[w] Lodge; def[t] by Tho[s] Stuart. Cont[d] to July. Jury Azeriah Dunn, Adam Clap, Matthew Luter[Lister?], Jacob Pinkley, Jn[o] Brooks, Eli Jones, Peter Fry, Jn[o] Robins, William Deloach, Joseph Choate, Hugh Simpson, Zach[h] Cox who find for Def[t]; Def[t] to recover ag[t] pl[tf] his costs of suit

p.222 Isaac Robertson ass[ee] Cha[s] Quary vs Nicholas Conrod. Debt. Jan[y] 1802 pl[tf] by Matthew Lodge; def[t] by Tho[s] Stuart. Cont[d]. July Jury Azariah Dunn, Adam Clap, Matt[w] Luter, Jacob Pinkley, John Brooks, Rich[d] Hutchins, Peter Fry, John Robins W[m] Deloach, Joseph Choate, W[m] Grimes, Walter Stark who find for Pl[tf] 83 Dollars 20 cents; also costs of suit expended

Isaac Robertson ass[ee] Cha[s] Quary vs Nich[s] Conrod. Debt. Jan[y] 1802 pl[tf] by Matt[w] Lodge; def[t] by Tho[s] Stuart. Cont[d]. July Jury Azariah Dunn, Matthew Luter, Peter Pinkley, Jn[o] Brooks, Adam Clap, Richard Hutchins, Peter Fry, John Robins, William Deloach, Joseph Choate, Eli Jones, Walter Stark who find for pl[tf]; assess damage to 9 Dollars 67 cents; also his costs

p.223 Matthew Brooks vs Henry M Lawson. Debt. Ap[l] 1802 pl[tf] by John C Hamilton, def[t] by Peter R Booker. July Jury Benj[n] Coates, Ja[s] Stark, Ja[s] Elliott, John Gardner, Ja[s] Stuart, W[m] Stark, And[w] Washington, Ja[s] Jones, William Deloach, Matthew Day, Philip Parchment, Jacob Pinkley find for pl[tf] his debt

150 Dollars; damage 17 Dollars 87½ cents; also costs of suit

Order Shff refund to John Chewning money he paid on purchase of Wm Nelsons land for 1800 & 1801 Tax except printers fees, Clerk & Shff having relinquished their costs; clerk to omit sending sd account to Treasurer

Will of Thomas Stark proven by Tho⁵ Johnson & Wᵐ Grimes; Rachel Stark & Walter Stark exᵗʳˢ appᵗᵈ in sᵈ will took oath

Deed David McCall to Thomas Beaty 1000 acres proven by Thoˢ Johnson
Deed Henry Rutherford to Henry Hyde 378 acres proven by Thoˢ Johnson
Deed James Karr to Henry Johnson 125½ acres proven by Thomas Johnson
p.224 Road Springfield to Port Royal to be altered from Purnell branch to leave Elias Lawrences bottom field a few rods North, to intersect road now cleared out, nearest & best way

Deed Philemon Thomas by attʸ/fact William Vawter to George Briscoe 340 acres proven by Thoˢ Johnson
Deed Nathˡ Harbin to Matthew Day 75 acres ackd
Deed George Briscoe to Jacob Fulk 140 acres proven by Thomas Johnson
Deed James Haynes to Thomas Haynes 320 acres proven by William Haynes
Deed George Briscoe to John Chewning 200 acres proven by Thomas Johnson
Deed Charles Simmons to Thomas Savage 60 acres proven by Thomas Johnson
Deed Elijah Carney to John Carney 100 acres proven by Jacob Pinkley
Deed Jonathan Latimer to Daniel Latimer 240 acres proven by Jonathan Latimer
Deed Grisham Coffield to Nicholas Conrod 281 acres proven by James Norfleet
Deed William Johnson to James Vaughn 100 acres ackd
Deed Jonathan Latimer to Jonathan Latimer 640 acres proven by Daniel Latimer

Order Van Walker, Wᵐ McClish, Thoˢ Napier, Ellis Tycer, Thoˢ Simpson be Patrolers for Captⁿ Samˡ Walkers company

Will of John Tennison proven by Joel Vaughn and William Sale

John Carr appᵗᵈ admʳ estate of Dickeson Carr decᵈ; bond 4000 Dollars, Lawrence Carr and John Sherod his securities

B/S Lemuel Sugg to Joseph Choate proven by James Karr

p.225 Court Adjourns untill tomorrow Morning 9 OClock

Tuesday Morning July 20ᵗʰ 1802
Present Benjamin Menees, Isaac Philips, James Norfleet

County Commissioners allowed for 2 years past the sum of Ten Dollars each
Clerk and Sheriff allowed 40 Dollars each for exoficio services for the last past year

Order County Trustee to receive from Collector certificates given State Witnesses on cases where State fails & it is not taxable on prosecutor

Order the new road laid off in 1801 to be cleared; begins at County line above David Stuarts, passes Sulpher Lick, thence to Kentucky Road between Summers Branch & Lucas. John James to oversee from beginning; William Haynes from end of James part to intersection with Kentucky road; James Crabtree Esq, Charles Bradon, and James Yates to divide the road and hands between the overseers aforesaid

Samuel Tucker vs John Hebdon. Dismissed by Plaintiff; Julius Elmore assumes all costs. John James a witness proves 2 days attendance

Deed James Menees Sheriff to Meredith Walton 640 acres ackd
Deed George Briscoe to William Briscoe 64 acres ackd
Deed John Young and James Norfleet commʳˢ to John and Edward Simmons a lot in Springfield ackd
Deed John Young & James Norfleet commʳˢ to Meredith Walton a lot in Springfield ackd

p.226 [a loose sheet of paper at this page]: Robertson County. Febʸ term 1804. Anunedab complains of Furdinand Dreadnaught in a plea of Trespass in Ejectment....Anunedab by P W Humphreys his attʸ saith that William P Anderson on 15 March 1802 had demised to Anunadab 640 acres in Robertson on east side Sulpher fork of Red river.... east boundary of Ezekiel Polks survey... Cantrals line running north...Fansurs corner ...granted by North Carolina to Alexʳ Allen by Patent 629 15 Septʳ 1787, to sᵈ Anunedab from 1 March 1802 for 15 years... sᵈ Furdenand on 25 March 1802 with force and arms entered sᵈ 640 acres which William had demised to Anunedab and ejected Anunedab out of same to damage of Anunedab 500 Dollars. P W Humphreys

To John Gardner. Gardner in possession of premises mentioned in Declaration of Ejectment. I being sued as casual ejector

114

and having no claim or title to same do advise you to appear
at next Court...Furdenand Dreadnaught.

Menees Sh^{ff} of Robertson County maketh oath that April 1804
he delivered a copy of the Declaration hereto annexed to Jn°
Gardner...told him it was a Declaration of Ejectment...

W^m P Anderson vs Dreadnaught. Ej^t

p.226 [July 1802 Term continues]
Deed John Couts to Epaphroditus Benton 60 acres ackd

Deed Mathias Yocum & Sevinah Yocum to Thos Hampton 320 acres
admited to record by its being recorded in Shelby County KY
with clerks certificate & county seal

Deed John Young & James Norfleet comm^{rs} to Meredith Walton 1
lot in Springfield ackd
Deed Wm Hutchison to John Hutchison 50 acres ackd
Deed William Wilson to John Hutchison 50 acres proven by W^m
Hutchison
Deed Jonathan Price to John Couts 110 acres proven by John
Krisel
Deed Jonathan Price to John Couts 228 acres proven by John
Krisel

Josiah Fort Esqr app^{td} County Trustee gave Bond, Elias Fort
Junr & Wm Deloach his securities

Eppa Lawson to oversee New Road from county line near Portroyal to Robertson Court House as far as Purnells branch, is
intitled to hands Elias Fort S^r, Elias Fort J^r, Wm Deloach,
Caty Williams, Sugg Fort, Noah Woodard, George Connelly

Ordered Elias Lawrence oversee new Road from Purnells branch
to road by Benjn Menees Esqr, to have hands between s^d Road
& Sulpher fork & Tyre Fikes

Ordered that John Robins be overseer of road from War trace
creek to John Donelsons, hands Nathan Clark, Wm Crunk, Titus
Benton, Robert Galespie

Wm Briscoe to oversee road, War trace creek to Karrs creek,
same hands as used for that road

John Lipscomb to oversee the road from the fork of road near
Mr Wheatons to ridge near Betts's, same hands as usual

Deed James Menees Sh^{ff} to Richd Hutchins 640 acres ackd
Deed John J Dorris to Wm Crocket a lot in Springfield proven

by Saml Crocket

p.227   Isaac Dorris app^{td} constable; bond 620 Dollars, William Dorris and Samuel Doris his securities; took oath

James Menees Esquire duly elected Sheriff; bond 12500, Bazel Boren, Jacob Young, John Brooks, securities; took oaths

Ja^s Menees Esqr app^{td} Collector of State & County Tax; bond 2000 Dollars, Benjamin Menees & George Briscoe securities

Jurors to next County Court   Mark Noble, Asa Woodworth, John Cheatham,   Philip Parchment, Elias Fort Junr, Caleb Winters, Jno Crane, Willis Skinner, James Johnson, Sugg Fort, William Haynes, John Hardin, Thomas George, Andrew Washington, James Atkins, Noah Woodard, John Baker P C, Saml Crocket, Jonathan Stephenson,   Joseph Wimberley, Ge^o Clark,   Israel Robertson, Wm Pate, Ja^s Blackwell, William Dorris, Abel Williams, James Long, Nathl Harbin, Elias Fort M C, Josiah Skinner
Court Adjourns untill tomorrow Morning 9 OClock

Wednesday Morning July 21st 1802
Present   John Philips, Benjn Menees, Martin Duncan, Esquires

Order William Sanders to oversee, clear out & keep in Repair road as far as the County Line

County Trustee to pay Josiah Fort 12 Dollars 51 cents for Wm Connels services at supoena court as a state witness

p.228 Valuors of property:
Captn J Blackwells Company: Henry Gardner, Jiles Connel, and
        Jesse Martin
Captn J Youngs C^o: Samuel Crocket, James Long, Matthew Day
Captn J Dardins C^o: William Johnston, John Gardner, Elias
        Fort Junr
Captn J Bryants C^o: Levi Moore, William Perry, Arthur Pitt
Captn C Simmons C^o: James Appleton Senr, John Couts, David
        Jones
Captn A Youngs C^o: James Yates, John Hardin, Wm Armstrong J^r
Captn S Walkers C^o: Thomas Bounds, W^m McClish, Samuel Walker

Deed George Briscoe to Matthew Brooks Junr 640 acres proven by Matthew Brooks Senr
Deed James Menees Sh^{ff} to James Robertson 640 acres ackd
Deed James Menees Sh^{ff} to Joseph Motheral 50 acres ackd

Following tracts exhonerated from Tax for which they were sold: 274 acres in the name of Wm Jackson, 640 in name of W^m

Alford for 1801, which Lands have been paid by Josiah Fort

Martin Duncan Esqr delivered Tax List, Captn Saml Walkers C^o

Will of John Hardin proven by John Parks

Lovick Ventress at Liberty to Build on his Land on Sychamore Creek
Order John Bryan to oversee road, Logan to Springfield, from State Line to fork, one road leading to Betts, the other to Springfield; all hands within one mile west of road from the Line to Ja^s Karrs, also the other side all in Captn Bryants C^o on Red River to include Bazel Boren

John Dorris son of Isaac to oversee road from Springfield to Portroyal from fork north of Sulpher fork to Menees's; hands between s^d road & Sulpher fork work on same

p.229 Ltrs/Admn granted to Theos Rogers on estate of Nathan^l Rogers decd; bond one thousand Dollars, Tyre Fikes and Simon Fikes his securities; took oath of an administrator.

Miles Kerby, Charles Wheaton and Joseph Robertson apptd commissioners for four years to settle with Collectors agreeable to Act of General Assembly

Elisha Chick to oversee road in room of Robert Clark
Court Adjourns untill Court in Course
                    John Philips, Benjamin Menees, Martin Duncan

p. 230 Robertson County. Monday Morning October 18th 1802. Springfield.   Present the Worshipfull Benjamin Menees, John Hutchison, Wm Connell, Esquires

Grand Jurors: Sugg Fort foreman, Josiah Skinner, John Crane, Elias Fort Junr, John Cheatham, Philip Parchment, James Atkins, Joseph Wimberley, Elias Fort M C, Nathl Harbin, Abel Williams, James Johnson, Wm Pate

Thos Farmer allowed to pay taxes on 640 acres for 1801

James Yates records his stock mark
John Siglar records his stock mark
Benjamin Stowell Esqr produced Licence as an Attorney and is admitted
Isaac Johnson exhonarated from payment of tax for 117 acres

for 1802, sd land lying in Montgomery
Extr of Thos Stark decd delivered inventory

Ltrs/Admn granted Joel Vaughn on the estate of John Tennison
decd; bond one thousand Dollars, William Sale and John Baker
his securities; took oath by law required

William Flewellen records his stock mark
Admx estate of Nathl Rogers decd delivered inventory
Israel Robertson excused from serving as juror this Term
William Haynes excused from serving as juror this Term

Deed James Vaughn to Barton Coates 56 acres ackd
Deed Henry D Downs to James Robertson & Adam Shepherd 114
acres proven by Robert Drake
p.231 Deed Thomas Smith to Nathaniel Simmons 200 acres prov-
en by Norman Pick
Deed Christopher Funkhowser to Jacob Young 50 acres proven
by John Young
Deed Isaac Robertson to George Murphey 92 acres proven by
Benj[n] Menees
Deed John Donelson to James Watson 366 acres proven by Tho[s]
Stuart
Deed James Watson to Edward Butler 366 acres proven by Tho[s]
Stuart
Court Adjourns untill tomorrow Morning 10 oClock

Tuesday Morning October 19th 1802
Present Benj[n] Menees, Martin Duncan, Isaac Philips, Esquires

Deed James London Jr to John London admitted on Certificate
& County Seal of Amherst County, Virginia
Executor of W[m] Fort Dec[d] delivered amount of Sale, sold 18th
March 1802. Executors of W[m] Fort dec[d] at liberty to sell re-
maining perishable property of estate; also to lease mills &
so much of land of s[d] estate as they think proper

Deed James Norfleet to Cordial Norfleet 123 acres ackd
Deed James Montgomery to Zachariah Cox 160 acres proven by
Thomas Johnson
Deed James Wheeler to Arthur Oneal 23 acres proven by Mat-
thew Manning
Deed Joseph Barns to Holland Dardin 250 acres proven by Jon-
athan Dardin
Ordered that the Tax be received for 640 acres belonging to
the heirs of John Gray for 1802

p.232 Dann Lynn vs John Powers. Trespass. April 1802 Pl[f] by
John C Hamilton & Tho[s] Stuart; def[t] by Peter R Booker. Oct[r]

1802 Jury John Hardin, Ja^s Long, Caleb Winters, James Mays, Chas Simmons, Jo^s Washington, David Spence, And^w Irwin, Edwd King, Abraham Tippy, Jesse Martin, Bazel Boren, who find for Def^t. Def^t to recover ag^t Pl^{tf} his costs and charges in this Suit expended. Jacob Cook witness proves 2 days attendance; Jno Hendley 2 days, Lewis Powers 2 days, Thos Powers 2 days, Thomas Woodard 1 day

Thomas Woodard Constable allowed 2 Dollars for guarding John Volentine a criminal to District Jaol at Nashville. William Hunter allowed 1 Dollar 33 1/3 cents for service as guard in above business

Ordered Philip Parchment to oversee road in room of Patrick Martin; same hands to work on the road

Deed Jesse Jones to Augustine Cook 31 acres ackd
Deed Abraham Tippy to Jesse Jones 106½ acres proven by Thos Johnson
Deed Uel Lampkin by Jonathan Ramsey his att^y/fact to Thomas Hopkins 200 acres proven by Thos Johnson
Deed Benjamin McNew to Burrill Pitts 66 acres proven by Wm Holland
Deed Joseph Childress to Wm Briscoe 64 acres 126 poles proven by Thos Johnson
p.233 Deed James Bell & Thomas Johnson Ex^{trs} of Joseph Carmack dec^d to Abraham Tippy 6½ acres; ack^d by Johnson; signature of James Bell proven by Peter R Booker

County Trustee to pay Jesse Martin for attendance as a state witness agt Henry Morris at May Term of Superior Court 1799

Henry Johnson exhonarated from payment of Taxes this year on 640 acres, that amount overcharged

Joseph Barns vs James Norfleet. July 1802 pl^{tf} by Wm Smith; def^t by Bennet Searcy. Octr 1802 Jury Jno Hardin, Caleb Winters, John Krisel, Saml Crocket, Peter Browner, Chas Bradon, Jno James, Robt Lancaster, Zachariah Cox, Wm Dickeson, Jacob Pinkley, Wm Wilson. Pl^{tf} called & non Suited. William Connel, witness, proves 2 days attendance; Jesse Martin 2 days; Lemuel Sugg 2 days.

Thomas Woodard app^{td} Constable; gave bond 620 Dollars, Richd Nuckolls & Andw Irwin his securities; took oaths

p.234 Jno Siglar to oversee road from Richd Couts in Springfield in room of John Strain

Jurors to next Superior Court: Isaac Philips, Matthew Day,

John Brooks, Thomas Johnson, Thomas Strain
Court Adjourns untill tomorrow Morning 9 OClock

Wednesday Morning October 20ᵗʰ 1802
Present Benjamin Menees, Martin Duncan, James Crabtree

Order David Henry oversee Road in room of William Grimes; &
the same hands work under him

Jurors to next County Court: Wᵐ Benson, Wᵐ Spiller, Francis
Boren, Charles Wheaton, Charles Bradon, William Huddleston,
Anthony Jones Sʳ, James Mays, James Stark, Robert Galispie,
Walter Stark, Benjamin Porter, Jesse Jones, Wᵐ Crocket, Samˡ
Crocket, Nimrod McIntosh, Jaˢ Bell, Jacob Pinkley, Lawrence
Carr, Jiles Connel, Mark Noble, James Elliott, James Walker,
Henry Airs (Caleb Creek), Isham Rogers, Lovick Ventress, Jaˢ
H Bryan, Patrick Martin, Benjamin Koen, Jacob Young

Order John Crane, Shaderick Rawls, Caleb Winters, Moses Winters, & James Stuart to view & mark a road from Springfield
to Majʳ Smiths Mill as far as the Kentucky line

Order Benjamin Menees Esqʳ take Lists of Taxable property in
that part of Robertson County South of Cumberland River
John Philips Esqʳ for Captⁿ Jacob Youngs Co
Isaac Dortch Esqʳ for Captⁿ Jas Blackwells Co
Charles Miles Esqʳ for Captⁿ Dardins Co
Thomas Strain Esqʳ for Captⁿ A Youngs Co
John Hutchison Esqʳ for Captⁿ Simmons Co
Martin Duncan Esqʳ for Captⁿ Bryans Co

Deed Samuel Tucker to John D Robins about 50 acres proven by
Charles Simmons
Deed Samuel Tucker to Silas Tucker about 110 acres proven by
Charles Simmons

p.235 Order John Philips & Thomas Johnson Esqʳˢ to value the
property of estate of Nathˡ Rogers decᵈ; make return next Ct

Deed William Tucker to Samuel Tucker 100 acres proven by Jno
D Robins
Deed John Young & James Norfleet Commʳˢ to John Cheatham one
lot in Springfield ackd
Deed John Young & Jas Norfleet Commʳˢ to Levi Noyes one lot
in Springfield ackd.   [5 more deeds Commʳˢ to Levi Noyes]

Deed John Young & James Norfleet Commʳˢ to John Cheatham one
lot in Springfield ackd
Deed John Young & James Norfleet Commʳˢ to Thomas Johnson &

James Menees one lot in Springfield ackd

Order estate of Jn° Tucker dec^d pay to Mrs Betsey Tucker one Dollar p^r week for the time she has kept Samuel the child of John Tucker dec^d

Joel Lewis allowed out of estate of John Tucker dec^d 20 Dollars for keeping Riggs Tucker & John Tucker, children of Jn° Tucker dec^d one year, to be paid at expiration of time

Peggy Tucker bound by indenture to Charles Simmons untill she arrives to age 18 years, also Nancy Tucker bound to Joseph Philips untill she arrives to age 18 years

p.236 Sarah Tucker bound by Indenture to Silas Tucker untill she arrives to age 18 years.   Henry Tucker bound to Silas Tucker untill he arrives to age 21 years

Letters/Adm^n on estate of John Tucker dec^d granted to John Robins; bond 7000 Dollars, Joseph Robertson, Silas Tucker, Joseph Castleberry, & William Dorris his securities

Ltrs/Admn on estate of Samuel Tucker decd granted to Betty Tucker & Charles Simmons, who gave Charles McIntosh & Joseph Philips their securities

Adm^r/estate of John Tucker dec^d allowed to sell perishables of s^d estate, giving 10 days notice by advertisements

Enoch Tucker entitled to draw from estate of Jn° Tucker dec^d 13 Dollars for keeping some orphan children of Decd to now

Ordered Clerk & Sheriff have Liberty to report any Lands not given in for taxation
Court Adjourns untill Court in Course
John Philips, Martin Duncan, Benjamin Menees, Isaac Philips

Robertson County, Monday Morning January 19th 1803
Present the Worshipfull John Philips, Isaac Dortch, James Crabtree, Esquires

Grand Jurors: Samuel Crocket foreman,   Jesse Jones, Jacob Pinkley, Nimrod McIntosh, Anthony Jones, Henry Airs, Mark Noble, John Krisel, Lawrence Karr, Patrick Martin, Walter Stark, Benjamin Koen, William Spiller

Parry W Humphreys produced licence to practice Law; was accordingly admitted
Clerk to receive Lists of Taxable property for present year

Ja^s Shannon app^{t d} overseer of Road in room of James McDonald

Henry Gardner to oversee the Road from Brush Creek to County Line, one to Clarksville, other to Portroyal; following work under him: Henry Gardner, Jiles Connell, Wm Connell, Major Baker, Jn° Yoes, Ja^s Atkins, Wm Atkins, Noah Woodard, Israel Robertson

Jonathan Stephenson to oversee Road in room of John Carr
Zachariah Cox to oversee Road in room of James Elliott J^r
Abell Williams to oversee Road in room of Jacob Pinkley
p.128   Deed Matthew Brooks J^r to Jacob Pinkley J^r 100 acres proven by John Brooks
Deed Zachariah Oneal to Thomas Holman 100 acres proven by James Holman
Deed Matthew Brooks to Frederick Cobb 200 acres proven by John Brooks
Deed Samuel Lampkin to Uel Lamkin 200 acres proven by William Briscoe
Deed Sampson Matthews to Amos Cohea 40 3/4 acres proven by John Hutchison
Relinquishment/Mortgage given by Joseph Childress to Jacob Pinkley ackd by s^d Pinkley
Deed Nicholas Conrod to Lawrence Carr 171/2 acres ackd
Deed John Tennison to James Vaughn 200 acres proven by James Benton
Admr^s estate of Saml Tucker dec^d delivered Inventory
Elisha Fikes to oversee Road in room of Joseph Washington
Power/Atty Uel Lamkin to Jonathan Ramsey proven by William Briscoe
Admr estate of John Tennison delivered an Inventory
James Crabtree Esqr delivered Tax List for Captⁿ A Youngs C°

Adm^r estate of Dickison Carr dec^d delivered an Inventory

James Henderson vs Warren Sams. Attach^t. Levied on 72½ acres on Spring Creek of Sychamore; judg^t entered by Benjⁿ Menees Esqr for 20 Dollars & costs. Court ordered land sold to satisfy Judgement & costs
Court Adjourns untill tomorrow Morning 9 OClock

p 239 Tuesday Morning January 18th 1803
Present John Philips, Thomas Strain, Charles Miles, Benjamin Menees, Isaac Philips, Esquires

John and William Bell released from double tax on three 640 acre tracts for 1802 upon taxes being paid for same

John Philips Esqr delivered tax list for Captn J Youngs Company; Charles Miles Esqr for Captn Dardins Company

Deed Gilbert Sellars to Thomas Johnson 640 acres proven by Robert Galespie
Deed Matthew Day to David Spence 25 acres ackd
George Browning apptd overseer of Road in room of Anderson Cheatham
B/S Gresham Coffield to Isaac Dortch for a Negro man, proven by William Connell
Administrator estate of John Tucker decd delivered amount of sales of sd Estate
Phebe Tucker bound by indenture to Traviss Elmore untill she arrives at age eighteen, Andw Irwin his security
Mrs Betsey Tucker allowed out of monies arising from estate of John Tucker dec^d seventy five Dollars for keeping of Saml a child of John Tucker decd one year from this time

Isaac Dortch Esqr delivered Tax List, Captn Blackwells C^o. Benjn Menees for South of Cumberland R. John Hutchison Esqr for Capt Simmons Co. Martin Duncan Esqr for Capt Krisels C^o

p.240   Whereas Nicholas Conrod about 2 June 1802 purchased 3840 acres advertised as Thos Persons to discharge Taxes for same, which 3840 acres is Capt James Turners, not Thos Person's, therefore order Nicholas Conrod released from paying to Sheriff the money he bid, except the cost which he is directed to pay; Nicholas Conrod relinquishes his purchase so made, and Clerk to certify same to the Treasurer

Henry Box vs Josiah Fort. Jacob Kenedy witness failing to appear, order he forfeit agreeable to Act of Assembly. Elias Fort Jr proves 2 days attendance as Witness

Deed Thomas Bethany to Drury Christian 100 acres proven by Sterling Brewer

State vs Martha Stark. Recognizance for 50 Dollars, called & forfeited. Order Scire facias issue for her to appear next Court to show cause why forfeiture should not be absolute

State vs Henry Gardner & James Ford. Recog. 25 Dollars each; called & forfeited. Scire facias to issue [worded as above]

Adm^r estate of John Tucker dec^d delivered Inventory
Adm^{rs} of Samuel Tucker dec^d granted liberty to sell property of estate on 27th Inst by advertising agreeable to Law

John Philips & Tho⁸ Johnson app^td last Term to appraise the estate of Nathl Rogers Dec^d delivered appraisement

p.241 Samuel Crocket vs Adam Shepherd & Co. Debt. July 1802 pltf by John C Hamilton; Def^t by Tho⁸ Stuart. Sh^ff levied on furnace, pig iron, scalps, flasks, patrins, open sandware, 6 horses, 4 waggons & harness, cattle & hogs of Shepherd & Co. Robert Drake came into Court & replevied property attached & entered Special Bail for Adam Shepherd. Jany 1803 Jury Isham Rogers, James Mays, Robt Galespie, Benjn Porter, James Walker, Matt^w Day, William Sale, And^w Washington, Elijah Bridgewater, James Pike, Joel Lewis, Nicholas Conrod, who find for pl^tf his debt 400 Dollars, Damage 98 Dollars & costs. George Neville witness proves 4 days attendance & 100 miles travel. David Brigham 2 days, 84 miles, 2 ferriages

Theor Rogers admr estate of Nathl Rogers decd delivered into Court a supplementary inventory
Order for Road from Browns fork to Browns ford on Red River recinded
Order road laid off from Montgomery line on middle fork Bartons Creek to Wm Tayes on Yellow Creek; to mark same: Captn Nisbet, Jeremiah Nisbet, Charles Tayes, Wm Giffen, William Tays Jr, and that Wm Tayes Jr cause same to be cleared, with all convenient hands to work under him
p.242   Court adjourns untill tomorrow Morning 9 OClock

Wednesday Morning January 19th 1803   Present
John Philips, Wm Connell, Isaac Philips, Archer Cheatham

Robert Warren app^td Constable, Bond 620 Dollars, William Milsap and Charles McIntosh his securities

Power/Att^y Philemon Thomas to Wm Vawter admitted to record by certificate and county seal of clerk of Mason County, KY

Deed Thomas Johnson to Levi Noyes Lot in Springfield ackd

James Johnson to oversee road Springfield to Smiths Mill, as formerly marked, from Menees Road at head of Buzzard C^r to State Line; hands John and Dorsey Cromwell, Jesse Lawrence, Josiah Skinner, Willis Skinner, John Harrel, the Masons at Suggs place, Isaac Philips, & all hands on North side of Red River in bounds of Captn Dardins C^o

George Patterson to oversee in room of Wm Haynes, Patterson is authorized to cut from James Crabtree nearest & best way to State Line to meet the Kentucky Road; all hands within 3

miles each side and all Capt[n] Youngs company on West side to
work on same

Enoch Tucker, gdn for Jane Tucker while she was a Lunitick,
made choice of Negro for her & in so doing acted fraudulent-
ly; Court discharges sd Guardian. Jane, now wife of Joseph
Engleman, with consent of sd Engleman, to chose for herself;
she with Husband makes choice of woman by name of Easter

Order W[m] Atkins, James Atkins, Rob[t] Perry, Pray Whipple, Jn[o]
Foster, John Yoes, W[m] Gosset be patrolers for Capt[n] Blackwells Company; they shall meet & ride at least once a month
and oftener if they think necessary

p.243 Petition of Edward Butler for erecting a water grist
mill on Sulpher fork of Red River; order County Surveyor attend at place stated in petition, there lay off & value one
acre on East side sd Creek; Freeholders to attend and value
with Surveyor are John Couts, John Johnson, Samuel McMurry,
James Appleton; make report to next Court

Order James Menees, Collector, have credit with State Treasurer for $5.85.9½ also with County Trustee $4.17.8 the whole
being for delinquents for 1799, 1800, & 1801; if he receive
any of those monies hereafter he is to refund it

James Crabtree Esq[r] allowed 8 Dollars for time he has kept
Daniel McDonald to the present time

Order following Land exposed to Sale for Taxes for 1799, being advertised in Nashville Gazette--Adam Hampton 640 acres,
W[m] Bowman 640 acres, W[m] Bowman 640, John Rice & Jn[o] Sappington 640 acres
Also for year 1800 as above. Adam Hampton 640 acres, W[m] Bowman 640, W[m] Bowman 640, David Edwards 640, John Rice & John
Sappington 640. Also for year 1801 Adam Hampton 640, W[m] Bowman 640, W[m] Bowman 640, David Edwards 640, John Rice & John
Sappington 640
Also for year 1802 Adam Hampton 640, W[m] Bowman 640, W[m] Bowman 640, David Edwards 640, John Rice & John Sappington 640,
Judgement is Entered against s[d] Land; ordered Collector proceed to sell agreeable to Law

Order all Lands which Collector shall report to Clerk previous to next Court he shall forthwith transmit to the printer
of Nashville Gazette to be published agreeable to law

p.244 Ordered that the county survey & the following jurors
Levi Moore, Tho[s] Yates, John Siglar, W[m] Sale, Joel Vaughn S[r]
attend on premises, estate of Adam Fleener dec[d], on Red Riv-

er River and lay off the dower of the widow agreeble to law

Jurors to next Court Abraham Young Senr, Chas Kilgore, James Wharton, Bartimias Pack, Josiah Skinner, Joseph Payne, Willis Skinner, Dorsey Cromwell, John Hardin, Wm Johnson R R, John Johnson Jr R R, Eppa Lawson, John Payne R R, Jesse Lawrence, Wm Deloach, James H Bryan, Lovick Ventress, Jonathan Dardin, Holland Dardin, Henry Gardner, John Gardner, Azariah Dunn, Jesse Martin, Matthew Luter J^r, John Carr, Archibald Mahon, Noah Woodard, Robert Perry, Mark Noble, Elias Fort M C, James Atkins

State vs Ja^s Latham. Order Ja^s Latham for contempt to Court pay Ten Dollars, which money was paid into the office. From the Testamony of Danl McKinley. Order James Latham give good security for his good behaviour toward Danl McKinley & every other citizen for one year. James Latham ackd himself bound in sum 1000 Dollars, Jonathan Stephenson and Joseph Johnson his security, each bound in sum of Five Hundred Dollars
Court Adjourns untill Court in Course
John Philips, William Connell, James Crabtree

p.245 Robertson County, Monday Morning April 18th 1803 Springfield. Present the Worshipfull Benjamin Menees, John Hutchison, John Philips, Esquires

Grand Jurors John Gardner foreman, John Payne, Elias Fort, Bartimias Pack, Lovick Ventress, Arch^d Mahon, Dorsey Cromwell, Abraham Young, William Deloach, John Carr, Robt Perry, James Wheeler, John Hardin

Will of William McClish proven by John Johnson & Peter Renfro. Jane McClish & George Lamb ex^{tx} & ex^{tr} took oaths. John Nisbit, Robert Nisbit, Thomas Simpson, and Samuel Walker to appraise the personal property of estate of W^m McClish dec^d

Wm Connel & Hardy S Bryan Esq^{rs} to settle with Benjamin Koen adm^r estate of Abraham Koen Dec^d relative to business of s^d Estate & make return to this Court, which they made

On oath of Saml Fulk in open Court, James McIntosh gives security for good behaviour for one year & one day toward person & property of Samuel Fulk & other citizens, bound in sum 100 Dollars, Bazel Boren & John Duncan his securities, bound in sum of fifty Dollars each p.246 Thomas Payreson vs Shaderick Rawls. Appeal. Pl^{tf} by John C Hamilton; def^t by Thomas Stuart. Jury Matthew Lister Jr, Azariah Dunn, Noah Woodard, Philip Parchment, James Atkins, Jesse Martin, Josiah Skinner, Ja^s H Bryan, Jo^s Payne, Willis Skinner, Charles Kilgore, Joseph Washington, who find for Def^t. Motion for a new tryal overruled

Joseph Choate to oversee road in room of Thomas Choate
Mark Noble excused from serving as a juror this Term
Eppa Lawson excused from serving as a juror this Term

John Wilson vs Joseph Dorris & Isaac Doris. Hugh Henry Esqr defendant's appearance bail surrendered him. Defendant gave Elisha Chick as further bail

George Briscoe vs George Bell. Attachment. Wm Briscoe a garnishee swears he owes s^d Bell 37½ cents; at time he was summoned he owed 4 Dollars 37½ cents; he has since paid Bell's agent 4 Dollars. John Robins as garnishee swears he owes Ge^o Bell 35 Dollars, & estate of John Tucker dec^d is indebted to s^d Bell something but he knows not what amount

Collector to have credit for 80 cents State & County Tax due on 320 acres given in by James Johnston and Elijah Hamilton; s^d Johnson is released from his part

Will of William Sanders was proven by Benjn Darrow
Joseph Woolfork admited to administer the estate of William Morris; bond 500 Dollars with Nicholas Conrod his security

p.247 Adm^r estate of Samuel Tucker decd delivered amount of sales of s^d Estate
Power/Atty John Burnley to John Trice ackd
Power/Atty John Trice to John Burnley ackd
Deed James Menees Sh^{ff} to Levi Moore ackd
Deed David Patterson to Ephraim Pool 148 acres proven by Elias Fort
Deed Mark Noble to John Noble 75 acres ackd
Deed William Haynes to John Trice 316 acres proven by Elisha Chick & John Burnley
Deed John Carney to Daniel Gonsalus 100 acres proven by Jacob Pinkley
Deed Jonathan Marsh & Nancy Marsh to Willie Cherry 640 acres admited to record on certificate of the presiding Justice of Beaufort County N Carolina with county seal annexed

Deed John Chewning to John Watkins 200 acres ackd
Deed Augustine Cook to Wyatt Bishop 131 acres proven by Thomas Johnson
Deed Nicholas Choate to George Golladay 100 acres proven by

Joseph Choate
Deed James Henderson to Thomas Hail   107 3/4 acres ackd

Joseph Washington, Aaron Winters, Saml Bellamy, Benjn Wood,
Moses Winters, James Stuart to work under James Stuart over-
seer of New Road from Menees ford to half mile below Demsey
Coffields plantation, being s^d overseers part of s^d road

p.248 Elias Fort M C to oversee New Road to Iron works from
the Mare Lick to half mile below Demsey Coffields Plantation
and Elisha Pilant, Wm Pool, Silas Crane, Whitmill Arrington,
Robert Perry, John Yoes, Wm Atkins, Elias Fort work thereon.
Court Adjourns untill Tomorrow Morning 9 OClock

Tuesday Morning, April 19th 1803   Present the Worshipfull
John Philips, Martin Duncan, James Crabtree, John Hutchison
and Isaac Philips, Esquires

Beverley A Allen vs George Evans.   Plaintiff was called and
nonSuited.   Samuel Hollis witness proves 2 days attendance;
Thomas Choate 2 days, Joseph Choate 2 days, Col^o James Ford
7 days, 96 miles traveling

John Philips and Martin Duncan Esq^{rs} to settle with adm^x of
estate of Daniel Holland dec^d relative to estate;   who made
report same day; ordered to be recorded

George Patterson to oversee road in room of Wm Haynes; he is
authorized to cut from Birds Creek where James's part stops,
thence to Strains thence to Crabtrees thence agreeable to 2^d
order to the State Line where Kentucky Road intersects;   all
hands within 3 miles east of the road and all Captain Youngs
Company on the West side to work on same

Jurors to next Superior Court   James Crabtree, John Hutchison, Daniel Mckinley Senr, Matthew Day, and Philip Parchment

p.249 Jurors to next Court John Appleton, David Huddleston,
And^w Irwin, Richard Matthews, Saml McMurry, Walter Stark, W^m
Spiller, Moses Winters, And^w Washington, Thomas Sellars, W^m
Crocket, John Burnley, Joseph Latimer, Jacob Young, Holland
Dardin, William Atkins, Lawrence Carr, James Gardner, Nimrod
McIntosh, James Blackwell, Cordial Norfleet, James Elliott
J^r, Peter Browner, Asaph Parker, John Crane, James Jones J^r,
Peter Pinkley, James Walker, Matthew Mathes, Thomas Little

Deed Peter Fry to Philip Parchment 105 acres proven by Jacob
Pinkley
Deed Jacob Young to Levi Noyes one Lot in Springfield ackd

Deed James Menees Sh^{ff} to James Ford 274 acres ackd
Deed Comm^{rs} of Springfield to Levi Noyes one Lot ackd
Jesse Martin to oversee Road in room of Matthew Luter
Deed Philip Parchment to Anthony Hinkle 105 acres ackd

David Jones vs John Flynn and Jacob Young. Judgement for 31
Dollars 90 Cents Debt and Costs 50 cents before a Justice of
the Peace, execution for which has been levied on 200 acres
the property of John Flynn. Sheriff to sell agreeable to Law
to satisfy judgement & costs

Ordered that Wm Karr oversee road from Springfield agreeable
to s^d Karrs former order
B/S Gabriel Rawls to Samuel Crocket proven by Isham Rogers

p.250   1803 County Tax: each hundred acres 12½ cents; each
white pole 6 2/4 cents; each black pole 12½ cents, each town
lot 10½ cents; each stud horse for covering mares 25 cents

A Petition of William Tait for rectifying a mistake made by
Sec^y/State of North Carolina in making out a grant for 640
acres. Kept over untill next Court to produce Testamony

James Menees Sh^{ff} app^{ld} Collector for present year gave Bond
5000 Dollars, Wm Armstrong and Philip Parchment securities

Archer Cheatham Esqr admited to keep an Ordanary one year;
bond 500 Dollars, Bazel Boren and Lemuel Sugg his securities

Jonathan Stephenson admited to keep an Ordanary for one Year
gave Bond 500 Dollars, Isaac Johnson his security

Following tracts to be exposed to sale or so much of each as
shall satisfy Taxes & costs due thereon for Taxes for 1799:
Philip Bush 300 acres, Jonathan Magness 213 1/3 acres.
For 1800: Martin Armstrong 960 acres, Daniel Curd 200 acres,
Melcher Oyler 213 acres, Wm Clark 640 acres
p.251 For 1801: Thomas Barry 640 acres; David Clandins 824
acs; Danl Curd 200 acs; John Carvon 320 acres; James Doherty
70 acres; David Davis 640 acres; Alexander Fletcher 100 ac;
Thos Molloy 640 ac; Melcher Oyler 300 ac.
Also following Tracts not given in for Taxation: for 1799:
John Fords heirs 640 acres; David McCree 1000 acres
Year 1800: John Fords heirs 640 acres; David McCree 1000 ac;
Adam Fleeners heirs 320 acres
For 1801: Kirby Vick 96 ac; John Fords heirs 640 ac; David
McCree 1000 ac; Adam Fleeners heirs 320 acres
For 1802: Kirby Vick 96 ac; John Fords heirs 640 acs; David
McCree 1000 ac; George W Darnald 1214 acres; Adam Fleeners
heirs 320 acres.

Judgement is hereby entered against aforesaid Tracts; order
Sheriff to proceed to sell agreeable to Law
Court Adjourns untill Court in Course
    Benjn Menees, Isaac Philips, Martin Duncan, John Philips

p.252   Robertson County,   Monday Morning   July 18th 1803,
Springfield.   Present the Worshipfull Martin Duncan, Isaac
Dortch, James Norfleet, Esquires

Grand Jury James Blackwell foreman, Andrew Washington, Peter
Pinkley, Joseph Latimer, Nimrod McIntosh, Wm Atkins, Matthew
Matthews, David Huddleston, John Burney, Wm Crocket, Samuel
McMurry, James Walker, James Elliott

Deed William Surry to James Murphree 320 acres ackd

W^m P Anderson may list his Taxable property for last year, &
pay amount to the Collector, Clerk to furnish Treasurer with
same, am^t of property listed 1280 acres

Joseph Washington is granted credit for Tax on 376 acres for
present year

Elisha Chick who was Security for Joseph Dorris in suit John
Wilson ag^t s^d Doris & Isaac Doris, surrendered s^d Joseph
Isaac Doris, son of Samuel, and James Menees ack^d themselves
s^d Dorris's in afs^d suit

Arthur Jones granted credit for tax on 640 acres given in by
Maj^r Baker, s^d land lies out of the County
Bartimias Pack to oversee Road in room of Elisha Chick
Jacob Pinkley to oversee road in room of David Spence
Order the Clerk to receive all the Lists of Taxable property
which may be presented during this Term

p.253   John Wilson vs Joseph Doris & Isaac Doris. Covenant.
Jany 1803 pl^{tf} by John C Hamilton; Def^t by Thos Stuart. July
Jury Asa Parker, Thos Sellars, James Gardner, Ja^s Jones J^r,
Richd Matthews, Henry Gardner, John Crane, Wm Spiller, Moses
Winters, John Payne, Sugg Fort, John Lipscomb, who find for
pl^{tf}, assess damage 250 Dollars. Motion for New tryal over-
ruled. Pl^{tf} to recover damage & costs of suit

Peter Brawner to oversee road from fork above Millers Creek
toward Nashville to where road from Springfield to Weakleys
ferry crosses same; & all hands on Millers creek above James

Elliotts to work on same

Deed Jonathan Oyler to Henry Johnson Senr 300 acres ackd
Deed/Trust John Burnley to John Trice ackd
Deed James Menees Sh^{ff} to Elisha Chick 640 acres ackd
Deed William Henry Hill to Ezekiel Noris for individed moity
or half of 2468 acres proven by Wm Norris
p.254 Deed James Menees, Collector, to Archibald Mahon 900
acres ackd
Deed James Menees Collector to Arch^d Mahon 200 acres ackd
Deed Jonathan Oyler to Wm Perry 218 acres ackd

Ex^{trs} estate of William Fort dec^d delivered am^t of sales of
estate; also additional inventory

James Bell to oversee road in room of Jno Lipscomb; Benjamin
Porter, Thomas Johnson, Joseph Robertson, Jesse Jones, John
McIntosh, James McIntosh, Jacob Fulk, Samuel Fulk, Ja^s Bell,
John Lipscomb, and Joseph Castleberry work thereon under him

Ltrs/Admn granted Isabella Butler & W^m P Anderson on estate
of Edward Butler Dec^d; bond 4000 Dollars, George Bell, John
Somerville & Bennet Searcy securities; took oath
Transfer of Land Warrant & Entry William Lurry[Surry?Jurry?]
to Patrick Patterson ackd
Court Adjourns untill tomorrow Morning 9 OClock

Tuesday Morning July 19th 1803   Present John
Philips, Benjamin Menees, Isaac Philips, John Hutchison

Bill/Sale Christopher Stump to Archer Cheatham for Negro boy
proven by W^m B Vinson
Deed James Menees, Collector, to Archer Cheatham and Thomas
Johnson 460 acres ackd
Deed James Menees, Collector, to Archer Cheatham and Thomas
Johnson 640 acres ackd
p.255 James Menees, Collector, to Archer Cheatham and Thos
Johnson 520 acres ackd
Deed James Menees, Collector, to Archer Cheatham and Thomas
Johnson 580 acres ackd

Ex^{trs} of W^m McClish delivered Inventory & Appraisement of s^d
estate

George Bell vs James Latham. Attachment. Following persons
sworn as garnishees is indebted Nothing: Thomas Dorris, William Clark, Daniel Holman (says his Daughter owes 50 c^{ts}),
George Sprouse, John Crummill, James Walker, Robert Warren

George Bell vs Jacob Feltner as Garnishee for James Latham. The Def^{dt} being Legally summoned made oath he is indebted to James Latham 19 Dollars 15 cents. Judgement ag^t Feltner behalf George Bell for af^{sd} sum

George Bell vs Joseph Doris garnishee for Ja^s Latham. Def^{dt} made oath he is indebted to Ja^s Latham 147 Dollars 91 cents; judg^t ag^t Joseph Doris behalf Ge^o Bell for af^{sd} sum

Admr estate of Wm Morris delivered Inventory of estate

p.256 George Bell vs Levi Noyes as garnishee for Ja^s Latham. Def^{dt} made oath he is indebted to James Latham 14 Dollars 91 c^{ts}; judg^t ag^t Noyes behalf Ge^o Bell for af^sd sum

George Bell vs Jacob Pickren as garnishee for James Latham. Def^{dt} made oath he is indebted to James Latham 8 Dollars 50 cts. Judg^t ag^t Pickren behalf Ge^o Bell for af^{sd} sum

George Bell vs Anderson Cheatham as Garnishee of Ja^s Latham. Def^{dt} made oath he is indebted to James Latham 10 Dollars 81 ½ c^{ts}; judg^t ag^t s^d Cheatham behalf George Bell for af^{sd} sum

George Bell vs Jacob Young as Garnishee of Ja^s Latham. Def^{dt} made oath he is indebted to James Latham 104 Dollars; judg^t is entered ag^t said Young in behalf George Bell for af^{sd} sum

George Bell vs Thomas Johnson as garnishee of James Latham. Def^{dt} made oath he is indebted to James Latham 22 Dollars 50 cents to be paid in cotton next fall; therefore judg^t is entered ag^t s^d Johnson behalf George Bell for af^{sd} sum

George Bell vs Polly Hunter as garnishee of Ja^s Latham. Def^t made oath she is indebted to James Latham 3 Dollars. Judgement ag^t s^d Hunter in behalf George Bell for af^{sd} sum

George Bell vs Wm Johnson as garnishee of James Latham. Def^t made oath he is indebted to James Latham 16 Dollars 32 c^{ts}; judgement ag^t s^d Johnson behalf George Bell for af^{sd} sum

Ge^o Bell vs John Cheatham as garnishee of Ja^s Latham. Def^{dt} made oath he is indebted to Ja^s Latham 81 Dollars 86 cents; judgement against Cheatham behalf George Bell for af^{sd} sum

Ge^o Bell vs Elijah Bridgewater as garnishee of James Latham. Def^t made oath he is indebted to Ja^s Latham 7 Doll^s 82½ c^{ts}; judgement ag^t s^d Bridgewater behalf George Bell for af^sd sum

George Bell vs Eli Jones as garnishee of James Latham. Def^{dt} made oath he is indebted to James Latham 10 Dollars 87½ c^{ts};

judgement against Jones in behalf George Bell for af^{sd} sum

p.258 Granted Joseph Washington liberty to build a mill on Calebs Creek oppisit Andrew Washingtons and following jurors to view & condemn premises: John Crane, James Stuart, Silas Crane, John Carr, Archd Mahon, Jesse Martin, Moses Winters, Aaron Winters, Caleb Winters, Wm Flewellen, Philip Parchment, Silas Bankston, Isaac Menees, Elisha Fikes

Isaac Menees records his stock mark

George Bell vs George Briscoe. Motion by Defendant's attorney that certiorari be dismissed; overruled

Deed Robert Beaty to Thomas Johnson, John Simmons Senr, and Edward Simmons 640 acres ackd; also Certificate of John and Edward Simmons conveying a part to Charles Simmons was ackd

Deed Thomas Haynes to Thomas Smith 320 acres ackd
Deed W^m T Lewis to Richd Hutchins 222 acres proven by Thomas Johnson
Deed James Menees Sh^{ff} to John Payne 74 acres ackd
Deed James Menees Sh^{ff} to Jacob Fulk 640 acres ackd
Deed Ja^s Meness Collector to W^m P Anderson 500 acres ackd
Deed James Menees Collector to W^m P Anderson 640 acres ackd

Power/Att^y Ge^o W Darnald to Heydon Wells & Nicholas Darnald proven by Ja^s Menees

p.259 Adm^r estate of Edward Butler dec^d delivered Inventory

Order James Appleton, Thomas Johnson, & Anderson Cheatham to value property of estate of Ed^{wd} Butler dec^d, so much thereof as the adm^{rs} do not see cause to sell

County Trustee to pay Daniel Holman Coroner Four Dollars for services in Inquisition on dec^d child of Rebekah McConnell

Order Daniel McKinley Jr, David Jones Jr, James Appleton Jr, and Thomas Appleton allowed one Dollar fifty cents each for services in guarding Dan Lynn to Nashville Jaol. Robert Warren, Constable, allowed three Dollars 93 3/4 cts for conveying sd Lynn to Nashville Jaol ´

Clerk & Sheriff allowed 40 Dollars each for Exoficio service for the past year

Philip Parchment made Oath he has lost a note of Hand given by John Tucker to Peter Pinkley for 99 Dollars, and given by Pinkley to Parchment. Balance due on Note when Lost and not

yet paid is 51 Dollars 83 Cents
Court Adjourns untill tomorrow Morning 9 Oclock

p.260   Wednesday Morning July 20th 1803.
Present Benjn Menees, Isaac Philips, Martin Duncan, Esquires

Deed Sampson Matthews to John R McShehee   36 acres proven by
John Hutchison

Bustards & Eastin vs John Flynn. Attachment. Levied by Robt
Warren Constable on 200 acres. Judgement entered by A Cheatham Esqr for 6 Dollars 30 c^{ts}. Ordered that land or so much
thereof as will satisfy Judgement & costs be sold.

Order Jacob Pickren Constable allowed 3 Dollars 30 cents for
summoning 11 witnesses in suit State vs Rebekah McConnel

Order John Baker, Martin Duncan, John Hutchison Esq^{rs} be inspectors for election on first Thursday in August & succeeding Day; Sugg Fort & Thos Johnson to be Cl^{ks} for s^d election

Charles Wheaton, Wyatt Bishop, & Abraham Philips app^{td} County commissioners to settle with county trustee & Collector;
gave bond, with Wm Grimes and Wm Briscoe their security

Enoch Tucker to oversee Road from Springfield to Port Royal
from fork of road near Springfield to Menees Road, all hands
between sd Road & Sulpher fork work on same, & Henry Johnson

Order Anthony Jones S^r oversee Road in room of John Appleton

p.261   Deed James Menees Sh^{ff} to W^m B Vinson 640 acres ackd

Commissioners of Springfield to contract with workman to fix
good steps to doors of Court House, a Table for the Clerk, a
Lock to one Door, and bolt to the Other; draw on the County
Trustee for amount sd work may cost

William Crunk appointed Constable; bond one Thousand Dollars
with David Henry & Wm Spiller his securities; took Oath

Surveyor & Jurors to condemn one acre for purpose of Captain
Edward Butlers Mill made return: Feby 18th 1803.... line of
Jas Jones on West side of Creek... the whole of this land of
James Jones is overflowd with a common flood but distance as
above stated is the truth from low water mark. Value of acre
is one Dollar. Henry Johnson, SRC; John Couts, James Appleton, John Johnson, Saml McMurry jurors

p.262   On Motion of Enoch Tucker, order Benjn Menees J^r as
Surveyor attend on premises of 640 acres lying on Spring Cr,
property of heirs of John Tucker dec^d, with following jurors
Nathan Arnet, Benjamin Menees Senr, Ja^s Long, James Walker,
Matthew Matthews, who are to lay off tract amongst legatees
of John Tucker Dec^d, value s^d Lots, and make report

Deed James Williams to John Robins 365 acres proven by Peter
Young
Deed George Galespie to John Robins 50 acres proven by Saml
Robins

Jurors to next Court: Josiah Skinner, Samuel Miles, Dorsey
Cromwell, Jno Cromwell, John Gardner, Nathan Yoes, James At-
kins, James Young, Levi Dunn, Elias Fort Junr, Wm Deloach,
Cordal Norfleet, Walter Stark, James Sawyer, Thomas Bounds,
James Mays, Wm Huddleston, Hugh Henry, Wm Pate, Wm Armstrong
Jr, Conrod Coon, John McMillon, William Gilbert, Moses Hard-
in, William Wills, Jacob Pinkley (Sych), Isaac Sanders, Ja-
cob Lewis, Ephraim Pool

John Philips & Archer Cheatham Esqrs to divide hands to work
on roads between George Browning and Wm Briscoe, overseers

Jacob Pickren exhonarated from Tax on stud horse, the horse
not being kept for covering mares
Court Adjourns untill Court in Course
     Isaac Philips, Benjn Menees, John Hutchison, John Philips

p.263   Robertson County. Monday Morning   October the 17th
1803. Springfield. Present the Worshipfull Benjamin Menees,
John Hutchison, James Crabtree, and Isaac Philips, Esquires

Grand Jurors: James Sawyers foreman, Wm Huddleston, John Mc-
Millon, Nathan Yoes, Ja^s Young, Saml Miles, Cordal Norfleet,
Dorsey Cromwell, Conrod Coon, Jacob Lewis, William Pate, Jno
Cromwell, Hugh Henry

Henry Hunt records his stock márk; also Joseph Choate and
James H Bryan record their stock marks

Clerk to receive all Lists of Taxable property which may be
presented at this Term for year 1803 on taxes being paid

Order that at all succeeding Terms this Court will on first
day of Term enter upon Civil Docket either to try or to con-

tinue agreeable to Law

Ltrs/Admn on estate of John Wade granted to James Robertson;
bond 500 Dollars, Wm Caldwell & Benjn Mason his security

Deed Thomas Ramsey to James Farmer 100 acres proven by Robt
Heaton
Adm^r estate of John Wade dec^d delivered Inventory of estate

p.264 Power/Atty Josiah Hundley to Wm Hundley ackd
Charles Kilgore app^t^d overseer or Road in room of Jno Siglar

Deed John Hutchison to Elijah Bridgewater 150 acres ackd
Deed Thos Choate to John Randolph (illegible word) and Annis
Hansley for 110 acres proven by Joseph Choate
Deed Arthur Oneal to Thomas Holman 23 acres proven by Daniel
Holman
Deed Josiah Ramsey to Philip Parchment 213 acres proven by
Saml Hollis
Deed Josiah Ramsey to Philip Parchment 200 acres proven by
Saml Hollis
Deed John Caffery to Henry Hunt 300 acres proven by Joseph
Choate
Deed Thomas Ramsey to And^w Sanders 270 acres proven by Benjn
Weakley
Deed Nathl Dickison to Ja^s H Bryan 200 acres ackd; also the
certificate of Thos Johnson ackd
Court Adjourns untill tomorrow Morning 10 OClock

Tuesday Morning October 18^t^h 1803   Present Benjamin
Menees, Thos Strain, William Johnson, Isaac Dortch, Esquires

Deed James Menees Sheriff to David Rounsavall 100 acres ackd
B/S Jacob Pinkley to Isham Rogers for a Negro woman ackd
The Ex^t^r of estate of John Kitts dec^d delivered to court the
account of the amount of sales of said Estate

p.265 Adam Shepherd & Co vs David Smith. Debt. July 1803 pl^f
by Thos Stuart; Def^t by Matt^w Lodge. Octr Jury Ephraim Pool,
Isaac Sanders, Wm Deloach, John Gardner, Levi Dunn, James
Yates, William Ragsdale, Thos Kilgore, Samuel McMurry, Jesse
Martin, Edward King, William Wills who find for Pltf; assess
damage 60 Dollars 55 cents; also his costs of Suit

George Briscoe vs George Bell. Attachment. Jury Josiah Skinner, Chas Kilgore, Eli Jones, Wm Dorris, Ja^s Gardner, Bazel
Boren, James Pike, Andrew Washington, Ja^s Mays, Whitmill Arrington, Isham Rogers, George Browning after which Plaintiff
suffered a NonSuit

Order Matthew Day, John Hutchison, Jas Sawyers, Josiah Fort, Asa Woodard attend next Superior Court as Jurors

p.266 Deed Nathan Smith to Hardy S Bryan 40 acres proven by Asa Bryan
Deed Thomas Barker to Joseph McDowel 228 acres proven by Jas Gambril
Deed Thos Britain atty/fact for John Russel McShehee to Jas England 70 acres proven by Jas Sawyers
Deed Jacob McCarty to John Dorris 66 acres proven by Henry Johnson

Jacob Pickren app^td Constable; Bond 500 Dollars, Jno Wilson, Joseph Robertson, Benjn Menees Jr securities; took oath

Samuel Miles app^td Constable; Bond 500 Dollars, Jacob Lewis & Conrod Coon his securities; took oath
Court Adjourns untill Tomorrow Morning 9 OClock

Wednesday Morning October 19th 1803
Present John Philips, James Crabtree, Martin Duncan, Esqrs

Jury to lay off and value 274 acres for Joseph Washington's mill made report
Deed James Menees Sh^ff to John D Robins 124 acres ackd

p.267 James Latham vs James Menees. Ass^t & Battery. Ap^l 1803
Pl^f by Thomas Stuart; Def^t by Wm Smith & Bennet Searcy. Oc^tr Jury Isham Rogers, Isaac Dorris, Edward King, Joseph Robertson, Nimrod McIntosh, Jno Siglar, Wm Wills, Charles Wheaton, John Cheatham, Bazel Boren, John Wilson, William Sale, find for Pl^tf, damage 25 cents. Def^t obtained appeal to Superior Court; Cordal Norfleet & Hugh Henry his securities

p.268 George Bell vs George Briscoe. Certiorari. July 1803
Pl^tf by Bennet Searcy; Def^t by Thos Stuart. Oc^tr Jury Josiah Skinner, Wm Deloach, Isaac Sanders, Ephraim Pool, Levi Dunn, David Jones, Saml McMurry, James Shaw, Thomas McIntosh, And^w Morris, Moses Davidson, Leml Sugg, who find for Pl^t; assess damage to 25 Dollars 25 cents; also costs. Motion by Def^dt's attorney for new tryal overruled. Henry Johnson, a witness, proves 4 days attendance

William Ragsdale vs Patrick Patterson. Ass^t/Battery. Def^t in proper person confessed Judgement 175 Dollars with assent of Plaintiff. Each party pays own attornies & witnesses; Clerks & Sheriffs fees to be equally divided between them

p.269   Stothart & Bell vs Joseph Doris. Covenant. July 1803
pl[f] by Bennet Searcy; def[t] by Tho[s] Stuart. Oct[r] Jury Matthew
Day, Dan[l] Holman, Sam[l] Robins, Jacob Fry, Amos Cohea, Julius
Elmore, Ja[s] Mays, Sam[l] Henry, Willie Skinner, Jesse Martin,
Abraham Pinkley, Patrick Patterson who find for pl[tf]; assess
damage 82 Dollars 36½ cents; also costs of suit

p.270   William Crunk vs James Latham. Ass[t]/Battery. July pl[tf]
by Bennet Searcy & John C Hamilton; Def[t] by W[m] Smith, Matt[w]
Lodge & Tho[s] Stuart. Oct[r] Jury Josiah Skinner, W[m] Deloach,
Isaac Sanders, Ephraim Pool, Levi Dunn, David Jones, Samuel
McMurry, James Shaw, Thomas McIntosh, Andrew Morris, Matthew
Matthews, John Couts who find for pl[tf], assess damage to 25
cents; also costs of suit in that behalf expended

Patrick Patterson vs William Ragsdale. A/B. Pl[tf] in proper
person dismissed suit; def[t] in proper person assumes to pay
his own attorney & his own witnesses, and one half of clerk
& sheriff fees

p.271   James McCoun vs Montgomery Bell. Case. July 1803 pl[tf]
by P W Humphreys; def[t] by Mattw Lodge. Oct[r] Jury Isham Rogers, Isaac Dorris, Edward King, Nimrod McIntosh, John Cheatham, Charles Wheaton, W[m] Wills, Jesse Martin, Uriah Swann,
Joel Lewis, Abraham Pinkley, John Wilson, who find for pl[tf];
assess damage 119 Dollars 36 c[ts]; also costs of suit; Josiah
Marr witness proves 3 days attendance, 50 miles, 2 ferriages

p.272   John C Hamilton vs Stephen Boren. Covenant. July 1803
pl[f] by Tho[s] Stuart; Def[t] by P R Booker. Oct[r] Jury Matt[w] Day,
Sam[l] Robins, Jacob Fry, Amos Cohea, Julius Elmore, Ja[s] Mayo,
Samuel Henry, Willie Skinner, Abraham Pinkley, Jesse Martin,
Sam[l] McMurry, George Browning who find for pl[tf]; damage 310
Dollars. Def[dt] obtained appeal to Superior Court, bond 650
Dollars; Bazel Boren & Isaac Dorris securities. Samuel Mc-
Murry witness proves 3 days attendance; Jesse Martin 3 days

Deed Isaac Dorris to Isaac Dorris 28 acres ackd
P/A Shaderick Rawls to John Akin ackd
Court Adjourns untill Tomorrow Morning 9 OClock

Thursday Morning October 20th 1803
Present John Philips, Benj[n] Menees, James Crabtree, Esquires

p.273   Wyatt Bishop vs Jacob Young. Debt. July 1803 pl[tf] by
Bennet Searcy; d[ft] by P W Humphreys. Oct Jury William Wills,
W[m] Deloach, Levi Dunn, Joseph Robertson, Nimrod McIntosh, W[m]
Wilson, Charles Murphey, Daniel Pinkley, Isham Rogers, Uriah
Swann, Tho[s] Kilgore, Titus Benton, who find for Pl[tf]; assess

damage to 66 Dollars 99 cents; also costs

B/S George Briscoe to Wm Briscoe proven by Thos Johnson

General Andrew Jackson app^{td} guardian for orphan children of Captn Edward Butler dec^d: Caroline S Butler, Eliza Butler, George W Butler, & Anthony Wayne Butler, gave bond 8000 Dollars, with Bennet Searcy & George Bell his securities

p.274   Andrew Morris vs John Cromwell. Appeal. Pl^{tf} by Thos Stuart; d^{ft} by John C Hamilton. Jury James Mays, Saml Henry, Jacob Young, Henry Airs, Uriah Swann, Josiah Skinner, William Sale, Ja^s Yates, Jacob Pinkley, Jo^s Payne, John Cheatham, Julius Elmore, who find for Pl^{tf}; assess damage to one Dollar 62½ cents; also costs of suit in this behalf expended

Deed James Menees Sheriff to John D Robins 640 acres ackd

Surveyor & jurors apptd by last Court to divide & value land of John Tucker dec^d between legatees, returned Plat, which Court refused to receive, owing to one Lots being given to a Legatee without drawing Lots with the other Legatees

Deed James Menees Sh^{ff} to Josiah Skinner   240 acres 40 poles ackd

p.275   State vs John Young. Indictment for Assault/ Battery. July 1803   Wm Smith County Solicitor; def^t by Bennet Searcy. Octr Jury Wm Wills, Wm Deloach, Levi Dunn, Joseph Robertson, Nimrod McIntosh, William Wilson, Charles Murphey, Danl Pinkley, Isham Rogers, Edwd King, George Browning, Abraham Dean, who find Def^t Guilty as Charged. Def^t fined 40 Dollars with Costs of suit. Wm Johnson witness proves 4 days attendance; George Bell 4 days, Julius Elmore 2 days, Charles Simmons 2 days, James Mayo 2 days, Titus Benton 4 days.
Court Adjourns untill tomorrow Morning 9 OClock

Friday, October 21st 1803   Present John Philips, James Crabtree, Martin Duncan, Archer Cheatham, Esquires

p.276   State vs Edward King. Presentment. Wm Smith, County Solicitor; def^t by John C Hamilton. Jury Wm Ragsdale, Jacob Siglar, Jo^s Payne, Isaac Dorris, Jacob Young, Wm Wills, Levi Dunn, Wm Sale, Henry Johnson, Moses Davidson, Jno McElhainy, Abraham Dean who find Def^t Not Guilty. Court orders Prosecutor to pay all Costs

Ordered Henry Hyde oversee Road in room of Philip Parchment

State vs George Browning. Presentment. Jury Wm Ragsdale, Jacob Siglar, Joseph Payne, Jacob Young, Wm Wills, Levi Dunn, Wm Sale, Henry Johnson, John McElhainy, Abraham Dean, Nimrod McIntosh, Isham Rogers find Def^t Not Guilty. Prosecutor to pay all Costs. Abraham Dean witness proves 4 days attendance

Thomas G Walk vs Shaderick Rawls. Judgememt $1.25, costs one Dollar. Execution levied on 200 acres claimed by said Rawls the 29th July 1803. Lem^l Sugg Constable

Robert Warren vs Shaderick Rawls. Execution 50 cents. Levied on above 200 acres July 29th 1803. Lem^l Sugg Constable

Thomas G Walker vs Shaderick Rawls. Judgem^t $4.87½, costs 50 cents. Execution levied on above 200 acres July 29th 1803. Lem^l Sugg Cons^{le}
Ordered that the afsd 200 acres be sold or so much thereof as will satisfy above judgements & costs

p.277 State vs Enoch Holman. Indictment. Wm Smith County Solicitor; def^t by John C Hamilton. Jury Ge^o Browning, Isaac Dorris, Jacob Young, Wm Wills, Levi Dunn, John McElhainy, Abraham Dean, Edwd King, Thos McIntosh, Isham Rogers, Peter Young, Nimrod McIntosh who find Def^t Not Guilty. Wm Ragsdale witness proves 5 days attendance, Jacob Siglar 5 days

Following Justices to take Lists of Taxable property for the ensuing Year; make return to our next Court

James Crabtree Esqr	for Captⁿ Abraham Youngs Company
Joseph Doris Esqr	Captⁿ Charles Simmons Co
Wm Johnson Esqr	Captⁿ John Krisels Co
Archer Cheatham Esqr	Captⁿ Wm Briscoe's Co
Isaac Philips Esqr	Captⁿ J Skinners Company
James Norfleet Esqr	Captⁿ J Blackwells Co
Hardy S Bryan Esqr	Captⁿ John Bryans Co

Wm Connell Esqr for that part of Robertson South of Cumberland River

Jurors to next Court: Joseph Robertson, Stephen Boren, John Cheatham, Jacob Pinkley, Chas McIntosh, Jo^s Fry, Jno Sommerville, Moses Beason, Jno Strain, Thomas Byrd Jr, Levi Moore, Thos McIntosh, Wm Perry, William Benson, Arthur Pitt, Tignal Martin, Walter Stark, Nathan Clark, Charles Bradon, Ja^s England, Saml McMurry, James Appleton S^r, James Wheeler, Moses Beason, Philip Parchment, James Stark, Wm Sale, Joel Vaughn Senr, Barton Coates, Nimrod McIntosh

John Childress bound by Indenture to Danl Pinkley untill he arrives to age twenty one years

p.278   Order patrollers for Captains Krisel & Simmons compa-
nies: William Crunk Captain,   Titus Benton, James Appleton,
Tignal Martin, Ja^s Mayo, Ja^s Niell, Wm Clark.   Captn Black-
wells, Briscoes & Skinners Companies: Robert Warren Captain,
And^w Washington, Moses Winters, Ja^s Gardner, Joshua Gardner,
Isham Rogers, Budy Browning, Charles Murphey. Captain Youngs
Co: James Yates Captn, Ja^s Wheeler, Wm Armstrong Jr^r, Thomas
Kilgore, Charles Kilgore, Patrick Patterson, Adam Clap

State vs John Young. Indictment. John Young called & failing
to attend   forfeited his recognizance.   Also Daniel McKinley
security for s^d Young forfeited his recognizance

Sheriff to have credit for Taxes due on 16360 acres which
was reported & would not sell for the Taxes

James Menees Collector of State & County Tax for 1801 report
land as not being given in for purpose of paying Taxes:
Peggy Allen 640 acres waters of Sulpher fork;   John Drew 640
Sulpher fork.   Also for year 1802: Abisha Thomas 545 acres,
Peggy Allen 640 ac, David Shelton 274 ac Red River,   Charles
Simmons 640 Red River, John Drew 640 Red River. For 1803: W^m
Hoods heirs 640 Sulpher fork, Abisha Thomas 545 acres waters
Sychamore, Peggy Allen 640 Sulpher fork, David Shelton 274
Red River, Chas Simmons 640 Red River, John Fords heirs 640
Sychamore, Martin Armstrong 866 ac; Jno Carson 280; Jno Rice
& John Sappington 636; David Edward 575 Sychamore; John Drew
640 acres Sulpher fork
p.279   Order Clerk cause af^{sd} Land to be twice published in
Nashville Gazette, once in Gazette at Knoxville, with amount
of Taxes & costs due thereon.

Court Adjourns untill Court in Course
John Philips, Benjn Menees, Martin Duncan

p.280   Robertson County.   Monday Morning, February 6th 1804.
Present the Worshipfull Benjamin Menees, James Crabtree, and
William Johnson Esquires

Thos Woodard constable sworn to attend Grand Jury
Deed Martha Stark to Elisha Bellemy 50 acres proven by Asa
Woodward
James H Bryan took oaths required of Justice/Peace

State vs Charles Bowls. Indictment. Jesse Walker, Robt Dunning, Saml Horsley, Benjn Volentine ack^d selves each bound to

State 100 Dollars for appearance to give Testamony on behalf State ag^t Charles Bowls

State vs John Young. Indictment determined last Court, Def^t fined 40 Dollars. This Term it was moved by Def^t attorney to have fine mitigated. Court mitigates fine, sum Twenty Doll^s and costs. County solicitor prayed appeal to Superior Court. Def^t paid s^d Sum of Twenty Dollars

p.281 Deed James Menees Sh^{ff} to Wm Black 640 acres ackd
Deed William Milsap Senr to William Dickson 196 acres proven by Benjn Menees Esqr
Deed John Baker to Martin Walton 320 acres proven by Wm Sale
Deed John Caffery to And^w Jackson 640 acres proven by Leven Donelson
Deed John Hutchins to And^w Jackson 624 acres proven by Leven Donelson
Deed James Menees Sheriff to William Milsap 196 acres ackd
Deed James Menees Collector to Robert Nelson 640 ac^s originally John Porterfields ackd
Deed James Menees Collector to Robert Nelson 274 ac^s originally Wm Caswells ackd
Deed Wilber Cherry to Saml Hollis 266 acres proven by Matt^w Luter(Suter?) Senr
Deed John D Robins to Anthony Jones 110 ac^s proven by Waddy Jones & Richard Nuckolls

Harbert Flewellen app^{td} Constable; bond 500 Doll^s, Whitmill Harrington, Wm Flewellen and Shaderick Rawls his securities

B/S William Haggard to Wm Johnson proven by Henry Johnson

Deed John D Robins to heirs of Edward Butler 62 acres proven by Thomas Johnson
Deed James Menees Sheriff to George Hauser 1027 acres ackd
Deed/Gift Wm Heath to Elijah Heath admitted on certificate & seal of Garrard County, Kentucky

p.282 Whitmill Harrington before Benjn Menees a Justice of Robertson County made oath he had a Note on Larkin Ryle date Jany 5 or 2 1797 to amount of 180 Dollars, which note he has lost. Also sworn in Open Court Feby 6th 1804. Thomas Johnson

James Appleton S^r excused from serving as a Juror this Term. Also John Sommerville

Jonathan Young Junr app^{td} Constable; bond 500 Dollars, John Young & Adam Clap his securities

James Payne appt^d Constable; bond 500 Dollars, Thomas Yates

& John Payne his securities
Court Adjourns untill tomorrow 10 OClock A.M.

Tuesday Morning February 7ᵗʰ 1804   Present John Philips,
John Hutchison, Martin Duncan, Charles Miles, James Norfleet

Nathaniel A McNairy Esqʳ produced Licence and is admitted to
practice Law as an Attorney.
Thomas J Overton Esqʳ produced a License to practice Law and
was accordingly admitted

Thomas Norris Senʳ recorded his stock mark
Moses Winters recorded his stock mark

p.283 John Doe on demise of Wᵐ P Anderson vs Ezekiel Polk.
Robert Nelson & Thomas Johnson appᵗᵈ surveyors to survey the
disputed claim; Jnᵒ Baker, Elias Fort Jʳ, Jnᵒ Gardner, Jiles
Connell jurors to attend with surveyors; return three plots
of their proceedings to next Court

Joshua Bowden vs Elisha Chick. A/B. Present Jnᵒ Philips, Jaˢ
Norfleet, Chas Miles, John Hutchison, Isaac Philips, Martin
Duncan, J Crabtree Esqrs. April 1803 plᶠ by John C Hamilton;
defᵗ did not appear; Octʳ 1803 Judgement by Default agᵗ Dᶠᵗ.
Febʸ 1804 jury Moses Beason, Tignal Martin, John Cheatham, Wᵐ
Sale, James Stark, William Benson, Jaˢ England, Chaˢ Bradon,
Arthur Pitt, Levi Moore, Bazel Boren, Jacob Shores, who find
for Plᵗᶠ; assess damage one Cent; also costs of suit

Thomas Appleton to oversee Road in room of Anthony Jones
B/S Isaac Clark to Samuel McMurry proven by John Appleton

p.284 Jnᵒ Holland vs Joseph Dorris. Case. Present Jnᵒ Phil-
ips, Jaˢ Norfleet, Chaˢ Miles, Jnᵒ Hutchison, Isaac Philips,
Martin Duncan, James Crabtree Esqʳˢ. July 1803 plᵗ by Thoˢ
Stuart; defᵗ by Jnᵒ C Hamilton. Febʸ 1804 jury Moses Beason,
Tignal Martin, Jnᵒ Cheatham, Wᵐ Sale, Jaˢ Stuart, Wᵐ Benson,
James England, Chaˢ Bradon, Arthur Pitt, Levi Moore, Anthony
Jones, Jacob Shores, find for Plᵗᶠ damage 10 Dollˢ; & costs

Isaac Johnson vs James Latham. Attachment. Eli Jones, garnishee, swears he owes sᵈ Latham $10.87½. Anderson Cheatham
owes $10.81½. Thomas Johnson owes 17.50. Polly Hunter owes
1.00. William Johnson owes 16.32. Levi Noyes owes 14.91.
Elijah Bridgewater swears he owes nothing

Deed Elijah Hamilton to James Johnson 320 acres proven by
Josiah Fort
Deed Smith Oglevie to Sugg Fort 274 acres proven by Joseph

Fort
B/S Martin W Wickliff to Henry Johnson for Negro Boy proven
by Budy Browning

p.285 Order road laid off from Springfield to Russelville as
far as State Line, to meet the road opened by order of Logan
Court. Jury John Williams, Henry Johnson, Simon Fikes, Chas
McIntosh, John McElhainey, Nimrod McIntosh, Willie Skinner

Order James Menees Shff released from Taxes for 1802 on 3840
acres in name of Oliver Smith, listed twice for that year

B/S Zachariah Betts to Jno Appleton for Negro proven by Saml
McMurry
B/S Isaac Turman to John Appleton for Negro proven by Archer
Cheatham
Jacob Childress bound by Indenture to Jacob Pinkly untill he
arrives to age twenty one years

Jurors to next Court John Carr, James Stuart, John Gardner,
James Atkins, Jesse Martin, Wm Conyers, Ezekiel Polk, Philip
Parchment, Wm Johnston R R, James Johnston, Elias Fort Junr,
Eppa Lawson, Volentine Choate, Elijah Bridgewater, Sampson
Matthews, James McDonald, James Sawyers, John Simmons Senr,
Charles Wheaton, Wm Edwards, Benjamin Porter, James Bell, Wm
Crocket, Jno Hyde, Thos Hunter, Jas Hunt, Jacob Moake, David
Henry, John Crocket, Richd Nuckolls, Jno Krisel, John Couts,
Abraham Young Senr, Thomas Kilgore Jr, William Armstrong Jr,
Charles Kilgore, William Byrd, Joseph Payne
Court Adjourns untill Tomorrow Morning 9 OClock

Wednesday Morning Feby 8th 1804
Present John Philips, Thomas Strain, Charles Miles, Esquires

B/S William Benson to Archer Cheatham, two Negroes ackd
Nimrod McIntosh recorded his stock mark

p.286 Thomas Hopkins vs Abraham Standley. Case. Present John
Philips, Thos Strain, Isaac Philips, Wm Johnson Esqrs, Octr
1803 plff by Wm Smith; deft by Thos Stuart. Feby jury Moses
Beason, Tignal Martin, Charles Bradon, John Cheatham, James
England, Levi Moore, Arthur Pitt, James Stark, Wm Sale, Wm
Benson, Asa Parker, Whitmill Harrington who find for Plff &
assess his damage 60 Dollars 11 cents; also costs of suit

Deed Daniel Young to Hardy S Bryan 250 acres proven by John
Earthman
Deed John H Hauser to John Chowning 400 acres proven by Thos
Johnson

Ltrs/Admn granted Whitmill Harrington on estate of Robert
Adair. Bond 500 Doll^s, Moses Winters & Shadrick Rawls secur^y

Jurors to next Superior Court Henry Gardner, Josiah Skinner,
Obediah Bounds, Lovick Ventress, William Karr

p.287 Stephen Boren vs Thos G Walke & Joseph Johnson. Debt.
Present John Philips, Benjn Menees, Martin Duncan, Ja^s Crab-
tree. Octr 1803 pl^f by Peter R Booker; def^t by Bennet Searcy
& Thos Stuart. Feby jury Moses Benson, Tignal Martin, Chas
Bradon, John Cheatham, Ja^s England, Levi Moore, Arthur Pitt,
James Stark, William Sale, William Benson, Asa Parker, Whit-
mill Harrington who find for pl^{tf} debt 108 Dollars, damage 5
Dollars 6 cents; also costs of suit in that behalf expended

Shaderick Rawls vs Thos G Walke. Appeal. Present John Philips, Martin Duncan, Ja^s Crabtree. Feby 1804 appeal Returned,
Pl^{tf} by Jno C Hamilton; Def^t by Thos Stuart. Jury Moses Benson, Tignal Martin, Chas Bradon, John Cheatham, Ja^s England,
Levi Moore, Arthur Pitt, James Stark, Wm Sale, William Benson, Asa Parker, Whitmill Harrington, find for Pl^{tf}; assess
Damage to 16 2/3 cents; also costs of suit

p.288 Tennessee vs Robert Warren. Indictment against King &
Browning wherein Robert Warren was prosecutor, was malicious
or frivolous; it is opinion of Court that said Warren prosecutor shall pay the attornies fee, and the attorney Imployed
by Edward King & George Browning

Order that County Trustee & State Treasurer refund to Benjn
Menees & Philip Parchment the amount of money for which Ja^s
G Bickhouse's land was sold for taxes of 1800 & 1801, it ap-
pearing that there was no such Land

State vs Charles Bowls. Benjn Volentine witness proves three
days attendance, 100 miles traveling

Following land advertised in Knoxville & Nashville gazettes:
For 1802 Abraham Thomas 545 acres, David Shelton 274 acres,
Charles Simmons 640 acres, John Drew 640 acres
For 1803 Abisha Thomas 545 ac^s, David Shelton 274 ac^s, Chas
Simmons 640 ac^s, John Fords heirs 640 ac^s, Martin Armstrong
866 ac^s, John Carson 280 ac^s, John Rice & Jno Sappington 636
ac^s, David Edwards 575 ac^s, John Drew 640 ac^s. Judgement entered against s^d Lands for taxes, costs & charges due thereon. Sheriff to sell as much of each tract as shall be sufficient to pay taxes & costs due thereon

John Philips & Martin Duncan Esq^{rs} app^{td} to settle with adm^x
of estate of Daniel Holland dec^d delivered the settlement

Court Adjourns untill Court in Course
                    Benjamin Menees, Isaac Philips, Martin Duncan

p.289   Robertson County.   Monday Morning May 7th 1804
Presesent the Worshipfull   John Philips, Benjn Menees, Hardy
S Bryan, William Johnson, and John Hutchison, Esquires

Grand Jurors   Ezekiel Polk foreman, Volentine Choate, Elisha
Bridgewater, Jesse Martin, Richd Nuckolls, Philip Parchment,
Chas Wheaton, Thos Kilgore Jr, Sampson Matthews, John Gard-
ner, John Couts, Abraham Young Senr, Elias Fort Junr, Joseph
Payne, William Conyers

Hutchins G Burton Esqr produced Licence to practice Law, and
was admitted accordingly

Benjn Chapman recorded his stock mark
James Bell recorded his stock mark
Archer Cheatham admitted to keep an ordinary one year; bond
500 Dolls, Wm Milsap & Stephen Boren securities
Nancy Pankey admitted to keep an ordinary one year; bond 500
Dolls, Volentine Choate & John Simmons securities
John Huey admitted to keep an ordinary one year; gave bond
500 Dollars, Wm Briscoe & Wm Crunk his securities
Deed David Smith & Obedience Smith to Eppa Lawson   200 acres
proven by Sugg Fort
Deed Matthew Luter to Matthew Luter Junr   75 acres proven by
Isaac Dortch
Deed Isham Rogers to Matthew Morris   125 acres ackd
Deed Sampson Matthews to John Hutchison   6 acres ackd

p.290 Deed/Gift James McElyea to children of Mary Wit: Wil-
liam, Thomas, Sarah, Phebe, proven by Bazel Boren
Deed Elisha Bridgewater to Jno Hutchison 150 acres proven by
James Sawyers
Deed Samuel Crocket & Patrick Martin to Samuel Hollis, Peter
Brawner, Benjn Wood, Thomas Martin & William Carter, 2 acres
ackd
Power/Atty Leml Sugg to William Fort proven by Sugg Fort

Eppa Lawson excused from serving as a Juror this Term
Court Adjourns for one Hour. Court met. Present John Philips, Benjn Menees, Isaac Philips

William Flewellen vs John Cheatham. Case. Present John Philips, Benjn Menees, Isaac Philips. Jany 1803 Pltf by John C

Hamilton & Bennet Searcy; def^t by Thos Stuart. May 1804 Jury Ja^s Stuart, Wm Crocket, John Simmons Senr, Ja^s McDonald, Jno Hyde, Jacob Moake, Jno Crocket, Thos Hunter, David Henry, Wm Byrd, Benjn Porter, Wm Johnston find for Pl^{tf}; assess Damage 40 Dollars; also costs.   Joseph Wimberley witness 4 days, Isham Rogers 1 day, 70 miles, 2 ferriages

p.291 Isaac Johnson vs James Latham. Attachment. Eli Jones a garnishee swears he owes Ten Doll^s 87½ c^{ts}

John Stump vs And^w Morris & John Blackburn. Judgement before Justice/Peace for $47.03½ & 50 c^{ts} costs. Levied on 181½ ac^s on Buzzard Creek property of And^w Morris.   Court orders Sh^{ff} sell af^{sd} land to satisfy judgement & costs
Court Adjourns untill tomorrow Morning 9 OClock

Tuesday Morning May 3rd 1804.   Present the Worshipfull Benjamin Menees, Charles Miles, William Connell, Esquires

Daniel Holman vs Uriah Swann. Appeal. Present Benjn Menees, Chas Miles, Wm Connell, Esq^{rs}. Octr 1803 pl^f by Bennet Sear- cy; df^t by J C Hamilton. Jury (blank) find for pl^f; assess damages (blank). Def^t obtains new tryal. Continued. May 1804 Jury James Stuart, Wm Crocket, Jno Simmons S^r, Ja^s McDonald, John Hyde, Jacob Moake, John Crocket, Thomas Hunter, David Henry, Wm Byrd, Benjn Porter, Wm Johnston find for Def^t. Ja^s Yates witness proves 4 days attendance. Thos Kilgore 6 days

p.292 Order James Norfleet and John Philips Esqr let to low- est bidder the maintainance of Isaac Williams for one year from Feby Term 1804, he being a poor man now on the parish

Isaac Dortch Esqr, Commissioner of the Revenue, returned his List of Taxable property taken by him under the late law, & for his services the Court allow him Sixty Dollars

Roger B Sappington adm^r of Mark B Sappington dec^d vs Jesse Martin. Case. Present Benjn Menees, John Hutchison, Thomas Strain, Esqs. Octr 1803 pl^f by W Smith; def^t by Thos Stuart; Cont^d. May 1804 Jury Ja^s Stuart, Wm Crocket, Jno Simmons S^r, Ja^s McDonald, Jno Hyde, Jacob Moake, Jno Crocket, Thos Hunt- er, David Henry, Wm Byrd, Benjn Porter, Wm Johnston who find for def^t. Thomas Choate witness proves 3 days attendance 160 miles traveling & 4 ferriages; Nicholas Conrod 2 days

Order Matthew Luter Sr oversee in room of Jesse Martin, road from Jonathan Stephenson to Nashville to ford of Sychamore, and same hands work under him that worked under sd Martin

147

Whitmill Harrington adm^r of estate of Robert Adair delivered
inventory; order adm^r sell property of s^d estate

p.293   John Doe on demise of W^m P Anderson vs Ezekiel Polk.
Ejectment. Present Benjn Menees, Jno Hutchison, Wm Johnson,
Esqrs. February 1804, pl^{tf} by P W Humphreys; def^t by Bennet
Searcy. Def^t Ezekiel Polk comes into Court, ack^d service of
Writ of Declaration. May Jury John Carr, James Sawyers, John
Krisel, Wm Edwards, Ja^s Atkins, Nathan Clark, Jiles Connell,
John Gardner, Wm Briscoe, Elias Fort Junr, Joseph Robertson,
Willie Skinner who find Defendant Not Guilty. Elias Fort J^r
juror proves 3 days attendance; John Gardner 3 days as juror

Jacob Neill vs Henry Fiser. Attachment. Present Thos Strain,
Benjn Menees, Martin Duncan, Wm Johnson, Esq^{rs}. Peter Fiser
garnishee says he has no property of Henry Fiser, nor knows
of no other person who has

Moses Winters to oversee road in room of Ja^s Stuart
W^m B Vinson apptd overseer of road in room of Wm Briscoe

Deed Jacob McCarty to James H Bryan 2 acres ackd
Deed William Johnson to Barton Crates 298 acres ackd

p.294   Roger B Sappington adm^r of Mark B Sappington dec^d vs
James Foster. Attachment. Present Benjn Menees, Wm Johnson,
Martin Duncan, Thos Strain, Esqrs.   Writ returned Octr 1803
"Not found." Judicial Attachment issued, returned Feby Term
1804 "Levied on 12 ½ cents." Pl^{tf} by Wm Smith; def^t failing
to appear, judg^{mt} by default. May Jury Ja^s Stuart, Wm Crock-
et, John Simmons S^r, Ja^s McDonald, Jacob Moake, Jno Crocket,
John Hyde, Thos Hunter, David Henry, Wm Byrd, Benjn Porter,
James Sawyers assess pl^{tf}'s damage to 106 Dollars; and costs

B/S Wm Ragsdale to Thomas Yates proven by W^m B Vinson
B/S Wm Flewellen & Harbert Flewellen to Jesse Martin proven
by Elijah Hughs

James Norfleet & Jno Philips report they let Isaac Williams,
now on the Parish, to Thomas Hunter, lowest bid, for 45 Dollars untill 1st Monday in Feby next. Hunter's bond 200 Doll^s

James Stuart excused from serving longer as juror this Term

Jury apptd to lay off road from Springfield to Kentucky line
made report

p.295 Deed Levi Noyes to Wm Easten 7 Lots in Springfield ack
Deed William Karr to Michael Fiser 102½ acres ackd
Deed William Karr to Jacob Damewood 117½ acres ackd

Augustine Cook appt^d Constable; bond 1000 Dollars; Volentine Choate & Meredith Walton his securities; took oaths Court adjourns untill tomorrow Morning 9 OClock

Wednesday Morning May 9th 1804   Present John Philips, Benjn Menees, Thomas Strain, John Hutchison, Charles Miles, Esqrs

Richard Napier vs Montgomery Bell and Ge^o Lamb. [Present the justices named above] Feby 1804 Pl^{tf} by Bennet Searcy; def^t by Matthew Lodge. May Jury William Crocket, John Simmons, James McDonald, John Hyde, Jacob Moake, John Crocket, Thomas Hunter, David Henry, William Byrd, Benjn Porter, John Carr, James Atkins who find for Pltf; assess damage to 378 Dollars 68 cents & 4 mills; also his costs

p.296 Wm Johnston excused from Serving longer this Term as a Juror

Deed James Menees Sheriff to James Karr, Wm Karr, John Karr, Robt Karr, 640 acres ackd

Stephen Jett vs Elisha Cheek. A/B. Present Jno Philips, Thos Strain, Benjamin Menees, Chas Miles, Esq^{rs}. Feby 1804 pl^f by Bennet Searcy, d^{ft} by Jno C Hamilton & Thos Stuart. May 1804 jury Ja^s Sawyers, John Krisel, Wm Edwards, Nicholas Conrod, Shaderick Rawls, Peter Fiser, Levi Noyes, Joseph Fry, Bazel Boren, Wm Briscoe, Jo^s Wimberley, Joseph Robertson, who find for Def^t. Pl^{tf} obtained appeal to Superior Court; bond with Bennet Searcy & Chas Miles his securities. Maj^r John Young, witness, proves 2 days attendance

Isaac Johnson vs James Latham. Attachment. Polly Hunter garnishee swears she owes Latham 1 Dollar.

Jurors to next Court Hugh Henry, Andrew Irwin, David Jones, Ja^s Mayo, Benjn Chapman, Isaac Doris Jr, John Hardin, Joseph Latimer, Thos Holman, John Trice, Robt Wilson, Wyatt Bishop, Stephen Boren, Anderson Cheatham, John Duncan, Jesse Jones, David Spence, John Robins, James Gambril, John Siglar, Theophilus Morgan, Wm Spiller, Jacob Cook, Richard Hutchins, Wm Deloach, William Dorris, John Baker, James Blackwell, Silas Crane, John Crane, Nicholas Conrod, Ja^s Elliott, James Gardner, George Murphey Junr, Henry Hyde, Allen Parker, Michael Shannon, Robert Perry, William Hunt

p.297 Philip Hornbarger vs John Knight. Appeal. Present Jno Philips, Thos Strain, Hardy S Bryan Esq^{rs}. May 1804 pl^{tf} by Thos Stuart; Jury Wm Crocket, Jno Simmons Sn^r, Ja^s McDonald, Jno Hyde, Jacob Moake, John Crocket, Thos Hunter, David Henry, William Byrd, Benjn Porter, John Carr, James Atkins, who find for pl^{tf}, assess damge to 27 Dollars 11 cents; also his costs of suit. Nicholas Conrod witness proves 2 days attendance; Benjn Menees 2 days

W^{m} D Dorris records his stock mark
Nathan Clark app^{td} Captain of Patrollers in room of Wm Crunk

Isaac Johnson vs James Latham. Attachment. Anderson Cheatham Garnishee owes $10.81+. Thomas Johnson garnishee owes 17.50. Levi Noyes garnishee owes 14.91. Wm Johnson g^{ee} owes 16.32

On petition of James Mayo attorney for Julius Elmore one of the Legatees of Samuel Tucker dec^{d}, ordered that Jno Hutchison Es^{q}r attend as Surveyor with Jurors James Sawyers, James Appleton S^{r}, David Jones S^{r}, James Jones S^{r}, Saml McMurry on the premises to lay off and value lands of the estate agreeable to Law amongst legatees of s^{d} Tucker dec^{d}

John Crocket to oversee road in room of David Henry
Deed W^{m} P Anderson to John Cheatham 1 lot in Springfield proven by W^{m} B Vinson

p.298 William P Anderson vs John Gardner. Ejectment. Order Thomas Johnson attend on premises & find the interference in dispute, following jurors attend: Ezekiel Polk, Elias Fort J^{r}, Jiles Connell, Thomas Polk; surveyor & jurors to meet on third Monday in June next. The same as to Henry Gardner & s^{d} Anderson

Benjamin Menees J^{r} app^{td} Collector of Taxes for present year gave Bond 2000 Dollars with Benjn Menees Senr, Philip Parchment, William Flewellen his securities; took oath

Court Adjourns untill Court in Course
John Philips, Benjn Menees, Thomas Strain, Joseph Doris

p.299 August 6th 1804. Springfield. Present the Worshipfull Benjamin Menees, William Johnson, John Hutchison, James H Bryan, Esquires

Grand Jurors John Baker foreman, John Harden, George Murphey Junr, James Elliott, Theophilus Morgan, James Mayo, Thomas Holman, William Doris, Richard Hutchins.
James Payne, constable, sworn to attend on the Grand Jury

Roger B Sappington vs Ja^s Doherty. Original attachment. Levied on 70 acres joining Springfield; Judgement before Justice/Peace $46.24 and 50 cents costs. Court orders property attached be sold to satisfy judgment & costs

Deed John Dobbins to John Syraker 10 acres proven by George Parks
Deed Josiah Turpin to William Reed 100 acres proven by Ge° Parks
Deed Josiah Turpin to Edmund Turpin 100 acres proven by Ge° Parks
Deed Joseph Dickson to Jonathan Pairs 228 acres proven by Wm Hammond
Deed Robert Wilson to Michael Shannon 160 acres ackd
Deed Jonathan Piairs, Israel Mials 228 acres proven by William Hammond

p.300 Shaderick Rawls vs Lemuel Sugg. Feby 1804 pl^{tf} by Thos Stuart; Def^t by Bennet Searcy & P R Booker. August 1804 jury William Hunt, Wyatt Bishop, Henry Hyde, David Spence, Joseph Latimer, Jesse Jones, Andrew Irwin, William Deloach, Robert Perry, Isaac Dorris Junr, James Gardner, David Jones. After which the pl^{tf} is Non suited.

John Baker J^r summoned as witness in above suit behalf Shaderick Rawls did not appear; order he forfeit; Si fa to issue

John Sherod to oversee road from Calebs Creek to Brush Creek leading from Springfield to Clarksville, to have same hands formerly alloted to John Carr

Jacob Shore vs Isham Rogers. Case. Octr 1803 pl^{tf} by Thomas Stuart; def^t by Jn° C Hamilton. Augt 1804 Jury Wm Hunt, Wyatt Bishop, Henry Hyde, David Spence, Joseph Latimer, Jesse Jones, And^w Irwin, William Deloach, Robert Perry, Isaac Dorris J^r, James Gardner, David Jones who find for pltf; assess damage 11 Dollars 45 cents; also his costs

Deed Alexander McNeely to James Vaughn 127 acres proven by Wm Spiller

p.301 Roger B Sappington adm^r M B Sappington dec^d vs Benjn Wallace. Present John Philips, Isaac Dortch, James Crabtree, Benjn Menees. July 1802 writ ag^t Benjn Wallace; returned Oct 1803 "Not found." Judicial attachment issued 27 Octr 1803; returned by Sheriff Feby 1804 "Levied on 12+ cents" at which Term pl^{tf} appeared by Wm Smith his att^y. Def^t not appearing, judgement by Default. Augt 1804 jury Allen Parker, John Duncan, John Robins, Hugh Henry, William Spiller, Robt Willson, Stephen Boren, John Crane, John Gardner, Nimrod McIntosh,

Sampson Matthews, Perry Cohea, who find for pl^{tf}; damage 70 Dollars 20 cents; also costs of suit

Obed Davis delivers himself to Court in exhonaration of his bail in suit William Gulledge against s^d Davis; John Brooks ack^d himself s^d Davis's security

Deed W^m D Watson to Thomas Woodard 450 acres proven by Thos Johnson
Deed James Menees Sh^{ff} to Levi Moore 320 acres ackd
Will of Thomas Norris dec^d proven by William Norris

p.302 Nathan Arnet vs Jno Robins adm^r of John Tucker. Debt. Feby 1804 pl^{tt} by P W Humphreys; def^t by Wm Smith. Augt 1804 Jury Wm Hunt, Wyatt Bishop, Henry Hyde, David Spence, Joseph Latimer, And^w Irwin, Robert Perry, Isaac Dorris, James Gardner, David Jones, William Spiller, John Duncan, who find for Pl^{tt} 20 Dollars 92 Cents. Also costs of suit. Abel Williams witness proves 4 days attendance; Griffith Williams 3 days

Deed Susannah Hart to David London 640 acres proven by George Turner
Deed Robert Prince to James Blackwell 320 acres ackd
Deed James Karr to Solomon Squire 100 acres proven by Henry Johnson
Deed Elisha Bellemy to William Connell 50 acres proven by Archibald Mahon

Isaac Dorris app^{td} Constable; bond 1000 Dollars, John Dorris & John Hutchison his securities; took oath

James Miles app^{td} Constable; bond 1000 Doll^s, Aaron Winters & Nicholas Conrod his securities; took oath

p.303 William Emson and Rebekah Emson bound by Indenture to Elijah Biggs until they arrive to full age
Caleb Emson bound by Indenture to Dickison Hall until he arrives to the age of 21 years
Perry Cohea admited to keep an Ordinary for one year; bond 1000 Dollars, John Hutchison & Augustine Cook, securities
Thomas Norris to oversee road in room of Jacob Pinkley
Michael Shannon excused from serving as a Juror this Term
Jacob Cook excused from serving as a Juror this Term
Wm Armstrong Junr to oversee road in room of Bartimias Pack
Benjamin Porter to oversee road in room of James Bell
John H Bowen Esqr produced Licence to practice law as an attorney; accordingly admited
Court Adjourns untill tomorrow Morning 9 OClock

Tuesday Morning Augᵗ 7ᵗʰ 1804
Present Benjamin Menees, Isaac Philips, Charles Miles, Esqr

James Menees Esqʳ, Collector of State & County Tax for 1803,
reported following tract not returned for taxation: George
Hook 274 acres lying on Bartons Creek. Order Clerk transmit
copy of same to printers of Knoxville and Nashville Gazettes
together with amount of taxes costs & charges thereon

p.304 Robert Prince vs Benjⁿ Menees Jʳ. Ejectment. Aug 1804
jury Wᵐ Hunt, Wyatt Bishop, Henry Hyde, David Spence, Joseph
Latimer, Jesse Jones, Andʷ Irwin, Wᵐ Deloach, Robert Perry,
Isaac Dorris Junʳ, James Gardner, David Jones, who find the
Defᵗ Guilty; assess damage to one cent; also costs of suit

John Irwin vs Montgomery Bell. Case. Febʸ 1804 plᶠ by Bennet
Searcy Esqʳ; defᵗ by Matthew Lodge Esqʳ. Augᵗ 1804 jury Wil-
liam Hunt, Wyatt Bishop, Henry Hyde, David Spence, Joseph
Latimer, Jesse Jones, Andrew Irwin, William Deloach, Robert
Perry, Isaac Doris Jʳ, James Gardner, David Jones, find for
pltf; assess damge to 167 Dollars 49½ cents; also costs

Deed James Menees Sheriff to John Simmons and Edward Simmons
640 acres ackd

p.305 Benjamin Shaw vs Isaac Johnson. Trespass with force of
arms. May 1804 plᶠᶠ by John C Hamilton; defᵗ by Thoˢ Stuart.
Augᵗ 1804 Jury William Hunt, Wyatt Bishop, Henry Hyde, David
Spence, Joseph Latimer, Jesse Jones, Andʷ Irwin, Wᵐ Deloach,
Robert Perry, Isaac Dorris Junʳ, James Gardner, Allen Parker
who find for Plᶠᶠ; damage 30 Dollars; also his costs. Elijah
Spiller witness proves 1 day attendance

Deed Nathan Smith to Nancy D Hatch 60 acres proven by John W
Bryan

Report of arbitrators of controversy wherein Samˡ Robins is
plᶠᶠ and John Young defᵗ. Find for the defᵗ. Augᵗ 7ᵗʰ 1804.
David Jones, James Appleton, Thomas Kilgore, James Yates.
Richard Nuckolls a witness proves 2 days attendance; Julius
Elmore 5 days, 70 miles & 2 ferriages; Levi Noyes 2 days

Isaac Dortch Esqʳ allowed 40 Dollars in addition to that allowed him last Term for his services as Revenue officer

p.306 Elected John Cheatham sheriff for ensuing two years,
bond 10,500 Dollars, with William Milsap, Joseph Robertson,
Joseph Castleberry his securities; took oath

Josiah Fort Esqʳ app'd County Trustee; gave Bond with Wyatt

Bishop & Matthew Day his securities

Archibald Mahon elected coroner; bond 5000 Dollars, William Deloach & Jacob Pinkley his securities

State vs Stuart Thornton. A/B. Thornton's Appearance bond 100 Dollars, John Krisel & Jacob Pickren each 50 Dollars, s^d Thorntons security

Wm Deloach excused from serving as a juror this Term

Clerk and Sheriff allowed 50 Dollars each for their exoficio services for the past year

John Philips & James Crabtree Esqrs to let to lowest bidder Daniel McDaniel, who is on the parish

Order Nicholas Conrod be repaid his taxes on 640 acres sold in name of Jesse Nelson three times, which James Meness Collector is ordered to pay sd Conrod

John Chowning to oversee road of Charles Bradon & have same hands
Peter Spence to oversee road in room of Abel Williams
John Cromwell to oversee road in room of James Johnston; the same hands to work under him

p.307 Ordered that a road be laid off from County Line near Thos Harrisons to the Logan Road near Bazel Boren, following jurors to mark same: Joseph Boren, Isaac Dorris, Benjn Chapman, Amos Cohea, John Hutchison; persons who signed the petiton for s^d road shall open the same

B/S William Homes to Samuel Crocket for Negro girl proven by Allen Parker

Isaac Dortch, Commissioner of Revenue, reported land not given in for taxation

Pierce Asbels heirs	70 ac^s joining Springfield & one lot in Springfield
Richard Cook	50 ac^s joining Renfro on Bush Creek
Isaac Roberts	548 on Sychamore
Isaac Williams	140 on Spring Creek of Sulpher fork where he lives
And^w Brakie	640 acres Gilkison Creek
James Glasgow	1000 acres mouth of Sychamore
James Greenlee	640 Elk fork
William Holeness	640 Karrs Creek--double tax p^d into office
Robert Hopkins	640 acres Sychamore

154

James M Lewis	2560 acres Millers Creek
do	1280 acres on the ridge
Thomas Williams	640 acres waters Sychamore
Martin Armstrong	866 Karrs & Millers Creeks 2 tracts
John Cummins	1000 acres on Sychamore
Benjn McCullochs heirs	274 joining Moses Winters
"	joining J G Buhon waters Red River
"	640 waters of Red River
"	640 Winters Creek
"	640 between Millers Cr & Sychamore
Laughlin Flynn	640 head of Calebs Creek
John Sutton	100 Red River
Robt Stothart	100 where Henry Wigle lives
Doctr Butler	228 Sulpher Fk pd double tax & cost
Joseph Shaw	540 head of Sulpher fork
John Coleman	640 Sychamore
Thos Davis	640 joining survey wich includes Turnbulls Clay lick
p.308 Uel Lamkin	200 acres Calebs Creek
Levin Powel	640 west boundary of Jacob McCarty on Sulpher fork
"	640 Spring Creek of Red River
"	640 east of road from Harkins to Barren River
"	640 Red River
William Macbean	640 incl Goose pond. pd to clerk
William Surry(Lurry?)	640 on N side Middle fork Red River
Zarubabul Staks heirs	one lot in Springfield
Charles Simmons	one lot in Springfield
Jesse Rascoe	one lot in Springfield
John Pankey	one lot in Springfield

Ordered Clerk transmit list to printers of Knoxville & Nashville Gazettes together with amount of taxes & costs due
Court Adjourns untill Tomorrow Morning 9 OClock

Wednesday Morning August 8th 1804
Present John Philips, Charles Miles, James H Bryan, Esqrs

John Duncan to oversee road in room of Geo Browning

On a Petition of Isabella Butler to have her dower laid off, order Sheriff summon county surveyor and 12 jurors to attend on premises to lay off afsd widows dower

Order Elisabeth Tucker be allowed out of the estate of John Tucker decd 20 Dollars for the past 6 months keeping a child of sd John Tucker

Deed John Hardin and Moses Hardin to John Parks 110 acres

proven by Joseph Latimer

Matthew Morris admited to keep an ordanary for one year;
bond 500 Dollars, Matthew Day and John Brooks securities

p.309 William P Anderson vs Dann Lynn. Covenant broken. May
1804 pl^{tf} by P W Humphreys; def^t by Wm Smith. August jury W^m
Hunt, Wyat Bishop, Henry Hyde, David Spence, Joseph Latimer,
Jesse Jones, And^w Irwin, Robt Perry, Isaac Dorris J^r, James
Gardner, Allen Parker and John Duncan find for Pl^{tf}; assess
damage to 52 Dollars 19 cents; also costs of suit

Isaac Johnson vs James Latham. Attachment. May 1804 pl^{tf} by
Thos Stuart; pl^{tf}(sic) failing to appear by himself or att^y,
Judgement by default; writ of Enquiry ordered. Augt Jury W^m
Hunt, Wyatt Bishop, Henry Hyde, David Spence, Jo^s Latimer,
Jesse Jones, And^w Irwin, Robert Perry, Isaac Dorris J^r, Ja^s
Gardner, Allen Parker, John Duncan, inquire what damage the
pl^{tf} had sustained by his Writ of Enquiry, assess his damage
to 94 Dollars 25 cents 3 mills. Considered by Court that pl^t
recover ag^t def^t 94 Dollars 20 cents 3 mills; also costs

p.310 Isaac Johnson vs Polly Hunter, garnishee for Ja^s Latham. Def^t made oath she is indebted to James Latham 1 Dollar,
Judg^t ag^t Polly Hunter behalf Isaac Johnson for one dollar

Isaac Johnson vs Anderson Cheatham [worded as above] for Ten
Dollars 81½ cents
Isaac Johnson vs William Johnson [worded as above] for six-
teen Dollars 32 cents
Isaac Johnson vs Thos Johnson [worded as above] for 17 Dol-
lars 50 cents
Isaac Johnson vs Levi Noyes. [worded as above] 14 Dollars 91
cents
Isaac Johnson vs Eli Jones [worded as above] Ten Dollars 87½
cents

p.311 Order heretofore made for payment of wolf scalps in
this county is hereby rescinded

James Menees, Collector of State & County Tax has credit for
tax of 1098 acres for 1801. Also, a credit for 14,520 acres
which was a double tax

Deed James Menees, Sh^{ff}, to Samuel Crocket 264 acres ackd

Commissioners app^{td} to let to lowest bidder Daniel McDaniel
who is put on the Parish, has let him to Thomas Woodard for
one year for forty nine Dollars

William Dorris to oversee road in room of Enoch Tucker

John Sevier Governor vs James Menees Collector of County Tax
for 1801 & John James, Joseph Robertson, Andrew Cheatham his
securities; Judg^t is entered for 79 Dollars 97 cents 3 mills

John Sevier Governor vs James Menees [worded as above] for
406 Dollars, 13 cents 2 mills
John Sevier Governor vs James Menees [worded as above] for
371 Dollars 63 cents 5 mills

p.312 State vs Stuart Thornton. Presentment. Def^t submits to
Court; fined one Dollar; fine paid into office

Commissioners app^{td} by Court to settle with County Trustee,
Sheriff & Clerk up to present term, each allowed 10 Dollars

Deed James Menees Sh^{ff} to Nicholas Conrod 40 acres ackd

Jurors to next Court: James Hunt, Jacob Moake, Jacob Lewis,
W^m J Perry, Thos Savage, Richard Matthews, Jno Johnson, John
Pike, Saml Dorris Senr, William Wills, Jno McMillion, Joseph
Payne, Danl Holman, Wm Pate, Adam Clap, Nathan Simmons, An-
derson Cheatham, William Briscoe, Henry Johnson, John John-
son, Jacob Pinkley, John Huey, Nimrod McIntosh, Wm Perry,
Meredith Walton, Levi Moore, Walter Stark, John Krisel, John
Cromwell, Lemuel Sugg, Thos Sellars, Willis Skinner, Holland
Dardin, Jiles Connell, Matthew Luter Jr, John Carr, William
Atkins, James Stewart, Thomas Polk, Mark Noble
Court Adjourns untill tomorrow Morning 9 OClock

Thursday Morning August 9th 1804
Present Benjn Menees, Charles Miles, Archer Cheatham, Esq^{rs}

Jurors to Superior Court: David Jones Senr, Thomas Strain,
James Yates, Josiah Fort

On Motion of Thomas G Walk by his att^o to enter Judgment ag^t
Robt Warren constable for monies by him collected on Judgements, notes & accounts that was put in his hands by s^d Thos
G Walk and which he has not paid & accounted for, upon which
motion the Court ordered continuance untill next court

Benjamin Menees returns one lot in Springfield for taxes of
present year, also one lot in name of John J Dorris
Archer Cheatham returns 640 acres joining Appleton in name
of James Watson for taxes of this year
Levi Noyes returns one Lot in Springfield in name of Nathan
Clark

Court Adjourns untill Court in Course
Benj[n] Menees, Charles Miles, John Hutchison, A Cheatham

p.313   Robertson County. Monday Morning November 5th 1804.
Present the Worshipfull John Philips, Benjamin Menees, John
Hutchison, Esquires

Grand Jurors: John Huey foreman, Richard Matthews, Matthew
Luter Jun[r], Thomas Polk, Nimrod McIntosh, Holland Dardin, W[m]
Pate, John Johnson, William Briscoe, Meredith Walton, Willis
Skinner, Jacob Pinkley, Adam Clap, Sam[l] Dorris Sen[r], William
Wills

Nathaniel W Williams produced a licence to practice law and
was accordingly admited

Samuel Miles security for appearance of Peter Pinkley in
suit Sam[l] Crocket vs s[d] Pinkley surrendered Pinkley to Court

Deed John Stewart to James Felts 200 acres ackd
Deed Robert Weakley to John Stewart 200 acres proven by Ja[s]
Stewart
Deed Jn[o] C Hamilton to Tho[s] J Overton one lot in Springfield
ackd
Deed Lewis Barker to Joseph McDowel 200 acres proven by Ja[s]
Gambril
Deed Lewis Barker to Alex[r] Gordon 200 acres proven by James
Gambril
Deed William Atkins to John Yoes 100 acres proven by W[m] Con-
nell
Deed James Menees Collector to Henry Johnson 89 acres ackd
Deed James Menees Sheriff to Henry Johnson 311 acres ackd

p.314 Nathan Arnet vs John Weakley. Case. May 1804 plt[f] by P
W Humphries; d[ft] by Tho[s] Stuart. Nov[r] 1804 jury Jn[o] Krisel,
Anderson Cheatham, Nath[l] Simmons, Henry Johnson, Mark Noble,
Tho[s] Sellars, Daniel Holman, Jiles Connell, W[m] J[L?] Perry,
Tho[s] Savage, Jacob Moake, Jn[o] Pike who find for pl[tf]; assess
damage 56 Doll[s]; costs. Benj[n] Darrow witness proves one days
attendance; Abel Williams one day, Griffith Williams one day

John Den lessee of Sam[l] Crocket vs Peter Pinkley. On motion
John Cochran the Land Lord comes into Court and prays to be
made Defendant in this suit; granted; brings John Chowning,
Eppaphroditus Benton, and Augustine Cook as his special bail

Power/att^y John Yoes, Wm Atkins, & Nathan Yoes to W^m & Jiles
Connell proven by Pray Phipple
Aaron Lamberts Taxable property for 1804 rec^d by Court: 640
acres on Sychamore. Lovick Ventress agent
B/S Henry W Lawson to Elias Fort for Negro girl proven by
Jiles Connell
John McMillon excused from serving as a Juror this Term
Nathan Clark granted liberty to build a mill on Sulpher fork
on his own Land
p.315 Court Adjourns untill Tomorrow Morning 9 OClock

Tuesday Morning Novr 6th 1804   Present the Worshipfull
Benjamin Menees, James Norfleet, Archer Cheatham, Esquires

Power/att^y Burrwell Bunn to Josiah Fort admited to Record on
Certificate & seal of Nash County, also Certificate of Red-
man Bunn, Chairman of said Court

John Anderson & James Weir vs John Young. Case. August 1804
pl'f by Thomas Stuart; def^t by Bennet Searcy. Novr Term Jury
Anderson Cheatham, Nathl Simmons, Henry Johnson, Mark Noble,
Thos Sellars, Daniel Holman, Giles Connell, William J Perry,
Thomas Savage, Jacob Moake, John Carr, John Pike, who find
for Pl'f; assess damage to 109 Dollars 27 cents; also costs

Order made last Court to lay off road from near Harrisons to
the road near Bazel Borens continued, & same persons to view
it with addition of Bazel Boren, Wm Johnson, and Arthur Pitt

p.316   Hardy S Bryan guardian for Wm Bryan vs Philip Parchment and James H Bryan. Judgement obtained from Benjn Menees
Esqr for 42 Dollars 64 cents, 75 cents costs, on which James
Miles Constable returned "Levied on 228 acres of Land lying
on Calebs Creek." Ordered s^d land be sold

Hardy S Bryan g^du for Wm Bryan vs Philip Parchment & James H
Bryan. Judg^t before Benjn Menees Esqr for 42 Doll^s 64 c^ts, &
50 c^ls costs, on which Ja^s Miles Constable returned "levied
on 228 acres lying on Calebs Creek." Order said land be sold

In consequence of Death of James Hunt who had bound to him a
child James Crow, Court release Hunt's Heirs from any Damage
which might accrue from the Indenture, and ordered that Mary
Crow mother of s^d child be at Liberty to take the Child

Ordered Phebe Tucker child of John Tucker dec^d who was bound
to Travess Elmore released from her Indenture, Jane Engleman
mother of s^d child at liberty take her, with consent of said
Elmore, and Elmore is hereby released from any Damages which

might accrue in consequence of said Indenture

Order road from Springfield to Mrs Butlers altered from the Black Branch, to run to the War Trace Creek; Joseph Robertson, Benjamin Porter, & Wyatt Bishop to lay it off; Anderson Cheatham to be overseer in room of Wm B Vinson

Deed Josiah Skinner to Wᵐ Lunsford 241 acres 41 poles proven by Lemuel Sugg
p.317 Deed /Release from Augustine Lunsford, John Smith and Stephen Lunsford to Wᵐ Lunsford 50 acres proven by Lemˡ Sugg

State vs Benjamin Menees and Anderson Cheatham. Presentment A/B. Defᵗˢ submit, fined one Dollar each & costs

State vs James Hogan. Presentment, A/B. Defᵗ submits; fined one Dollar

John Den Lessee of Samuel Crocket vs Peter Pinkley and John Cochran. Ordered that Henry Johnson & Robᵗ Weakley attend on Premises & make survey and return to our next Court

Order Thoˢ Appleton, James Jones Jʳ, Wm Briscoe, Joseph Robertson, Benjamin Porter, Joshua Smith, Anthony Jones & Silas Tucker be added to Patrollers which Nathan Clark is captⁿ of

Order road laid off from Richard Cavets to Williams Mill on Red River, jury to mark same: Barton Coates, Richᵈ Hutchins, Wᵐ Benson, Wᵐ Johnson, Charles Kilgore; make return to Clerk who is to issue order to Wᵐ Dorris overseer without delay to open sᵈ road. Hands to work under him: Bazel Boren, Wᵐ Holland, Jaˢ Lynn, Dann Lynn, Jaˢ Luck, Jaˢ Benton, Jnᵒ Grimes, Garlant Williams, Larkin Edwards, Simon Fike, Jesse Mason, Josiah Skinner, Thomas Johnson Junʳ, Joseph Pitts, Murrell Pitts, Willis Holland, Elisha Bridgewater, Wᵐ Spiller, Richᵈ Benson, Wᵐ Perry

Order road laid off from Springfield to Jesse Williams Mill on Red River, persons to mark same: Nimrod McIntosh, Thomas McIntosh, George Browning, John McElhainy, William Dorris, John Cromwell. That John Cromwell oversee the road, and that Jesse Williams hands open sᵈ road

p.318 Order a road laid off from Springfield to State Line near Thomas Travess on the far fork of Red River; persons to view & mark: Charles Wheaton, Wᵐ Edwards, Wᵐ Johnson, Abraham Moore, William Sale. John Siglar to be overseer; following work under him: Jacob Siglar, Wᵐ Ragsdale, George Henly, John Henly, James Gambril, James McElyea and Webster Gilbert

Order road from Springfield to Russelville altered: to leave old road one or two hundred yards south of the creek, cross creek below John Couts & Henry Johnsons mill, then intersect old road. Following to mark same: Nimrod McIntosh, George Browning, Thos McIntosh, Edward Cheatham, Anderson Cheatham. Soon as possible after road is laid off John Duncan overseer is to cause it to be opened

Deed James Menees Shff to Alexr Work 640 acres ackd
Deed John I[?] Wiggins & wife to Jas Maxwell 640 acres proven by Bennet Searcy
Deed Henry Johnson to Noah Woodard 400 acres ackd

Titus Benton to oversee road, War Trace Creek to Mrs Butlers & John Couts, John Krisel & Richd Nuckolls & those living on their plantations work on same with the former hands

George Leeland bound by Indenture to Peter Browner untill he arrives to the age of Twenty one years
Deed Matthew Brooks to David Spence 55 acres proven by Peter Pinkley
p.319 The Petition of John Cromwell, Dorsey Cromwell, Rosey Lawrence wife of Jesse Lawrence, Winnifred Cromwell, Garrard Cromwell by John Cromwell his guardian, received by Court, the object is to rectify a mistake on a deed of Conveyance
The Court Adjourns untill tomorrow Morning 10 OClock

Wednesday Morning Novr 7th 1804   Present the Worshipfull
John Philips, Benjamin Menees, Archer Cheatham, Esquires

Levi Noyes app'd Inspector of Cotton gave Bond 1000 Dollars, Henry Gardner and James Norfleet his securities; took oath

Land reported for Nonpayment of Taxes for 1803: 96 acres of which John Dickson is reputed owner on East fork of Bartons Creek, part of 640 acres granted Jno Dickson...Hugh Williamsons line...copy to be published together with amount of tax & costs due thereon

Collector for 1804 to have credit with treasurer for tax due on 640 acres, being twice given in in name of Robert Lee

Edward Cheatham 297 acres admited for taxes of 1803
Order John Couts & Henry Johnson admited to build a mill on Sulpher fork on their own land
A Jury of View app'd last Court to lay off dower of Isabelle Butler widow of Captain Edward Butler decd returned verdict

p.320 Beverley A Allen vs George Evans. Verdict in favour of

Def^t; Judgement given ag^t pl^{tf} for costs. Si fa to issue ag^t Beverley A Allen to revive s^d Judgement for costs af^{sd}

Bazel Boren to oversee Logan Road, from fork where one leads to Springfield, to State Line; John Philips Esqr and Elisha Bridgewater to divide hands between Boren & William Dorris

Elias Lawrence overseer of road to have John Gardners hands to work under him
Due to Josiah Fort, County Trustee, $11.35½ as appears by a settlement this Day made with the Commissioners

Jurors to next Court: James Atkins, Nathan Yoes, Cordal Norfleet, Elijah Pilant, Wm Atkins, Robert Perry, Nicholas Conrod, Ezekiel Polk, Joseph Robertson, John Brooks, Frederick Cob, Edward King, B Jacob Pinkley, Ge^o Browning, Jno Hardin, Wm Armstrong, Abraham Young, Robt Brown, Chas Bradon, Sampson Matthews, Jno Appleton, Andrew Irwin, Richd Jones S^r, Mr Watkins S^r, James Bell, Daniel Pinkley, Danl McKinley, Jacob Damewood, James Long, Lemuel Sugg, Michael Fiser, Wm Crocket

Order County Trustee pay James Menees Three Dollars 37 cents

Order William Connell, Henry Watkins Senr, Thos Kilgore Junr attend ensuing Military Election as Inspectors; Jesse Isaacs & Wyatt Bishop clerks to said Election

Order that Logan Road be altered as Mr Porter has cleared it leading by his house
Anderson Cheatham admited to keep an Ordinary for one year; bond 1000 Dollars, Wyatt Bishop & Arch^d Mahan his securities

Order James Yates be Captain of Patrollers, and that he have liberty to appoint the hands which is to act with him
p.321 Court Adjourns untill Court in Course
John Philips, Benjn Menees, John Hutchison

Records of Robertson Court Feby Term 1805.   Monday Morning February 4th 1805. Springfield.   Present the Worshipfull John Philips, Benjamin Menees, William Johnson, Esquires

Grand Jurors   Abraham Young foreman, George Browning, Jacob Damewood, Andrew Irwin, Richard Jones S^r, Sampson Matthews, James Long, Elisha Pilant, William Atkins, William Crocket, Nathan Yoes, B Jacob Pinkley, Joseph Robertson, Robt Perry, Daniel Pinkley

Thomas Hopkins vs Abraham Standley. Abraham Tippy garnishee swears he is indebted to Abraham Standley for Lott sold for Standley 40 Dollars, one half in country Linning, the other half in money which is booked but not Collected. At Succeeding Term sd Garnishee paid into office $20 and 28½ yards of white country linning and 8 3/4 yards of mixed cotton cloth

William Russel & Archibald Harris vs John James. Wᵐ Shannon security for defᵗ delivered him to Court; Defᵗ gives as bail John Hutchison and Chaˢ Simmons, who in open court in proper persons acknowledge the same

Jacob Lewis excused for his nonattendance last Term as Juror

p.322 Deed William Atkins to Mark Noble 50 acres ackd
Deed Joseph Robertson to Benjamin Porter 60 acres ackd
Deed David London to James Hodges 640 acres proven by Robert Perry
Deed Dann Lynn to James Lynn Senr 74 acres proven by Joshua Rice
Deed or Release Samuel Crocket to James Lee 264 acres proven by Thomas Johnson
Deed James Elliott Senr to James Elliott Jr 150 acres proven by Samuel Elliott
Deed Thomas Whitford to Robert Brown 74 acres proven by Abraham Young
Deed John Brooks to Peter Fiser 109½ acres proven by Michael Fiser
Deed Richard Martin to James Kile 50 acres ackd
Deed Archer Cheatham & Thos Johnson to Richd Jones 320 acres ackd

The Will of James Hunt proven in open court by Miles Kerby & John Hyde subscribing witnesses thereto. Sion Hunt and John Hunt, executors, took oath and recᵈ Letters Testamentary

B/S Joseph Woolfolk to Henry Johnson for a Negro girl proven by Isaac Johnson

The jury to lay off a road from Thomas Harrisons to Logan Rᵈ near Bazel Borens made return
Court Adjourns untill tomorrow Morning 9 OClock

Tuesday Morning Febʸ 5ᵗʰ 1805
Present John Philips, Benjamin Menees, Charles Miles, Isaac Philips, James H Bryan, John Hutchison, Martin Duncan, Esqʳˢ

p.323 Samuel Robins vs John Young. Assᵗ & Battery. Octʳ 1803 pl^{tf} by Jn° C Hamilton, Wm Smith & Thos Stuart; def^t by Bennet Searcy. Con^t untill August 1804 when refered to arbitrament & award of James Appleton Senr, David Jones Senr, James Yates and Thomas Kilgore Junr; if they do not agree for them to choose a fifth man, their award to be judgement of Court. August 7th 1804 arbitrators of opinion pl^{tf} not entitled to damages; consequently find for def^t. Pl^{tf} att^y moved to set aside the award; Novr 1804 Court set aside af^{sd} award. Feby 1805 Jury Frederick Cobb, Henry Watkins, Edward King, Lemuel Sugg, Robert Brown, Michael Fiser, Chas Bradon, Matthew Day, John Gardner, Thos Polk, John Dorris, Francis Boren who find for Def^t. Pl^{tf} obtained appeal to Superior Court; bond with Jn° D Robins & Jn° Chowning securities. Richd Nuckolls, witness, two days attendance; Julius Elmore 7 days, 70 miles, & 2 ferriages; Levi Noyes 2 days; Charles Simmons 3 days; Wm Johnson 9 days; Titus Benton 2 days, [illegible] Mays 8 days

p.324   Order Daniel McKinley Senr, George Browning, Matthew Day and John Brooks to divide hands to work on roads between following overseers: Anderson Cheatham, John Duncan, Thomas Norris, Henry Fiser, Edward King

Commissioners Charles Wheaton, Wyatt Bishop, Ab^m Philips allowed Ten Dollars each for settling with County Trustee for past years since their appointments

Deed Eli Jones to Edmund Edwards 30 acres ackd
Deed James Vaughn to William Johnson 100 acres proven by Wm Benson
Deed Richard Matthews to Thos Harrison for a Lot in Springfield ackd
Deed Eli Jones to Edmund Edwards 200 acres ackd
Deed Richard Jones to James Jones 146 acres 76 poles ackd
Deed John Beason to Moses Beason 100 acres proven by John Siglar
Deed Matthew Manning to Frederick Hunter 228 acres proven by Isaac Johnson
Deed Ezekiel Polk to Thomas Polk 365 acres proven by Elias Fort Junr
Deed James McElyea to Nathl Harbin 8 acres ackd
Deed Absolom Hooper Senr to William Pace 140 acres proven by Obed Davis
B/S Edmund Edwards to Eli Jones for a Negro ackd

Henry Fiser to oversee road from Springfield to Karrs creek at John Brooks. The following hands to work under him: John Brooks, Peter Fiser, Michael Fiser, Jacob Damewood, Wm Hays, James Hays, Robert Hays, Wm Crocket, Joel Lewis, Thos Boren

Samuel Woolsey to oversee road in room of George Patterson

p.325 Thomas Woodard apptd Constable; bond 620 Dollars; Noah Woodard & Andw Irwin his securities; took oath
Release from Daniel Rowan to Counties of Montgomery and Robertson ordered to be filed
Sampson Matthews to oversee road in room of Thomas Appleton
B/S James Ragsdale to William Sale for a Negro proven by Jno Krisel

Order the following hands work on road of which Zachh Cox is overseer: Wm Carter, James Elliott, Saml Elliot, Joseph Egnight, Duke Pincen, Wm Pincen, Abm Pinkley, Wm Fleuellen, Nichl Darnald, Harbert Fleuellen, Shaderick Rawls, Isaac Winters, Robert Hogan
Court Adjourns untill tomorrow Morning 9 OClock

Wednesday Morning February the 6th 1805 Present John Philips, Charles Miles, James Norfleet, Isaac Philips, Esqrs

B/S Samuel Warren to Margaret Karr one Negro proven by Henry Johnson

The road from Springfield to Port Royal is to be turned from upper end of Charles Miles Esqr plantation to go through his lane and into sd road below so as to intersect the old road below Elias Lawrences

Deed Levi Noyes to Bustard & Easten 2 lots in Springfield & a cotton ginn & Press ackd

Will of Thomas Byrd decd proven by Jas Crabtree Esqr

p.326 A Seekright lessee of Wm P Anderson vs John Gardner. Ejectment. Present Jno Philips, Jno Hutchison, Jas Norfleet, Charles Miles, Isaac Philips. May 1804 Plf by P W Humphreys; Jno Gardner prays to become deft in room of Casual Ejector & is admited; his attorney John C Hamilton. February 1805 Jury Frederick Cobb, Henry Watkins, Edward King, Leml Sugg, Robt Brown, Michael Fiser, Charles Bradon, Richard Crunk, Ledford Payne, John James, Joseph Castleberry, John Huey find Deft Guilty; assess damage to six cents; pltf recovers possession of land, damage six cents, & his costs. Elias Fort Junr witness proves 4 days attendance; Henry Johnson 2 days as surveyor, 24 miles travel, 3 days as witness; Thomas Johnson 1 day as surveyor, 24 miles travel, 3 days as witness

A Rect for Direct Tax from James Menees, Collector of Direct Tax, to Aaron Lambert proven by Benjn Menees Jr

Order Jn° Philips, Ja⁵ Norfleet, John Hutchison Esq⁷ˢ comm⁷ˢ
to contract for building frame addition to west end of Court
House 12 f⁵ long, as high as House, with plank partition to
make 2 Jury Rooms, a window in each, brick or stone chimney
with a fireplace in each room terminating in one funnel, all
to be done in as workmanlike manner as present Court House,
of as good materials; also to repair the House

p.327 Order following Tracts sold for Nonpayment of 1803 Tax
-- 96 acres, John Dickson reputed owner, on Bartons Creek;
274 acres, George Hooks reputed owner, Bartons Creek
Court Adjourns untill tomorrow Morning 9 OClock

Thursday Morning Feb⁷ 7⁵ʰ 1805   Present the worshipfull
Isaac Philips, James H Bryan, Charles Miles, Esquires

Hannah Porter vs Jesse Lawrence. Covenant. Present above and
John Philips. Aug⁵ 1804 pl⁵ by Thomas Stuart; Def⁵ by Bennet
Searcy. Cause cont⁴; Feb⁷ 1805 Jury Frederick Cobb, Henry
Watkins, Edward King, Lem¹ Sugg, Rob⁵ Brown, Michael Fiser,
Charles Bradon, John D Robins, Stewart Thornton, Wᵐ Briscoe,
Amos Cohea, James Stark who find for Pl⁵ᶠ, assess damage to
55 Doll⁵ 3½ c⁵ˢ; Motion of pl⁵ᶠ for new tryal granted; pl⁵ᶠ
(sic) with assent of pl⁵ᶠ confessed Judgement 76 Dollars 36
cents 9 mills, with costs of suit.

p.328 Hadley & Rawlings vs Joseph Dorris and Isaac Dorris.
Covenant. Justices as above. Aug⁵ 1804 pl⁵ᶠ by John C Hamilton; Def⁵ by Thoˢ Stuart; Cont⁴. Feb⁷ 1805 Jury John James,
Thoˢ Neely, David Jones, Wᵐ Sale, Wᵐ Milsap, Joseph Castleberry, Shadᵏ Rawls, Hugh Henry, Richᵈ Crunk, William Coates,
Francis Boren, John Chowning find for pl⁵ᶠ damages 95 Doll⁵
87 cents 6 mills; also his costs

Lemuel Sugg vs Shaderick Rawls. Appeal. Court as above. Pl⁵ᶠ
by Bennet Searcy; def⁵ by Thoˢ Stuart. Jury Frederick Cobb,
Henry Watkins, Edwᵈ King, Robert Brown, Mich¹ Fiser, Charles
Bradon, Stewart Thornton, Wᵐ Briscoe, Amos Cohea, Jaˢ Stark,
Anthony Hinkle, Levi Noyes find for Pl⁵ᶠ, damages 4 Dollars
50 cents; also his costs

Thomas Woodard allowed seventeen Dollars for the time he has
kept Daniel McDaniel up to this Day

p.329 Order John Philips and Benjamin Menees Esq⁷ˢ let to
lowest bidder the clothing & maintainance of Daniel McDaniel
now put on the parish for one year. They let him to Thomas
Woodard for 68 Dollars fifty cents

Order following to mark a road the convenient way from Black branch to War trace Creek and report to Overseer: Jn° Hutchison, John Johnson, Ab^m Young, Wm Briscoe, David Jones, Thos Kilgore J^r, Jn° Simmons, Bazel Boren, Sampson Matthews, Danl Holman, Jn° Chowning, Jn° McMillion, Jn° McIntosh Senr, Amos Cohea

Following Justices/Peace to take lists of Taxable property for present year

Archer Cheatham	Captain Briscoes Company
Isaac Philips	" Skinners "
Martin Duncan	" Krisels "
James H Bryan	" Blackwells "
Hardy S Bryan	" Moakes "
Thomas Strain	" Kilgores "
John Hutchison	" Bounds "

Jurors to next Court Henry Gardner, Mark Noble, Peter Brawner, Jiles Connel, John Polk, Jesse Martin, Ja^s Gardner, Jo^s Washington, David Huddleston, Volentine Choate, George Pool, John James, James Jones, Jn° Simmons, Jn° Cromwell, Whitmill Harrington, Pat^k Martin, Stephen Boren, Wyatt Bishop, Joseph Castleberry, David Spence, James Wheeler, Charles Kilgore, Moses Hardin, Jn° Burney, Daniel Holman, Daniel McKinley J^r, Jacob Hunter, Jacob Moake, John Hyde, W^m J Perry, Wm Benson, John Crocket, John Couts, David Henry, Solomon Squire, Silas Tucker, Lovick Ventress, James Elliott

Jurors to next Superior Court Isaac Philips, Thomas Hunter, Wm Johnson, James Blackwell

p.330 Shaderick Rawls vs Lemuel Sugg. Present John Philips, Isaac Philips, Chas Miles. Pl^tf by Thos Stuart; def^t by Bennet Searcy. Jury Fred^k Cobb, Henry Watkins, Edwd King, Robt Brown, Michael Fiser, Chas Bradon, Stuart Thornton, Wm Briscoe, Amos Cohea, James Stark, Anthony Hinkle, John Cromwell, who find for plaintiff three Dollars; also his costs of suit

Daniel Pinkley to oversee road from Karrs Creek to Ironworks as far as former overseers part of s^d road
Court Adjourns until tomorrow Morning 9 OClock

Friday Morning February 8th 1805 Present the Worshipfull John Philips, Isaac Philips, Charles Miles, Esquires

Benj^a Menees J^r Collector for 1804 to have a Credit with the State Treasurer for the taxes on 1142 acres given in by Thos Dillon agent for Thos Persons twice for same year, also Thos Deaderick 540 acres twice given in

Benjamin Menees Esqr Collector for 1804 Reports Taxes remain
unpaid on following tracts and there is no personal property
on which to Distress: Susannah Hart 2560 acres; John Chislom
640 acres; Dorias Grey 640. The Clerk is to transmit copy to
printer to be published agreeable to Law

p.331   Joseph Roberts 640 acres Sulpher fork ordered to be
recd for 1804 Tax; also 640 acres in name of Wm Crabtree

John B Cheatham app^td Guardian for Nancy Tucker; gave bond
one thousand Dollars, Wm Milsap & Edward Cheatham securities

John Cromwell & others vs Hannah Porter & others. Petition
to rectify error in Deed given by John McCoy Alston to Alex-
ander Cromwell; petiton granted, from which Judgement Hannah
Porter obtained appeal to Superior Court; bond one Thousand
Dollars, Hugh Henry & Benjn Menees Jr securities
Court Adjourns untill tomorrow Morning 9 OClock

Saturday Morning Feby 9th 1805 Present the Worshipfull John
Philips, Isaac Philips, Archer Cheatham Esquires

Petition of Joseph Castleberry, Joseph Robertson, & William
Dorris, securities for Jno D Robins admr of Jno Tucker decd,
& heirs of John Tucker decd and John Cheatham guardian, Pray
appointment of John Hutchison & A Cheatham, Esqrs, to settle
with admr agreeable to Act of Assembly; & settlement so made
to be rendered in to Next Court

p.332   George Hardin vs Edward Cheatham. Attachment. On a
Demurer, after argument heard, order that original attachment be quashed

Order Collector have Credit for Taxes on 357 acres sold for
1801 and 1802 Taxes name of James G Beckhouse, it appearing
there is no such Land, & that s^d Collector refund to Edward
Cheatham af^sd Taxes, he being the purchaser

Edward King to oversee road in room of Wm Karr

p.333   William Coates vs John D Robins admr of John Tucker
decd. Present John Philips, Isaac Philips, Chas Miles, Benjn
Menees, Esq^rs. Novr 1804 pl^tf by Jno C Hamilton; def^t by W^m
Smith. Feby Jury Frederick Cobb, Henry Watkins, Edwd King,
Lemuel Sugg, Robt Brown, Mich^l Fiser, Charles Bradon, Joshua
Smith, Stewart Thornton, Richard Crunk, James Stark, Elisha
Bridgewater, who find for Pl^tf, assess damage to 191 Dollars
66 2/3 cents; also his costs of suit. Enoch Tucker, witness,
proves three days attendance

Thomas G Walke vs Robt Warren, Wm Milsap, Charles McIntosh.
Present John Philips, Isaac Philips, Martin Duncan, Benjamin
Menees, Chas Miles, Esq^rs. Motion to enter Judgement for sum
of $100.10½ for a Receipt given by Robert Warren, Constable,
to Thos G Walke under the hand of Robert Warren in following
words: "Novr 13th 1803 then rec^d and now in my hands a balance of Judgement & Notes amounting to one Hundred Dollars &
10½ cents which I promise to make due returns of as my office or the Law Directs on or before the first Day of January next as Witness my hand" signed Robt Warren Cons^le. Test
Peter Young. Considered by Court that Pl^tf take nothing by
his Motion, s^d Pl^tf to pay to Def^ts their costs expended

Court Adjourns untill Court in Course
John Philips, Benjn Menees, A Cheatham, Isaac Philips, James
Norfleet, Charles Miles

State of Tennessee, Robertson County, Monday, May 6th 1805
Present the Worshipfull John Philips, Benjamin Menees, James
Crabtree, and Joseph Dorris, Esquires

Grand Jurors: Wyatt Bishop foreman, Solomon Squire, Moses
Hardin, Joseph Castleberry, David Henry, Joseph Washington,
William J Perry, David Spence, James Wheeler, Jiles Connel,
Lovick Ventress, George Pool, Stephen Boren, James Elliott

Jacob Cook registers his stock mark
Archibald Mahon, Coroner, resigned his appointment

Edward Ward released from 1804 Taxes charged on his personal
property, & Collector to have credit with Treasurer for that
amount

p.335 Wm Gulledge vs Obed Davis. Augt 1804 plt^f by Bennet
Searcy; def^t by Thos Stuart. May Jury Volentine Choate, John
Cromwell, John Polk, Ja^s Gardner, David Huddleston, Patrick
Martin, John Simmons, John Couts, Charles Kilgore, Ja^s Bell,
Asaph Parker, James Stark who find for Def^t; Def^t to recover
from Pl^tf his costs of suit. John Stump, witness, proves 1
Days attendance, 40 miles traveling; Merrel Philips 7 days,
120 miles; Caleb Bosman 7 days, 120 miles; John B McCormack
7 days, 108 miles; Jacob Pinkley 1 day; Frederick Pinkley 2
days, 72 miles; Henry Pinkley 1 day, 38 miles.

Deed George Gollady to Wm Gulledge and Wm Kearney 107 acres
proven by W^m J Perry

Deed James Menees Sheriff to William Findley 140 acres proven by Isham Tredway

p.336 Joseph Engleman allowed Thirty Dollars from estate of John Tucker dec^d for keeping two children of s^d John Tucker decd named Riggs Tucker and John Tucker to present Day with all contingent expenses

Deed Thomas Holman to Jesse Golson 123 acres proven by Isaac Johnson
Deed Moses Hardin to Jacob McKee 40 acres ackd
Deed George Murphey Junr to Fanny Green 92 acres proven by Marvel Lowe
Deed James Menees Sh^ff to Isham Tredway 177 acres proven by Wm Findley
Deed James Vaughn to Wm Perry 100 acres proven by Wm Spiller
Deed James Menees Sh^ff to John Lipscomb 557 acres proven by Thomas Johnson
Deed James Menees Sh^ff to George Gordon 630½ acres proven by Wm Stark
Deed Robert Hays to John Richardson 640 acres proven by Wm Atkins
Deed Moore Stephenson to Robert Perry 1000 acres proven by Wm Perry
Deed John D Robins to Isaac Johnson 725 acres proven by Thomas Johnson

Mark Noble excused from Serving as a Juror this term

Elijah Hughs app'd inspector of Cotton; bond 1000 Dollars. Ja^s H Bryan & Philip Parchment, securities; took oath

Elias Lawrence to oversee road from Springfield to Portroyal from Menees road to Purnells branch, leaving Fikes field to the left, passing through Charles Miles Esqr lane, thence to Purnells branch; having hands between sd road & Sulpher fork and John Gardners hands

p.337 Power/Attorney Moses Armstrong to James Stewart proven by Isaac Dortch

Moses Hardin, William Armstrong, Thomas George & George Patterson to view a road opened by the inhabitants leading from James Wheelers and Jacob Cooks to State line; also the Road leading by Harrisons Mill; report to next Court in favour of the road which they deem nearest & best way

Nathaniel Simmons to oversee road in room of Charles Kilgore

Will of Richard Jones decd proven by Samuel Scott and Edward

Jones; Peter Jones & Edward Ward, executors, took oath

James Crabtree Esqr delivered into Court the Tax list, Captn Kilgores Compy. Jas H Bryan Esqr, Captn Stuarts Compy. John Hutchison Esqr, Captn Bounds; Hardy S Bryan Esqr, Captn Robertsons; Archer Cheatham Esqr, Captn Briscoes; Isaac Philips Esqr, Captn Suggs
Court Adjourns untill tomorrow Morning 9 OClock

Tuesday Morning May 7th 1805. Present the worshipfull Benjn Menees, Charles Miles, Isaac Philips, James Norfleet, Esqrs

Power/Atty Jacob Johnson & Margaret Johnson to Jacob Johnson proven by John Johnson
Deed Charles Miles to John Crane 100 acres ackd
Deed Peter Brawner to Elijah Hughs 271 acres proven by Jas H Bryan

p.338 Thomas Neely vs Abraham Pinkley. Certiorari. Charles Miles, James Norfleet, Jno Philips, James Crabtree, Esquires August 1804 pltf by J C Hamilton; deft by Thos Stuart. Contd May jury: Volentine Choate, John Cromwell, John Polk, James Gardner, David Huddleston, Patrick Martin, Jno Simmons, John Couts, Charles Kilgore, Lemuel Sugg, Eppa Lawson, John Crane who find for Plf; assess damage to 31 Dolls 63 cts; also his costs. Isaac Houdashall, a witness proves 3 days attendance, Benjamin Menees Junr 10 days, James Norfleet 2 days, Nathan Yoes 7 days

Deed John Powers to Joseph Pitts 228 acres proven by John Pitts

Road from Springfield to War Trace Creek to continue the New Road, passing Anderson Cheatham's house, thence to Old Road near a Honey Locust. then with Old Road to sd Creek

p.339 Shaderick Rawls vs Lemuel Sugg. Present Chas Miles, Jno Philips, Isaac Philips, J Dorris, Benjamin Menees Esqrs. Novr 1804 pltf by Thos Stuart; deft by Bennet Searcy. Contd. May Jury Volentine Choate, Jno Cromwell, Jno Polk, Jas Gardner, David Huddleston, Patk Martin, Jno Simmons, John Couts, Chas Kilgore, John Crane, Thos McIntosh, Isaac Williams who find for Deft. Deft to recover agt Pltf his costs of suit. Josiah Fort. a witness. proves 2 days attendance

James Menees Collector 1802 State & County Tax to have $3.20 credit with Treasurer for land in the name of John Williams, there being no such land; also with County Trustee

Martin Duncan and John Hutchison Esquires to settle with the
administrators of estate of Samuel Tucker decd; make report

Joseph Washington was duly elected Coroner for 2 years; bond
2000 Dollars, Joseph Wimberley & Josiah Fort his securities

p.340   Wm Russell & Archibald Harris vs John James. Present
Jno Philips, Ja^s Crabtree, Wm Johnson, Jno Hutchison, Esq^{rs}.
Novr 1804 pl^f by Ja^s H Bowen & Wm Smith; D^{ft} by Thos Stuart.
May 1805 Jury Vol Choate, Jno Cromwell, Jno Polk, Ja^s Gard-
ner, David Huddleston, Pat^k Martin, Jno Simmons, John Couts,
Chas Kilgore, Lem^l Sugg, Joseph Robertson, Edwd Cheatham who
find for Def^t. Previous to Jury delivering Verdict, Pl^{ff} Non
Suited; wherefore considered by Court that Def^t recover from
Pl^{ff} his costs of suit. Perry Cohea, witness, proves 6 days
attendance; James Hutchison 2 days; James Cain 4 days & 140
miles Traveling

Jno McElhainy to oversee road from Springfield to Logan; his
Bounds extend from North side Sulpher fork to where s^d Road
intersects Old Logan Road; all hands residing on North side
of s^d Fork who formerly worked under John Duncan are to work
under s^d John McElhainey

Deed James Cain to Richd Nuckolls 41 acres proven by Augus-
tine Cook
Deed Ezekiel Polk to John Polk 240 acres proven by Wm Polk
Deed George Hendley to George Pelly Leach 74 acres proven by
William Johnson
Martin Duncan Esqr delivered Tax List for Captn Krisels Co
p.341   Deed Hugh Henry, Sheriff, to Bennet Searcy 320 acres
ackd
Deed Ezekiel Polk to William Polk 318 acres proven by John
Campbell
Deed Noah Woodard to Ezekiel Polk 465 acres proven by Thomas
Polk
Deed Ezekiel Polk to John Campbell 225 acres proven by Wil-
liam Polk
Executors of estate of James Hunt decd delivered Inventory
Court Adjourns untill tomorrow Morning 9 OClock

Wednesday Morning May 8th 1805   Present the Worshipfull
Benj^u Menees, Martin Duncan, Charles Miles, Archer Cheatham

County Tax for present year: Each White pole 5¼ Cents; Each
Hundred acres 6¼ Cents; Each Black pole 12½ cts; Each Stud
Horse 12½ cents; Each Town Lot 12½ cts; Each store of Mer-
chandize 2.50

Jacob Pickren fined fifty cents for swearing in presence of the court; fine paid
Grand Jury Discharged
Elisabeth Tucker allowed Twenty Dollars for keeping Samuel a child of John Tucker dec^d for the present year

p.342 State vs Daniel McKinley Junr. Present Joseph Dorris, Benjn Meness, M Duncan, J Hutchison, J Philips, A Cheatham, C Miles, J H Bryan, I Philips, James Crabtree, Esquires. Wm Smith, County Solicitor, behalf State; Jno C Hamilton & Thos Stuart for Deft. Jury Volentine Choate, John Cromwell, John Polk, James Gardner, David Huddleston, Pat^k Martin, Jno Simmons, John Couts, Charles Kilgore, Theophilus Morgan, Peter Pinkley, Wm Dorris find Def^t Not Guilty. Def^t pay all costs. Motion to Tax prosecutor with Costs overruled. Thos Figures witness proved 3 Days attendance; William Lundsford 2 days

John Couts vs Saml & John D Robins. Covenant. Present J Dorris, J Hutchison, J Philips, M Duncan. Feby 1805 plt^f by J C Hamilton; def^ts by Wm Smith. May Jury Volentine Choate, John Cromwell, Jno Polk, James Gardner, David Huddleston, Patrick Martin, Jno Simmons, Charles Kilgore, Peter Pinkley, Wm Dorris, Isaac Johnson, Thos Dorris find for pl^{tf}, assess damage to 535 Dollars 62 cents; also costs of suit.

p.343 John Hutchison and Joseph Dorris Esq^{rs} to settle with adm^{rs} estate of John Tucker dec^d & make report

B/S William Huddleston, John Huddleston and Jonathan Huddleston to Charles Wheaton, Negro woman, proven by John Duncan

John J Dorris allowed 30 Dollars for present year to be paid by County Trustee

Philip Parchment, Moses Winters, Shaderick Rawls, Ge^o Murphey, Danl Pinkley to lay off a road from Springfield to the Iron Works, to run left of Matthew Day, then nearest & best way to join Old Road near Ramseys hay field
Court Adjourns untill Tomorrow Morning 9 OClock

Thursday Morning May 9th 1805   Present the Worshipfull John Philips, Benjamin Menees, John Hutchison, Esquires

Elisabeth Tucker is allowed Thirteen Dollars for keeping a Negro child one year belonging to estate of John Tucker dec^d to be paid out of the monies of s^d estate

John B Cheatham, Sheriff, apptd Collector State and County Taxes for present Year; bond 5000 Dollars, Edward Cheatham and William Johnson his securities; took oath

Matthew Matthews to oversee road in room of William D Dorris

p.344 Levi Noyes vs Samuel & John D Robins. Present Benjamin
Menees, Chas Miles, Martin Duncan. Feby 1805 plf by J B Reynolds, deft by Wm Smith. May Jury Vol Choate, John Cromwell,
Jno Polk, Jas Gardner, David Huddleston, Patrick Martin, Jno
Simmons, John Couts, Chas Kilgore, Edward Cheatham, Wm Briscoe, Stuart W Thornton who find for pltf, assess damage to
80 Dollars; also his costs of suit

Israel Robertson vs James Miles. Certiorari. Previous Motion
to quash Execution as no Judgement was given by a Justice of
this County agt deft, which sd Execution was quashed. Joseph
Woolfolk witness proves 3 days attendance, 30 miles traveling; Reubin Grayson 3 days, 30 miles; Eppa Lawson 3 days

Samuel Miles to oversee road in room of Isaac Sanders
John Tucker bond by Indenture to Nehemiah Varnon untill he
arrives to age twenty one years

Volentine Choate allowed 20 Dollars to keep Riggs Tucker one
year, a child of John Tucker decd, to be paid out of estate
of sd John Tucker decd, who has this day received the Child

p.345 Jurors to next Court: Joseph Payne, Bartimias Pack, Wm
Byrd, James Yates, George Patterson, Daniel Holeman, James
Johnson, Wm Sale, Walter Stark, Bazil Boren, Francis Boren,
Titus Benton, James Bell, William Briscoe, Matthew Morris,
William Crocket, Henry Fry, Benjamin Porter, Charles Bradon,
Hugh Henry, Samuel McMurry, James McGuire, John Simmons Jr,
Walter Brown, Jesse Martin, Jno Crane, Jno Carr, William At-
kins, Thomas Polk, Elijah Hughs, Philip Parchment, Asa Wood-
worth, George Murphey, John Hyde, Luke Rawls, James Hunt, Wm
Johnson R R, John Williams Spring Cr RR, Barton Coates

On oath of Enoch Tucker, it appears John Tucker had made do-
nation of a colt to Hannah Tucker his daughter, that sd John
traded sd colt to Asaph Parker, sd John agreeing with Hannah
for a good creature. Hannah chose a mare at sale of John's
estate to satisfy John's debt to Hannah, which mare was sold
to Hannah by the admr for 50 Dollars. Ordered by Court that
Hannah be exhonarated from payment of afsd 50 Dollars which
mare sold for, and that the admr have credit for that amount
in his settlement of estate of John Tucker decd

Martin Duncan and John Philips, Esquires to settle with admr
estate of Nathaniel Rogers decd & make report to next Court

Clerk to transmit to Knoxville and Nashville Gazettes a list
of lands reported by James Menees & Benj[n] Menees J[r] for Non
payment of Taxes. List reported by Ja[s] Menees is as follows
p.346. For Year 1799
James Mabins   640 acres Battle ground Creek
John Nelson   430 waters Karrs Creek
       For Year 1800
Thomas Bethany 100 on Harpeth & 1 white pole
William Clark   640 Elk fork
John Haynes   320 Red River & 1 Black pole
George H Hauser 400 Sulpher fork waters
W[m] B Powel   1 Lot in Springfield & 1 white pole
David Young   39 Karrs Creek & 1 white pole
       For Year 1801
Robert Black   210 Sulpher fork & 1 white pole
George Hook   320 Bartons Creek
Philip Johnson 200 Red River & 1 White pole
Moses Larisy   340 Spring Creek, 1 white & 1 black pole
Edward Lucas   540 Harpeth 1 white pole
Robert Nelson   320 situation not known
Jonathan Price 160 Beaver Dam
David Young   39 Karrs Creek
       For Year 1802
Robert Beatty   1000 Battle ground Creek
Joseph Childress 60 War trace & 1 white pole
W[m] Cochran   1063 Bartons Creek
W[m] Dennis   415 Beaver Dam
Robert Hopkins 640 Sychamore
John Hinds   300 War trace
John Kirney   100 Sychamore & 1 white pole
Edw[d] McGowen 640 situation not known
Robert Nelson   600 Karrs Creek & War trace
Jonathan Price 260 Beaver Dam
Harriet S Rice 640 situation not known
       For year 1803
Darius Grey   640 situation not known
Daniel Hogan   100 Sulpher fork
John H Hooser   400 Sulpher fork waters
George Hook   250 Bartons Creek
W[m] Lurry   1280 waters Red River
Aaron Laws   1000 waters Red River
p.347 W[m] Lusk 228 Beaver Dam
James Latham   1 lot in Springfield & 2 Black poles
Joseph Lawrence 50 acres Red River & 1 white pole
James McClellen 640 Bartons Creek
Alex[r] McNeely 127 Barrens
Daniel Wheaton 640 acres --
       For Year 1804
Matthew Brooks 640 waters Red River
W[m] Blackfan   640 Duck branch

Isaac Caldwell   60 waters Red River & 1 White pole
James Huling   640 on Sychamore
Henry W Lawson   640 Sturgeon creek
Samuel Davis   228 joining Simmons
David McCree   1000 Sychamore
Robert Nelson   997 Millers Creek & Red River

Signed Benj[n] Menees, John Philips, Joseph Dorris, Cha[s] Miles

p.348   State of Tennessee, Robertson County. Monday Morning
August 5[t]h 1805. Springfield. Present the Worshipfull Benj[n]
Menees, Isaac Philips, James H Bryan, James Norfleet, John
Philips, Esquires

Clerk to receive Lists of Taxable property

Grand Jurors W[m] Sale foreman, John Williams, Barton Coates,
Francis Boren, George Patterson, Cha[s] Bradon, Jesse Martin,
John Simmons Jr, Henry Fry, W[m] Crocket, Samuel McMurry, Luke
Rawls, W[m] Johnston R R, John Hyde, Matthew Morris
Isaac Dorris, Constable, sworn to attend the Grand Jury

Thomas Hunter allowed 45 Dollars for keeping Isaac Williams,
now on the Parish, untill first Monday in February next

James Norfleet, Isaac Dortch, and Ja[s] H Bryan to settle with
executors of estate of William Fort Dec[d]; make report

Tavern rates continue as heretofore made with addition of 50
cents for each half pint of French Brandy or Rum

Volentine Choate to oversee road in room of John Chowning
Peter Pinkley to oversee road in room of Thomas Norris
Deed Aquilla Sugg to Gulley Moore 50 acres proven by William
Moore
Court Adjourns for one Hour.   Court met.   Present Benjamin
Menees, Isaac Philips, Martin Duncan, Esquires

p.349 John Philips and Martin Duncan, Esq[rs], app[td] to settle
with adm[r] estate of Nathaniel Rogers dec[d], report that adm[r]
is indebted to estate to whole amount of appraisement of s[d]
Estate 649 Dollars 74¼ Cents

Order of last Court for settlement with adm[rs] of Sam[l] Tucker
dec[d] revived, to be returned to next Court

George Murphey Junr to oversee the New Road as lately marked from Springfield to Old Iron work Road near Ramseys old Hay field, that Matthew Day and William Crocket designate hands which s^d overseer is to have

Benjamin Menees Collector of 1804 State Tax to have a credit for $1.25, the am^t of delinquents this day produced to Court

Asa Woodard excused from serving as a Juror this Term

Archer Cheatham admited to keep an Ordinary for one year in this County gave Bond 1000 Dollars, James Sawyers & Benjamin Menees Jr his securities

Order James Shannon to oversee the road from the ridge near Betts to Browns fork, to have the following hands: James McDonald, Carnes Logue, Walter Brown, Michael Withen, Burrel Robertson, Jacob Johnson, Ja^s Jones, Asa Jones, Garlin Tidwell, Mark Robertson, Henry Wiggle

Ltrs/Admn granted to Wm Johnston on estate of Saml Johnston dec^d; bond 1000 Dollars, James Norfleet his security; took oath; also delivered an Inventory of said estate

p.350 Order a road laid off from where Nashville road crosses Millers Creek, intersecting Davidson ferry road where it crosses Persons creek, thence to County Line, following persons mark same: James Blackwell, Robert Perry, Elias Fort, Saml Pearson, Mark Noble. Petitioners and persons residing within one mile of the road to open it

Wm Briscoe excused from serving as a Juror this Term
Deed John Trice to Elijah Eubanks 450 acres proven by J C Hamilton
Deed Jesse Golden to John Young 50 acres proven by Abraham B Young
Deed James Menees Shff to Robert Nelson 640 acres ackd
Deed James Menees Shff to Richard Nuckolls & Thomas Johnson 640 acres ackd
Deed James Menees Shff to Robert Nelson 274 acres ackd
Deed James Menees Shff to Benjn Weakley 640 acres ackd
Deed John Huey to Wm Johnson 64 acres proven by Augustine Cook
Deed John Huey to Wm Johnson 64 acres proven by Augustine Cook
Court Adjourns until tomorrow Morning 9 OClock

Tuesday Morning August the 6th 1805 Present the Worshipfull John Philips, Benjamin Menees, John Hutchison, Esquires

Thomas Polk excused from Serving as a Juror this Term

p.351   Executors of Wm Fort dec^d exhibited account current
ag^t s^d estate; examined by James Norfleet, Hardy S Bryan and
Isaac Dortch; rec^d by them & sanctioned by the Court.   Also
a settlement examined by af^s^d Justices between the executors
& Jeremiah Fort, Sarah Fort, Ja^s Fort, William A Fort, Jacob
Fort, Josiah Fort and Mary Fort, orphans of s^d Wm Fort dec^d;
also rec^d by them, sanctioned by Court, ordered recorded.
James Norfleet, Isaac Dortch and Wm Farrior to divide estate
of William Fort dec^d amongst Legatees agreeable to will.
Ex^t^r^s estate Wm Fort dec^d to deposit vouchers Clerk's office

Admrs Henry Sherod dec^d to sell personal estate of dec^d

Bustard & Eastin vs Levi Noyes. Case. Plaintiffs & Def^t in
proper person agreed to refer cause to Genl Thomas Johnson &
Col^o Archer Cheatham; their award to be rule of this Court

Levi Noyes vs W^m B Vinson agent for Bustard & Eastin. Case.
Pl^t^f & def^t in proper person refer cause to Thomas Johnson &
Archer Cheatham; their award to be rule of this Court

p.352 George Chapman vs Thomas Bell. Case. Benjn Menees, Jno
Philips, I Philips, Charles Miles, Esq^r^s. - May 1805 pl^t^f by
Thos Stuart; def^t by Wm Smith. August Jury John Carr, Daniel
Holman, Elijah Hughs, Ge^o Murphey, Jo^s Payne, Walter Stark,
Richd Crunk, James Hogan, Jonathan Oyler, James Mayo, Samp-
son Matthews, James Appleton Junr who find for pl^t^f & assess
damage to 31 Dollars 12½ cents. Also costs. John Duncan wit-
ness proves 2 days attendance

Levi Noyes vs William B Vinson. Trespass breaking close. Pl^f
& def^t in proper persons agree to refer this cause to Thomas
Johnson & Archer Cheatham; their award to be rule of Court

Thomas Woodard exhonarated from payment of Tax on 200 acres,
to be deducted from his Tax List, being more than he owns, &
entered by mistake; Collector to have credit with Treasurer

p.353 John Den Lessee of Bustard & Eastin vs Levi Noyes and
Jno Den. Ejectment. Pl^t^f^s & def^t^s, to wit Levi Noyes s^d Levi
confesses he is guilty of Trespass as charged; pl^t^f^s to recover their Term and costs of suit; Plaintiff may have Writ
of Possession for same when called for

Caven Witty vs Henry Gardner. Appeal. Benjamin Menees, John
Philips, Wm Johnson Esq^r^s. Pl^t^f by Thos Stuart; def^t by J C
Hamilton. Jury Daniel Holman, Elijah Hughs, George Murphey,

Joseph Payne, James Bell, Richard Crunk, Jas Hogan, Jonathan
Oyler, Walter Stark, James Mayo, Sampson Matthews, James Appleton Junr, find for deft. Shaderick Gardner witness proves
one day attendance

Jurors to next Superior Court: Samuel Crocket, Isaac Dorris
Senr, William Johnson, Thomas Polk

Clerk & Shff each to receive fifty Dollars for Exoficio services for past year

Order made at Novr Term for laying off & opening a road from
Springfield to Williams Mill to be revived

Deed John Richardson to James McConnell 320 acres proven by
Henry Johnson
p.354   Deed Wm P Anderson to Thomas Polk 32 acres proven by
Wm Connell
Deed Daniel McKinley to William Huddleston 80 acres proven
by James Sawyers
Deed Robert Nelson to Eppa Lawson 640 acres proven by Sugg
Fort
Deed William Briscoe to John Huey 64 acres ackd
Deed William Briscoe to John Huey 64 acres 126 poles ackd
Deed Solomon Squire to Arthur Pitt 278 acres proven by Isaac
Johnson
Deed William Johnson to John Huey 342 acres proven by Benjn
Porter
Deed William Crunk to Lewis Wells 137 acres proven by Augus-
tine Cook; Certificate of Richard Crunk thereto annexed was
proven by Thomas Johnson
Deed William Robertson to Lewis Wells 137 acres 58 poles
proven by Thomas Johnson
Deed William Johnson to Thomas Johnson 370 acres ackd

B/S David Smith to William Deloach, Negro Girl, proven by
Sugg Fort

Ltrs/Admn estate of John Polk decd granted to Martha Polk,
Wm Polk, and John Campbell; Bond 10,000 Dollars; Thomas Polk
& Joseph Wimberley their securities

Jacob Damewood to oversee road in room of Peter Spence

John Huddleston to oversee road in room of John Duncan

p.355 Abraham Moore to oversee New Road from Levi Moore to
State Line at or near Travess; following to work under him:
Travess, Wm Ragsdale, Thomas Yates, John Hudson, Levi Moore,
James Gambril, Webster Gilbert, M Fulton, Saml Woolsey, Jas

p

Leach, M Story, Jesse Williams, Mr Humphreys, Wm Yates

Jurors to next Court: George Browning, Joseph Castleberry, Matthew Day, Anthony Hinkle, John Duncan, Jacob Fry, James Long, David Spence, Wm Cole, J^{no} Chewning, Wm Huddleston J^r, George Pool, Benjⁿ Holman, William Armstrong, Wm Byrd, John Burney, Adam Clap, Wm Gilbert, Jacob Warren, Elias Fort, Ja^s Johnston, Joseph McDowel, Joseph Choate, John Hunt, Wm Hunt, Marvel Lowe, Titus Benton, Meredith Walton, Silas Tucker, Richd Nuckolls, James Gambril, Henry Gardner, James Gardner, Archibald Mahon, Patrick Martin, Philip Parchment, James Stuart, Aaron Winters, & James Young
Court Adjourns untill Tomorrow Morning 9 OClock

Wednesday Morning Augt 7th 1805.   Present the Worshipfull John Philips, Martin Duncan, Archer Cheatham, Esquires

Deed Hannah Porter to Jesse Lawrence 64 acres 94 poles ackd

B/S John D Robins to John Johnson, for a Negro

Petition Joseph Engleman & wife against John Robins admr of John Tucker decd filed; order Clerk to issue Summons against him, returnable to Next Court together with copy of petition

p.356 Jacob Pinkley vs Bazel Boren and Stephen Boren. Si fa as bail for Isham Rogers. Def^{ts} failing to appear, Judgement entered against defendants

Ordered Wm Crocket to work on the Road under Henry Fiser and James Kile under Edward King

James Appleton vs John Shannon. Original Attachment. Levied on 200 acres Joining North & East Boundaries of Jn° Chowning where he now lives. A Cook Cons^{le} Augt 3rd 1805. Judg^t behalf plaintiff for 15 Doll^s 56¼ c^{ts}. Costs $1.25. A Cheatham J P. Order land af^{sd} be sold to satisfy judgment

Judgement Entered against following Land for Nonpayment of Taxes. For 1799
James Mabine   640 acres Battle Ground Creek
John Nelson   430 acres Karrs Creek
      For Year 1800
Thomas Bethany 100 on Harpeth, 1 White pole, 2 Black poles
Wm Clark   640 Elk fork
John Haynes   320 Red River & 1 Black pole
George H Harris 400 waters Sulpher fork
W^m B Powel   1 Lot in Springfield & 1 White pole
David Young   39 on Karrs Creek, 1 White pole

```
            For Year 1801
Robert Black     210 Sulpher fork & 1 White pole
George Hook      320 Bartons Creek
Philip Johnson   200 on Red River & 1 White pole
Edward Lucas     540 Harpeth & 1 White pole
Robert Nelson    320 situation not known
Jonathan Price   160 Beaver Dam Cr
David Young      29 Karrs Creek
            For Year 1802
Robert Beatty    1000 Battle Ground Creek
Joseph Childress 64 War Trace
Wm Cochran       1002 Bartons Creek
Wm Dennis        415 Beaver Dam
Robert Hopkins   640 Sychamore
John Hinds       300 War Trace
John Kerney      100 Sychamore & 1 White pole
Edward McGowen   640 situation not known
Robert Nelson    600 Karrs Cr & War trace
Jonathan Price   260 Beaver Dam
Harriot S Rice   640 situation not known
            For Year 1803
Darius Grey      640 situation not known
Danl Hogan       100 Sulpher fork
John H Hooser    400 Sulpher fork
George Hook      250 Bartons Creek
Wm Lurry         1280 Red River
Aaron Laws       1000 Red River
Wm Lusk          228 Beaver Dam
Joseph Lawrence  50 Red River & 1 White pole
Jas McClellan    640 Bartons Cr
Alexr McNeely    127 Barrens
Clk to issue fi  fas & Shff to sell agreeable to Law
```

p.358 Judgement entered agt following Land for Nonpayment of Taxes for 1804

```
Wm Blackfan      640 acres Duck branch
Isaac Caldwell   60 Red River & 1 White pole
Henry W Lawson   640 Sturgeon Creek
Saml Davis       228 joining Simmons
David McCree     1000 Sychamore
Robert Nelson    997 Millers Creek & Red River
Clerk issue fire facias & Shff sell agreeable to Law
```

B/S William Robertson to Archer Cheatham 2 Negroes proven by Anderson Cheatham
Deed Robert Prince to Benjamin Menees Jr 90 acres proven by Thos Johnson

Admr estate of Samuel Johnson decd to sell personal property of decd, giving legal credit

181

Luke Rawls registers his stock mark

Jury to view road from Springfield by Matthew Morris's, and New Road from Springfield intersecting Old Road near Ramseys Hay field; report which is nearest & best, as quick as convenient. Agreeable to their report, overseer must work. Jury Hardy Bryan, Patrick Martin, Sam¹ Crocket, Lovick Ventress, Henry Fry, George Murphey Junr, Allen Parker, Thomas Norris

John Hutchison Esquire delivered settlement made with John D Robins adm^r estate of John Tucker dec^d; received and ordered recorded; notes & vouchers lodged in Clerks office

B/S David Haley to Archer Cheatham, a Negro, proven by Wm B Vinson
B/S Lewis Wells to Archer Cheatham, a Negro, proven by Wm B Vinson
B/S Jacob Pickren, constable, to Archer Cheatham, a Negro, proven by Wm B Vinson

p.359 Archer Cheatham records his stock mark
James Sawyers records his stock mark

Perry Cohea is admited to keep an Ordinary for one year, his bond 1000 Doll^s, Jacob Pickren & James Sayers his securities

Order Joseph Castleberry to oversee road from Big Clay lick towards Betts as far as County line and following hands work under him: John Lipscomb, John Baldwin, John McIntosh, John McIntosh Junr, Jeremiah Boren, Jacob Fulk, James Bell, Henry Watkins two hands--

State vs John Duncan. Presentment. Deft submits; fined 6 ¼ cents and costs

Henry Johnson appointed guardian for orphan children of John Tucker dec^d: Hannah, Henry, Sally, and Peggy; gave bond 1500 Dollars, Jacob Pinkley and James Sawyers his securities

John B Cheatham app^t^d gd^n for orphan children of John Tucker dec^d: Phebe, Riggs, John, & Samuel Tucker, bond 1500 Dollars with James Sawyers and Daniel Pinkley his securities

Order Clerk deliver to guardians of children of John Tucker decd all notes lodged in his office by the Commissioners who settled with the administrator

p.360 State vs Daniel Pinkley. Presentment. Deft submits; fined 6¼ cents & costs
Court adjourns untill tomorrow Morning 8 OClock

Thursday Morning August 8th 1805
Present John Philips, Martin Duncan, Archer Cheatham, Esqrs

Petition of Nancy, Phebe, Riggs, John & Saml Tucker by John
B Cheatham their guardian against John D Robins admr of John
Tucker was filed; order Clerk issue summons ag^t him return-
able to next Court together with copy of Petition

The Petition of Hannah, Henry, Sally, Peggy Tucker by Henry
Johnson their guardian ag^t John D Robins adm^r of John Tucker
filed; order Clerk issue summons ag^t him returnable to next
Court together with copy of Petition

Court Adjourns untill Court in Course
                    John Philips, Martin Duncan, Archer Cheatham

p.361 State of Tennessee, Robertson County. Monday Morning
November the 4th 1805. Present the Worshipfull John Philips,
Hardy S Bryan, Benjn Menees, James Norfleet, & Isaac Philips

Order Clerk to receive all Lists of Taxable property for the
present year which may be Delivered to him this Term
Nathaniel Dickeson exhonarated from Poll Tax for present and
all succeeding years, he being a Cripple
Grand Jurors: Richard Nuckolls foreman, John Hunt, Anthony
Hinkle, Wm Byrd, Ja^s Long, James Stuart, Silas Tucker, Arch^d
Mahon, Aaron Winters, Jno Chowning, George Browning, Matthew
Day, Marvell Lowe, Joseph Castleberry, Elias Fort. Augustine
Cook, constable, sworn to attend the Grand Jury

Anderson Cheatham vs John D Robins. John Huey Def^{ts} appearance bail, delivered him. John Johnson in proper person ack^d
himself Def^{ts} bail in room of John Huey

State vs Robertson Murphey. James Green appearance bond 50
Dolls, condition he attend Court as prosecutor & witness behalf State agt Murphey. Robert Green also bound as above

p.362 Elisabeth Tucker and Charles Simmons adm^{rs} of Samuel
Tucker dec^d vs James Menees. Wm Hendley, def^t's appearance
bail, delivered def^t. Def^t brought George Murphey Junr and
Thomas Sellars who ack^d selves said Menees's bail in s^d suit

State vs Wm Ragsdale. John Siglar appearance bond 50 Dollars
as prosecutor and witness in behalf the State ag^t Ragsdale
Another bond, same persons, worded as above

Samuel Pearson to oversee road in room of Moses Winters

State vs James McIntosh. Appearance bond of John Watkins to prosecute & witness behalf State

E Tucker & C Simmons admrs vs James Norris and James Menees. Elisha Fikes and Stuart W Thornton appearance bail for James Menees surrendered him. Elisha Fikes & Jas Darnald ack themselves Menees's security in afsd suit

Archer Cheatham vs Stephen Boren. James G Heard security for deft delivered him. Charles Colgin acknowledged himself said Borens security in sd suit

p.363 Court orders admrs of John Polk decd to advertise and sell as much of estate as will satisfy claim of Maria Harris daughter of admx by a former marriage. Appoint Charles Miles Esqr, Wm Connell Esqr, & Elias Fort Junr to appraise remainder of sd estate and equally divide same between Martha Polk relict & Olivia Polk dau of sd decd. Further ordered that if upon division any part assigned to Olivia Polk is incapable of being increased for benefit of Olivia Polk, admrs are to advertise and sell same; return list of sales to next Court

Admrs estate of John Polk decd deliver inventory of estate; also account current of sd estate as it came into the hands of sd decd at the time of his marriage

Admr of the estate of Saml Johnston decd delivered amount of sales of said estate
Deed William Dickson to William Spiller 137 acres proven by Wm Johnson
Deed Thos Hale to John Morris 100 acres proven by Wm Hunt
Deed Lewellen Phips to Robt Bates 60 acres proven by James McDonald
Deed James Hodges to John Yoes 640 acres proven by William Connell
p.364 Order James Young to oversee road in room of Elias Fort (M C)

Will of Levi Moore proven by James Gambril & John Siglar, & Abraham Moore, Amos Moore & Joel Moore, executors, took oath

Josiah Wright apptd constable; his bond 620 Dollars, Stephen Stewart and William Atkins his securities
Jacob Pickren apptd constable; bond 620 Dollars, John Huey and Joseph Robertson his securities

Benjamin Holman excused from serving as a Juror this Term

Deed Benjamin Koen to Sam[l] Hollis 320 acres proven by Allen Parker
Deed Jesse Jones to Robert Carson 106½ acres ackd

William Polk app[d] guardian for Maria Harris, a minor; bond 6000 Dollars, James Mcfarlin and John Sherod his securities

Deed William Dickson to Benjamin Spiller 137 acres proven by William Johnson
Deed James Menees Sh[ff] to John Payne 94 acres ackd
Deed W[m] Briscoe to Archer Cheatham 110 acres proven by Tho[s] Johnson
Deed James Menees Sh[ff] to Thomas Sellars 1096 acres ackd

Giles Connell app[d] constable; bond 620 Dollars, Henry Johnson & Matthew Day his securities
Moses Benson app[d] constable; bond 620 Dollars, Patrick Patterson & Perry Cohea his securities

p.365 Order that the former markers to view road from Brush Creek, Mark Nobles ford, to intersect the old road about one miles from sd creek so as to leave Elias Forts plantation on the South, and make return to the overseer which is the most convenient way. Ordered that James Blackwell be overseer of sd road, persons work from Millers at James Youngs and hands within one mile of sd road

James Gardner apptd goverseer of road in room of John Sherod

Peter Brawner to oversee road beginning at fork of the road agreeable to his former order, to work toward Hardy S Bryans on Sychamore the distance of 4½ miles
Court Adjourns untill tomorrow Morning 9 OClock

Tuesday Morning Nov[r] 5th 1805   Present the worshipfull John Philips, Charles Miles, Martin Duncan, Esquires

John C Hamilton vs Philip Shackler. Judgement by an original attachment before a Justice/Peace for $12.50. Levied on 100 acres in the Barrens at a large spring about two miles N. E. course from Alex[r] Gordons on Red River. Jacob Pickren, con[le] Court Orders af[sd] land sold to satisfy judgement and costs

Josiah Wright, James Atkins, Ambrose Hutchison, Alexander Calhoon, Benjamin Edwards, John Groves, Matthew Luter Jr and Holland Luter appointed searchers and patrollers in Captain John Campbells company for the ensuing year

p.366 Deed William Johnson to John Biggs 50 acres ackd
Deed Martin Duncan to Alexander Chesnut 427 acres ackd
Deed George Pool to David Jones 20 acres ackd
Deed Joseph B Nevell Shff to Demsey Coffield 446 acres proven by Micajah Philps
Deed Rebekah Hinds to Wm Karr one third of 640 acres proven by Humphrey Hogan
Order James Crabtree Esqr and Danl Holman to designate hands which is to work under Nathl Simmons overseer of a road

John Hutchison Esqr admited to keep an Ordinary 1 year; bond 1000 Dollars, James Hutchison & James Sawyers his securities
Court adjourns untill tomorrow morning 9 OClock

Wednesday Morning, Novr 6th 1805
Present Charles Miles, Archer Cheatham, James Norfleet Esqrs

Order heirs of Nathan Robey pay Thomas Bell 100 Dollars for his trouble of going to North Carolina to sell lands of the estate &c

B/S William Dorris to Ezekiah Dorris proven by Bazel Boren

State vs John Siglar. Willliam Ragsdale appearance bond 100 Dollars, condition he attend Court in behalf of the State

p.367 State vs Robertson Murphey. James Green appearance bond 100 Dollars to prosecute and give Testamony behalf the State. Robert Green as a witness as above, same sum

Deed John Strother attorney/fact for John Gray Blount & Edward Harris to Philip Trammel 428 acres proven by Adam Clap

Deed James Menees, Collector of Direct Tax, to Wm P Anderson 280 acres ackd

State vs James McIntosh. John Watkins prosecutor and witness appearance bond 100 Dollars, behalf of the State

George Hardin vs Edward Cheatham. Pltf and deft by their attorneys. Pltf to recover agt deft 110 Dollars, & 16 Dolls 50 cts interest thereon, & 6 Dollars 59 cents costs of suit
Grand Jury discharged

p.368 Deed James Menees Sheriff to Wm Karr 150 acres ackd
Deed James Menees Shff to Wm Karr and John Flynn 640 acres ackd
Court Adjourns untill tomorrow Morning 9 OClock

Thursday Morning November the 7ᵗʰ 1805   Present
John Philips, Archer Cheatham, James H Bryan, Esquires

Jurors to next Court: James Johnston, Daniel Johnston, Eppa
Lawson, Thomas Byrd, Robt Brown, Walter Brown, William Craf-
ford, Charles Bradon, Obediah Bounds, Sampson Matthews, Ben-
jamin Chapman, William Benson, Francis Boren, Nathan Clark,
John Couts, James Bell, Wm Crocket, Frederick Cobb, Andrew
Cheatham, Jnº Dorris, Michˡ Fiser, John Lipscomb, John Hyde,
Jacob Lewis, Gabriel Rawls, Robert Saunders, Henry Airs, Jaˢ
Atkins, Geº Hanly Jʳ, John Sherod, Wᵐ Conyers, Jnº Campbell,
Jacob Pinkley, George Murphey, John Payne, Volentine Choate,
James Yates, Benjamin Menees Junʳ, Samuel Crocket

Deed James Vaughn to James Benton 100 acres proven by Wm
Johnson
Anderson Cheatham admited to keep Ordinary 1 year; bond 1000
Dollars, W B Vinson and Jacob Robertson his securities

Order James H Bryan & Thomas Johnson Esqʳˢ compleat the settlement of estate of John Tucker decᵈ with John D Robins the
administrator and report to this Court
Order John D Robins be allowed 108 Dollars 37½ cents out of
the estate of John Tucker decd for serving as administrator

Archer Cheatham apptd Inspector/Cotton gave bond 1000 Dollˢ
Anderson Cheatham and John B Cheatham his securities

p.369 The following land, advertised agreeable to Law, to be
sold, or so much thereof as shall satisfy taxes & costs due
thereon
Pierce Asbells heirs   70 acres joining Springfield
        Dº   one Lot in Springfield
Richard Cook   50 ac joining Renfro on Brush Cr
Isaac Roberts   548 ac Sychamore
Isaac Williams   140 ac Spring Cr of Sulpher fork
Andrew Braker   640 ac Gilkisons Creek
James Greenlee   640 ac Elk fork
Robert Hopkins   640 ac Sychamore
James M Lewis   2560 ac Millers Creek
        Dº   1280 ac on the ridge
Thomas Williams   640 ac waters of Sychamore
Martin Armstrong   800 ac Karrs & Millers Cr, 2 tracts
John Cummins   1000 ac Sychamore
Benjn McCullochs heirs   274 ac joining Moses Winters
        Dº   640 ac joining J G Brek on Red River
        Dº   640 Red River
        Dº   640 Winters Creek
        Dº   640 Millers Creek

Laughlin Flynn	640 ac head Calebs Creek
John Sutton	100 ac Red River
Robert Stothart	274 ac joining Mrs Karr
D°	100 ac where Henry Wigle lives
John Coleman	640 ac Sychamore
Thomas Davis	640 ac joining the tract [blank]
William Lurry	640 ac N side of Middle of Red River
Zarababul Starks heirs	1 Lot in Springfield
Charles Simmons	1 D° D°
Jesse Rascoe	1 D° D°
John Pankey	1 D° D°

p.370 Deed Martin Duncan to James Irwin 113 acres ackd

Order Martin Duncan & John Hutchison (formerly app^td) settle with adm^r of Saml Tucker dec^d and make return to next Court; also to value the Negroes belonging to s^d Estate

Commissioners appointed to settle with John D Robins adm^r of John Tucker Dec^d made report; examined & sanctioned

Henry Johnson guardian for orphans of Jn° Tucker decd vs Jn° D Robins adm^r of estate of John Tucker dec^d. Prayer of Petitioners granted; judgement entered for sum found due by commissioners app^td by Court to settle with s^d Robins

John B Cheatham guardian for orphans of John Tucker dec^d vs John D Robins adm^r estate of John Tucker dec^d. Same Judgement as entered for Henry Johnson

On petition of Enoch Tucker, order Thomas Johnson and Archer Cheatham appraise Negroes of Jn° Tucker dec^d & with the heir now of age, the adm^r and guardians of minors apportion & divide estate between legatees on or before 1 January next

Geo Murphey Junr to oversee road from Joseph Frys to Ramseys old Hay field on the Ironwork road; Wm Crockett and Matthew Day to designate hands to work under him

Court Adjourns untill Court in Course
                    John Philips, Martin Duncan, Archer Cheatham

p.371 State of Tennessee, Robertson County. Monday Morning Feby 3rd 1806. Present the Worshipfull Ja^s Norfleet, Martin Duncan, John Philips, Benjn Menees, James Crabtree, Esquires

Thomas Swann Esqr produced a Licence to practice Law in this state and is accordingly admited

Grand Jurors William Benson foreman, Walter Brown, Volentine Choate, Thomas Byrd, Jn° Hyde, Wᵐ Crocket, Henry Airs, James Johnston, Michael Fiser, Jacob Lewis, John Dorris, Benjamin Chapman, John Sherod, Wᵐ Crafford, Sampson Matthews. Giles Connell, constable, sworn to attend the Grand Jury

Thomas Hunter who had for one year Isaac Williams now on the Parish, the time being expired, delivered Williams to Court

Ordered estate of Joseph Hart decd pay to Aquilla Sugg three Dollars for making settlement between the estate of sd Hart and the estate of Noah Sugg deceased

State vs Nathaniel Dickeson. James Elliott and Peter Brawner securities for Nathˡ Dickeson delivered him. Wᵐ Dickeson and Henry Johnson acknowledge themselves Dickesons security

George Sprouse to oversee road in room of Sampson Matthews George Hendley excused from serving as a Juror this Term Deed James Menees Shff to Thomas Johnson & Richard Nuckolls 640 acres ackd

p.372 Order the admr of John Polk decd to advertise & sell as much of personal property of John Polk decᵈ as will fully satisfy claim of Maria Harris, daughter of relict by former marriage. Further ordered that Majʳ Charles Miles Esqʳ, William Connel Esqʳ, and Elias Fort are appᵗᵈ commissioners to appraise remainder of estate and divide same between Martha Polk, relict, and Olivia Polk, daughter of decᵈ: they shall lay off & assign to relict one third of land in sᵈ county to include the mansion & improvement as dower for life, and one third personal property they shall assign to sd relict. The Remaining two thirds they shall assign to Olivia Polk. Any part assigned to Olivia Polk incapable of increasing for her benefit, admʳ shall advertise and sell to highest bidder

Power/Attorney Dempsey Coffield to Micajah Philps admited to record on Certificate and county seal of Clerk of Livingston County, Kentucky, certifying it was proven in that Court

Deed Philip Trammel to Adam Clap 220 acres proven by Adam Clap
p.373 Deed William Hughs to Samuel Hollis 98 acres proven by Sarah Plasters
Deed James Menees Shᶠᶠ to Richard Nuckolls 82 acres ackd
Deed James Menees Collector of Direct Tax to Josiah Burt [or

Bull?Bult?] 274 acres ackd
Deed Johnson Kilgore to James Yates 150 acres proven by Thos
Yates
Deed Thomas Rose to Reddick Robertson 100 acres proven by
Ephraim Harrin
Deed Thomas Rose to Ephraim Herrin 100 acres proven by Red-
dick Robertson

Adm^r of estate of Henry Sherod Dec^d delivered supplementary
inventory of estate, also an account of sale of said estate

Adm^r of the estate of John Polk dec^d delivered supplementary
inventory of said estate. Wm Polk one of adm^{rs} of John Polk
dec^d allowed 55 Dollars 87 + cents for his trouble and money
expended on business of s^d estate, as per account rendered

William Polk released from guardianship of Maria Harris

Order Wm Connel and James Norfleet Esq^{rs} settle with adm^r of
estate of Noah Sugg dec^d and make return to this Court

Order Thomas Johnson and Anderson Cheatham settle with adm^r
and adm^x estate of Captⁿ Edward Butler dec^d and make return

p.374 Richd Nuckolls to oversee road in room of Titus Benton

Nathan Morris to oversee the Iron work road from Karrs Creek
to Ramseys old Hay field; Saml Crocket, Patrick Martin, Isaac Anderson, Mr Culverson, Wm Norris, William Blisard, Philip Parchment, Peter Fry, and Mr Farmer are to work under him
Court adjourns untill tomorrow Morning 10 OClock

Tuesday Morning February 4th 1806   Present the Worshipfull
John Philips, William Connel, Benjamin Menees, Esquires

Clerk to receive lists of Taxable property for year 1805
Wm Hendley to oversee road in room of Jno Cromwell

Philip Hornbarger vs John Knight.   Judgement May Term 1804.
Motion of def^t for Writ of Error to remove cause to Superior
Court; writ allowed upon his giving Bond

State vs James Elliott.   Nathaniel Dickeson appearance bond
to give Testamony in behalf of the state

John Philips & James Crabtree Esqrs to let to lowest bidder
Isaac Williams and Daniel McDaniel for one year made report:
they let Isaac Williams to John Williams for 45 Dollars, who
was lowest bidder; also Daniel McDaniel to Noah Woodard for

42 Dollars 75 cents, who was lowest bidder. John Williams & Noah Woodard agree to furnish sd Isaac [p.375] & Daniel with sufficient good comfortable clothes, good holsome provisions and good comfortable lodging. John Williams will receive Ten Dollars at next Court, balance as expiration of the year

James Norfleet, Isaac Dortch & James H Bryan Esq^{rs} to settle with ext^{rs} of William Fort dec^d and make return this Court

Thomas Woodard appointed guardian for the orphan children of Daniel Holland dec^d; bond 15000 Dollars with Martin Duncan & Noah Woodard his securities

Deed Archer Cheatham & Miles Kerby to Isaac Dortch 100 acres proven by James Norfleet
Deed Archer Cheatham to Isaac Dortch 320 acres proven by Ja^s Norfleet
Deed James Menees Sh^{ff} to John Vanzant 181+ acres ackd
Deed Willis Hix to Joseph Barns 100 acres proven by Benjamin Menees
Deed Joseph Barns to James Norfleet 100 acres proven by John Carr
Deed George Bell to Perry Cohea Lot 15 in Springfield proven by William Johnson
Deed Joseph Barns to James Norfleet 200 acres proven by Isaac Dortch
Deed Joseph Huey to William Robertson 60 + acres proven by Thos Johnson
Deed William Johnson to William Robertson 450 acres ackd
Deed Wm Karr to Joel Lewis 50 acres proven by Henry Johnson

p.376 A Seekright lessee of W^m P Anderson vs Henry Gardner. Ejectment. Present Jno Philips, Isaac Philips, Benjn Menees. May 1804 pl^{tf} by P W Humphreys; def^t by Jno C Hamilton. Henry Gardner Def^t in room of Furdinand Dreadnaught enters common rule, pleads Not Guilty. Cont^d. Feby 1806 Jury: Obediah Bounds, Wm Conyers, John Couts, Ja^s Bell, Robt Brown, George Murphey, Jno Lipscomb, Eppa Lawson, Jacob Pinkley, James Atkins, Chas Bradon, David Henry find for Def^t. Pl^{tf} obtained appeal to Superior Court; bond 500 Dollars, P W Humphreys & Thomas Stuart, securities. Henry Johnson witness proves 12 days attendance, as surveyor one day, mileage as surveyor 60 miles. George Neville witness two days, 46 miles traveling. Robert Nelson witness two days, 50 miles; Francis Prince six days, 340 miles, 4 ferriages at 6 , c^{ts} and two at 50 cents. Ordered by Court that mileage of Francis Prince proven above shall only be calculated from state line on a direction from Robertson Court House to the United States Saline

James Norfleet & Isaac Dortch Esq^{rs} appt^d to value estate of

Wm Fort dec^d and make distribution in conformity to Fort's will made report which is sanctioned and ordered recorded

Deed Archer Cheatham & Thos Johnson to Wm Robertson 640 acres ackd
W^m D Menees to oversee road in room of Elisha Fikes, to have same hands with the addition of Milsaps hands
p.377 Obediah Bounds to oversee road that crosses the ridge at David Stuarts, from the County line to Byrds fork of Red River; old Mr Stringer to be overseer of s^d road from Byrds fork to the mouth of Simmons branch; Thos Kilgore J^r and Wm Byrd will designate hands to work under them, allowing hands to work the Robertson Road and the old Kentucky Road

William Carter to oversee road in room of Zach^h Cox
Arthur Pitt to oversee road in room of John Crocket
Court Adjourns untill tomorrow Morning 10 OClock

Wednesday Morning Feby the 5th 1806. Present the Worshipfull John Philips, Benjⁿ Menees, Archer Cheatham & Charles Miles

Commissioners app^{td} to have built an addition to Court House report: Col^o Archer Cheatham has compleated work agreeable to contract, for which he was to receive $240. Order County Trustee or Sheriff to pay s^d sum
James Norfleet and John Young allowed 37 + Dollars each for services as Commissioners of Town of Springfield, for laying off s^d Town, making Deeds, &c
Thomas Johnson allowed Ten Dollars for his services in lay-ing off Town of Springfield, making Plats of Town, &c
John Philips, Ja^s Norfleet & Jno Hutchison Esqrs allowed 400 Doll^s 50 c^{ts} each for services in leting the buildings
Solomon Ledford allowed 1 Dollar 50 c^{ts} for work done about Jaol as p^r acc^t filed

p.378 State vs Robertson Murphey. A & B. Def^t in proper per-son submits to Court; fined one Dollar and all costs

State vs Jacob Pickren. A & B. Def^t submits & is fined five Dollars & costs. Giles Connell proves 1 Day attendance

Benjamin Menees & John Hutchison Esq^{rs} app^{td} to settle with administrator of Daniel Holland dec^d & report to this Court

State vs Nathl Dickson. S^d Dickesons securities discharged

Isaac Dortch, James Norfleet, & James H Bryan Esq^{rs} app^{td} to settle with Ex^{trs} of Wm Fort dec^d made report

Grand Jury presents that children of Mary Crow is in a likely way to suffer; order that Mary be summoned to next Court and bring s^d children with her

John Hutchison and Benjn Menees Esq^rs, Comm^rs to settle with adm^rs of Daniel Holland dec^d, report; sanctioned

Deed James Lynn Senr to Wm Stricklin 74 acres proven by Joseph Pitts
Wm Conyers excused from serving as a Juror this Term

p.379 Volentine Choate & Charles Bradon designate hands to work on Captn Bounds road from Top of Ridge to Byrds Creek

Deed James Benton to Joseph McDowel 100 acres proven by Ja^s McDowel
Comm^rs to settle with adm^rs of Samuel Tucker dec^d delivered settlement; sanctioned
Court adjourns untill tomorrow Morning 9 OClock

Thursday February 6th 1806 Present
John Philips, Charles Miles, John Hutchison, Esquires

State vs James McIntosh. A & B. Def^t submits; fined 50 cents and costs. Jacob Pickren, witness, proves 4 days attendance

B/S Samuel Robins to John B Cheatham, two Negroes, proven by Thomas Johnson, also certificate of Nathan Clark annexed to s^d Bill of Sale was also proven. Ordered registered

Israel Robertson vs James Miles. Motion to take deposition of [blank] Clements at his house in Indianna Territory at or near Lusks ferry across the Ohio; Court appoint Robert Kirk and Richard Ferguson or either to take s^d Deposition

Eppa Lawson excused from serving as a Juror this Term

p.380 Joseph Engleman & wife Jane vs John D Robins adm^r of Jno Tucker dec^d. Jury Obediah Bounds, Jno Couts, James Bell, Robert Brown, George Murphey, John Lipscomb, James Atkins, Charles Bradon, Shaderick Rawls, Matthew Day, David Spence, Nathaniel Dickeson who assess the plaintiff's damage to 64 Dollars & costs of suit

Joseph Engleman & wife Jane vs Jno Robins adm^r of Jno Tucker decd with Will annexed. Petition for a Legacy. John Philips, Ja^s H Bryan, Chas Miles, Justices. John D Robins not having performed Last Will & Testament of John Tucker decd, decree that John D Robins pay sd Joseph & Jane sd 64 Dollars. When

193

Judgement is recovered against Robert Nelson by Jn° D Robins in suit mentioned in Petition, money arising therefrom admr to pay sd Jane annually during her life the Interest arising from sd Money, and John D Robins to pay costs of this suit

B/S Bazel Boren to William Benson for a Negro ackd

p.381 Jacob Robertson vs James Darnell. Pltf obtained Judgement before a Justice/Peace agt deft, and obtained execution agt goods & chattels of deft; officer could find no personal property and levied on 1840 acres. Ordered to sell so much land was will satisfy debt and costs

Jacob Pickren vs James Darnell. Pltf obtained Judgement agt deft before Justice/Peace; obtained Execution which was returned no personal property found; levied on 1840 acres Ordered to sell so much land as will satisfy debt and costs

Grand Jury discharged the fourth Day

Elisabeth Tucker & C Simmons Admrs of Samuel Tucker decd vs James Menees. Debt. Novr 1805 Pltf by N W Williams; deft by Wm Smith. Feby 1806. Jury Obediah Bounds, John Couts, James Bell, Robt Brown, George Murphey, John Lipscomb, Jacob Pinkley, James Atkins, Chas Bradon, Shadk Rawls, D Spence, Nathl Dickeson who find for pltf 54 Dollars 54 cents. Also costs p.382 Court Adjourns untill Tomorrow Morning 10 OClock

Friday Morning Feby 7th 1806   Present the Worshipfull John Philips, Benjamin Menees, Martin Duncan, Esquires

Archer Cheatham jaoler, Robertson County, exhibited his acct against Jacob Fulk for Jaol fees while he was imprisoned, & also account for officer who served warrant & other services amounting to Ten Dollars 33 1/3 cents. Judgement entered; & clerk to issue execution for the same

Jurors to next Court: Wm Byrd, Moses Hardin, Thomas George, Charles Kilgore, William Armstrong Jr, Walter Stark, William Spiller, William Robertson, Francis Boren, Jas Stark, George Browning, Joseph Castleberry, Jn° Duncan, Henry Fiser, Jacob Fry, Elisha Fikes, James Hays, Henry Johnson, Joseph Choate, Henry Hunt, Jacob Moake, Allen Parker, Jacob Pinkley, James Jones Sr, David Huddleston Sr, Richd Matthews, Jn° Chowning, Obediah Bounds, William Cole, Mark Cole, William Deloach, John Williams, Lemuel Sugg, Joshua Gardner, James Blackwell, John Crane, John Karr, Thomas Polk

Jurors to Superior Court: Abraham Philips, Isaac Dorris Sr,

Elias Fort, William Connell

Thos Johnson & Anderson Cheatham Esqre appt^d to settle with
adm^x & adm^r of Captn Edward Butler dec^d made report.
Adm^x and adm^r of Edwd Butler Dec^d delivered amount of sales;
also an additional inventory

Thomas Johnson Clerk allowed Ten Dollars, price he gave for
Iredells Revisal of the Laws of N Carolina for use of this
Court, Also 2 Dollars for the purchase of a small bound Book
for the use of the Clerks office

p.383 Following persons to take Lists of Taxable property

James Norfleet Esqr	Captn Campbells Company
James Crabtree	" Kilgores "
Joseph Dorris	" Bounds "
Martin Duncan	" Krisels "
John Philips	" Thorntons "
Isaac Philips	" Suggs "
James H Bryan	" Brawners "
Hardy S Bryan	" Murpheys "

John B Cheatham Esqr Collector State & County Tax for 1805
Reports tracts not given in for purpose of paying Taxes

Richard Cook	50 acres joining Renfro, Brush Creek
Isaac Roberts	548 Half pone Creek
Isaac Williams	140 Spring Creek of Sulpher fork
Robt Hopkins	640 Sychamore
James M Lewis	2560 Millers Creek
D^o	1280 on the ridge
Thos Williams	640 Sychamore
Martin Armstrong	800 Karrs and Millers Cr, two tracts
John Cummins	1000 Sychamore
Laughlin Flynn	640 head of Calebs Creek
John Sutton	100 on Red River
Thomas Davis	410 joining Turnbulls Clay Lick
William Lurry	640 waters of Red River
Joseph Pankey	Lot 17 in Springfield
John Thompson	640 Karrs Creek
Aaron Laws	1000 Red River
Lewis Barker	400 Red River
James Glasgow	1000 mouth of Sychamore
William Crafford	640 Red River, Crafford preemption
Darrias Grey	640 Cumberland River
Josiah Howel	320 Karrs Creek
p. 384 Thomas Hickman	640 acres bought for Taxes
D^o	D^o
Edmund Hickman heirs	274 joining Goose pond
[blank] McCormick	640 joining Wm Johnson in Barrens
John Irwin	1920 waters Red River

```
Robert Lee                  640 Millers Creek
Mary Watson heir of John Ford  640 acres waters of Sychamore
Amos Rounsavall             Lot 35 in Springfield
Wm Renfro's Heirs           415 Brush Creek
Wm Taitt                    640 Winters Creek
Edward Ward                 1280 waters Sulpher fork
Samuel Dorris Senr          Lot 57 in Springfield
James McGill                Lot 5 in Springfield
Richard Matthews            Lot 26 in Springfield
Nicholas Conrod             Lot 60 in Springfield
        D°       423 Sulpher fork
        D°       320      D°
        D°       181 Millers Creek
        D°       one half of 274 on Sulpher fork
        D°       220 waters Millers Creek & 1 black pole
John Wilson        640 mouth War Trace Creek on Sulpher fork
Frederick Cook     640 head of Persons Creek
John McCormick     640 joins above on Persons Creek
Above to be published agreeable to Law
```

Ordered David Lucas be Captⁿ of patrollers in Captain Bounds Company; Elijah Harris, Robᵗ Bradon, James England, Obediah Bounds be patrollers under him. That George A West, John W Bryan, Matthew Galt, Samuel Elliott, Asa Woodward be patrollers in Capᵗ Brawners Company. That Stuart W Thornton, Peter Young, Jacob Robertson, John Strain, Leonard Sale and Wᵐ Milsap Jʳ be patrollers for Captⁿ Thorntons Company

Order that the small room in the addition of the Court House be appropriated to the Clerks office, as shall be sufficient for the good accommodaiton of sd office, so as to have in sd Room a sufficient space when it is necessary for the Jury to be there.
Court Adjourns untill Court in Course
                Benjⁿ Menees, Archer Cheatham, Martin Duncan

p.385   State of Tennessee, Robertson County.   Monday Morning, May 5ᵗʰ 1806. Present the Worshipfull Benjamin Menees, Isaac Philips, Charles Miles, Esquires

Grand Jurors sworn: John Williams foreman, Jacob Moake, Elisha Fikes, Francis Boren, Richard Matthews, Charles Kilgore, John Crane, Joshua Gardner, Moses Hardin, John Chowning, Wm Spiller, William Cole, John Duncan, Allen Parker, Geo Browning. Josiah Wright, constable, sworn to attend on Grand Jury

William Mason records his stock mark
Hardy S Bryan Esqr to take list of Taxable property in Captⁿ
Murpheys Company, make return to Next Court
James Miles resigned his appointment of Constable
Thomas Sellers records his stock mark

Order Sheriff refund to Robert Perry one Dollar twenty cents
being Tax on 640 acres in name of John London, it appearing
sd tract was before paid by Allen Parker

James Norfleet and Isaac Dortch Esqrs to settle with admr of
estate of John Tennison decd & make report to this Court

Jacob Siglar to oversee the road in room of John Siglar from
Springfield to Joel Moores, & following hands to work under
him, Thomas Morgan, David Siglar, George Isbell, Thos Morgan
Jr, Wm Huey, Wm Robertson, Mr Steel, Thos Johnson, John Huey

James Norfleet Esqʳ returned list Taxable property for Captⁿ
Campbells Company
p.386   James H Bryan   Capt Browners Company
Isaac Philips   Capt Suggs Company
John Philips   Capt Thorntons Company
Martin Duncan   Capt Krisels Company
Joseph Dorris   Capt Bounds Company
James Crabtree   Capt Kilgores Company

Deed Thomas Yates to Mary Isbell 150 acres ackd

Order Road leading from John Karrs turned from the corner of
Carrs fence next to John Sherods, leading to Brush Creek so
as to leave sᵈ Sherods improvement to the left, intersecting
the old road at the lower corner of Sherods plantation, the
nearest and best way. Jury to mark same: James Stuart, John
Carr, Archᵈ Mahon, Jesse Martin, James Gardner

Admʳˢ of John Polk decᵈ delivered a list of property sold by
order of Court to satisfy claim of Maria Harris, also an account of the hire of the Negroes of Olivia Polk

Wᵐ Connell, Charles Miles & Elias Fort Jʳ delivered accounts
of personal property of John Polk decᵈ appraised & assigned
for Martha Polk relict of sd decd and for use of Olivia Polk
dau of sᵈ decᵈ. Also two plats of land being the division of
land of sᵈ decᵈ in this County, between Martha Polk, relict,
and Olivia Polk, daughter of sᵈ decᵈ

Deed James Menees Shᶠᶠ to Wᵐ Mason 181½ acres ackd
Deed Ezekiel Polk to Henry Gardner 155 acres proven by Elias
Fort Jʳ & Joshua Gardner

B/S Thomas Shaw to Joseph Choate for two Negroes ackd
B/S Bazel Boren to Francis Boren, a Negro, ackd
p.387   Deed Philip Parchment to George Murphey 280 acres
ackd
Deed James Menees Sh^{ff} to Lemuel Sugg 28 acres ackd
Deed James Menees Sh^{ff} to George Donnell 640 acres
Deed William Wells to David Lucas 200 acres ackd

James Sawyers, Obediah Bounds, Volentine Choate, & Chas Bradon to divide hands amongst overseers of road from the ridge
at David Stuarts to Byrds fork; Charles Bradon is to oversee
from Robertson Road to County line on af^{sd} road

Will of Margeret Karr proven by Thomas Johnson, Mary Smith,
Elisabeth Long and Jane Hardin subscribing witnesses thereto

Joshua Smith to oversee road from Springfield to Smiths mill
from town to Menees Road near the head of Buzzard Creek in
room of Edward King, and have same hands to work under him

Charles McIntosh to oversee road from Springfield to Logan,
his bounds from N^o side Sulpher fork to where s^d road intersects old Logan Road; hands on N^o side s^d fork who formerly
worked under John McElhainy are to work under Chas McIntosh
Court Adjourns untill tomorrow Morning 10 OClock

Tuesday Morning May 6th 1806
Present John Philips, Benjamin Menees, Charles Miles, Esq^{rs}

James Stark records his stock mark

p.388 James Darnell vs Jacob Pickren. Present John Philips,
Isaac Philips, Benjn Menees, Chas Miles, Esq^{rs}. August 1805
pl^{tf} by Thos Stuart; def^t by John C Hamilton & N W Williams.
Feby 1806 jury Obediah Bounds, Jno Couts, James Bell, Robert
Brown, Ge^o Murphey, John Lipscomb, Eppa Lawson, Jacob Pink-
ley, James Atkins, Charles Bradon, Ja^s Miles, Wm Edwards who
assess plaintiffs damages to 85 Dollars; new tryal granted.
May 1806 Jury Walter Stark, Mark Cole, Jacob Pinkley, Andrew
Irwin, Henry Hunt, Henry Johnson, William Byrd, Lemuel Sugg,
Jacob Fry, Jno Carr, William Deloach, Ja^s Shannon who assess
pl^{tfs} damage to 120 Dollars. Pl^{tf} obtains appeal to Superior
Court; bond 500 Dollars, Lemuel Sugg, Jno B Cheatham & James
Sawyers his securities.   Witnesses: Wm Flewellen proves 6
days attendance.   Nathan Fikes 8 days & 40 miles traveling;
Booth Malone 5 days & 100 miles traveling;   Shaderick Rawls
7 days; Joel Lewis 2 days

Order John Williams receive from County Trustee Ten Dollars

198

for time he has kept Isaac Williams to his death, who was on
the parish, being for funeral expences, &c
William Edwards records his stock mark
Augustine Cook app'd Constable; bond 620 Dollars, Jn° Duncan
& Epphra⁵ Benton his securities; took oath

p.389   Bustard & Eastin vs Samuel Robins. Present John Phil-
ips, Jo⁵ Dorris, M Duncan, Esqʳˢ. Novʳ 1805 plᵗᶠ by Bennet
Searcy; defᵗ by Thoˢ Stuart. May 1806 jury Mark Cole, Jacob
Pinkley, Andrew Irwin, Henry Hunt, Henry Johnson, Wᵐ Byrd,
Lemuel Sugg, Jacob Fry, Jn° Carr, Wᵐ Deloach, Wᵐ Sale, James
Shannon who assess plᵗᶠˢ damage to 112 Dollars 40 3/4 cents.
Also his costs of suit

County Tax for present year: each 100 acres 6¼ cents
                            each black pole   12½
                            each white pole   6¼
                            each town Lot   12½
                            each store for retailing goods $2.50
                            each stud horse   12½

Ordered Emanuel Skinner be allowed Thirty Dollars for keeping Sally Moore, one year, now on the parish
p.390   Deed William Matthews to Sampson Matthews 156 acres
proven by Michael Kerny
Deed Archibald Mahon coroner to Isaac Dortch 380 acres ackd
Deed Joel Vaughn to Theophilus Morgan 200 acres ackd
Deed Benjamin Menees Jʳ to Thomas Norris 228 acres ackd

James Mcfarlin admited to keep an ordinary 1 year; bond 5000
Dollars, Giles Connell & Nicholas Conrod, securities
Orphan Joseph Childress bound to Henry Fry untill he arrives
to age of 21 years
Court Adjourns untill tomorrow Morning 10 OClock

Wednesday Morning May 7ᵗʰ 1806   Present the worshipfull
John Philips, Benjamin Menees, Isaac Philips, Esquires

Mortgage for Negro Hannah from John Ferguson to David Mcfaddin proven by James Mcfarlan, subscribing witness; & also by
Archibald Mahon who was present and saw Ferguson sign seal &
acknowledge sd Mortgage though not a subscribing witness

p.391   James Berry vs James Darnell. Two Judgements agᵗ Darnell before a J/P: 70 Dollˢ 54 cᵗˢ on 5 Apˡ 1806, subject to
credit 17 Dollˢ 77 cᵗˢ 20 Apˡ 1806. Shᶠᶠ returned execution
levied April 14ᵗʰ on 1149 acres property of James Darnell on
Sturgeon Creek. Sheriff to sell so much as shall satisfy the
judgements and costs

William Flewellen vs James Darnell. Present Isaac Philips, Joseph Dorris, Martin Duncan, Esq^{rs}. May 1806 Pl^{tf} by Bennet Searcy; def^t by William Smith. Jury Walter Stark, Mark Cole, Jacob Pinkley, Andrew Irwin, Henry Hunt, Henry Johnson, Wm Byrd, Jacob Fry, William Deloach, Wm Sale, Matthew Day, John Mcfarlan who find for Def^t. Pl^{tf} to pay all costs. Witnesses: Shaderick Rawls proves 3 days attendance; Nancy Rawls 1 day; Isaac Philips 3 days

Deed Benjamin Menees Senr to Archer Cheatham 37 acres ackd

John B Cheatham app^{td} Collector of State & County Tax; bond 3000 Dollars; Josiah Fort, Elias Fort Jr, Wm Deloach, John Hutchison, Augustine Cook, Joseph Castleberry his securities

p.392 Ordered that Thomas Figures be overseer of the road in room of Anderson Cheatham
Stuart W Thornton to oversee road from Springfield to Karrs Creek at John Brooks
Court Adjourns untill tomorrow Morning 10 OClock

Thursday Morning May 8th 1806   Present the Worshipfull
John Philips, Benjamin Menees, Isaac Philips, Esquires

State vs George Murphey. A/B. Present [as above]. Presentment: George Murphey on 10 January 1806 did beat, wound, and ill-treat Peter Brawner to his great damage. Wm Smith. Def^t by attorney[blank]. May 1806 jury Mark Cole, Jacob Pinkley, Andrew Irwin, Henry Hunt, Henry Johnson, Wm Byrd, Jacob Fry, Wm Deloach, Matthew Day, David Spence, John Huey, Peter Fry, who find Def^t not Guilty. Order Prosecutor Peter Brawner to pay all costs as being malicious. Witnesses: Robertson Murphey 3 days; William Jefferson 3 days; John Murphey 3 days

Deed James Menees Sh^{ff} to Archer Cheatham & Thos Johnson 640 acres ackd
p.393 Deed Robert Prince to James Mcfarlin 147 acres proven by Thos Johnson

Having been published in the gazettes, the following tracts are to be sold by the Sheriff
Richard Cook	50 acres joining Renfro's preemption
Isaac Roberts	548 on Half pone
Isaac Williams	140 Spring Creek of Sulpher fork
Robert Hopkins	640 on Sychamore
James M Lewis	2560 Millers Creek
D^o	1280 on the ridge
Thomas Williams	640 Sychamore

Martin Armstrong	800 Karrs Cr & Millers Cr, 2 tracts
John Cummins	1000 Sychamore
John Sutton	100 Red River
Thomas Davis	410 Turnbulls Clay lick
Joseph Pankey	Lot 17 in Springfield
John Thompson	640 Karrs Cr
Aaron Laws	1000 Red River
James Glasgow	1000 mouth of Sychamore
Darias Grey	640 Cumberland River
Tho[s] Hickman	640 bought for Taxes
D[o]	2755 bought for Taxes
Edwin Hickmans heirs	274 joining Goose Pond
[blank] McCormick	640 Barrens joining W[m] Johnson
John Irwin	1920 Red River
Robert Lee	640 Millers Creek
Amos Rounsavall	Lot 35 in Springfield
W[m] Renfros heirs	415 Brush Creek
Sam[l] Dorris	Lot 57 in Springfield
Ja[s] McGill	Lot 5 in Springfield
John Wilson	640 mouth of War Trace, Grant #665
Frederick Cook	640 head Persons Creek
John McCormack	640 joining above tract

p.394 Elisha Bridgwater vs Benj[n] Menees Sen[r]. Appeal. Present John Philips, M Duncan, Isaac Philips, Esq[rs]. May 1806 Pl[tf] & def[t] by[blanks]. Jury: Mark Cole, Jacob Pinkley, And[w] Irwin, Henry Hunt, Henry Johnson, W[m] Byrd, Jacob Fry, W[m] Deloach, Matthew Day, David Spence, John Huey, Peter Fry, find Pl[tfs] damages 12 Doll[s] 58 c[ts]. Also costs. Witnesses: John Hutchison proves two days attendance; Nancy Rawls one day; Archer Cheatham 2 days

P/A Peter Pinkley to John Fry was signed sealed and ack[d] in open court; County seal annexed & delivered to s[d] Pinkley

Volentine Cheatham allowed Five Doll[s] of estate of Jn[o] Tucker dec[d] for Curing Riggs Tucker of the Riptures

John Philips, John Hutchison, and Martin Duncan Esq[rs] to determine which records of the Registers Office to transcribe, agreeable to Act of General Assembly. Bazel Boren, app[td] for that purpose, is immediately to transcribe s[d] records

John B Cheatham Sheriff given credits for following taxable property delinquents: 12 white poles

Benj[n] Menees Esq[r] Collector 1804 Tax granted credit for Harmon Little 1 white & 1 black pole; Ge[o] Hargrove 1 white pole & 2 black; John Simmons 1 white pole twice given in; Dow[or Doett?] L Noyes 1 Lot & 3 Lots not sold Double Taxed

p.395 Riggs Tucker bound by Indenture to Henry Fiser untill
he arrives to age 21; William Hays and James Darnell, Fisers
securities for his true performance of the Indenture

John B Cheatham Sheriff reports 1805 taxes unpaid on following land; that there is no personal property on which he can
distress. Tracts to be advertised agreeable to Law. W[m] P Anderson 1280 acres; John Brown 640; John & W[m] Bell 1920; John
Childress 1920; Rob[t] Goodwin 640; David McCree 1000; Joseph
Roberts 640; John Chick 426 2/3; Rob[t] Fenner 1477; W[m] Green
228; W[m] Verrell 357; John D Robins 1407 acres, 1 white pole,
3 black, 3 town Lots, and one stud horse.

Jurors to next Court: Joseph McDaniel, Rich[d] Hutchins, James
Johnston, Eppa Lawson, Wm Dorris, Jacob Cook, Henry Airs,
Ja[s] Blackwell, W[m] Conyers, Sam[l] Crocket, Holland Dardin, Ja[s]
Elliott Sen[r], Jn[o] Gardner, John Coleman, James Stuart, Benj[n]
Porter, Wyatt Bishop, Jacob Pinkley Jr, W[m] Crocket, William
Huddleston, Henry Fiser, John Cromwell, W[m] Alexander, W[m] Ma-
son, Jn[o] Sherod, James Long, Elijah Hughs, Arch[d] Mahon, Dan[l]
Johnson, Robertson Murphey, Marvel Lowe, Conrod Coon, James
Appleton J[r], John Robertson, William Robertson, Ja[s] Holland,
Richard Nuckolls, Henry Watkins Sen[r], Robert Carson, James
Bell, James Mcfarlan.

Order Augustine Cook, James Appleton J[r], Titus Benton, Rob[t]
Fairliss, Nathan Clark, John Hardin, and Benjamin Porter to
be patrollers for Captain Krisels Company

Court Adjourns untill Court in Course
                John Philips, Archer Cheatham, Isaac Philips

p.396 State of Tennessee, Robertson County, August 4th 1806
Present the Worshipfull John Philips, Joseph Dorris, Martin
Duncan, James Crabtree, and Hardy S Bryan, Esquires

Grand Jurors, John Coleman foreman, William Robertson, James
Johnston, Henry Fiser, Marvel Lowe, Holland Dardin, Jacob
Pinkley Jr, Henry Airs, John Gardner, Elijah Hughs, William
Mason, James Elliott, John Robertson, Daniel Johnson, Wyatt
Bishop. Isaac Dorris, constable, sworn to attend Grand Jury

John Morris records his stock mark
James Johnston records his stock mark
Clerk to receive lists of delinquent Taxes during this Term
B/S Ballas Corder to Abraham Young Sen[r] proven by Jacob

Young & Abraham Young Jun[r]
Extx of George Pool dec[d] to sell personal property of dec[d]
giving 15 days notice of sale & 9 months credit
Thomas Sellars records his stock mark

David Standley vs John Leeper.   Thomas Yates and W[m] Yates,
security for Def[t], delivered s[d] Leeper.

John B Cheatham vs Jane Norris. Matthew Morris, bail for the
Def[t], delivers her. Nath[l] Dickeson & James Norris ack[d] themselves defendants Bail

p.397   John B Cheatham vs William Norris. Matthew Morris security for Def[t] delivered him. Nath[l] Dickeson & James Norris
ack[d] themselves s[d] defendants Bail

Deed James Menees Sheriff to Thomas Hale 84¼ acres ackd
Deed Robert Weakley to Robert Jackson 100 acres proven by
Marvel Low & Mary Jackson
Deed/Gift Mary Isbell to Lewis Ragsdale 50 acres proven by
Joel Ragsdale and William Yates
Deed James Fitts[Felts?] to Marvel Lowe 21 acres proven by
Conrod Coon and Henry Hyde
Deed W[m] T Lewis to Rich[d] Hutchins 247 acres 53 poles proven
by Thomas Johnson and John B Cheatham
Deed Joseph Choate to Thomas Shaw 200 acres proven by Henry
Hunt
Deed Ansellim Goodman to Jesse Goodman 103 acres ackd
Deed Thomas Hale to John Karney 89¼ acres ackd
Deed Cordal Norfleet to Samuel Bellemey 123 acres proven by
Benjamin Wood and Aron Winters
Deed James Norfleet to Benj[n] Wood 120 acres proven by Samuel
Bellemy and Aaron Winters
Deed Elias Fort to John Barber 200 acres proven by James
Young and Arch[d] Mahon
p.398   Deed William Conyers to James Young 55 acres proven
by John Bowers and Matt[w] Luter J[r]
Deed Robert Ewing to John Young 30 acres proven by Adam Clap
and Adam Clap
Hardy S Bryan Esq[r] returned Tax list for Capt[n] Murpheys C[o]
Deed Meredith Walton to Joel Walton 640 acres ackd
Deed George Gordon to Sam[l] Hendley 630 acres proven by
Joshua Hendley and W[m] Hendley
John Sherod excused from serving as a Juror this Term
Ja[s] Holland excused from serving as a Juror this Term

Eppa Lawson app[t]d constable; bond 620 Dollars, Joseph Rob-
ertson & Thomas Appleton his securities
Will of George Pool dec[d] was proven by Martin Walton, Milley
Dorris, David Jones & Nathan Frizel; Chloe Pool ext[x]

L^{trs}/Adm^{n} estate of John Cromwell dec^{d} granted to Winferd Cromwell; bond, Wm Stark & Wm Lundsford securities
Giles Connell to oversee road in room of Henry Gardner

Order following hands to work under James Blackwell overseer of road: Reuben Bowers, John Noble, John Perry, Robt Perry, Ge^{o} Henley, William Henly, John Henley, Wm Atkins, Jeremiah Goins, James Burns, Cordel Norfleet, Cavin Witty, Elias Fort

p.399 Order following hands work under James Young overseer of road: Elisha Pilant, Wm Barron, Wm Pool, Jno Barber, John Yoes, Nathan Yoes, Jo^{s} Stroud
James Fitts[Felts?] to oversee road in room of Henry Hyde
Court Adjourns untill tomorrow Morning 9 OClock

Tuesday Morning Augt 5th 1806   Present the Worshipfull
John Philips, Isaac Philips, Charles Miles, Esquires

Henry Minor Esqr produced Licence to practice Law as an attorney in this State and was accordingly admited
Wyatt Bishop and Charles Wheaton, Comm^{rs} to settle with the County Trustee, made report; ordered recorded

At election for Robertson County for electing a Sheriff for ensuing two years, after poles closed and votes counted out, John B Cheatham was constitutionally elected; bond sum 12000 Dollars; John Yoes, William Milsap, Richard Matthews, James Sawyers his securities; took the oaths by Law required

Josiah Fort unanimously elected County Trustee; gave bond 3 thousand Dollars, Elias Fort Junr and Wm Connell, securities

p.400 Elisabeth Tucker & Chas Simmons adm^{x} & adm^{r} Saml Tucker dec^{d} vs John D Robins & Enoch Tucker. Debt. Present John Philips, Isaac Philips, Wm Connell. Novr 1805: pl^{tf} by N W Williams; def^{t} by Thos Stuart. Augt 1806: pl^{tf} by P W Humphreys; def^{t} att^{y} af^{sd}. Jury Henry Watkins S^{r}, Saml Crocket, Wm Crocket, Wm Dorris, James Stuart, James Long, John Couts, Thos Savage, Lemuel Sugg, Peter Fry, Joseph Robertson, Thos Dorris, who find John D Robins has not paid debt 60 Dollars, and assess pl^{tfs} damage by nonpayment thereof to 10 Doll^{s} 95 c^{ts}; further find def^{t} Enoch Tucker at time of executing s^{d} writing obligatory was under age of 21 years, age 19; therefore pl^{tfs} to recover ag^{t} def^{t} John D Robins 60 Dollars and damage 10 Doll^{s} 95 c^{ts} & costs of suit. Jane Engleman a witness proves 2 days attendance, 54 miles travel, 2 ferriages

Michael Fiser to oversee road in room of Jacob Damewood

AUGUST 1806

William Armstrong and Jacob Young to oversee Old County line
Road from Nashville to Kentucky; Armstrong & Young to divide
the road and hands as they shall agree; not to concern with
hands that belong to other Roads

p.401 Daniel McKinley J^r vs Jn° Watkins. Present Wm Connell,
Ja^s H Bryan, Chas Miles, Esq^rs. Feby 1806 pl^tf by Thos Stu-
art; def^t by Bennet Searcy. Jury Obediah Bounds, John Couts,
James Bell, Robert Brown, Ge° Murphey, John Lipscomb, Jacob
Pinkley, Ja^s Atkins, Charles Bradon, Shaderick Rawls, David
Spence, Nathl Dickeson who find for Def^t; New tryal granted.
Augt 1806 Jury Saml Crocket, Wm Crocket, James Stuart, James
Long, Thomas Savage, Lem^l Sugg, Peter Fry, Joseph Robertson,
Anthony Jones, Peter Spence, John Appleton, Matthew Day, who
find for Def^t. Pl^tf to pay all costs. John Luke, a witness,
proves 6 days attendance and 120 miles travel

Daniel McKinley Junr vs John Watkins. Sally Bashaw a witness
failing to appear after being solemnly called, forfeits

Matthew Morris to oversee Iron work road from Nashville road
between Springfield and Tucker's old place to Millers Creek;
with hands: Saml Crocket, Patrick Martin, Thos Martin, Isaac
Anderson, Mr Culberson, Wm Norris, Wm Blizard, Philip Parchment, Peter Fry, Mr Farmer, Saml Hunter

Deed William Milsap to John Hignight 174 acres ackd
Deed Ja^s Menees Sh^ff to Josiah Fort 274 acres ackd
p.402 Deed John Young & James Norfleet Comm^rs of Springfield
to John Wilson Lot 7 proven by John Hutcheson
Deed Robert Carson to James Bell 106½ acres proven by Wyatt
Bishop and Colin Bishop
Luke Rawls to oversee road in room of Saml Miles
John McIntosh Senr to oversee road in room of Joseph Castle-
berry
Deed William Polk to Elias Fort Junr 40 acres proven by W^m
Connell & Pray Whipple
Deed William Robertson to Thomas Johnson 141 acres 143 poles
proven by Lewis Wells

P/A Joel Bunn & Charity Bunn to Josiah Fort admited on Certificate & Seal of Clerk of Nash County N Carolina and Certificate of Chairman of sd Court

L^trs/Adm^n on estate of Alexander Tennen dec^d granted to Mary
Tennen and Wm Anderson; bond 5000 Dollars, Nathl Simmons and
Isaac Dorris securities; returned inventory of s^d estate

Archibald Huddleston app^td constable; bond 620 Dollars, with
Henry Dare his security

Court Adjourns untill tomorrw Morning 9 OClock

Wednesday Morning August 6ᵗʰ 1806   Present the Worshipfull
John Philips, Isaac Philips, and Charles Miles, Esquires

Order Elisabeth Tucker have credit for 102 acres and 1 Black
pole given for 1806 Tax, before given in by Charles Simmons

Ordered Nathaniel Bradley to oversee road from Isaac Philips
Esqʳ from River bank to State line; all hands in Captⁿ Suggs
Company North of Red River to work under him

p.403   Agreeable to Court Order, I have commited to Flames
certificates to amount of $931.29 ¼, Nᵒˢ of sᵈ Certificates
are in hands of Clerk & Commissioners. John Philips

Isaac Dorris apptᵈ constable; bond 620 Dollars, Wᵐ Dorris &
Bazel Boren his securities
Deed James Menees Shᶠᶠ to Wᵐ Milsap Senʳ 274 acres ackd

Allen Parker to oversee road in room of Peter Pinkley
County Trustee or Shᶠᶠ to pay Bazel Boren, Esqr, Register, 8
Dollars for purpose of buying Books for Registers office

Order that Clerk & Sheriff receive 50 Dollars each for their
exoficio services for the past year

Commissioners Wyatt Bishop, Charles Wheaton, & Abram Philips
allowed 5 Dollars each for settling with County Trustee

State vs James G Heard. Wᵐ Landsford appearance bond behalf
the state; Lemˡ Sugg appearance bond behalf the state

p.404 Commissioners report examination of Registers office:
Book A containing ninety instruments; Book C containing 233
instruments; Book D containing 131 instruments; Book E containing 206 instruments, the whole of which requires to be
transcribed.   10 May 1806. John Hutchison, John Philips,
Martin Duncan

Bazel Boren took oath for true performance transcribing the
Registers office agreeable to Act of General Assembly passed
30 October 1805. 10 May 1806. Bazel Boren. John Philips J.P.

Order Jacob Siglar overseer of road to have following hands
added to his List: John Siglar, Thomas Everton, Thoˢ Yates,
Joseph Huey, Wᵐ Moore, Robert Moore, Eleazer Smith, Wᵐ Sale,
Wᵐ Morgan

Isham Rogers vs James Menees. Motion to enter Judgement ag^t def^{dt} for monies detained in suit Isham Rogers ag^t Wm Lowry. After argument thereon, motion of plaintiff overruled, order by Court the pl^{tf} pay all costs. Asa Parker, witness, proves one day attendance, Jane Norris 1 day, Benjn Menees J^r 1 day

p.405   State vs James G Heard. Indictment. Appearance bond to answer charge of state against him. John Coleman and Levi Noyes his securities, for charge of A/B on Wm Lundsford

Elisabeth Tucker & Chas Simmons adm^x & adm^r of Samuel Tucker decd vs James Norris and James Menees. Present John Philips, Isaac Philips, Jo^s Dorris, Esq^{rs}. Jury Henry Watkins, Samuel Crocket, Wm Crocket, Wm Dorris, Ja^s Stuart, Ja^s Long, Joseph Robertson, Thos Appleton, Peter Pinkley Senr, David Spence, Edward King, Matthew Day make a mistrial
Court Adjourns untill tomorrow Morning 9 OClock

Thursday Morning August 7th 1806   Present the Worshipfull John Philips, Isaac Philips, and Joseph Dorris, Esquires

State vs Robert Hays. Affray. Def^t submits; fined 5 Dollars & costs

p.406   State vs Robert Hays. Affray. Def^t submits; fined 5 Dollars & costs

Sheriff granted credit with State Treasurer for Ten Dollars 95 cents, seven and three fourth miles, for lands that would not sell for 1805 Taxes. Also with County Trustee for five Dollars 47 cents & 8 miles

State vs Solomon Ledford. Affray. Def^t submits; fined five Dollars and costs

State vs Joshua Browning. Assault on Wm Norris. Presentment found May 1806. Def^t submits & is fined one Dollar & costs. Elisha Fikes, a witness, proves 4 days attendance

p.407   Jacob Pickren vs William Flewellen. Debt. Present Jno Philips, Isaac Philips, Jo^s Dorris, Esqrs. Pltf by P W Humphreys; def^t by Bennet Searcy. Augt jury Henry Watkins S^r, Wm Crocket, Wm Dorris, James Long, Wm Hays, Peter Fry, Esaph Parker, Peter Pinkley, Joshua Smith, Wm Huddleston, Thomas Cheatham, Edward King who find for Pl^{tf} his debt of 65 Doll^s and damage 4 Dollars 52 cents; also costs of suit.

Jacob Pickren vs Ja^s Darnel. Debt. John Philips, Isaac Philips, Joseph Dorris, Esq^{rs}. May 1806 pl^{tf} by P W Humphrey;

def^t by Wm Smith. Augt Jury H Watkins Senr, Wm Crocket, Wm
Dorris, Ja^s Long, William Hays, Peter Fry, Asa Parker, Peter
Pinkley, Joshua Smith, Wm Huddleston, Thomas Cheatham, Edwd
King who find for pl^{tf} his debt of 65 Doll^s, damage 4 Doll^s
52 c^{ts}; also his costs of suit

p.408   John Brooks vs Levi Noyes and Joseph Robertson. John
Philips, Isaac Philips, Joseph Dorris, Esq^{rs}. May 1806 pl^{tf}
by Thomas Stuart; def^t by J B Reynolds. Augt jury Henry Watkins Senr, Wm Crocket, Wm Dorris, James Long, Wm Hays, Peter
Fry, Esaph Parker, Peter Pinkley Senr, Joshua Smith, Wm Huddleston, Thomas Cheatham, Edward King who find for Pl^{tf} his
debt 96 Dollars 33½ cents which is unpaid; assess pl^{tfs} damage for the nonpayment thereof to 4 Dollars 33½ cents; also
his costs of suit

Bart Stuart vs James Lynn. Debt. Jno Philips, Isaac Philips,
Joseph Dorris, Esq^{rs}. May 1806 pl^{tf} by W Smith; def^t by J B
Reynolds. Augt jury Henry Watkins Senr, Wm Crocket, Wm Dorris, Ja^s Long, Wm Hays, Peter Fry, Asaph Parker, Peter Pinkley, Joshua Smith, Wm Huddleston, Thomas Cheatham, Edwd King
who find for pl^{tf} his debt sixty dollars, damage 1 dollar 70
cents & costs.

p.409   Larkin Edwards to oversee road from Williams Mill to
Richard Cavits as far as Logan Road; hands convenient to s^d
road not belonging to other roads are to work under him
William Benson to oversee sd road from Logan Rd to where it
intersects the Springfield Road; all hands convenient to s^d
road not belonging to other overseers are to work under him

Deed John Hardin to John Egnew 265 acres ackd
Perry Cohea admited to keep an Ordinary for 1 year; bond 500
Dollars, Henry Johnson and James Sawyers his securities

Jurors to next Court   Alex^r Gordon, Edmond Edwards, Abraham
Moore, Alex^r Chesnut, Jo^s Winfield, Chas Seal, Wm Wells, Ja^s
Pike, Chas Bradon, Thos Kilgore Jr, Abraham Young S^r, Josiah
Payne, Wm Byrd, Jno Krisel, James Neil, Charles Kilgore, Jno
Brooks, Peter Fiser, Richd Hutchins, Wm Conyers, Wm Alexan-
der, Ja^s Young, Arch^d Mahon, Ja^s Mcfarlin, Thos Polk, Henry
Gardner, Jno Karr, Robertson Murphey, Henry Hyde, Jacob Lew-
is, Jacob Pinkley, Nimrod McIntosh, Edward King, Thos McIn-
tosh, James Bell, Noah Woodard, Chas Murphey, John Williams

Jurors to Superior Court in Nashville Charles Wheaton, John
Chowning, Josiah Fort, James Sawyers

Bazel Boren allowed seven dollars in addition to sum allowed
for the purpose of buying books for the Registers office

p.410 B/S Henry McMurtry to John McMurtry ackd
Archer Cheatham Esqr admited to keep an Ordinary for 1 year;
bond 620 Dollars, James Sawyers & John Huddleston securities

Court adjourns untill Court in Course
                    John Philips, Isaac Philips, Martin Duncan

p.411   State of Tennessee, Robertson County. Monday November the 3rd 1806. Present the Worshipfull Benjamin Menees, James H Bryan and James Norfleet, Esquires

Grand Jurors: Archibald Mahon foreman, William Conyers, Peter Fiser, Thomas McIntosh, Alex^r Gordon, Henry Hyde, Nimrod McIntosh, Noah Woodard, John Williams, Thomas Kilgore, James Bell, Jacob Lewis, John Krisel, William Wills, John Brooks. Josiah Wright constable sworn to attend the Grand Jury

Nathan Yoes records his stock mark
John Yoes records his stock mark
Jacob Pinkley records his stock mark
Clerk to receive lists of Taxable property for present year

Adm^x of estate of John Cromwell dec^d at liberty to sell personal estate of s^d decd
B/S John Bowers J^r and John Barber for two Negroes proven by Reuben Bowers and James Young
Deed James Menees Senr to Moses M Donelson 133½ acres proven by Benjn Menees & Benjn Menees J^r

p.412 Henry Gardner excused from serving as Juror this Term
Geo A West to oversee road in room of Peter Brawner
Adm^x estate of John Cromwell dec^d delivered Inventory of s^d estate
Deed Thos Farmer to George Williams 640 acres ackd

P/A John Chisum to James Chisum admited to record on Certificate of two Justices of Jackson County & Certificate of the Clerk with seal of office affixed.

Adm^x of estate of James Muller dec^d delivered inventory
Deed Jacob McCarty to James H Bryan 113 acres proven by John W Bryan & Edmund Bryan
Deed Jesse Goulden to Matthew Kell 68 acres proven by James Wheeler & Robt Kell
Deed Shaderick Rawls to James Martin 100 acres ackd
Deed Philip Parchman to Wm Carter 175¼ acres proven by Thos

Farmer and Isaac Anderson
John Carr excused from Serving as a Juror this Term
Ex^{tx} estate of George Pool dec^d delivered Inventory
Court adjourns untill tomorrow Morning 10 OClock

p.413 Tuesday Morning Novr 4th 1806 Present the Worshipfull
Benjamin Menees, James H Bryan, James Norfleet, Esquires

Wyat Bishop, one of Comm^{rs} app^{td} to settle with County Trustee, delivered papers belonging to Comm^{rs} in his possession

John Grimes vs William Crunk. Appeal. Justices as above. May
1805 pl^f by J C Hamilton; def^t by Thos Stuart. Novr 1806 pl^f
by Wm Smith, def^t by Thos Stuart. Jury Jo^s Winfield, Josiah
Payne, Ja^s Neill, Charles Murphey, Joseph Fry, Joshua Smith,
Matt^w Day, Wm Dickeson, Jo^s Castleberry, Hosea Donily, Budy
Browning, Lem^l Sugg who find for pl^{tf} & assess his damage to
8 Dollars, & his costs. John Grant, witness, proves 11 days
attendance; Charles Johnson 4 days, 300 miles, 6 ferriages

p.414 John Hill to oversee the Ironwork Road from Montgomery
County line towards Springfield as far as 9 Mile tree; per-
sons to work under him John Rawls, Abel Rawls, Joseph Rawls,
John Hill, Wm Lewis, David Beasley, Gabriel Beasley, Jacob
Moake, Robert Sanders, William Sanders, Thos Hunter, Andrew
Sanders, Daniel Sanders, Frederick Fisher

Israel Robertson vs James Miles. Appeal. Justices as above.
Novr Term 1805 pl^{tf} by Thomas Stuart; def^t by Bennet Searcy.
Novr 1806 Jury Nathan Yoes, Edwd King, Enoch Tucker, George
Browning, Titus Benton, Nimrod Browning, Theop^s Morgan, John
Edwards, Wm Edwards Senr, Thomas Dorris, Wm Lundsford, Jesse
Jones who find for pl^{tf} his damage 27 Doll^s ½ c^{ts} & costs on
original Judg^t 75 cents. Joseph Woolfolk, a witness, proves
10 days attendance, 90 miles travel. Eppa Lawson 12 days

Ordered the Adm^x of James Muller[Mullis?] dec^d at liberty to
sell the personal property of s^d estate
Deed Mark Noble to Wm Connell 103 acres proven by Elias Fort
Jr & Giles Connell
Deed John Fort to Elias Fort 100 acres ackd
p.415 Deed John Campbell to James Norfleet 225 acres ackd
Deed William Johnson to James Stark 84 acres proven by Wil-
liam Edwards & Gravet Edwards
Volentine Choate admited to keep an Ordinary one year; bond
1000 Dollars, Sampson Matthews & Charles Simmons, securities
Court Adjourns untill tomorrow Morning 10 OClock

Wednesday Morning Novr 5th 1806. Present the Worshipfull

James Norfleet, Archer Cheatham, William Connell, Esquires

State vs Kellian Creek[Cruk?], Jabus Townsen, Light Townsen, James Johnston, Payton Nowlin. Jas Darnell, prosecutor, appearance bond.

James Johnston appearance bond; David Smith and Josiah Fort his securities

p.416 Deed Bustard & Eastin to Archer Cheatham nine lots in Springfield proven by Stuart W Thornton & Thomas Johnson

B/S Bustard & Eastin to Archer Cheatham 1 cotton ginn, proven by Stuart W Thornton & Thomas Johnson

John Hutchison Esqr admited to keep an Ordinary 1 year; bond 1000 Dollars, James Sawyers his security

James Sawyers presented his commission as Justice/Peace, and took oaths by Law required

State vs Isaac Philips. Indictment. Appearance bond. David Smith his security

Ordered Executors of William Fort dec^d be at liberty to sell the grist mill stones and the Irons of the saw & Grist mills

Deed William Johnson to Hiram Rice 100 acres ackd

p.417 State vs Isaac Dorris & Joseph Dorris Junr. Appearance bond of Eppaphroditus Benton as prosecutor and witness

Jurors to next Court: Ja^s Blackwell, Ja^s Atkins, Mark Noble, George Hendley, Elias Fort M C, Wm Gosset, Wm Barrow, Reuben Bowers, Ja^s Elliott J^r, Peter Brawner, Henry Hunt, Az^b Dunn, John Gardner, Wm Johnston, Sampson Matthews, Samuel McMurry, David Huddleston S^r, John Johnson, Charles Kilgore, Patrick Patterson, Thomas Yates, Abraham Young S^r, William Gilbert, John Pike, John Couts, John Appleton, Wm Benson, Wm Perry, Richd Nuckolls, Henry Johnson, William Huddleston J^r, Joseph Castleberry, Jno Huddleston, Jno Duncan, Jno Lipscomb, Jacob Pinkley Junr, Benjamin Porter, Matthew Day, Joseph Robertson

On petition of Martha Robertson, relict of Wm Robertson decd Lewis Wells is admr on estate, bond 5000 Dollars with Josiah Fort and Anderson Cheatham his securities

Ordered Henry Johnson surveyor attend on lands of Wm Robertson decd in this county with jurors Richd Nuckolls, William Perry, Wm Benson, Silas Tucker, Nathan Clark, John Krisel, Anthony Jones, James Appleton J^r, James Stark, Walter Stark, Arthur Pitt and John Procktor to lay off dower of the widow, also provisions necessary for support of widow & family for one year, agreeable to petition of the widow

p.418 James McFarlan vs Lemuel Sugg. Trover. Feby 1806 pl^{tf}
by Thos Stuart; def^t by Bennet Searcy & Ja^s B Reynolds. Nov^r
1806 jury Joseph Winfield, Josiah Payne, Ja^s Neill, Charles
Murphey, Joseph Fry, Joshua Smith, Edwd King, Budy Browning,
James Hays, Volentine Choate, Ge^o Browning, John Baldwin who
find Def^t guilty of trover & conversion as stated in Declaration, and find for Plaintiff seventy five Dollars & costs.
Def^t obtained appeal to Superior Court, bond 300 Doll^s, Joseph Robertson & William Deloach his securities. Wm Connell a
witness proves 2 days attendance; Giles Connell 4 days; Jeffery Sanders 6 days, William Deloach 5 days.

Adm^r estate of William Robertson dec^d delivered Inventory of
s^d estate
p.419 Court Adjourns untill Tomorrow Morning 10 OClock

Thursday Morning Novr 6th 1806   Present the Worshipfull
John Hutchison, Archer Cheatham, James Sawyers, Esquires

Lemuel Sugg vs David Smith. Josiah Fort and Joseph Wimberley
Defendant's bail delivered him into Court. William Deloach &
Giles Connell def^t's bail

State vs James G Heard. Indictment. John Hutchison, Ja^s Saw-
yers, Joseph Dorris, Esq^{rs}. The Grand Jury say James G Heard
with force & arms on 6 Augt 1806 at Springfield assaulted W^m
Lundsford to great damage of s^d Lundsford. At Novr Term 1806
Wm Smith Esqr att^y in behalf State; P W Humphreys and Bennet
Searcy for def^t. Jury Joseph Winfield, Josiah Payne, James
Neill, Chas Murphey, Peter Young, S W Thornton, Solomon Ledford, Thomas Figures, Richd Newman, George Browning, Rowlin
Allen, Joshua Smith find def^t Not Guilty as Charged. Opinion
of Court that Prosecution was malicious; is ordered by Court
that prosecutor Wm Lundsford pay all Costs. Giles Connell a
witness proves 2 days attendance

p.420 Thomas Smith records his stock mark
John Huddleston records his stock mark

State vs Isaac Philips. Def^t appearance bond, indictment for
altering and passing base & counterfeit coin. Josiah Fort &
Giles Connel securities for Philips, sum $2500 each.

Witnesses bound: William B Vinson, John Bell, John Hutchison, James Johnston, Shaderick Rawls, $125 each, to testify
in behalf State ag^t Isaac Philips. John Bell proves 4 days
attendance; James Johnston 4 days; Benjn Menees J^r 4 days

State vs Joshua Smith. Neglect of Road. Present John Hutchi-

son, Jo⁸ Dorris, Ja⁸ Sawyers, Esqʳˢ. Jury Joseph Winfield,
Josiah Payne, James Neile, Charles Murphey, Thomas Cheatham,
Titus Benton, Peter Young, S W Thornton, Solomon Ledford,
Tho⁸ Figures, George Browning, Rowlin Allen who find Defend-
ant guilty. Court fine him six & one forth cents. John Gard-
ner witness proves 4 days attendance; James Johnston 4 days

p.421 Robert Williams to oversee the Williams Mill road from
near Sulpher fork to sd mill in room of John Cromwell decd,
to have same hands, also those not belonging to other roads

Perry Cohea to oversee Nashville road from Sulpher fork near
the mill through Springfield to Karrs Creek in room of John
Huddleston. John Strain, Peter Young, Elijah Spiller, Peter
Fiser, Wm Huddleston, Jonathan Huddleston, Jno Duncan, Henry
Stults, Thomas Smout, Wm Huddleston, and John Huddleston are
to work thereon under him
Court Adjourns untill tomorrow Morning 10 OClock

Friday Morning Novʳ 7ᵗʰ 1806.   Present the Worshipfull
John Hutchison, Archer Cheatham, James Sawyers, Esquires

Bustard & Eastin vs Jacob Robertson. Attachment. Justices as
above. Augᵗ 1806 Shᶠᶠ levied on 2 town Lots, parcel of sole
leather, 1 candle stand, 1 barrel & some whiskey, [complete
list not transcribed]. Plᵗᶠˢ by P W Humphries; judgᵗ by default, cause contᵈ. Jury Joseph Winfield, Josiah Payne, Ja⁸
Neill, Charles Murphey, S W Thornton, Solomon Ledford, Peter
Young, Stephen Boren, Martin Walton, Ja⁸ Long, George Browning, Charles McIntosh who find the plᵗᶠˢ sustained damage 55
Dollars, 54 3\4 cents; Court order property attached be sold

p.422 James G Heard vs Daniel McKinley. AB & False Imprison-
ment. Jn° Hutchison, A Cheatham, Ja⁸ Sawyers Esqʳˢ. May 1806
Plᵗᶠ by Bennet Searcy & J B Reynolds; defᵗ by Thomas Stuart.
Novʳ Jury Joseph Winfield, Josiah Payne, Ja⁸ Neill, Charles
Murphey, Solomon Ledford, Stephen Boren, James Long, George
Browning, Titus Benton, Lewis Wells, Philip Parchment, Shad-
erick Rawls, who find for plᵗᶠ, assess damage to 12½ cents,
also his costs. Henry Watkins witness proves 9 days attend-
ance; Jn° Leak 9 days, 80 miles travel; S W Thornton 4 days.
Court Adjourns untill tomorrow Morning 8 OClock

Saturday Morning, Novʳ 8ᵗʰ 1806.   Present the Worshipfull
Martin Duncan, A Cheatham, James Sawyers, Esquires

John Hutchison Esqʳ elected Chairman of this Court Pro Tem

Thomas Johnson clerk allowed 8 Doll^s 87½ c^{ts} for three bound books purchased for use of Court, also 10 Doll^s 50 c^{ts} for examining and colating the transcribed Registers Books, it being seven days services

Order the Commissioners of Springfield to cause stocks to be erected on public square, also a stray pen to be built

p.423 Archer Cheatham gaoler allowed 3 Doll^s 16 c^{ts} for fees in commiting, releasing, and finding Simon Holland in gaol

Order the adm^r estate of Wm Robertson dec^d may sell personal property of s^d estate

John B Cheatham Sheriff allowed 5 Doll^s for summoning guards for purpose of guarding Lemon Holland in Springfield Gaol

John B Cheatham Collector of State & County Tax for 1806 reports land not given in for purpose of paying Taxes
[blank] McCormick   451 acres, Barrens, joins Wm Johnson
Thomas Williams   340 ac Sychamore
John Stuart heirs   320 Red River
     same   380 Millers Creek
John Richardson   320 tract includes Wheatons sink
Clerk transmit a copy to be published agreeable to Law

Court Adjourns untill Court in Course
John Hutchison, Archer Cheatham, Ja^s Sawyers, Martin Duncan

State of Tennessee, Robertson County, Monday January the 5th 1807. Present the Worshipfull Benjn Menees, Martin Duncan, William Connell, Esquires

Grand Jury Matthew Day foreman, Jacob Pinkley, John Duncan, Joseph Castleberry, David Huddleston, Sampson Matthews, Thos Yates, Samuel McMurry, Abm Young Senr, John Huddleston, John Pike, Wm Perry, Henry Johnson, George Henley. Jacob Pickren constable sworn to attend the Grand Jury

Peter Fiser records his stock mark
Clerk to receive lists of Taxable property for past year
Wm Johnston excused from Serving as a Juror this Term

George Murphey vs Zachariah Cox. Ejectment. Henry Johnson, surveyor, appointed to survey the interfering claims and return plats thereof to Court

Deed John Brisby and Lewis Martin to Thomas Martin 429 acres
proven by Samuel Hollis and Patrick Martin
Deed Thomas Martin to Partrick Martin 214 acres ackd
Deed John Chisum by James Chisum his atty in fact to Nathan
Arnett 140 acres proven by James Long & Robert Long
Deed Nathan Arnett to Griffith Williams 140 acres ackd
p.425 Deed Philip Trammel to Abraham Young 308 acres proven
by Robert Brown & David Biggs
Deed Adam Clap to Thomas Roper 220 acres proven by Jacob F
Young & Robert Brown
Court Adjourns untill tomorrow Morning 10 OClock

Tuesday Morning, January 6ᵗʰ 1807. Present the Worshipfull
Benjamin Menees, William Connell, Isaac Dortch, Esquires

George & Thoˢ Brown vs Stewart W Thornton. Charles Miles, Wᵐ
Connell, James Sawyers, Esqʳˢ. May 1806 plᵗᶠ by G W L Mair;
defᵗ by Thoˢ Stuart & J B Reynold. Janʸ 1807 Jury Jnᵒ Couts,
Peter Brawner, Reubin Bowers, Wᵐ Barrow, Mark Noble, James
Adkins, Elias Fort, Chaˢ Kilgore, John Appleton, James Bell,
Joel Lewis, Henry Fiser find defᵗ did not assume upon him-
self as plᵗᶠˢ alledged against him; he may recover agᵗ plᵗᶠ
costs of suit. Plᵗᶠˢ obtained appeal to Superior Court, Bond
200 Dollars, Joseph Woolfolk & Israel Robertson, securities.
James Kirkham a witness proves two days attendance

p.426 Deed Jonathan Huddleston to John Huddleston 170 acres
ackᵈ in open Court
Deed Lewis Wells to John Procktor 66½ acres ackd
Wm Crocket records his stock mark

Bazel Boren, Register, allowed 124 Dollars for transcribing
the Registers books assigned to him for that purpose

Admˣ estate of James Muller decᵈ delivered amount of sale of
sᵈ estate
Thomas Woodard appᵗᵈ constable; bond 620 Dollˢ, Noah Woodard
and Andrew Irwin his securities
Deed John B Cheatham to James Bell 140 acres ackd
Admˣ estate of John Cromwell decᵈ delivered amount of sales
of sᵈ estate
Deed Joseph Motheral to Henry Johnson 50 acres proven by
Archer Cheatham and Thomas Johnson
Deed Matthew Kell to Thomas Harrington 63 acres proven by
James Wheeler and Elizᵃ Harrington
Admʳ of estate of William Robertson decᵈ delivered amount of
sales of sᵈ estate
Court Adjourns untill tomorrow Morning 10 oClock

Wednesday Morning January 7th 1807   Present the Worshipfull
Benjⁿ Menees, Charles Miles, Wm Connell, Isaac Dortch, Esq^{rs}

p.427   Order Sheriff summons 12 freeholders to enquire into
the lunacy of Betsey Dardin, make return to next Court

Sheriff to have credit for 640 acres for 1806 listed in name
Robert Burton; s^d land is above the quantity he possesseth

John B Cheatham, possessor of a ginn in 1805, made oath that
he listed the ginn of 41 saws, but he did not work said ginn
in said year; therefore order Cheatham exhonarated from tax

Charles Wheaton exhonarated from penalty for not returning a
stud horse last year for taxation on his paying the price of
one season

Order William Connell Esqr take the list of Taxable property
in Capt Campbells Company

Benjamin Menees	Capt Suggs
Archer Cheatham	Capt Thorntons
James H Bryan	Capt Brawners
Hardy S Bryan	Capt Murpheys
Martin Duncan	Capt Krisels
James Sawyers	Capt Bounds
James Crabtree	Capt Kilgores

p.428   State vs Isaac Philips. Indictment. Wm Connell, Chas
Miles, J Crabtree, Isaac Dortch, Ja^s Sawyers, Benjⁿ Menees,
A Cheatham, Esq^{rs}.   Novr 1806 Grand Jury say Isaac Philips
with force & arms on 7 August 1806 did pass one counterfeit
likeness of a Spanish milled Dollar current coin of state of
Tennessee knowing same to be base to Charles Millbanks with
intention to defraud s^d Millbanks contrary to Act of General
Assembly. Wm Smith att^o for R.C. Archibald Mahon foreman of
Grand Jury A True Bill. Sheriff brought defendant to Court.
p.429.   Bond 1000 Doll^s, Security David Smith. Cause cont^d.
Appearance bond, $5000, Josiah Fort & Giles Connell his se-
curities $2500 each. Jany Term 1807 Wm Smith County Solici-
tor behalf State, Def^t by P W Humphreys, B Searcy & J B Rey-
nold pleads Not Guilty. Jury John Couts, Elias Fort, James
Atkins, Mark Noble, Chas Kilgore, Reuben Bowers, Wm Barrow,
Peter Brawner, Wm Hays, James Appleton Junr, Richd Matthews,
Theophilus Morgan who find Def^t Guilty as Charged.   Present
Charles Miles, Benjⁿ Menees   p.430   James Crabtree, Isaac
Dortch, James Sawyers, A Cheatham, Esq^{rs}, of opinion def^t be
fined fifty Dollars, costs and one months imprisonment. From
the verdict of Jury and sentence of Court the Def^t appealed

to Superior Court, Bond 1000 Doll^s, John Philips and Charles
Wheaton securities. Witnesses: Benjn Menees J^r 7 days, Mary
Johnston 2 days, Nathaniel Bradley 3 days, John Bell 7 days,
Foster Mason 3 days, Thomas Appleton 3 days, Holland Luter 6
days, Ja^s Johnston 7, Nathaniel Harbin 3, Shaderick Rawls 4,
Wm Flewellen J^r 6, Lem^l Sugg 3, Jno Hutchison 3

State vs Isaac Philips. Wm Flewellen a witness failed to appear; order he forfeit agreeable to Act of General Assembly.
Charles Millbanks, prosecutor, failed to appear; ordered he
forfeit his recognizance; si fa issues

Deed John Yoes to George Hendley 100 acres ackd
Peter Fry records his stock mark
Anthony Hinkle records his stock mark
Peter Pinkley records his stock mark

p.431   Deed Nicholas Darnell & Ge^o W Darnell by s^d Nicholas
Att^o in fact for s^d George to John Blackwell proven by Benjn
Menees and Benjn Menees Junr
Court Adjourns untill tomorrow Morning 9 OClock

Thursday Morning January 8th 1807   Present Wm Connell, Chas
Miles, Benjn Menees, Isaac Dortch, James Crabtree, Esquires

Jacob Pinkley, Sychamore, admited to keep an Ordinary for 1
year in this county; bond 1000 Doll^s, Adam Pinkley and Jacob
Pinkley, Big, his securities
David Huddleston Senr records his stock mark

Deed Leven Powell J^r, Sus^n Elisa Powell to Stephen G Roszel
admited, deed having been proven in County Court of Louden,
Virginia, with the seal of the county annexed

State vs James G Heard. Presentment. Wm Smith, County Solicitor, Def^t by att^y; Jury Jno Couts Elias Fort, James Atkins,
Mark Noble, Charles Kilgore, Reuben Bowers, Wm Barrow, Peter
Brawner, Thos Smart, John Yoes, John Bell, Silas Tucker, who
find Def^t Guilty as charged; fined 5 Dollars and costs.

State vs Perry Cohea and James G Heard. James Bell, witness,
proves 4 days attendance; Thos McIntosh 4 days; Noah Woodard
3 days

p.432   State vs Perry Cohea. Presentment. Wm Smith, County
Solicitor, def^t by att^y. Jury John Couts, Elias Fort, James
Atkins, Mark Noble, Chas Kilgore, Reuben Bowers, Wm Barrow,
Peter Brawner, Thomas Smart, John Yoes, Nathan Yoes, Joel
Lewis who find Def^t Guilty; Fined Five Dollars and costs

William Smith, County Solicitor, allowed Fifty Dollars for
his exoficio services for the past year

There being full Court and good reasons shewn, the road from
fork West side Calebs C^r to intersection with Nashville road
near James Mcfarlans discontinued; s^d road from him to Isaac
Philips on Red River discontinued

State vs Joseph Dorris Junr. Indictment. Benjn Menees, James
Sawyers, M Duncan, Esq^{rs}. Def^t submits, fined 25 C^{ts} & costs

State vs Joseph Dorris Junr and Isaac Dorris Senr. Wm Stark,
witness, proves 4 days attendance; James Appleton J^r 2 days

Jury app^{td} to lay off dower of Widow Robertson, relict of W^m
Robertson dec^d, delivered their return

p.433 Commissioners of Springfield agreeably to Court Order
lett building of Stocks & Stray pen to lowest bidder, Henry
Watkins Junr. Stray pen $9.99
        Stocks <u>14.96</u>
            $24.95
Above work rec^d as well done. A Cheatham, Thomas Johnson
Order County Trustee pay above sum to s^d Watkins

State vs John Williams. Appearance Bond William Rogers and
Robert Rogers to give testamony behalf State, $200 each

Robertson County. Present Wm Connell, M Duncan, Ja^s Sawyers,
Jno Hutchison. Samuel Crocket sworn maketh oath he hath paid
taxes in Robertson for all land he bought in name of Martin
Armstrong that was sold by Sheriff for taxes. Test T Johnson

Order jury of view James Jones, John Huddleston, Wm Huddleston J^r, John Duncan, Jonathan Huddleston, James Bell, Silas
Barr, to mark way for Nashville Road from Springfield, so as
to cross Karrs C^r near mouth of Huddlestons Spring branch, &
intersect old road between Karrs C^r & Norris's pond

p.434 William Benson to oversee road from Cavets to Williams
Mill on Red River to oppesit Bazel Borens; hands of Wm Benson, William Crafford, Meredith Walton, & Martin Walton are
to work under him

Samuel McMurry returns taxable property for 1806, one cotton
ginn with thirty six saws

Jurors to next Court: Patrick Patterson, Jacob Young, George
Patterson, Thomas George, James Payne, Moses Renfro, William

Yates, Jesse Martin, Jn° Sherod, William Gosset, Henry Hunt, Azariah Dunn, John Gardner, Thomas Polk, Robert Perry, John Young, David Lucas, Stephen Cole, Wm Cole, Mark Cole, John Chowning, Richd Jones, Francis Byrd, Benjamin Holman, Jacob Pinkley J^r, Jacob Damewood, Thos Smart, Jonathan Huddleston, Wyatt Bishop, Wm Huddleston Senr, John Brooks, Jesse Jones, Henry Fry, Nathan Clark, Ja^s Stark, Walter Stark, Wm Hunter, Thos Appleton, Jn° Grant, Jn° Crocket
Court Adjourns untill tomorrow morning 9 oClock

Friday Morning January 9th 1807   Present the Worshipfull John Hutchison, Martin Duncan, A Cheatham, Esquires

John B Cheatham Collector of 1806 Taxes reports taxes unpaid on 1850 acres & 1 white pole in name James Darnell; there is no personal property on which to distress; therefore ordered by Court that sheriff proceed to sell; also 1000 acres, name of David McCree, & 640 name of Robert Goodwin for 1805 taxes

John Strain allowed $1.12½; Rowland Allen 1.50; Perry Cohea .75 for guarding Lemon[Simon?] Holland in Springfield Gaol

Thos Figures vs Josiah Vinson. Attachment. Saml Hendly Junr summoned as garnishee failed to appear; order si fa to issue ag^t s^d Henley
Court Adjourns untill Court in Course
                M Duncan, Jn° Hutchison, Archer Cheatham

p.435   State of Tennessee, Robertson County. Monday Morning April the 6th 1807. Present the Worshipfull Benjamin Menees, James Crabtree, William Connell, Esquires

Order 1806 tax received on 75 acres and 2 black poles in the name of John Noble; also John Thompson 640 ac on Karrs Creek

Grand Jurors elected: William Cole foreman, John Crocket, Jacob Damewood, Jn° Chowning, William Huddleston, Jesse Martin, William Yates, Jonathan Huddleston, Stephen Cole, Nathan Clark, Francis Byrd, Jacob Pinkley Junr, George Patterson, John Sherod, William Hunter
Augustine Cook, constable, sworn to attend on the Grand Jury

Patrick Martin records his stock mark
Order James H Bryan and Benjamin Menees Esq^rs to settle with adm^rs of the estate of Henry Sherod dec^d

John Dodge vs Moses Philips, Holland Darden & Elisha Phelps, securities for def', delivered him

Order Lawrence Clinard, Peter Hinkle, Anthony Hinkle & Henry Fry added to hands of Matthew Morris, overseer of Road
Order Wm Blizard & Thos Martin added to hands of Allen Parker overseer of Road

Lemuel Sugg vs Burrell Bunns adm^r. Elias Fort Junr replevied property attached, and acknowledged himself special Bail

p.436   Thomas Figures vs Samuel Henley J^r. Conditional judg^t entered last Court set aside, & Defendant released therefrom

Order Enoch Tucker released from 1806 the Tax on a Town Lot, it appearing that s^d Lot was listed and paid by J B Cheatham

The Will of Jn° Payne S^r was proven by Moses Beason & Edward Brown. Josiah Payne, the surviving executor, took oath

Deed Andrew Mitchel to Saml Hollis   640 acres proven by Patrick Martin & Thomas Martin
Deed Thomas Holderness to Thomas Jones Senr   213 1\3 acres proven by Jacob V Johnson & Waddy Jones
Deed James H Bryan to Asa Woodard   225 acres ackd
Deed Saml Henley Senr to Wm Henley   110½ acres ackd
Deed Wm Rogers, Simon Fikes, and Dollytheo Fikes to David Taylor 150 acres proven by Wm Taylor & Joseph McElhainey
Deed Asa Woodard to James H Bryan 113 acres proven by Edmund Bryan & Ge° A West
Deed William Barron & wife Lyda Barron 33 1\3 acres ackd. Acknowledgement of Lyda Barron proven by Henry Gardner & Jn° Carr
Deed John Choate to Thomas Shaw   40 acres proven by Wm Hunt

Josiah Payne app^t^d constable, bond 1000 Dollars, Moses Beason & John Chowning his securities

James H Bryan & Benjn Menees Esq^rs delivered settlement with adm^rs of the estate of Henry Sherod dec^d
Deed Thomas Holderness to Waddy Jones   213 1\3 acres proven by Jacob V Johnson & Elijah Spiller
p.437   Deed Wm Edwards to Robert Cartwright   300 acres ackd

Martin Duncan Esq delivered Tax list for Captn Krisels Comp^y
Hardy S Bryan for Captn Murpheys; James Crabtree for Captain Kilgores; James H Bryan for Captn Brawners company

Wyatt Bishop excused from Serving as a Juror this Term

Order Lovick Ventress oversee road in room of Hardy S Bryan
Isaac Bridgewater to oversee road in room of James Shannon

Philip Parchment to oversee road from Calebs Creek to inter-
section with Iron work road, his hands are Zach^h Cox, Robert
Hogan, George Murphey, Robert Murphey, William Huston, Isaac
Winters, Lemuel Sugg

Order James Elliott oversee road from Miller Cr up to Calebs
creek; hands Samuel Elliott, Joseph Hignight, [blank] Beard,
Wm Conyers, Wm Andes, Wm Caster
Court Adjourns untill tomorrow Morning 9 OClock

Tuesday Morning April 7th 1807   Present the Worshipfull
Benjamin Menees, Joseph Dorris, James Sawyers, Esquires

Order Wm Connell & Benjamin Menees Esq^rs settle with adm^r of
estate of Daniel Holland dec^d
Order Isaac Dortch and James Norfleet Esq^rs settle with adm^r
of estate of Wm Fort dec^d

p.438 William Latham vs Jacob Fulk. Certiorari. James Crab-
tree, Wm Connell, Ja^s Sawyers, Esq^rs. Feby 1806 pl^tf by Thos
Stuart; def^t by J B Reynolds. Cont^d. April 1807 Jury Robert
Perry, Mark Cole, Thos Smart, Thos George, Benjamin Holeman,
John Brooks, Azariah Dunn, Henry Fry, Thomas Appleton, Fred^k
Cobb, Noah Woodard, Hugh Henry who find for Def^t, & costs of
suit. Jacob Johnson witness proves 9 days attendance; James
Jones 12 days

State vs Reuben Ross. Charles Murphey prosecutor appearance
bond 500 Dollars
Order John McMillen have a credit one Dollar, amount he paid
for 1804 Ginn tax above the am^t of saws of said ginn
Order Thomas Johnson & Archer Cheatham value the Negoes belonging to estate of John Tucker decd; make return to Guardians who is then authorized to settle with Lagitees of age.
Guardians to make return to next Court
Order Elijah Biggs released from the payment of Taxes on 200
acres listed for 1806
Isaac Dortch and James Norfleet Esq^rs report settlement with
adm^rs of estate of Wm Fort dec^d

p.439 David Smith vs Philip Parchment. Certiorari. The Def^t
confesses Judgement in favour plaintiff 20 Dollars with stay
of execution untill next Court, pl^tf pays Sheriff's fees

Deed Archer Cheatham and Thomas Johnson to Peter Hinkle 320
acres ackd

Deed Eppa Lawson to Thomas Appleton 100 acres proven by oath
of Elias Fort Jr & Daniel Johnston
Wm Hays to oversee Road in room of Joshua Smith
Release, Charles McIntosh to Henry Johnson & John Couts ackd

William Connell Esqr delivered into Court tax list for Captn
Campbells Compy. A Cheatham for Capt Thorntons; John Hutchison for Capt Pitts; James Sawyers for Capt Bounds

Jury appointed to inquire into Betsey Dardin's lunacy report
she is a Lunatick. Jonathan Dardin apptd guardian, who gave
bond one thousand Dolls, Wm Milsap & Josiah Fort, securities

Deed Isaac Clark to Josiah Fort 162 acres proven by James
Fort & Henry Fort
Deed Thomas Norris to Allen Parker 328 acres proven by Saml
Hollis & Ansellam Goodman
Deed Daniel Wilburn to John Shannon 272 acres proven by Wm
Cole & Saml Shannon
Walter Stark to oversee road in room of Arthur Pitt

p.440   William Sale to oversee road in room of Jacob Siglar
Court Adjourns untill tomorrow Morning 10 OClock

Wednesday Morning, April 8th 1807   Present the Worshipfull
James Crabtree, James Sawyers, Benjamin Menees, Esquires

Deed James Norfleet & Jno Young commissioners of Springfield
to Richard Nuckolls Lot #24 ackd
Order John Hutchison & James Crabtree Esqrs to let to lowest
bidder Daniel McDaniel now on the Parish for one year
Noah Woodard records his stock mark
Deed John B Cheatham Shff to Wm Black 640 acres ackd
Deed Richard Nuckolls to John B Cheatham Lot #50 in Spring-
field ackd

State vs John Williams. AB. James Sawyers, B Menees, J Norfleet, Esqrs. Deft submits; fined one Dollar and costs

Deadrick vs Wm Mason. Ejectment. Henry Johnson apptd to survey disputed land, to return plat to next Court

Thomas Smart to oversee new road from Springfield as lately
marked to where it intersects Old road beyond Karrs Creek, &
to have the same hands which Perry Cohea had

Benjn Menees Esqr delivered tax list for Capt Suggs company

Order Augustine Cook, constable, allowed one Dollar 25 cents for summoning guards to guard Lemond Holland, a prisoner in Springfield gaol

p.441 James Crabtree & John Hutchison Esqʳˢ report they let Daniel McDaniel to Benjⁿ Holman lowest bidder for 54 Dollars 25 cents. Benjⁿ Holman bond 200 Dollˢ; he provides McDaniel with holesome diet, lodging and good sufficient clothing for one year, the time he has taken sᵈ McDaniel

Nathaniel Davis vs Lemuel Sugg. Covenant. J Hutchison, James Crabtree, B Menees, Esqʳˢ. Novʳ 1805 plᵗᶠ by P W Humphries & Thomas Stuart; Defᵗ by B Searcy & J B Reynolds. Contᵈ. April 1807 jury Robᵗ Perry, Thoˢ Smart, Benjⁿ Holman, John Brooks, Azariah Dunn, Henry Fry, Benjⁿ Chapman, Chaˢ Murphey, Henry Watkins, Samˡ Crocket, Wᵐ Hutchins, James Leach who find in favour of Plᵗᶠ, assess damages by nonperformance of Covenant to 365 Dollars, also his costs. Defᵗ obtained appeal. Wᵐ T Lewis a witness proves 2 days attendance, 52 miles travel, 2 ferriages; John Hannah 7 days, 130 miles, 2 ferriages; Robert McCrory 10 days, 310 miles, 2 ferriages; Blake Rutland 9 days, 250 miles, 2 ferriages; Josiah Fort 3 days

p.442 John Hutchison Esqr allowed $4 for guarding Leml Holland to Nashville, & finding a horse for prisoner to ride.

Joshua Smith	a guard	$2.50
Garrot Flipps	do	2.50
Abraham Philips	do	2.50
Isham Philips	do	2.50

Jurors to next Supʳ Court to be held at Clarksville: Jiles Connell, William Connell, Abraham Young Senr, Jnᵒ Carr, John Coleman, David Jones Senʳ, James Johnston Senʳ, Josiah Fort, Lovick Ventress, Henry Hunt, Elijah Hughs

Wᵐ Karr exhonarated from 1806 Tax on 100 acres given in by mistake, Sheriff to have credit for same

Jurors to next Court: Isaac Dorris Junʳ, Hugh Henry, Richard Matthews, Jaˢ England, William Moss Sʳ, Henry Gardner, Mark Noble, Wᵐ Barrow, James Stuart, James Adkins, James Elliott Jr, Benjⁿ Wood, James Mcfarlan, Moses Winters, Samˡ Crocket, George Murphey, George A West, Joseph Payne, Daniel Holman, Bartimias Pack, Thoˢ Byrd, Moses Beason, Jaˢ Yates, Alexander Gordon, Burrell Pitts, John B Blackwell, Thomas Sellers, William Hendley, Anderson Cheatham, William Strickland, John Robertson, Edmond Edwards, James Hampton, Joel Moore, Henry Castle, Charles Wheaton, Anthony Jones Senʳ, Henry Fiser

County Tax for present year: Each white pole 6¼ cents, each Black pole 12½ cents; each stud kept for covering mares 100

cents; each Town [lot] 12½ cents; each retail store $5; each hundred acres 6¼ cents. The District Tax the same as above, retail stores excepted
The Grand Jury Discharged

p.443 Petition of Isaac Clark who by Military land Warrant #3687 from North Carolina to Robert & William Clark assee of Edward Robertson, located & entered 21 June 1792, surveyed 8 November, petitioner claims title. Surveyor in returning a Survey Certificate to Secretary, erred by inserting the name James Clark instead of Robert Clark, error appears when comparing the Certificate of Survey & Grant with that of Entry & Location. Jaᵃ Clark sold an interest in sd Tract to Hardin Perkins, innocent purchaser. To avoid litigation James Clark bought the interest of Hardin Perkins; title now compleatly vested in petitioner who prays to have evidence of his claim exhibited to commissioners of the Land office for Tennessee, petitions the Court for relief.
Upon consideration of petition, the Court order sd prayer be granted, Clerk to Certify same to Secretary of State of Tennessee in order that the Error commited by the Surveyor may be rectified.
Court Adjourns untill tomorrow Morning 10 oClock

Thursday Morning April the 9ᵗʰ 1807 Present the Worshipfull John Hutchison, Benjamin Menees, James Crabtree, Esquires

David Smith vs Philip Parchment. Certiorari. James Norfleet witness proves 4 days attendance
Charles Murphey records his stock mark
Deed Matthew Brooks to John Huddleston 160 acres ackd

Noah Woodard allowed Ten Dollars 17 cents for keeping Daniel McDaniel 2 months & 8 days longer than time which he was let
Court Adjourns untill tomorrow Morning 8 OClock

Friday Morning April 10ᵗʰ 1807 Present the Worshipfull John Hutchison, B Menees, James Crabtree, Martin Duncan, Esquires

Henry Fry[Hay?] records his stock mark

Sheriff to pay Jacob Pinkley one Dollar 20 cents, the tax he paid on 640 acres belonging to John Thompson for 1806; said Thompson had paid the tax for the same year for sᵈ land

p.445 Jesse Gardner vs Ann Gardner. Debt. Novʳ 1806 plᵗᶠ by Thomas Swann; defᵗ by P W Humphries. Apˡ jury Mark Cole, Azʰ Dunn, Henry Fry, Robert Perry, Thoᵃ Smart, Benjⁿ Holman, Jnᵒ Brooks, Uriah Swann, Wᵐ G Hutchison, Jaˢ Hays, Wᵐ Hays, S W

Thornton who inquire what £67.19 is in Dollars & cents, find
it to be 226 Dollars 50 cents, Interest 28 Dollars 88 cents.
Pl^{tf} to recover against defendant, also his costs of suit

Upon motion of Philip Parchment in case of John Sevier, Governor vs James Menees Collector of County Tax for 1803, & W^m
Armstrong & Philip Parchment his securities on Judgement obtained August Term 1804; upon examination of the records it
appears Parchment is entitled to a Judgement vs Wm Armstrong
for $140.86 & 5 mills. Ordered that Judgement be entered ac-
cordingly with costs

John B Cheatham Sh^{ff} app^{td} Collector of State and County Tax
for the present year gave bond 5000 Dollars, Thomas Figures,
Epps Benton, John Hutchison and Martin Duncan his securities

p.446 Rowland Allen vs Bazel Boren. Case. Augt 1806 pl^{tf} by
Thos Swann; def^t by Thos Stuart. April 1807 Jury Mark Cole,
Azariah Dunn, Henry Fry, Robt Perry, Thos Smart, Benjⁿ Hol-
man, John Brooks, Uriah Swann, William G Hutchison, James
Hays, William Hays, Stuart W Thornton find for Defendant. A
Motion for New Tryal over ruled by Court.

Henry Gardner vs William Ingram and Eppa Lawson on Judgement
obtained before Wm Connell Esqr for 26 Dollars 95 cents, and
a further sum of one Dollar costs. Sheriff returns: Levied
March 25th on 100 acres on Red River, property of Wm Ingram.
J B Cheatham Sh^{ff}. Ordered af^{sd} land be sold to satisfy the
judgement & costs.

Nathaniel Davis vs Lemuel Sugg. Exception being made by Pl^{tf}
atto to the Bail taken in his appeal, Court are of opinion
that Bail is insufficient and motion for appeal is dismissed

p.447 Ethreldred Hargrove vs William Lundsford. Debt. Jan^y
1807 pl^{tf} by Bennet Searcy; def^t by J B Reynolds. April 1807
jury Mark Cole, Azariah Dunn, Henry Fry, Robt Perry, Thomas
Smart, Benjamin Holman, John Brooks, Uriah Swann, William G
Hutchison, William Hays, James Hays, Stuart W Thornton, who
find for pl^{tf} his debt 81 Dollars & damage 1 dollar 62 cents
Also his costs

Perry Cohea vs James Benton S^r. Appeal. April 1807 pl^{tf} by J
B Reynold; d^{ft} by Thos Stuart. Jury Mark Cole, Azariah Dunn,
Henry Fry, Robt Perry, Thos Smart, Benjⁿ Holman, Jno Brooks,
Uriah Swann, W^m G Hutchison, Wm Hays, James Hays, Stuart W
Thornton who find for def^t. Pl^{tf} to pay all costs. Motion
for new tryal overruled. James Jones a witness proves 4 days
attendance; Epps Benton 2 days; Jacob Pickren 5 days

Court Adjourns untill Court in Course
                Benjamin Menees, Martin Duncan, Archer Cheatham

State of Tennessee   Robertson County,   Monday Morning July
6ᵗʰ 1807.   Present the Worshipfull John Hutchison, Martin
Duncan, James Sawyers, Esquires

Grand Jurors sworn Alexander Gordon foreman, Samuel Crocket,
George Murphey, James Mcfarlan, Richard Matthews, Wᵐ Strickland, Mark Noble, Isaac Dorris Jʳ, Joseph Payne, Jnᵒ Robertson, Anthʸ Jones Sʳ, Joel Moore, James England, Jnᵒ B Blackwell, Henry Castle. Isaac Dorris, Constable, sworn to attend
on the Grand Jury

Order Clerk receive Tax Lists delivered to him this Term
Order William Perry allowed 2 Dollars 50 cents for guarding
Lemon Holland to Nashville gaol

George Murphey vs Zachariah Cox.   Ansolem Goodman, security
for appearance of Defᵗ, delivered him.   Lemuel Sugg security
in the room of Goodman
Deed John B Cheatham Shᶠᶠ to Wᵐ Christmas 228 acres ackd
Lemuel Farmer to oversee Road in Room of John Stringer

p.449 Deed John Gosset Senʳ to Wᵐ Gosset 100 acres proven by
Willie Blount & Elijah Gosset
Deed Wᵐ Gosset to William Bunton 100 acres proven by Willie
Blount & Elijah Gosset
Deed James Kile to Jnᵒ Strain 50 acres proven by Jnᵒ Hutch-
ison & Robert Hays
Deed Jnᵒ Johnson to Jnᵒ Pike 100 acres proven by Isaac John-
son & Joseph Winfield
Deed John B Cheatham Shᶠᶠ to Thoˢ Johnson Lot 45 ackd
Deed John B Cheatham Shᶠᶠ to Thoˢ Johnson Lot 45 ackd
Charles Wheaton excused from serving as Juror this Term
Daniel Holman excused from serving as Juror this Term
Mortgage John Ferguson to Joseph Washington two Negroes ackd
Court Adjourns untill to Morning 9 oClock

Tuesday Morning July 7ᵗʰ 1807   Present the Worshipfull
Isaac Dortch, Benjamin Menees, Charles Miles, Esquires

Lovick Ventress exhonarated from payment of Tax on a stud
Horse given in by mistake for present year

The petition of John Stump for leave to build a grist mill a cross Sychamore Creek above Ramseys Spring Br, Stump being owner and proprietor of the Land on both sides of the Creek was produced; leave was granted to build aforesaid mill

p.450 Order County Trustee to pay Elisabeth Tucker Twenty-five Dollars for keeping the children of John Robins Dec[d] to present time; si fa to issue commanding Elisabeth to appear at next Court with children of s[d] Robins dec[d]

Howel Sellers & Tho[s] Sellers vs James Darnell. Jacob Pickren obtained a Judgement against Howel Sellers; Tho[s] Sellars as bail of James Darnell on a Si fa to amount Thirteen Dollars & one Cent; it also appearing that Howel and Thomas had paid same into this Court for use of Jacob Pickren, therefore on motion of Thomas Stuart their attorney, considered by Court that Howel Sellers & Thomas Sellars recover against Darnell Thirteen Dollars and one cent and costs of this motion

Jones and Owen vs Rowland Allen. Jacob Fry, def[t]'s security, delivered him. Perry Cohea security in room of Fry

Isham Uzzia to Nedom Hines 93 acres proven by Tho[s] Johnson & Henry Gardner
A supplementary return of property of W[m] Robertson dec[d] delivered by adm[r]
Demsey Coffield & Gresham Coffield to W[m] Barron[Barrow?] 270 acres proven by Jesse Martin [torn] Whitehead

p.451 Bustard & Eastin vs Levi Noyes. Case. Isaac Dortch, Benjamin Menees, Cha[s] Miles, Esq[rs]. May 1805 plt[t] by Bennet Searcy; def[t] by Ja[s] B Reynold. Cont[d]. July 1807 jury Henry Fiser, Bartimas Pack, Tho[s] Sellars, Edmond Edwards, W[m] Hendley, Hugh Henry, Ja[s] Stuart, Meredith Walton, Moses Beason, James Bell, W[m] Perry, Abraham Young who find for Def[t]. Pl[tt] pay all costs of suit. John Somervill, a witness, proves 1 days attendance, 50 miles Travel and 2 ferriages

Order Isaac Dortch and Benj[n] Menees Esq[rs] to make additional settlement with adm[r] of estate of Daniel Holland dec[d]

Nathaniel Davis vs Lemuel Sugg. W[m] Deloach security for Def[t] delivered him.
Jacob Pickren vs Howel Sellars & Tho[s] Sellers. Def[ts] failed to appear. Judgement according to Si fa $13.01 which sum def[ts] [torn] into Court & are thereof Discharged

p.452 Joel Moore to oversee road in room of Abraham Moore
Joseph Castleberry to oversee road in room of John McIntosh
Deed Henry Williams to John B Cheatham 320 acres proven by

Henry Johnson & Wᵐ Hays
Deed John Philips to Thomas Figures Lot in Springfield ackd
Deed Thoˢ Johnson to Thomas Figures half Lot 45 ackd
Deed Charles Simmons (long) to Thomas Dickson Lot in Spring-
field ackd
Deed John Richardson by Henry Johnson his attorney in fact
to Henry Williams 320 acres ackd

Power/attʸ John Richardson to Henry Johnson admited on Cer-
tificate of two Justices of Cumberland County, the presiding
Justice, and also of Clerk with seal of office
Robert Cartwright to oversee Road in room of Larkin Edwards
Court Adjourns untill tomorrow Morning 9 OClock

Wednesday Morning July 8ᵗʰ 1807   Present the Worshipfull
Benjamin Menees, Martin Duncan, Charles Miles, Esquires

p.453 State vs Isaac Doris Senʳ. Present Benjⁿ Menees, Chaˢ
Miles, Isaac Dortch. Novʳ 1806 Grand Jurors present Joˢ Dor-
ris Jʳ & Isaac Dorris Sʳ late of Robertson County with force
& arms on 30 Septʳ 1806 assaulted Eppaphroditus Benton. Wᵐ
Smith attʸ for R C. Archibald Mahon foreman. True Bill Eppˢ
Benton prosecutor. July 1807 I Dorris Sʳ by P W Humphreys;
Wᵐ Smith for State. Jury Henry Fiser, Bartimias Pack, Thoˢ
Sellars, Edmond Edwards, Wᵐ Hendley, Anderson Cheatham, Hugh
Henry, James Stuart, Moses Beason, James McDonald, Robertson
Murphey, Mattʷ Day who find Defᵗ not Guilty. Charles Simmons
a witness behalf Defᵗ proves 6 days attendance; Silas Tucker
witness behalf defᵗ 6 days

Isaac Dortch & Benjamin Menees Esqʳs returned settlement of
Daniel Hollands estate
Noah Woodard to oversee road in room of Charles McIntosh

p.454   Joel Bunn admʳ of Burrell Bunn decᵈ vs Lemuel Sugg.
Debt. Present B Menees, I Dortch, C Miles, Esqʳˢ. Augᵗ 1806
plᵗᶠ by Thoˢ Stuart, defᵗ by Jaˢ B Reynolds. July jury Chaˢ
Simmons, Henry Stults, John Couts, John Huey, Nathˡ Harbin,
Joel Lewis, Charles McIntosh, Silas Tucker, Nehemiah Varnon,
Richᵈ Crunk, John Krisel, Peter Fiser say Defᵗ has not paid
Debt, & has not performed condition of bond mentioned in the
Declaration; plᵗᶠs damage 1400; plᵗᶠ to recover agᵗ defᵗ his
debt with his costs, but this Judgement may be Discharged by
the payment of 1400 Dollars being the damages afˢᵈ & costs.
John Bell a witness proves 4 days attendance; James Johnston
witness proves 3 days

State vs Anderson Cheatham. John Boren prosecutor & witness
appearance bond

Grand Jury Discharged
p.455 Robertson Murphey app^{td} Constable; bond 1000 Dollars,
Whitmill Harrington & Lemuel Sugg, securities

Miles Draughon vs Enoch Tucker & Luke Sanders. Wm Hays & Ja^s
Hays securities for Luke Sanders delivered him; Thos Sellers
& Jeremiah Bath[Balk?] securities. And deliver Enoch Tucker;
Henry Johnson & Perry Cohea securities in room of Hays's
Court Adjourns untill tomorrow Morning 9 OClock

Thursday Morning July 9th 1807   Present the Worshipfull
Benjamin Menees, Martin Duncan, Isaac Dortch, Esquires

Deed Robert Weakley to Shaderick Hunt 200 acres proven by
Marvel Lowe & John Hunt
Jurors to next Court: Ja^s Elliott Jr, Ja^s Atkins, Moses Win-
ters, Danl Holman, Thos Byrd, James Yates, Henry Airs, Elias
Fort (M C), Wm Deloach, Arch^d Mahon, Jesse Martin, Jno Hunt,
Henry Hyde Jr, John Coleman, Lovick Ventress, James Bell, W^m
Crocket, Jo^s Castleberry, John Dorris, Wm Huddleston, James
Hays, Jesse Jones, Hen^y Johnson, Fred^k Batts, Elias Fort Jr,
Jno Sherod, James Holeman, Jno Hunt, Moses Hardin, Chas Kil-
gore, Francis Boren, Jno Crocket, Nathan Clark, Ja^s Gambril,
Jo^s Henry, Charles Bradon, Volentine Choate, David Huddle-
ston, John Pike

William Dickeson exhonarated from Tax on his stud horse for
present year, horse is not kept for covering mares

p.456 John Paca vs Rowland Allen. Appeal. I Dortch, M Dun-
can, B Menees, Esq^{rs}. Novr 1806 pl^{tf} by Thos Stuart; def^t by
[written over] Swann. July jury Henry Fiser, Bartimias Pack,
Edmond Edwards, Wm Hendley, Hugh Henry, James Stuart, Luke
Sanders, John Bell, Robertson Murphey, Whitmill Harrington,
Jesse Martin, Thos Sellers who find for pl^{tf} 31 Dollars 51½
cents, also costs. Francis Dellam witness proves 8 days attendance, 150 miles Travel, 6 Ferriages. Matthew Lodge, witness, 2 days attendance

Ordered James Crabtree, Henry Watkins & Henry Gardner be inspectors for ensuing Election for Governor, &c; & that John
Coleman and Thomas Swann be Clerks to said Election

Lemuel Sugg vs David Smith. Marvel Mcfarlan, witness, proves
5 days attendance; Josiah Fort, witness, seven days

p.457 Jackson & Hutchins vs John Glover. Case. B Menees, M
Duncan, I Dortch, Esq^{rs}. Ap^l 1807 pl^{tf} by Bennet Searcy; Df^t
[blank]. July jury Henry Fiser, Bart^s Pack, Thomas Sellars,

Edmond Edwards, Wm Hendley, Hugh Henry, Luke Sanders, John Bell, Whitmill Harrington, Wm Mason, Robertson Murphey, Ge^o Murphey who find for pl^tf his damages 136 Dollars 85 and 1/6 cents and costs.

Bustard & Easten vs James G Heard. Benjn Menees, I Dortch, M Duncan, Esq^rs. Ap^l 1807 pl^tf by Thos Swann; def^t by P W Humphries and J B Reynolds. July jury Henry Fiser, Bartimias Pack, Thos Sellars, Edmond Edwards, Wm Hendley, Hugh Henry, Luke Sanders, John Bell, Whitmill Harrington, Wm Mason, Robertson Murphey, George Murphey who find the plaintiff's damages 269 Dollars 37½ cents and costs.
p.458   Court Adjourns untill Tomorrow Morning 9 OClock

Friday Morning July 10th 1807   Present the Worshipfull A Cheatham, John Hutchison, Martin Duncan, Esquires

Stothart & Bell vs Jacob Pickren. Debt. Above justices. Ap^l 1807 pl^tf by Thos Swann; Def^t by Ja^s B Reynold. July jury: Henry Fiser, Bart^s Pack, Thomas Sellars, Edmond Edwards, Wm Hendley, Anderson Cheatham, Hugh Henry, James Stuart, Lewis Carter, Thomas Holman, S W Thornton, Peter Cheatham find for pl^tf, assess debt & damage to 202 Dollars 73 cents & costs

J B Cheatham Esqr, Collector of 1806 Tax, has credit with State Treasurer for delinquents for year 1806

p.459 Bustard & Easten vs Bazel Boren. Case. J Hutchison, B Menees, M Duncan, Esq^rs. April 1807 pl^tf by Thos Swann; def^t by Thos Stuart. July Jury Henry Fiser, Bartimias Pack, Thos Sellars, Edmond Edwards, Wm Hendley, Hugh Henry, Wm Walton, Lewis Carter, Thomas Holman, Enoch Tucker, Perry Cohea, Lawrence Owen who find for plaintiff, assess damage to 84 dollars 46 cents and costs.

Bustard & Easten vs John Huey. Debt. J Hutchison, B Menees, M Duncan, Esq^rs. April 1807 pl^tf by Thomas Swann; def^t by Wm Smith. July jury Henry Fiser, Bartimias Pack, Thos Sellars, Edm^d Edwards, Wm Hendley, Hugh Henry, Wm Walton, Lewis Carter, Thomas Holeman, Enoch Tucker, Perry Cohea, Lawrence Owen who find for plaintiff sixty five Dollars debt & damage one Dollar 95 cents and costs of suit.

p.460 Evan Wallace vs William McCormick. Attachment. Pl^tf by Thomas Swann; Def^t failing to appear, judgement by default, debt 200 Dollars, interest 15 Dollars, & also costs of suit. Clerk issues writ to sell property attached. Sheriff levied on 451 acres lying in the Barrens joining William Johnson

John B Cheatham Sh⁵ᶠ allowed 5 Dollars for summoning guard,
finding horse, and guarding John Robertson to Clarksville
gaol. Peter Young   a guard allowed $2
     Wᵐ Hays   "   " $2
     David Jones   "   " $2
     Nathˡ Harbin   "   " $2
Archer Cheatham, gaoler, forty days $10.66

Archer Cheatham Esqʳ admited to keep an Ordinary for 1 year
gave bond 1000 Dollˢ, Henry Johnson & Henry Fiser securities

John B Cheatham, Collector, reported following land has not
been given in for 1807 Taxes
David Ambrose   1000 on Sychamore
Willibough Williams   640 waters of Sulpher fork
David Davis   640 in the Barrens
Clerk to have the list published agreeable to Law

Court Adjourns untill Court in Course
          Benjamin Menees, Martin Duncan, Archer Cheatham

p.461 State of Tennessee, Robertson County, October the 5ᵗʰ
1807.   Present the Worshipfull Benjamin Menees, Hardy S
Bryan, William Connell, Martin Duncan, Esquires

Order Clerk receive lists of Taxable property
Leven D Powell Esqʳ produced his Licence to practice Law as
an attorney and was accordingly admited

Grand Jurors   John Coleman foreman, John Pike, John Sherod,
Moses Hardin, Henry Johnson, Thomas Byrd, Charles Kilgore,
Jaˢ Gambell, Jesse Jones, Moses Winters, Henry Aires, Daniel
Holeman, John Dorris, James Atkins, Francis Boren. Robertson
Murphey, constable, sworn to attend the Grand Jury

State vs James Wheeler. John Young appearance bond to give
testamony behalf the State; Abraham Young and Robert Brown
bond to testify behalf the state against James Wheeler

Elijah Spiller exhonarated from Taxes on 83 acres for 1807,
much more given in than he owns
Deed Jaˢ Menees Shᶠᶠ to Wᵐ Kenley 9½ acres ackd
Deed Zachariah Duncan to Daniel Darr 30 acres ackd
Deed Jesse Gardner to James Johnston 33 acres ackd
Deed Charles McIntosh to Nimrod McIntosh 23 acres proven by
Henry Johnson

231

p.462 Will of John Simmons proven by John Mcfarlan & Edward Choate. Jn° Simmons Jr, executor, delivered inventory
Deed Philip Alston by atty/fact John Gilbert 640 acres to Wm Harrison proven by Andw Miller & Elisha Bridgewater
Deed Sarah and Gabriel Sanders to Zachariah Duncan 70 acres proven by Wm Perry & Danl Darr

Jury to lay off dower of Mrs Emley Shaw relic of Samuel Shaw decd: James Sawyers, Richd Matthews, Sampson Matthews, Amos Cohea, Isaac Dorris Senr, Isaac Dorris Jr, Saml Dorris Senr, Plummer Willis, Isaac Bridgewater, James McDonald, Robert Bates, James Shannon.

Deed Philip Alston Junr by John Gilbert atty/fact 30 acres proven by Andrew Miller and Elijah Bridgewater [grantee not named]
Deed John Carney to John Mitchel 89¼ acres proven by Zachariah Duncan & Wm J Perry
Deed James Hays & Wm Hays to Richd M Harwell 100 acres, also Certificate annexed signed Jacob Damewood, proven by Thomas Figures & Thos Johnson
Nathan Clark excused from serving as a Juror this Term
Peter Kizer to oversee road in room of Allen Parker
Court Adjourns untill tomorrow Morning 9 OClock

Tuesday Morning October the 6th 1807. Present the Worshipfull B Menees, M Duncan, Jas Sawyers, Esqrs

George Murphey records his stock mark
p.463 State vs Jacob Cook. Appearance bond James Healthman to give testamony behalf State against Jacob Cook

Eppaphroditus Benton vs Isaac Dorris & Thomas Dorris. M Duncan, B Menees, J Norfleet, Esqrs. August 1806 pltf by Jas B Reynold; deft by Thos Stuart. Apl 1807 jury Robt Perry, Thos Smart, Thos George, Benjn Holeman, Jn° Brooks, Azariah Dunn, Henry Fry, Thomas Appleton, Fredk Cobb, Noah Woodard, James Jones, Hugh Henry who find for pltf, assess damage to $2.50 on Thomas Dorris & $2.50 on Isaac Dorris & Costs. New tryal granted. October 1807 jury Elias Fort (M C), Archd Mahon, Wm Crocket, James Holeman, Jesse Martin, Jacob Pinkley, Elijah Spiller, Isaac Johnson, Jn° Shannon, George Murphey, Plummer Willis, Jacob Pinkley Senr who find for pltf, assess damage agt Isaac Dorris to one Dollar & costs; find Thos Dorris not Guilty. Pltf to recover agt Isaac Dorris one Dollar & costs. Pltf to pay costs of Joseph & Thomas Dorris. Charles Murphey witness proves 7 days attendance; Thomas Appleton, 4 days

p.464 State vs Anderson Cheatham. Appearance bond of John

Boren to give Testamony on behalf the State

State vs Jacob Cook. Defendant's appearance bond

Lewis Wells, adm^r estate of Wm Robertson dec^d given liberty
to sell one or more Negroes of estate as necessary to discharge debts of s^d estate giving reasonable notice of sale

The adm^r of estate of James Hodges dec^d granted liberty to
sell personal property of s^d estate

Willis Holland vs William Johnson. Attachment. Lewis Wells
adm^r estate Wm Robertson summoned as garnishee, declares the
estate is indebted to William Johnson to about 500 Dollars

Deed Archibald Huddleston to Edwin Harris 100 acres proven
by James Felts & Howel Harris
Deed John Boren to Nimrod McIntosh 10 acres ackd
Deed William Brown to John Berry 237 acres proven by Elias
Fort & Noah Woodard
p.465 Deed John Matthews to Thomas Dixon Lot 59 in Spring-
field proven by Hugh Irwin & Tabitha H Dixon
Deed William McAdoe to Samuel McAbly 200 acres proven by Ja^s
Gambell & Alex^r Gordon
Deed Matthew Brooks to Peter Fiser 200 acres proven by James
Connell & Matthew Day
Deed Abraham Stuart, Wm Stuart, Elijah Stuart, Thos Grayson
by Thomas Johnson their att^y/fact to James Stuart for their
part of 640 acres ackd by Thos Johnson
Deed Abraham Stuart by Thos Johnson att^y/fact to James Stu-
art 120 acres ackd by Thos Johnson
Deed W^m T Lewis to Willis Holland 94 acres proven by Bennet
Searcy & Wm Baldry
Deed Elisha Stuart to Ja^s Stuart 102½ acres proven by Isaac
Dortch and Norfleet Dortch
Power/att^y Abraham Stuart to Thos Johnson admited to record
on Certificate of Ja^s Thompson & Matt^w Wilson, two justices
of Christian County, with the Clerks Certificate and County
seal annexed
Power/att^y Abraham Stuart, Wm Stuart, Elijah Stuart, Thomas
Grayson to Thomas Johnson admited to record on certificate
of James Thompson and Matthew Wilson, justices of Christian
County, Kentucky, Certificate clerk of Court, & County seal
annexed
Saml Robins & John Robins children of Jno Robins dec^d bound
by indenture to Samuel Tucker untill age twenty one; s^d Saml
Tucker gave John Johnson & John Shannon his securities
p.466 Deed Matthew McClain by att^y/fact John McClain to Ja^s
Stuart 220 acres proven by Thos Johnson & Jno B Cheatham
Deed James Stuart to Jesse Gardner 220 acres ackd

Power/att^y Wm Stuart to Thos Johnson admited on certificate of Matthew Wilson & James Thompson, Justices/Peace, Christian County, KY, Certificate of Clerk, County Seal annexed

Betsey and Polley Robins daughters of Jno Robins decd bound by Indenture to Elisabeth Tucker until age eighteen. John Johnson and John Shannon s^d Tuckers security

Hiram Hodges granted L^{trs}/adm^n on estate of Ja^s Hodges dec^d, bond 500 Dollars, with Nathan Yoes and John Yoes securities

Articles of Agreement between Jacob Cook and James Heathman proven by James Gambell
Perry Cohea admited to keep an Ordanery for one year; bond 1000 Dollars, with James Sawyers & Augustine Cook securities

Jacob Pinkley (Sych) to oversee Road in room of James Felts
Court Adjourns untill Tomorrow Morning 9 OClock

p.467 Wednesday Morning October 7th 1807 Present the Worshipfull William Connell, Archer Cheatham, James Norfleet

John Hutchison Esqr admited to keep an Ordinary for 1 year, bond 1000 Dollars, Josiah Fort & Augustine Cook, securities

Deed Jacob Damewood to Wm Adams 117½ acres proven by John Howel & Lewis B [blot]
Deed Jacob Pinkley to Henry Fry 160 acres ackd
Deed Jacob Pinkley to Anthony Hinkle 55 acres ackd

Duncan Robertson ass^{ee} Peter Brawner vs Whitmill Harrington. Debt. James Norfleet, Ja^s Sawyers, A Cheatham, Esq^{rs}. April 1807 pl^{tf} by George W L Marr; Def^t by Thos Stuart. October jury Jesse Martin, Arch^d Mahon, Joel Lewis, Henry Stults, Joseph Fry, Henson Day, Noah Woodard, Thomas Appleton, Theophilus Morgan, James Appleton Junr, Wm Mason, Abraham Young who find for pl^{tf} his debt 92 Dollars 77 cents; damage four Dollars 17 cents; also costs. George A West, witness, proves one day attendance; Elijah Wright proves one day

p.468 Deed Ezekiel Norman to Thos West 58 acres proven by Saml Spearman & Elijah Eubank

Jones and Owen vs Levi Noyes. James Norfleet, W Connell, Ja^s Sawyers, Esq^{rs}. April 1807 pl^{tf} by Thomas Swann; def^t by J B Reynold. Octr Jury Jesse Martin, Arch^d Mahon, Elias Fort (M C), Wm Crocket, James Holeman, Wm Sale, Willie Holland, Robt Hogan, Jonathan Huddleston, John Strain, Luke Sanders, Epp^s Benton assess pl^{tfs} damage to 80 Dollars 43½ cents, & costs

Deed Thomas Clark to Abraham Young   33 acres proven by Nath[l]
Simmons & W[m] Armstrong

State vs Jacob Pickren. State vs Thomas Figures. Appearance
bond of Rowland Allen in each suit, to appear next Court to
give testamony against Jacob Pickren and Thomas Figures

p.469   Deed Perry Cohea to John Strain   Lot 15 Springfield
proven by Levi Noyes & W G Hutchison
Deed James Clark to Abraham Young   274 acres proven by Nath[l]
Simmons & Flemmon Simmons

Miles Draughon vs Enoch Tucker & Luke Sanders.   Covenant. Wm
Connell, Ja[s] Norfleet, James Sawyers, Esq[rs]. July 1807 pl[tf]
by Bennet Searcy; def[t] by Thomas Swann. Oct[r] Jury Jesse Martin, Archibald Mahon, Elias Fort (MC), William Crocket, Ja[s]
Holeman, William Sale, Willie Holland, Rob[t] Hogan, Jonathan
Huddleston, John Strain, Noah Woodard, Epp[s] Benton who find
for plaintiff damages 96 Dollars and costs of suit

Deed Charles McIntosh to Henry Johnson and Archer Cheatham 9
acres ackd
p.470 Jacob Pinkley released from Tax on 640 acres, s[d] land
paid for by agent of John Thompson for year 1807

Willie Holland vs William Johnson. Attachment. Thomas Johnson, garnishee, deposeth he has note given by Wm Robertson
to Wm Johnson for 517 dollars 60 cents, [a lengthy explana-
tion by Tho[s] Johnson of his liability]   Thomas Johnson owes
p.471   only as above mentioned; knows of no one indebted or
who has any of W[m] Johnson's property except Charles Wheaton
who had some leather belonging to him some time ago
Court Adjourns untill tomorrow Morning 9 OClock

Thursday Morning October 8th 1807   Present the Worshipfull
William Connell, Archer Cheatham, James Norfleet, Esquires

B/S John Watson to Archer Cheatham for Negro man Joe proven
by Levi Noyes & Thomas Johnson

John Edmonston ass[ee] W[m] P Anderson vs Lemuel Sugg. Debt. Ja[s]
Norfleet, J Sawyers, W[m] Connell, Esquires. July 1807 p[lf] by
by Thomas Swann, def[t] by Ja[s] B Reynold; Oct[r] Jury Elias Fort
(M C), Arch[d] Mahon, W[m] Crocket, James Holeman, Jesse Martin,
W[m] Milsap, Peter Young, Peter Cheatham, S W Thornton, Perry
Cohea, Plummer Willis, Henry Fry who find for pl[tf] his debt
110 Dollars, damage 18 dollars 43 cents, also his costs

p.472 Henry Johnson g^{dn} of orphans of John Tucker dec^d produced settlement made with him by John Hutchison and Martin
Duncan. Court examined accounts of said guardian, allow him
100 dollars for his trouble & expenses

John B Cheatham gd^n for orphans of John Tucker dec^d produced
settlement made by John Hutchison & Martin Duncan Esq^{rs} with
him. Accounts of s^d g^{dn} examined; allow him for trouble and
expenses 106 Dollars

Bill/Sale Jesse Jones to Thomas Figures, two Negroes proven
by Thomas Swann & Thomas Johnson
Deed Edmond Hatch to Hardy S Bryan 60 acres ackd
Power/att^y Thomas Johnson to Benjn Coffield ackd & certified

John Philips, Justice of the Peace, resigned his commission
p.473 Isaac Philips, Justice/Peace, resigned his commission

John Fry J^r vs Joseph Robertson & And^w Cheatham. Wm Connell,
J Sawyers, J Norfleet, Esqr. July 1807 pl^{tf} by Thomas Swann;
def^t by James B Reynolds. Octr jury Elias Fort (M C), Arch^d
Mahon, Wm Crocket, Ja^s Holeman, Jesse Martin, Wm Milsap J^r,
Peter Young, Peter Cheatham, Perry Cohea, Plummer Willis,
Thomas Appleton, Epp^s Benton who find pl^{tf} his debt 133 Dol-
lars, damage 5 dollars 38½ cents, also costs

p.474 Winefird Cromwell vs Dorsey Cromwell. Attachment. W^m
Connell, James Sawyers, J Norfleet, Esq^{rs}. July 1807 Sh^{ff} re-
turn dated April, levied on 300 acres on Red River conveyed
by John Alston to Alex^r Cromwell, a forth part of tract said
Dorsey is intitled to for his share. J B Cheatham Sh^{ff}. P^{if}
by Bennet Searcy; Def^t failing to appear, judgement by default. October Jury Elias Fort MC, Arch^d Mahon, Wm Crocket,
James Holman, Jesse Martin, Wm Milsap J^r, Peter Young, Peter
Cheatham, Perry Cohea, Plummer Willis, Thomas Appleton, Epp^s
Benton, who assess pl^{tfs} damage to 60 Dollars, also costs.
[torn] property attached to be sold

p.475 John Philips ranger for Robertson County resigned his
appointment; John Hutchison Esqr app^{td} Ranger pro tem

Henry Johnson app^{td} gd^n for Nancy Tucker, Pheby Tucker, John
Tucker, Riggs Tucker, Samuel Tucker, children of John Tucker
dec^d in room of John B Cheatham resigned, bond 6000 Dollars
with Wm Crocket, Thomas Smart, and Augustine Cook securities

Deed Daniel Hogan to James Hays and Wm Hays 100 acres proven
by Francis Hays & Jacob Damewood

Jurors to next Court: Thomas Dorris, Wm Wills, John Johnson

OCTOBER 1807

Sr, Isaac Johnson, John Appleton, Jacob Pinkley Jr, Wm Hud-
dleston Jr, James Young, Abrm Young, Thomas Kilgore, James
Bell, Meredith Walton, Nimrod McIntosh, Richd Jones, Joseph
Wimberley, Wm Deloach, Mark Noble, Cordal Norfleet, Nicholas
Conrod, John Crane, Saml Henley S^r, Wm Atkins, Ja^s Shannon,
Jesse Gardner, John Siglar, Ja^s Appleton, Noah Woodard, Mar-
tin Walton, Thos R Butler, Richard Swift, Spencer Moss, John
Brooks, Walter Stark, John Chowning, James Long, Wm Byrd,
Matthew Day, Samuel Crocket, James McDonald, William Menees

p.476   Jurors to Sup^r Court Henry Gardner, Elias Fort J^r,
Wm Connell, Jiles Connell, John Couts, Wm Fletcher, Andrew
Shankling, Ja^s Johnson S^r, Sampson Matthews, James H Bryan,
John Coleman, William Perry

Disannull road Anderson Cheatham to Travess on Red River
Ordered road laid off from Ninkimpinch to Springfield; Felty
Farmer, Joel Moore, John Stringer, John Siglar, Thos Haynes,
John Farmer, James Crabtree, John Hudson, & George Farmer to
mark same

Gray Stringer admited to build a mill on Red River about ½
mile below the mouth of Simmons branch on his own land

Following land to be sold for 1806 Taxes & costs having been
advertised as Law directs
[blank] McCormick   451 acres Barrens joins W Johnson
Thos Williams   340 waters of Sychamore

p.477 Following land for 1807
David Ambrose   1000 on Sychamore
Willsbough Williams   640 waters of Sulpher fork
David Davis   640 in the Barrens

Clerk allowed fifty Dollars for exoficio services for past
year before July Court last

Sheriff allowed fifty dollars for exoficio services for the
past year before July Court last

Logan Road from fork in the Barrens near the Race paths to
the County line near Mr Bells is to be discontinued

Order a road laid off from Springfield to meet a road opened
by Davidson County on the ridge above Thos Harrisons; Henry
Johnson J^r, James McDonald, John Huddleston, Joseph Castle-
berry, James Bell, Wm Huddleston Jr, John Hutchison, Jacob
Pinkley Jr, John Lipscomb to mark same
Court Adjourns untill Court in Course
        James Sawyers, A Cheatham, Wm Connell, John Hutchison

237

BOREN (continued)
56 58 65 71 74 78 81-84 87 89
92 96 100 102 109 116 117 119
126 129 136-138 143 146 149
154 159 160 162 163 167 174
180 186 194 197 201 206 208
215 218 225 230 Francis 1 3 4
5 14 27 47 71 76 81 94 95 120
164 166 174 176 187 194 196
197 229 231 Jeremiah 182
John 1 32 228 233 Joseph 20
154 Moses 3 43 44 45 68 71 77
Sarah 32 Stephen 1 2 4-6 13 17
26-28 30 32 52 70 74 81 90
101 103 104 108 138 140 145
146 149 151 167 169 180 184
213 Thomas 164 William 9 42
44 45 50 52 59 87
BOSLEY John 77 84
BOSMAN Caleb 169
BOUNDS Captn 61 82 87 104 111
167 171 195-197 216 222 Jos
76 Obediah 55-57 76 94 96 97
145 187 191-194 196 198 205
Thomas 31 54 67 76 92 94 116
135 ---- 60 193
BOUNDS BRANCH 92
BOWDEN Joshua 143
BOWEN James 172 John 152
BOWERS John 46 84 203 209
Reuben 204 209 211 215-217
BOWLS Charles 141 142 145
BOWMAN Andrew 61 81 John 84
98 William 105 106 125
BOX Henry 123
BOYD John 105 106 Robert 91
BRADLEY/BRADLY George 105
106 Nathaniel 206 217
BRADON Charles 54 60 75 77 78
92 114 119 120 140 143-145
154 162 164-168 174 176 187
191 193 194 198 205 208 229
Robert 196
BRAKER Andrew 187
BRAKIE Andrew 154
BRAWNER Captn 195 196 216
220 Peter 130 146 167 171 185
189 200 209 211 215-217 234
BRAY William 25 48
BREK J 187
BREWER Sterling 123

BRIAN Morgan 8
BRICKEY Polly 64
BRIDGES John 15
BRIDGEWATER/BRIDGWATER
Elijah 124 132 136 143 144
232 Elisha 146 160 162 168
201 232 Isaac 221 232
BRIGHAM David 124
BRINER George 103
BRISBY John 215
BRISCOE Captain 141 167 171
George 4 11 12-15 16 20 21 29
30 33 34 40 42-45 47 48 50 52
64 65 67 73 81 82 87 93 95 96
98 100 107 110 111 113 114
116 127 133 136 137 139 John
32 44 45 50-52 54 55 Sarah 32
William 3-5 12 26-28 32 43 62
64 74 75 82 90 95 96 114 115
119 122 127 134 135 139 140
146 148 149 157 158 160 166
167 174 177 179 185
BRITAIN/BRITTON Thomas 86 91
93 137
BROCK Joseph 3 8
BROOKS John 34 44 50 59 62 84
96 102 103 112 116 120 122
152 156 162-164 200 208 209
219 221 223-225 232 237
Matthew 28 116 122 161 175
233
BROWN Edward 220 George 215
Hugh 67 91 Isaac 1 2 4 6 8 10
19 30 James 14 John 202
Joseph 80 Robt 162-168 187
191 193 194 198 205 215 231
Thos 215 Walter 174 177 187
189 William 2 6 8 12 14 16 28
47 67 233 ---- 12
BROWNER Captn 197 Peter 119
128 161
BROWNING Budy 141 144 210
212 Geo 95 102 107 108 123
135 136 138-140 145 155 160-
162 164 180 183 194 196 210
212 213 Joshua 207 Nimrod
210
BROWNS CR/FORD/FORK 6 7 13
22 27 29 53 85 87 103 124 177
BUSH CR 20 29 63-65 83 88 105
122 151 185 187 195-197 201

241

CRAWFORD Samuel 21
CREEK Kellian 211
CRICHLOE William 15
CRIPS Christian 39
CROCKET Jane 12 21 John 11 12
  20 25 56 57 85 86 102 107 110
  144 147-150 167 192 219 229
  Saml 11-14 20 22 25 27 28 32-
  35 38 40-42 48 49 52 54 62 63
  65 69 71 73 79-82 85 94 96 97
  110 116 119-121 124 129 146
  154 156 158 160 163 179 182
  187 190 202 204 205 207 218
  223 226 237 Wm 11 21 23 26
  38 71 79-82 85 115 120 128
  130 144 147-149 162 164 174
  176 177 180 187 189 202 204
  205 207 208 215 229 232 234
  235 236
CROCKETT William 10 188
CROLLY Mary 41
CROMWELL Alexr/Elexr 6 30 39
  41 42 44 56 59 89 90 99 168
  236 Ann 99 Dorsey 99 124 126
  135 161 236 Garrard 161 John
  124 135 139 154 157 160 161
  167-169 171-174 190 202 204
  209 213 215 Winnifred &c 161
  204 236
CROPS Christian 26
CROSS Richard 100
CROUCH Charles 9
CROW Jas 96 159 Mary 159 193
CRUMPLER Rafford &c 105 106
CRUK Kellian 211
CRUMMILL John 131
CRUMWELL ---- 103
CRUNK John 48 49 67 72 74 77
  78 85 Richd 72 165 166 168
  178 228 William 14 42 48 71 74
  76 77 94 96 102-105 107 108
  110 115 134 138 141 146 150
  179 210
CRUTCHER Anthony 57 Wm 57 86
CRYER/CRYOR John 105 106
CULBERSON Mr 205
CULVERSON Mr 190
CUMBERLAND COUNTY 228
CUMBERLAND FURNACE 73
CUMBERLAND R 8 13 61 67 83 93
  94 120 123 140 195 201

CUMMINS Jas 105 106 John 155
  187 195 201 Samuel 105 106
CURD Daniel 129
CURREY/CURRY Robert 51 62 72
  78 90
DABNEY Cornelius 2 12 13 17 18
  20 24 30 32 34 38 53 69
DAMEWOOD Jacob 148 162 164
  179 204 219 232 234 236
DANILY Tenor 103
DARDEN/DARDIN Ann 18 25 33
  Betsey 216 222 Capt 82 88 104
  109 116 120 123 124 Holland
  11 30 41 42 55 64 68 92 118
  126 128 157 158 202 220
  Jonathan 1 6 13 18 25 30 32-
  34 41 42 52 55 64 68 71 78
  118 126 222
DARE Henry 205
DARNALD George 106 129 133
  James 184 Nicholas 133 165
DARNEL/DARNELL James 194
  198 199 200 202 207 211 219
  227 George 217 Nicholas 217
DARR Daniel 231 232
DARROW Benjamin 127 158
DAVIDSON Moses 137 139
DAVIDSON COUNTY/FERRY 5 46
  56 91 95 177 237
DAVIS David 47 84 129 231 237
  Nathl 223 227 Obed 152 164
  169 Samuel 176 181 Thomas
  155 188 195 201
DAVIS FERRY 8
DAVY Jehu 91
DAY Henson 110 234 Matthew 18
  38 42 45 48 50 55 60 62 63 68
  74 77-80 82 85 89 95 101 102
  103 107 110 112 113 116 119
  123 124 128 137 138 153 156
  164 173 177 180 183 185 188
  193 200 201 205 207 210 211
  214 228 233 237
DEADERICK George 55 Thos 167
DEADRICK ---- 222
DEAN Abraham 7 11-13 108 139
  140 James 1
DELANY James 17
DELLAM Francis 229
DELOACH Milbery 47 William 9 10
  14-16 30-34 47 55 79 111 112

DUNCAN (continued)
213 214 216 219 220 224-226
228-232 236 Wm 1 3 8 12 13 17-
19 26 31 81 89 Zachariah 231
232
DUNN Azariah 14-16 37 41 75-78
89 92 108 111 112 126 127
211 219 221 223-225 232 John
107 Levi 135-140 Margaret 107
DUNNING Robert 141
DUPREE Howel 82
EARTHMAN John 144
EASTEN/EASTIN John 46 84 105
106 ---- 134 165 178 199 211
213 227 230
EASTER (slave) 125
EDMONSTON John 235
EDWARD/EDWARDS Benjamin
185 David 46 125 141 145
Edmd 164 208 223 227-230
Gravet 210 Jas 64 Jno 210
Larkin 160 208 228 N 101
Ninian 99 102 110 Thos 88 107
Wm 22 25 26-29 60 64 70 76
77 80 82 100 101 144 148 149
160 198 199 210 220
EGNEW John 208
EGNIGHT Joseph 165
ELDER James 61
ELLIOTT Jas 9 10 30 35 48 59 75
78 112 120 122 128 130 131
149 150 163 165 167 169 189
190 202 211 221 223 229
Martin 42 Saml 163 165 196
221 William 37 42 50 54 79
ELLIS John 82 98
ELMORE Julius 114 138 139 150
153 164 Travess 123 159
EMSON Caleb Rebekah & Wm 152
ENGLAND James 108 137 140
143-145 196 223 226
ENGLEMAN Jane 159 193 194
204 Joseph 125 170 180 193
ENNEVER Joseph 105 106
ENOCH David 22
ERWIN Joseph 98
EUBANK/EUBANKS Elijah 177
234
EVANS George 83 93 107 128 161
James 46 Kissey 45
EVERET/EVERETT William 47 67

EVERTON Thomas 206
EVINS Andrew 51
EWING James 14 54 89 90 94 108
John 16 Robt 4 54 203
FAIRLISS Robert 202
FAITH John 46
FAMILY FORGE 77
FANSUR ---- 114
FARMER Felty 237 Geo 237 Jas 66
136 John 237 Leml 226 Mr 190
205 Thomas 117 209 210 Wil-
liam 12 13 27-31 33 35 36 45
50 59 66 76
FARRIOR William 178
FARROW William 46 84
FAYETTE COUNTY KY 3
FAYETTEVILLE 59 65 82 94 100
FELTNER Jacob 132
FELTS Jas 158 203 204 233 234
FEN/FENN Richard 23 24 56
FENNER Richd 98 Robt 100 202
FENON Richard 98
FERGUSON John 199 226 Richard
193
FIGURES Thos 173 200 212 213
219 220 225 228 232 235 236
FIKE/FIKES Dollytheo 220 Elisha
122 133 184 192 194 196 207
John 106 Malaciah/Malakiah
106 Nathan 198 Simon 117 144
160 220 Tyre 115 117 ---- 170
FIN/FINN Richard 12 13 24
FINDLEY Wm 64 66 68-70 92 170
FISER Henry 148 164 180 194 202
223 231 Michl 148 162-168
187 189 204 215 227-230 Peter
148 149 163 164 208 209 213
214 228 233
FISHER Frederick 210
FITTS James 203 204
FLANNERY Elijah 23 37 Isaac 3 4
5 32 42 76
FLEANOR John 76
FLEENER Adam 46 125 129
FLEMING Ralph 4
FLETCHER Alexr 129 Wm 237
FLEUELLEN/FLEWELLEN Harbert
142 148 165 Wm 14 21-23 29
35 37 39 48 66 69 71 78 84
101 105 108 118 133 142 146
148 150 165 198 200 207 217

FLINN Geo 23 Wm 15 20 21 22
FLIPPS Garrot 223
FLYNN John 72-74 129 134 186
    Laughlin 155 188 195
FORD James 32 40 123 128 129
    John 129 141 145 196
FORT Benjn 87 David 27 Elias 7 9-
    11 29-34 41 43 47 56-58 62 63
    75 78 83 85 99 115-117 123
    126-128 135 143 144 148 150
    159 164 165 177 180 183-185
    189 195 197 200 204 205
    210 211 215-217 220 222 229
    232-237 Fredk 77 Henry 222
    Jacob 178 Jas 26 178 222
    Jeremiah 178 John 29 102 210
    Joseph 144 Josiah 2 13 20 31
    49 56 60 65 73 78 81 86 97 99
    100 101 103 105 109 115-117
    123 137 143 153 157 159 162
    171 172 178 200 204 205 208
    211 212 216 222 223 229 234
    Mary 178 Micajah 55 Sarah 109
    178 Sugg 16 39 43 44 47 72 90
    115-117 130 134 143 146 179
    Wm 1-4 6-8 10 13 16 17 25 27
    28 30 31 34-36 38 39 44 48 53-
    56 58-61 66 71 72 77 81 95-97
    99 101 103 105 109 118 131
    146 176 178 191 192 211 221
FOSTER James 148 John 125
FOWLER John 105 106
FRANKLIN COUNTY 8
FRAZER George 45
FRIZEL Nathan 203
FRY Henry 174 176 182 199 219
    220 221 223-225 232 234 235
    Jacob 92 93 138 180 194 198
    199-201 227 John 201 236
    Joseph 140 149 188 210 212
    234 Peter 107 112 128 190 200
    201 204 205 207 208 217
FRYER William 46
FULK Jacob 113 131 133 182 194
    221 Samuel 126 131
FULKISON Abraham 46 84 106
FULTON M 179
FUNKHOWSER Christopher 118
FURGESON Moses 73
FYKES ---- 105
GAINES/GAINS Anthy 106 ---- 111

GALESPIE/GALISPIE George 103
    135 Robert 97 99 101 103 105
    107 108 115 120 123 124
GALLAWAY Saml 50-52 55 62 82
GALT Matthew 196
GAMBELL James 231 233 234
GAMBLE Joseph 86
GAMBRIL James 102 137 149 158
    160 179 180 184 229
GARDNER Ann 87 224 Henry 7 20
    32 65 70 75 77 88 92 98-100
    116 122 123 126 130 145 150
    161 167 178 180 191 197 204
    208 209 220 223 225 227 229
    237 James 41 55 56 128 130
    136 141 149 151-153 156 167
    169 171-174 180 185 197 Jesse
    224 231 233 237 John 7 26 37
    41 55 58 108 112 114-116 126
    135 136 143 144 146 148 150
    151 162 164 165 170 202 211
    213 219 Joshua 141 194 196
    197 Shadk 179
GARNER ---- 111
GARRARD COUNTY KY 142
GASPERS RIVER ROAD 25
GATLIN Edward 76 86
GEORGE Thomas 58 69 96 116
    170 194 218 221 232
GIFFEN William 124
GILBERT Jno 232 Michl 17-19
    Webster 83 85 160 179 Wm 3
    17 30 56 57 135 180 211
GILKISON CREEK 154 187
GIVEN/GIVENS/GIVINGS Edward
    105 106 William 49 53 63
GLASGOW/GLASSGOW James
    105 106 154 195 201
GLEAVES Michael 19
GLOVER John 229 Samuel 85
    William 26 85 105 106
GOINS Jeremiah 204
GOLDEN Jesse 177
GOLLADAY/GOLLADY Geo 127
    169
GOLSON Jesse 170
GONSALUS Daniel 127
GOODMAN Ansellam &c 203 222
    226 Jesse 203
GOODWIN Robert 202 219
GOOSE POND 155 195 201

248

GORDIN/GORDON Alexr 158 185
208 209 223 226 233 George 7
23 82 170 203 Jno 105 106
GOSSET Elijah 226 John 226
William 125 211 219 226
GOULDEN Jesse 209
GOWER Russel 86
GRAHAM Francis 64 89 91 111
William 70
GRAINGER COUNTY TN 51
GRANT John 210 219
GRAY John 118
GRAYHAM Francis 83
GRAYSON John 73 74 Reubin 174
Samuel 61 65 66 73 74 77 79
90 Thomas 233
GREEN Fanny 170 James 183 186
Joseph 106 Robert 183 186
William 202
GREENLEE James 154 187
GREIDER Martin 39 49 80 100
GREY Darius &c 168 175 181 195
201
GRIDER/GRIEDER Martin 15 34
97 99
GRIMES John 8 78 82 160 210
Mary 78 Wm 9 48 72 74 77 79
83 86 95 98 102 103 110 112
113 120 134
GRISWILL James 64
GROVES John 185
GUBBINS Wm 98 105 106 ---- 84
GUFFEY Margaret 21 22
GULLEDGE William 152 169
GUTTERY Jas 77 80 Robt 75 77
GWIN Edward 18 William 53 64
HACKER George 21 53
HADLEY ---- 166
HAGGARD Edmond 102 John 102
William 4 6 13 18 19 20 23 26
27 49 89 91 105 142
HAIL/HALE Thomas 128 184 203
HALEY David 182
HALF PONE CREEK 93 195 200
HALL Dickison 152 Francis 14 44
John 46
HAMILTON Capt 76 82 88 David 6
8 17-19 32 34 40 44 55-57 66
81 Elijah 3 6 14 17 18 30 71 89
90 127 143 Hance 91 Isaiah 73
104 112 J 147 171 173 177

HAMILTON (continued)
178 210 John 26 34 51 52 56
59 62 68 69 74 77 78 80-82 86
87 90 92 94 96 97 102 108 110
112 118 124 127 130 138-140
143 145 147 149 151 153 158
164-166 168 185 191 198
Joseph 9 18 25 32-34 40 44 60
62 63 71 Robert 14 Thos 22 62
73 91
HAMMOND Samuel 96 William
151
HAMPTON Adam 26 39 125
Andrew 46 84 98 105 106
James 223 Thomas 73 115
HANDLEY Isaac 16 Jordan 66
Samuel 66
HANKS John 72 105 106 Richard
76 105 106 Thos 72 105 106
HANLY George 187
HANNAH (slave) 199
HANNAH John 223
HANSLEY Annis 136
HARBERT Nathaniel 77
HARBIN Nathl 96 97 102 108 113
116 117 164 217 228 231
HARDEN/HARDIN Abraham 20
Abram 11 22 Benjn 2 39 Geo
168 186 Jane 198 John 47 58
59 62 65 71 73 74 81 82 105-
107 116 117 119 126 149 150
155 162 202 208 Mary 7 12
Moses 64 66 68 69 79 90 102
107 135 155 167 169 170 194
196 229 231 Nathaniel 74 78
90 97
HARDWICK Thomas 77
HARGET/HARGETT F 106 Fredk
84
HARGROVE George 201
HARKINS ---- 155
HARMAN Richard 7
HARPER William 60
HARPETH RIVER 175 180 181
HARREL/HARRELL Jno 124 ----
103
HARRIN Ephraim 190
HARRINGTON Charles 11 Eliza
215 Thomas 16 215 Whitmill
105 142 144 145 148 167 229
230 234 Wm 3 6 11 16 20 73

249

HOBART/HOBERT (continued)
23 25 27 30 31 40 42 43 45 53
55 58
HODGES Hiram 234 James 163
184 233 234
HOGAN Daniel 1 39 106 175 181
236 Humphrey 105 106 186
James 160 178 179 John 27 39
Robert 165 221 234 235 William 105 106
HOGG Thomas 106
HOLDERNESS Thomas 220
HOLEMAN Benjn 221 232 Danl 2
3 6 10 102 174 231 Jas 229
232 234-236 Thomas 230
HOLENESS William 154
HOLIMAN Daniel 96
HOLLAND Danl 77 96 99 100 128
145 191 192 193 221 227 228
Elisabeth 96 James 109 202
203 John 143 Lemon 214 219
226 Lemond 223 Lemuel 223
Simon 219 Willie 234 235 Willis
160 233 Wm 119 160
HOLLIMAN Daniel 83
HOLLIS Samuel 12 14 23 31 54
128 136 142 146 185 189 215
220 222 ---- 54
HOLLIS MILL 85
HOLMAN Benjn 180 184 219 223-
225 Danl 27 54 107 108 110
131 133 136 138 147 157-159
167 178 186 223 226 229
Enoch 140 James 122 236 Thos
122 136 149 150 170 230
HOLMES Francis 77
HOMES William 154
HOOD William 19 28 141
HOODS BRANCH 22
HOOK/HOOKS George 106 153
166 175 181
HOOPER Absolam &c 109 164
HOOPERS HOLLOW 7
HOOSER David 52 John 175 181
HOPKIN/HOPKINS Robert 154 175
181 187 195 200 Stephen 105
Thomas 3 8 119 144 163
HOPTON Stephen 109
HORNBARGER Philip 149 190
HORSLEY Samuel 141
HOUDASHALL Isaac 171

HOWARD Elihu 7
HOWEL John 234 Josiah 195
HOWSE Lawrence 52
HOWSER David 48
HUDDLESON John 28
HUDDLESTON Archd 44 73 205
233 David 23 54 83 85 91 92
98 101-104 108 128 130 167
169 171-174 194 211 214 217
229 John 29 32-34 173 179
209 211-215 218 237 Jonathan
173 213 215 218 219 234 235
William 64 66 68 69 120 135
173 179 180 202 207 208 211
213 218 219 229 237
HUDSON Isaac 46 84 John 25 43
75 77 179 237
HUEY John 146 157 158 165 177
179 183 184 197 200 201 228
230 Joseph 191 206 Wm 197
HUGHS David 8 Elijah 148 170
171 174 178 202 223 John 26
William 106 189
HULING James 176
HULL Nicholas 4
HUMPHREY/HUMPHREYS/HUMPHRIES
Mr 180 P 114 138 148 152 156
158 165 191 204 207 212 213
216 223 224 228 230 Parry 122
HUNDLEY Joel 90 Josiah 65 70
136 Jurden 93 Lankston 93
Samuel 93 William 93 136
HUNT Henry 135 136 194 198-
201 203 211 219 223 James 96
144 157 159 163 172 174 John
163 180 183 229 Shadk 229
Sion 163 William 73 149 151-
153 156 180 184 220
HUNTER Allen 92 93 Dempsey 93
Frederick 164 Jacob 54 167
Polly 132 143 149 156 Saml
205 Thomas 72 76 94 95 111
112 144 147-149 167 176 189
210 William 119 219
HURT John 64
HUSE William 80
HUSK John 3
HUST John 66 68 69 Wm 14-16
26 27
HUSTON William 221
HUTCHINS John 106 Richard 112

JOHNSTON (continued)
49 60 116 144 147 149 176
177 211 214 ---- 103
JOINER Jesse 72
JONES Anthy 60 67 72 92 102
106-108 110 120 121 134 142
143 160 205 211 223 226 Arthur 130 Asa 177 Capt 104
David 23 30 46 47 59 83-86
116 129 133 137 138 149 150
151-153 157 164 166 167 186
203 223 231 Edward 171 Eli
17-19 21 22 39 70 87 101 112
132-133 136 143 147 156 164
Henry 38 James 23 27 30 60 64
67 72 96 112 128 130 134 150
160 164 167 177 194 218 221
225 232 Jesse 56 57 73 74 85
87 92 101 102 108 119-121
131 149 151 153 156 185 210
219 229 231 236 John 38 76
80 82 86-88 Jos 92 Peter 171
Richd 67 162-164 170 219 237
Thomas 68 92 220 Waddy 142
220 ---- 227 234
JURRY William 131
KANEDY Ann 33
KAR William 11
KARNEY 203
KARR Agness 12 James 11 12 19
24 32 34 87 94 96 107 113 117
149 152 John 12 37 149 194
197 208 Laurence &c 31 121
Margt 12 32 165 198 Mrs 188
Robt 12 24 149 Wm 12 21 32-
34 52 62 73 74 76 77 79 83 86
88 90 94 102 107 129 145 148
149 186 191 223
KARRS CR 5 6 17 20 29 34 52 54
62 78 80 85 87 103 115 154
155 164 167 175 180 181 187
190 195 200 201 213 218 219
222
KEARNEY William 169
KELL Mattw 209 215 Robt 209
KELLEY Giles 11
KELLY John 23
KENDLY Samuel 100
KENEDAY John 87 Margaret 77
KENEDY Ann 33 49 Jacob 123
KENLEY William 231

KENTUCKY LINE/ROAD 3 25 29
83 88 89 93 94 97 103 114 120
148
KENTUCKY MONEY/STATE 3 7 8
13 20 25 29 44 91 103
KERBY Miles 7 8 14 21 22 31 43
47 72 100 117 163 191 ---- 105
KERNEY John 181
KERNY Michael 199
KEYKENDALL 109
KILE James 163 180 226
KILGORE Capt 167 171 195 197
220 Chas 9 28 29 47 58 102
126 127 136 141 144 160 167
169-174 194 196 208 211 215-
217 229 231 John 6 7 98
Johnson 9 10 30 47 83 94 96
190 Thomas 1 22 54 58 94 95
136 138 141 144 146 147 153
162 164 167 192 208 209 237
KILTS John 21
KIMBREL John 66
KING Barnabas 16 25 Edward 69
73 74 88 119 136-140 145 162
164-168 180 198 207 208 210
212 Hugh 4 James 25
KIRBY Miles 37 39 72 99 109 ----
106
KIRK Robert 193
KIRKHAM James 215
KIRNEY John 175
KITTS John 16 99 100 136
KIZER Peter 232
KNIGHT John 28 149 190
KNOXVILLE 46
KOAN/KOEN Abraham 99 101 107
126 Benjn 66 73 80 99 101 107
120 121 126 185 Danl 80
KOVEL Benjamin 10
KRISEL Capt 123 141 167 172
195 197 202 216 220 John 30
32-34 72 94 101 115 119 121
140 144 148 149 154 157 158
161 165 208 209 211 228
LACY Jiner 9
LAMB George 126 149
LAMBERT Aaron 159 165
LAMKIN/LAMPKIN Samuel 122
Uel 122 155
LANCASTER Elijah 11 19 27 30 33
38 48 49 55 60 61 70 72 77 79

LANCASTER (continued)
80-82 86 92 95 97 Robert 1 3-5
17-19 24 25 27 30 56 58 59 61-
63 79 90 108 119
LANDSFORD William 206
LARISY Moses 6 16 25 27 50 56
58 59 64 66 68 69 77 83 175
LASITER Robert 98 105 106 108
LATHAM James 126 131 132 137
138 143 147 149 150 156 175
William 221
LATIMER/LATTEMER/LATTIMER
Daniel 113 Griswell 15 Jon-
athan 6 14 16 113 Joseph 14
128 130 149 151-153 156
LAURENCE Elias 26 41
LAURISY Moses 87
LAUTER Robert 18
LAW Marvel 102
LAWRENCE Elias 55 59 63 71 75
76-78 98 101 113 115 162 165
170 Jesse 103 124 126 161 166
180 Joseph 175 181 Rosey 161
LAWS Aaron 77 175 181 195 201
LAWSON Elizh 43 Epephroditus/
Eppa/Appa 41 56 62 63 76 83
85 86 98 100 101 111 115 126
127 144 146 171 174 179 187
191 193 198 202 203 210 222
Henry 62 77 92 109 112 159
176 181
LEACH Geo 172 James 180 223
LEAK John 213
LEDFORD Solomon 192 207 212
213
LEE James 84 163 Robert 161 196
201
LEELAND George 161
LEEPER John 203
LEMAR/LEMARR Nancy 2 5
LEREW Danl 25 50 Peter 32 38
LESTER Henry 34 Mattw 59 111
LEWIS Hugh 1 6 16 37 Jacob 37
71 72 135 137 157 163 187
189 208 209 James 72 155 187
195 200 Joel 121 124 138 164
191 198 215 217 228 234 Seth
4-6 10-12 16 19 20 23-28 32-
34 36-40 42 45 48 50 52 55 58
60 64 66 74 77 85 William 64
73 80 133 203 210 223 233

LIPSCOMB John 115 130 131 170
182 187 191 193 194 198 205
211 237
LISTER Matthew 112 127
LITTLE Harmon 201 Thomas 14
54 73 74 80 100 128
LIVELY Jeffery & Patience 45
LIVINGSTON COUNTY KY 189
LOCKART Capt 7 27 Jas 9 10 26
LOCUST Austin Betsy Elisabeth
Hannah Jas Moses 37 42 110
LODGE Matthew 99 103 112 136
138 149 153 229
LOES Marvel 88
LOFTON Jeremiah 61
LOGAN COUNTY/ROAD 5 7 39 46
52 81 101 117 144 154 162
163 172 198 208 237
LOGGANS/LOGGINS Milley 2 5
LOGUE Carnes 177 Elener 24 32
33
LONDON David 152 163 James
118 John 118 197
LONG Elish 198 James 20 22 28
29 71 79 116 119 135 162 180
183 202 204 205 207 208 213
215 237 John 61 80 Robert 215
William 61 66 93
LOUDEN COUNTY VA 217
LOVE John 84 105 106
LOVELACE/LOVELASS Vachel 40
64 78 95 101 George 101
LOW/LOWE Marvel/Marvell 88
170 180 183 202 203 229
LOWRY Jane 59 60 William 50-
52 56-60 62 68 207
LOYD Benjamin 28
LUCAS David 196 198 219 Ed-
ward 175 181 ---- 94 97 114
LUCK James 160 William 43
LUKE John 205 Matthew 78
LUNDSFORD/LUNSFORD Augus-
tine 160 Stephen 160 William
160 173 204 207 210 212
LUREY/LURRY William 67 131
155 175 181 188 195
LUSK Wm 9 10 25 27 59 83 85 86
94 98 99 108 175 181
LUSKS FERRY 193
LUTER Holland 185 217 Matthew
31 63 75 78 112 126 129 142

McDANIEL (continued)
190 191 222 223 James 33 78
95 Joseph 202
McDONALD Daniel 125 James 3
87 92 94 96 97 122 144 147
148 149 177 184 228 232 237
McDOWAL/McDOWEL James 193
Joseph 137 158 180 193 Nelson 61 94 95 Wilson 80
McELHAINEY/McELHAINY John
70 82 139 140 144 160 172
198 Joseph 220 Margaret 18
McELYEA James 10 18 38 146
160 164
McFADDIN David 199
McFARLAN/McFARLIN James 37
185 199 200 202 208 212 218
223 226 John 33 200 232
Margaret 37 Marvel 229
McFATTER Daniel 46 84 98 105
106
McGAUGH John & William 32
McGILL James 51 196 201
McGOWEN Edward 175 181
McGRAW Cornelius 66 101 David
61 66 72 82 91 93 101 Paul 66
80 93 Uriah 66 101
McGUIRE James 174
McINTOSH Alexr 25 47 Bazel 9
Benjn 2 3 5 6 8-10 12 13 17
20-22 24 25 27-31 34-36 40 41
43-46 50 52 60 Chas 3-5 17 18
21 22 37 44 48 49 52 55 58 62
73 79 121 124 140 144 169
198 213 222 228 231 235 Elish
47 J 74 James 126 131 184
186 193 John 3 9 10 47 75 82
83 131 167 182 205 227
Nimrod 3 5 9 11 18 33 34 38 41
46 47 52 55 62 73-75 83 85 94
97 102 103 108 120 121 128
130 137 138-140 144 151 157
158 160 161 208 209 231 233
237 Thos 4 5 9 11-13 26 30 45
47 56 57 68 74 81-84 97 137
138 140 160 161 171 208 209
217
McIVER Daniel 4
McKEE Alexander 22 Jacob 170
William 14 24
McKENLY Daniel 68

McKINDLEY Daniel 1 2 5 9 11 17
22 27 70 74
McKINLEY Daniel 76 82 87 89 90
95 97 105 110 126 128 133
141 162 164 167 173 179 205
213 James 83
McKROW James 94
McMILLEN/McMILLION/McMILLON
Hugh 16 John 76 110 135 157
159 167 221
McMURRY Samuel 3 7 9 23 27 37
48 69 72 125 128 130 134 136-
138 140 143 144 150 174 176
211 214 218
McMURTRY Henry 209 John 209
McNAIRY Nathaniel 143
McNEELY Alexr 80 151 175 181
McNEW/McNOW Benjamin 81 89
93 109 119
McNUT/McNUTT Isaac 18 19 23
34 40 44 48 50 52 69 71 73 74
81
McPHERSON John 62
McSHEHEE John 73 86 91 93 134
137 Miles 46 73 84
MELONE William 42
MENEES Benjn 1 2 4 5 13-15 17
19-22 25 26 28 30 36-39 41 42
47 48 50 51 53 55 57 59 60 61
64 67 69 71 75 76 78 79 86 88-
91 93 95-100 102-106 108 110-
112 114-118 120 121-123 126
130 131 134-138 141 142 146-
151 153 157-163 165-169 171-
178 181 183 187 188 190-194
196 198-201 207 209 210 212
214-222 224 226 227-232
Daniel 5 Isaac 2 18 37 60 133
James 25 31 33 37 42 43 47 54
57 59 60 62 65 67 69 72 73 77
85 87 89 93 96-99 101 102 105
108 114-116 121 125 127 129-
131 133 134 136 137 139 141
142 144 149 152-154 156-158
161 162 165 170 171 175 177
183-186 189 191 194 197 198
200 203 205-207 209 225 231
Wm 192 237 ---- 117
MENEES FORD/ROAD 94 103 111
124 128 134 170 198
MERCER John 2

NIELL James 141

NISBET/NISBIT Capt 124 Jeremiah 124 John 126 Robt 126

NINKIMPINCH ROAD 237

NOBLE John 127 204 219 Mark 6 9 25 37 49 50 79 80-83 88 111 116 120 121 126 127 157-159 163 167 170 177 185 210 211 215-217 223 226 237 William 83

NORFLEET Cordal 135 137 162 203 204 237 Cordial 118 128 James 4 6-8 10-13 21-23 31 32 34-36 38 39 43-45 49-55 59-61 64 67-70 72 73 79-81 86 91 100 104 109 112-115 118-120 130 140 143 147 148 159 161 165 166 169 171 176-178 183 186 188 190-192 195 197 203 205 209-211 221 222 232 234-236

NORIS Ezekiel 131

NORMAN Ezekiel 109 234

NORRIS Hannah 110 James 110 184 203 207 Jane 11 46 203 207 Thos 46 73 86 92 109 110 143 152 164 176 182 199 222 Wm 131 152 190 203 205 207

NORRIS POND 218

NORTH CAROLINA 73 114 186 224

NOWLIN Payton 211

NOYES Dow/Doett 201 Levi 120 124 128 129 132 143 148-150 153 156 157 161 164-166 174 178 207 208 227 234 235

NUCKELLS/NUCKLES/NUCKOLLS Richard 22 41 42 55 76 81 119 142 144 146 153 161 164 172 177 180 183 189 190 202 211 222

NYE Shadrick 20

OGLEVIE Smith 143

OHIO RIVER 193

ONEAL Arthur 118 136 Bryant 58 112 Zachariah 20 53 98 101 103 104 108 122

OVERTON Thomas 143 158

OWEN Lawrence 230 ---- 227 234

OWENS Benjamin 80 86 89 90 Elisha 86

OYLER Jonathan 79 84 91 93 95 107 131 178 179 Melcher 1 8 17-19 27 73 74 78 94 95 99 129

PACA John 229

PACE William 164

PACK Bartimas &c 54 76 102 126 130 152 174 223 227-230

PAIRS Jonathan 151

PALMER Thomas 70

PANKEY John 49 57 63 67 69 71 74 77 81 87 89 97 101 103 105 155 188 Joseph 51 195 201 Nancy 74 146 Polly 66

PARCHMENT John 21 22 25 32 37 44 45 50-52 63 Philip 3 15 20-22 35 38 42 45 48 50 54 56 58 59 63 76 89 92 93 98 101 107 110 112 116 117 119 127-129 133 136 139 140 144-146 150 159 170 173 174 180 190 198 205 213 221 225

PARISH Alexander 106

PARKER Allen 23 31 52 149 151 153 154 156 182 185 194 196 197 206 220 222 232 Asa 82 92 103-105 108 130 144 145 207 208 Asaph/Esaph/Isaph 45 92 128 169 174 207 208 Charles 23 80 Isham 12 14 15 23 30 37 Lucy 54 59 66 Thomas 81

PARKS George 151 John 117 155

PARR Noah 105 106

PATE Wm 116 117 135 157 158

PATTERSON Capt 25 34 39 45 49 David 8 11 54 59 78 127 Geo 64 70 79 124 128 164 170 174 176 218 219 John 42 59 64 70 Mary 64 Patk 98 99 131 137 138 141 185 211 218

PAYNE James 142 150 218 John 126 130 133 143 185 187 220 Joseph 3-5 54 59 70 73 75 86 96 101 126 127 139 140 144 146 157 174 178 179 223 226 Josiah 77 208 210 212 213 220 Ledford 165

PAYRESON Thomas 127

PAYTON John 17 39

PEARL Richard 15 16

PEARSON Samuel 177 184

PEAY Nehemiah 46

PENINGTON/PENNINGTON Jacob
1 23
PENNSYLVANIA 95
PERDUE-- 88
PERKINS Hardin 224 Nichs 70
PERRY Aaron 8 26 John 204 Nathan 12-14 Nathl 104 Robert
125 126 128 149 151-153 156
162 163 170 177 197 204 219
221 223-225 232 Thos 26 Wm
18 54 72 87 89 92 93 96 111
112 116 131 140 157-160 167
169 170 211 214 226 227 232
237
PERSON/PERSONS Thomas 105
106 123 167
PERSONS CREEK 177 196 201
PETER (slave) 42
PEVY Nehemiah 84
PHELPS Elisha 220
PHILIPS Abm 164 Abraham 134
194 223 Abram 206 Capt 49
Isaac 1 3 6 9 15 19 26 28 30 31
35 36 38 40 41 44 45 49 56-59
61 67-69 82 86-90 92 93 95 97
100 102-104 106 108 114 118
119 121 122 124 128 131 134
135 140 143 144 146 153 163
165-169 171 176 178 183 191
195-202 204 206-209 211 212
216-218 236 Isham 223 J 173
Jacob 49 John 1-7 9 10 12-14
16 19-21 25-28 30-32 35 36 39
41-45 47 49-53 56 58 59 64 66
69 75 79 82 83 85 86 95 97-99
102 103 106 108 110-112 116
117 120-124 126 128 131 135
137 138 141 143-151 154 158
161-163 165-169 171-174 177
178 180 183 185 187 188 190-
195 197-202 204 206-209 217
228 236 Joseph 26 36 52 64 73
121 Merrel 169 Moses 220
Philip 18 36 Saml 26 Wm 103
PHILPS Micajah 186 189
PHIPPLE Pray 159
PHIPS Joshua 87 Lewellen 55 59
61 62 78 184
PICK Norman 118
PICKREL/PICKRELL Jacob 26 34
44 45 52 56 62 72 74 82 97

PICKREN Jacob 90 97 103 105
132 134 135 137 154 173 182
184 185 192-194 198 207 214
225 227 230 235
PIKE James 124 136 208 John 14
62 63 157-159 211 214 226
229 231
PILANT Elisha 111 128 162 204
Elijah 162
PINCEN Duke 165 William 165
PINKLEY Abm 165 Abraham 138
171 Adam 217 Danl 107 138-
140 162 167 173 182 Fredk
169 Henry 88 169 Jacob 66 82
88 92-94 96-98 107 112 113
119-122 127 128 130 135 136
139 140 152 154 157 158 162
169 180 182 187 191 194 198-
202 205 208 209 211 214 217
219 224 232 234 235 237 John
79 83 87 88 96 Peter 79 82 88
96 102 107 108 110 128 130
133 158 160 161 173 176 201
206-208 217
PINKLY Jacob 144 Joseph 93
PIPKIN Lewis 31 32 61 64 69 71
91
PIRKEY/PIRKY Henry 91 John 84
PITT/PITTS Arther/Arthur 9 11-13
22 23 27 41 62 63 75 81 83 85
86 92 95 116 140 143-145 159
179 192 211 222 Burrel &c 111
119 223 Capt 222 John 171
Joseph 160 171 193 Murrell
160
PLASTERS Sarah 189
POE John 46 84
POLK Ezekiel 114 143 144 146
148 150 162 164 172 197 John
167 169 171-174 179 184 189
190 197 Martha 179 184 189
197 Olivia 184 189 197 Thomas
150 157 158 164 172 177 179
194 208 219 William 172 179
185 190 205
POOL Chloe 203 Ephraim 127
135-138 George 7 10 60 75 77
83 167 169 180 186 203 210
Mr 99 100 Wm 128 204
PORT ROYAL 88 94 103 111 113
115 117 122 134 165 170

259

PORTER Benjn 19 23 27-29 42 62
63 79 89 90 93 109 112 120
124 131 144 147-150 152 160
163 174 179 202 211 Hannah
39 59 66 80 166 168 180 John
8 27 Mr 162
PORTERFIELD Jno 84 98 105 106
POWEL/POWELL Cuthberth 83
Jas 52 56 58 59 62 Leven/Levin
83 155 217 231 Susn 217 Wm
31 34 42 52 55 56 58 59 62 67
68 175 180
POWERS John 3-5 37 56 64 66 68
69 76 79-81 96 110 111 118
171 Lewis 119 Thos 119
PRATT Ephraim 6 22
PRICE James 102 John 9 10 21 23
27 41 42 48 51 53 54 71-74 78
89 94 Jonathan 3 4 8-13 18 20
28 40 41 64 69 79 83 86 94 95
102 115 175 181 Joseph 28
PRINCE Francis 191 George 30
Robert 3 152 153 181 200
William 26 76
PRIOR Joseph 63
PROCKTOR John 211 215
PURNELL BRANCH 113 115 170
PURTLE Geo 32 Michael 24 33
QUARY Charles 112
QUICK David 86 William 86
RACCOON CREEK 93
RACE PATHS 4 8 237
RAGLIN Henry 93
RAGSDALE Joel 203 Lewis 203
William 109 136-140 148 160
165 179 183 186
RAMSEY David 58 77 Jonathan 88
94 100 102 119 122 Josiah 11
13 17 18 25 37 55 56 58 66 68
71 88 94 100 102 136 Thomas
136 ---- 66 173 177 182 188
190 227
RANDAL Aquilla 86
RANDOL Mrs 91
RANDOLPH John 136
RASCO/RASCOE Jesse 155 188
William 4 8 11 36 55
RASERE William 29
RASIN William 29
RAWLINGS ---- 166

RAWLS Abel 210 Elizabeth 70 86
Gabriel 129 187 John 210
Joseph 210 Luke 37 70 72 75
77 174 176 182 205 Nancy 200
201 Shadk 54 60 69 74 88 92
105 111 120 127 138 140 142
145 149 151 165 166 167 171
173 193 194 198 200 205 212
213 217 Widow 72 80
REASONS William 10
RED RIVER 5 7 13 22-24 29 39 40
41 44 49 54 81 83 88 103 117
124 125 141 155 160 175 176
180 181 185 187 188 192 195
201 206 214 218 236 237
REED Jesse 12 13 Wm 72 151
REES/REESE Ephraim 75 76 78
88 100
RENFRO Isaac 106 James 8 23
Moses 218 Peter 126 William 8
43 196 201 ---- 154 187 195
200
RENICK William 57
REYNOLD/REYNOLDS J 174 208
213 215 216 221 223 230 234
James 212 227 228 232 235
236
RHODES John 18
RICE Harriett 91 96 101 175 181
Hiram 211 John 125 141 145
Joshua 72 163
RICHARDS Rhody 50
RICHARDSON John 170 179 214
228 Sarah 98 105 106
RIGGS Jacob 74
RILEY ---- 23
ROAN Daniel 56
ROBERT/ROBERTS Isaac 66 105
106 154 187 195 200 John 23
Joseph 168 202 Moses 98
Thomas 99
ROBERTSON Burrel 177 Capt 171
Chas 98 105 106 David 109
Duncan 234 Edward 224 Eli-
jah 16 105 Ezekiel 95 Heze-
kiah 81 Isaac 28 92 107 112
118 Israel 116 118 122 174 193
210 215 Jacob 187 194 196
213 James 34 77 87 91 116
118 136 John 202 223 226 231

VENTRESS Lovick 46 59 60 66 72 73 94 95 97 117 120 126 145 159 167 169 182 221 223 226 229

VERRELL William 202

VINSON Josiah 219 William 212

WADE John 60 93 136

WALK/WALKE Thomas 140 145 157 169

WALKER Alexr 106 Allen 106 Capt 116 George 3 8 42 Jas 9 10 35 42 48 71 88 90 94 96 120 124 128 130 131 135 Jesse 141 John 100 Noel 97 Rachel 103 Samuel 113 116 117 126 Thomas 140 Van 113

WALLACE Benjn 151 Evan 230

WALTON Isaac 86 Joel 203 Martin 142 203 213 218 237 Meredith 22 32 39 70 76 80 101 112 114 115 149 157 158 180 203 218 227 237 Wm 230

WAR TRACE CR 5 24 115 160 161 167 171 175 181 201

WARD Eanis 106 Edward 169 171 196 Frederick 98 105 106 Stephen 73 91

WARNER Mary 7 38 50

WARREN Goodloe 94 Jacob 22 54 79 180 John 94 Robert 69 124 131 133 134 140 141 145 157 169 Samuel 165

WASHINGTON Andw 54 65 97 105 112 116 124 128 130 133 136 141 Joseph 37 47 75 80 96 97 102 104 109 119 122 127 130 133 137 167 169 172 226

WATERS John 67

WATKINS H 208 Henry 162 164-166 168 182 202 204 207 208 213 218 223 229 Jno 127 184 186 205 Mr 162 Noel 54 107

WATSON James 118 157 John 235 Josiah 68 Mary 196 Wm 152

WEAKLEY/WEAKLY Benjn 46 47 56 57 61 65 68 70 74 80 86 91 93 101 136 177 Capt 82 88 104 108 David 80 87 Isaac 26 42 46 56 57 61 65 70 93 107 John 80 158 Robert 37 47 54 65 73 158 160 203 229 Thos 61 Wm 80

WEAKLEY FERRY 72 76 80 83 89 93 104 130

WEIR James 159

WELBURN Daniel 43

WELLS Heydon 133 Lewis 179 205 211 213 215 233 William 198 208

WEST Eli 35 46 106 George 196 209 220 223 234 Thomas 234

WHARTON James 126 Jesse 79

WHEATON Charless 1 3 14-16 20 21 32 39 43 54 60 71 98 99 117 120 134 137 138 144 146 160 164 173 204 206 208 216 217 223 226 235 Danl 175 Mr 115

WHEATONS SINK 214

WHEELER James 4 20 25 29 65 83 104 108 118 126 140 141 167 169 170 209 215 231

WHILFORD Thomas & Willis 31

WHIPPLE Pray 125 205

WHITE Elisabeth 58 John 9 34 41 43-46 56 58

WHITEHEAD Richard 26 William 46 ---- 227

WHITFORD Thomas 163

WHITWORTH Findal 93 Tendale 66

WICKLIFF Martin 144

WIGGIN ---- 16 19

WIGGINS John 161

WIGGLE/WIGLE Henry 39 87 155 177 188

WILBURN Daniel 84 98 105 106 222

WILCOX Edmond 110 111

WILKISON Nathan 111 112

WILKS Francis 46 84

WILLIAMS Abel/Abell 72 82 116 117 122 152 154 158 Catherine 43 Caty 115 Dudley 87 Garlant 160 George 209 Griffith 152 158 215 Henry 227 228 Isaac 147 148 154 171 176 187 189-191 195 199 200 James 103 135 Jesse 1 9 14 15 20 68 88 108 160 180 John 15 87 104 144 171 174 176 190 191 194 196 198 208 209 218 222 Matthew 10 16 92 N 194 198

Heritage Books by Carol Wells:

Abstracts of Giles County, Tennessee: County Court Minutes, 1813–1816 and Circuit Court Minutes, 1810–1816

CD: Tennessee, Volume 1

Davidson County, Tennessee County Court Minutes, Volume 1, 1783–1792

Davidson County, Tennessee County Court Minutes, Volume 2, 1792–1799

Davidson County, Tennessee County Court Minutes, Volume 3, 1799–1803

Dickson County, Tennessee County and Circuit Court Minutes, 1816–1828 and Witness Docket

Edgefield County, South Carolina Probate Records, Boxes One through Three Packages 1–106

Edgefield County, South Carolina Probate Records, Boxes Four through Six Packages 107–218

Edgefield County, South Carolina: Deed Books 13, 14 and 15

Edgefield County, South Carolina: Deed Books 16, 17 and 18

Edgefield County, South Carolina: Deed Books 19, 20, 21 and 22

Edgefield County, South Carolina: Deed Books 23, 24, 25 and 26

Edgefield County, South Carolina: Deed Books 27, 28 and 29

Edgefield County, South Carolina: Deed Books 30 and 31

Edgefield County, South Carolina: Deed Books 32 and 33

Edgefield County, South Carolina: Deed Books 34 and 35

Edgefield County, South Carolina: Deed Books 36, 37 and 38

Edgefield County, South Carolina: Deed Books 39 and 40

Edgefield County, South Carolina: Deed Book 41

Edgefield County, South Carolina: Deed Books 42 and 43, 1826–1829

Genealogical Abstracts of Edgefield, South Carolina Equity Court Records

Natchez Postscripts, 1781–1798

Rhea County, Tennessee Circuit Court Minutes, September 1815–March 1836

Rhea County, Tennessee Tax Lists, 1832–1834, and County Court Minutes Volume D: 1829–1834

Robertson County, Tennessee Court Minutes, 1796–1807

Rutherford County, Tennessee Court Minutes, 1811–1815

Sumner County, Tennessee Court Minutes, 1787–1805 and 1808–1810

Williamson County, Tennessee County Court Minutes, July 1812–October 1815

Williamson County, Tennessee County Court Minutes, May 1806–April 1812

www.ingramcontent.com/pod-product-compliance
Lightning Source LLC
Chambersburg PA
CBHW061145220326
41599CB00025B/4360